WITHDRAWN

THE ARTIST'S GUIDE
TO GIMP EFFECTS

THE ARTIST'S GUIDE TO GIMP EFFECTS
Creative Techniques for Photographers, Artists, and Designers

Michael J. Hammel

NO STARCH PRESS

San Francisco

Printed in Canada

11 10 09 08 07   1 2 3 4 5 6 7 8 9

ISBN-10: 1-59327-121-2
ISBN-13: 978-1-59327-121-3

Publisher: William Pollock
Production Editors: Elizabeth Campbell and Megan Dunchak
Cover and Interior Design: Octopod Studios
Developmental Editors: Jim Compton and Tyler Ortman
Copyeditor: Christina Samuell
Compositor: Riley Hoffman
Proofreader: Jim Brook
Indexer: Nancy Guenther

For information on book distributors or translations, please contact No Starch Press, Inc. directly:

No Starch Press, Inc.
555 De Haro Street, Suite 250, San Francisco, CA 94107
phone: 415.863.9900; fax: 415.863.9950; info@nostarch.com; www.nostarch.com

Library of Congress Cataloging-in-Publication Data

Hammel, Michael J.
  The artist's guide to GIMP effects : creative techniques for photographers, artists, and designers
/ Michael J. Hammel. -- 1st ed.
        p. cm.
  Includes index.
  ISBN-13: 978-1-59327-121-3
  ISBN-10: 1-59327-121-2
 1. Computer graphics. 2. GIMP (Computer file) I. Title.
T385.H329558 2007
006.6'86--dc22
                                         2007001652

To the love of my life, Brinda, and for the love of my child, Ryann.
You both keep me going. Without you, this book would be just another unfinished project.

ACKNOWLEDGMENTS

The GIMP development team, with specific thanks to Sven Neumann for keeping the project going for many years and David Neary for helping me get motivated again when I started this book.

Paul Hudson, Julian Jefferson, Andrew Gregory, Rebecca Smalley, Nick Veitch, Matt Nailon, and the rest of the great staff at *Linux Format* (past and present) for staying interested in and supportive of my GIMP tutorials column for such a long time. And for staying interested in me even after I decided I need to write about something—ANYTHING—else for awhile!

Bill Pollock, Patricia Witkin, Liz Maples, Christina Samuell, Jim Compton, and Elizabeth Campbell at No Starch Press for eagerly accepting the idea for this book. Without their help, this book would be nothing more than a bunch of text files and screenshots.

Extra kudos to Jonathan Corbet for always answering tough questions (usually about the Linux kernel) and to Sean Reifschneider, Evelyn Mitchell, Kevin Fenzi, and the rest of the great gang at tummy.com in Fort Collins, Colorado for keeping my colocated server running and safe from serious harm for so many years.

Special thanks to my sister, Cathy, her husband, Jeff, and their family for letting me stay with them for four months while I was moving from Houston to Colorado. They gave me room, board, support, and companionship while my wife and daughter were so very far away, not to mention the fact that they provided me a second-floor porch with a terrific view from which to keep working.

Additional thanks to my mom for letting me use a photo of her from her high school days in Chapter 2. I know I wouldn't want my high school pictures used for anything except fireplace kindling.

And to Reba and Bailey, the two most wonderful golden retrievers in the world, for keeping my feet warm under the desk night after night after night. . . .

Credits

Several images in this book came from these royalty-free collections:

BigStockPhoto.com   http://www.bigstockphoto.com

iStockphoto.com   http://www.istockphoto.com

PDPhoto.org   http://www.pdphoto.org

morgueFile   http://www.morguefile.com

Stock.xchng   http://www.sxc.hu

My knowledge of how to use tools like the GIMP was born from reading many early texts on using Photoshop. When I taught myself how to use the GIMP, all I did was translate those Photoshop techniques into the button pushes and filter munging required to reproduce the concepts using the GIMP. The interesting thing about learning the GIMP this way is that I never actually used Photoshop until many years later, when my wife started to use it. Though I know where everything is in Photoshop because of those texts, I find I enjoy using the GIMP much more. We all have our comfort zones. Use what makes you happy. That's what software is supposed to do, anyway.

TABLE OF CONTENTS

Chapter 5
Type Effects 249

Chapter 6
User Interface Design 297

Index 337

INTRODUCTION

I've been writing about the Linux operating system in general and the GIMP in particular since 1996. I've written for every kind of publication, from countless print articles and magazine columns to website musings to this book, which is the third book on the subject that I've written on my own (I've co-authored two other titles). In 2001 I wrote an article called "Linux goes to the movies" for Salon.com, which discussed how Linux and the GIMP were starting to make waves in the special effects industry. It's hard to believe that an article like that was written seven years ago. Or that the GIMP is more than ten years old!

The GIMP started out as a class project at UC Berkeley, built on top of the venerable Motif toolkit, which at the time was really the only full-featured software library for X11-based windowing systems. GIMP 0.54 was my first taste of the program in this form. Later, the GIMP Toolkit (GTK+) was born and replaced Motif for various technical reasons. Somewhere between version 0.54 and version 0.99, I ported John Beale's Sparkle code to a GIMP plug-in. For that ancient and yet still meaningful work, I'm listed as a contributor to the project. It even got me into the Red Hat friends and family plan when they had their IPO (I should have sold when it was at its peak—dopey me). Eventually, my association with the project led me to write for the Linux Gazette and later *Linux Journal*, which led me to write my first book on the GIMP—the first book on the GIMP ever, in fact—called *The Artist's Guide to the GIMP*. You could say I've followed Linux and the GIMP from day one, and that would be just about right.

What This Book Is About

Of course, after all these years I'm no longer the only one writing on this subject, and the GIMP has become much more than a class project. Plenty of texts can show you which button opens which dialog, and the world is now quite familiar with the GIMP's buttons and dialogs. In this book, I hope to go where no one else has tried to go. It just isn't enough to show the reader where all the buttons, dialogs, and menus are anymore. We need to go beyond the application itself. In this book, I'll show you how to use the GIMP to do real work.

Linux and the GIMP have grown up together, and they are no longer youngsters in the computing world. Linux comes with a serious desktop (actually, more than one), and the GIMP is a serious application. It's time to get down to business—the business of graphic design. This book is about learning the techniques that will enable you to be more creative and efficient in the real world.

What This Book Is Not About

What you won't find in this book is a bunch of manual pages for each filter, menu, or feature. I won't explain each icon as you encounter it or tell you why each of the dialogs looks like it does. Instead, this book's tutorials show you how to use the GIMP's filters just as if they were a set of tools in a toolbox. It's a rare project that will only need a hammer. The GIMP provides the hammer, the saw, the drill, even the kitchen sink. With this book, I hope you'll learn to use all the tools in the toolbox, separately and in combination.

Linux vs. Mac vs. Windows

Starting with GIMP 2.0, users of all three major platforms have been able to harness the power of the GIMP. Ports to both Windows and Mac machines were completed a few years back using improved cross-platform libraries such as GTK+. This means that the user interfaces for Linux, Windows, and Mac are essentially the same. And that makes this book relevant to all three platforms.

NOTE *The use of the CTRL and ALT keys are described as they are used under Linux. Windows and Mac users should map these keystrokes to the equivalents on those platforms.*

How This Book Is Organized

The book is divided into six chapters, each of which contains several sections. Each chapter covers a different area of graphic design: fundamental techniques, photography, web design, advertising, typography, and user interface design. Each chapter opens with introductory material on the subject at hand and ends with a set of tips related to that area of design.

Chapter 1: Fundamental Techniques

This chapter provides a set of core tips for common tasks such as using the toolbox, working with scanned images, and manipulating text. These are not tutorials per se, but this general information will prove useful and is relevant to the other chapters in the book. Users new to the GIMP should read this chapter thoroughly, whereas more advanced users may only need to reference it occasionally or may be able to skip it altogether.

Chapter 2: Photographic Effects

This chapter is for photographers. The GIMP's raster processing is ideal for working with photographs and stock imagery. The number of effects you can create is limitless, but this chapter will help you get started using the most common techniques.

Chapter 3: Web Design

This chapter is all about graphic design for the Web. While most web design is implemented with programming and display tools like Macromedia Flash, there are still many areas of web design where static images play key roles. Features like background images, menus, buttons, and logos are important web design elements, and you can use the GIMP to create all of them.

Chapter 4: Advertising and Special Effects

This chapter will take you to the world of advertising design. Like photography, advertising makes heavy use of stock images. In this chapter, you'll find techniques for creating 2D and 3D designs for products that range from movies to cell phones to underwater adventures.

Chapter 5: Type Effects

This chapter covers type effects. The GIMP is wonderful at turning boring fonts into fantastic logos and 3D designs. This chapter will give you step-by-step instructions for re-creating some commonly used text effects.

Chapter 6: User Interface Design

We close out the book with a look at graphic design for computer user interfaces. Anyone who's used an MP3 player or a DVD player on a computer has seen some of the wild user interface designs that are possible. Because user interfaces of this kind are highly complex, this chapter takes a unique approach by using each section as a building block on the way toward creating the interface for a simple video player.

What You Need to Know About the Tutorials

Each chapter contains several sections, and (with the exception of Chapter 6) each section is a tutorial that stands on its own. Each tutorial begins with a summary of the project at hand and an explanation of how this technique is applicable in the real world. The tutorials are designed so that, by following along with the steps, you can use the GIMP's default tools and features to quickly re-create the effect shown.

Unless otherwise noted, you should start with a canvas set to the default size (400 × 320 pixels). This size will work fine for web design, but it's not appropriate for print projects, so you'll need to scale up the process if you intend to use one of these techniques in a project destined for print. In that case, you'd just increase the amount of blur, adjust the number of pixels by which to offset a layer, and so on. The thing to remember in each tutorial is the basic set of steps: Add text, apply a filter, offset a layer, duplicate and rotate, and so on. The settings you'll use will change as the scale of the project changes, and print projects tend to use significantly larger canvases.

NOTE *Don't create a print project at the default canvas size and then try to scale it up later! The result will be grainy and unusable.*

How Should I Read This Book?

New GIMP users should start by reading Chapter 1 to get an overview of the program. Both new and experienced users will find that the rest of the chapters and sections can be read in any order. With the exception of Chapter 6, each section of each chapter stands as an independent project, so the order in which you try the tutorials doesn't matter. For Chapter 6, readers should read the sections in order if they wish to reproduce the video player design as shown.

I won't be referencing keyboard shortcuts very often—with a few exceptions like Select All (CTRL-A) and Deselect All (SHIFT-CTRL-A)—because the GIMP allows you to configure shortcuts to suit your needs. Instead, I'll reference the default menu paths where necessary. If a feature has a keyboard shortcut, it will be listed next to that option in the menu. Start committing those to memory if you want to move through these tutorials even more quickly.

Because the GIMP is constantly evolving as an application, it is possible that the default menu paths will change before this book makes it into your hands. I've done my best to keep up to date with changes as they've been made, but you may need to dig around a little if the application menus have changed since GIMP 2.2 was released.

Can't find a dialog referenced in the text? Access the Dialogs menu in any canvas window or from the File menu in the toolbox. Clicking a menu entry jumps to that dialog if it's already open or opens it if necessary.

Keyboard entries are always given with uppercase letters to make the keystroke sequence easier to read. Unless the SHIFT key is specifically listed in the keystroke sequence, it does not need to be used. The same is true of the CTRL and ALT keys.

Terminology

In this book, the terms *canvas* and *image window* are interchangeable. The official GIMP documentation refers to the main drawing area as an *image window*. I prefer to use the term *canvas* because the term *image* is somewhat vague—it can mean more than one thing, depending on the context in which it is used. Besides, an artist works on a canvas, right? It just makes better sense to me.

Looking Ahead to GIMP 2.4

The GIMP is an actively developed open source project, and as is the case with any open source project, improvements are inevitable. This book is based on GIMP 2.2, which was released for Linux/Unix in December 2004 and has since been released on Windows and Mac OS X systems. When this book was started in early 2005, there was already talk of GIMP 2.4, but at the time of this writing, that release is still in development. When GIMP 2.4 is available, you'll be able to download it from the GIMP website, http://www.gimp.org.

Even though I've chosen to cover GIMP 2.2, it is possible to compile the latest developer version of GIMP 2.4 to find out how its changes will affect the tutorials in this book. The upcoming release will include many important improvements. Most of them are "under the hood," however, and are not directly visible or accessible by an end user. The user interface in GIMP 2.4 won't change dramatically from the 2.2 version, and fortunately, where the tutorials in this book are concerned, you won't notice much of a difference at all. Keep in mind the following differences between GIMP 2.2 and GIMP 2.4:

- The Drop Shadow filter has moved. In GIMP 2.4 you access it by choosing Filters ▸ Light and Shadow ▸ Drop Shadow.

- The Layer ▸ Colors menu you accessed in GIMP 2.2 is available as a top-level Colors menu in GIMP 2.4.

- The top-level Script-Fu menu in GIMP 2.2 has been integrated with the Filter menu in GIMP 2.4.

- After you've created a path in GIMP 2.4, you can use a menu option in the Layers dialog to align text to that path.

- Under the Filters ▸ Noise menu, the Scatter RGB and Scatter HSV filters in GIMP 2.2 have been renamed *RGB Noise* and *HSV Noise* in GIMP 2.4.

Other changes in GIMP 2.4 that you should be aware of include the following:

- The Print dialog in GIMP 2.4 has changed drastically from GIMP 2.2. It is significantly simplified.

- In GIMP 2.4, the alpha channel appears as its own entry in the Channels dialog.

And, of course, there are some new features that you'll want to explore when GIMP 2.4 finally arrives. Some of the most interesting ones include the following:

- Startup time has been greatly reduced in GIMP 2.4. The GIMP no longer needs to scan all your font files at startup, for example, which will greatly increase the speed of application startup on systems that have a large collection of fonts.

- GIMP 2.4 offers a Healing tool that makes it easier to remove scratches and other blemishes from photos.

- GIMP 2.4 also offers a new Foreground Select tool. This tool uses a simple, paint-based selection mechanism that is intended to make it easier to make selections of foreground objects.

- A Zoom tool has been added to the toolbox in GIMP 2.4, making it a little easier to zoom in and out of large images.

- An Alignment tool has been added in GIMP 2.4; it is an improved version of the alignment dialog (found under Layer ▸ Align Visible Layers in GIMP 2.2) that includes an easier to use, icon-based interface integrated into its Tool Options dialog.

- GIMP 2.4 offers an alternative Clone tool called Perspective Clone. This tool allows you to clone an area while mapping it into a perspective view that you define.

- Limited color management has been added in GIMP 2.4, including initial support of embedded color profiles in image files. Image operations are still done in RGB colorspace, however, and no CMYK colorspace operations are available yet.

- GIMP 2.4 offers improved support of multi-page TIFF files.

- GIMP 2.4 also offers added support for loading Photoshop .abr brushes.

- GIMP 2.4 for Windows features added support for large (greater than 2GB) XCF files.

- The performance of the Transform tools has been improved in GIMP 2.4.

- The Ellipse and Rectangle tools in GIMP 2.4 feature interactive interfaces that allow you to drag their edges and use hot spots to modify the shapes directly in the canvas.

- Support for rounding the corners of a rectangular selection has been integrated directly into the Rectangle Select tool's Tool Options dialog in GIMP 2.4, although it is still possible to enable the feature using Select ▸ Rounded Rectangle.

- GIMP 2.4 offers extensive support for Python-based plug-ins.

- When the lcms library is installed, a color-managed CMYK color selector is available in GIMP 2.4.

- GIMP 2.4 features improved hardware support, including support for multiple processors and MMX.

- A red-eye removal plug-in has been added to GIMP 2.4; you can find it under Filters ▸ Enhance ▸ Red Eye Removal.

This is by no means a comprehensive study of the upcoming release, but rather a heads up about what's in store for GIMP artists and how the differences between GIMP 2.2 and 2.4 relate to the tutorials in this book. With only minor modifications, you should be able to use either version of the GIMP to complete these tutorials.

GIMP

CORE FEATURES

1

FUNDAMENTAL TECHNIQUES

The *GNU Image Manipulation Program* (just the *GIMP* to its fans) is one of the world's most popular open source projects. It allows everyday users on a budget to harness the graphical abilities of virtually any computer. It's open source, meaning that anyone is free to improve the program, and it's free to download.

To install the GIMP, go to http://www.gimp.org and find the download and installation instructions for your operating system. The GIMP runs on all three major platforms: Mac, Windows, and Linux. In fact, if you use Linux, it's probably already installed on your machine. You'll need to be running GIMP 2.2 in order to follow along with the tutorials in this book. Come back once you've got it up and running! The tutorials throughout this book provide plenty of practice and guidance in using the GIMP's features, but they don't spend much time holding your hand when it comes to the program's basic tools and features. The book assumes that you'll learn best by experimenting and combining effects with one another. If you're a beginner, read the first section in each chapter carefully, and check out the GIMP's official user manual if you get confused (http://docs.gimp.org/en).

For the benefit of readers transitioning from other image-editing software programs and for those of you completely new to the GIMP, we'll begin with a quick introduction to the most important elements of the GIMP interface: the toolbox and the image window. If you're already a GIMP enthusiast, you may want to skip ahead to Section 1.1. If you haven't used the GIMP before, or you'd like to refresh your memory, read on.

The GIMP Toolbox

The *toolbox* holds all of the GIMP's core tools. The toolbox is also the only window that is always open, though you can hide it when you run the GIMP in full-screen mode.

This table shows the icons for each tool available in the toolbox and briefly describes that tool's abilities. Each tool also has a Tool Options dialog, which allows you to fine-tune how each tool is applied and achieve exactly the effect you desire. We'll discuss the Tool Options dialog in just a moment.

The GIMP toolbox

Toolbox Icons

Tool		Function
	Rectangle Select	This tool allows you to create rectangular selections, which you can then manipulate. Use the Tool Options to specify how the new selection should be combined with existing selections. Use the SHIFT key while selecting to create a perfect square.
	Ellipse Select	The Ellipse Select tool is just like the Rectangle Select tool, except that the shape of the selection is elliptical. Use the SHIFT key to create a perfect circle.
	Free Select	Another selection tool, the Free Select tool allows you to draw a freehand outline to create your selection.
	Fuzzy Select	The Fuzzy Select tool selects pixels based on their similarity in color and proximity to the point you click in the image window. Using higher Threshold settings in the Tool Options dialog will cause more pixels to be selected. Check the box next to the words *Sample merged* to choose pixels in all layers instead of in just the current layer.
	Select by Color	The Select by Color tool is similar to the Fuzzy Select tool, except that the chosen pixels do not need to be in close proximity to one another.
	Scissors	This is an intelligent tool that finds edges in an image, making it easier to outline an oddly shaped figure and create a selection around it.
	Paths	Paths are the vector component of the GIMP and consist of a series of nodes connected by straight or curved lines. You can edit paths to change the position of nodes and the arc of lines. The Paths tool allows you to create a new path or edit an existing one.
	Color Picker	Use this tool to change the foreground or background colors in the toolbox. With the Color Picker tool active, just click any pixel on the canvas.

Toolbox Icons (continued)

Tool		Function
	Magnify	Use the Magnify tool to zoom in on a section of an image. Drag a box around an area to zoom in on that spot.
	Measure	Use the Measure tool to measure angles in an image. These measurements are useful when used in combination with the Rotate tool.
	Move	This tool provides a means of moving elements of an image around the image window. You can move layers, text, and masks with this tool.
	Crop and Resize	The Crop and Resize tool is the best way to crop images quickly. You can also use it to resize images, though there are other tools that are easier to use for resizing images and layers.
	Rotate	The transform tools can be applied to an image or a layer. Use the Rotate tool to perform a rotation on either.
	Scale	Another transform tool, the Scale tool is used to resize a layer or image.
	Shear	Use the Shear tool to keep opposite sides of a bounding box parallel while moving pixels within the box left/right or up/down.
	Perspective	The Perspective tool stretches the bounding box. Imagine that you're viewing a square photo from head on. Tilt the photo away from you, and you'll notice that the far edge appears shorter than the near edge. That's perspective.
	Flip	Use the Flip tool to flip a layer or image horizontally or vertically.
	Text	If you want to add text to a project, you'll need to use the Text tool. The Tool Options dialog allows you to specify font size and family, along with alignment options.
	Bucket Fill	Use the Bucket Fill tool to fill a portion of a layer with a solid color or pattern.
	Blend	The Blend tool applies a smooth color transition (known as a *gradient*) to a portion of a layer that follows. Click and drag to apply a gradient with the Blend tool. Many stock gradients are available.
	Pencil	Paint tools use the active brush and the current foreground or background color. The Pencil tool draws hard-edged lines that are not antialiased, even if the brush itself has a soft edge.
	Paintbrush	Use the Paintbrush tool to draw with soft-edged strokes and the active brush.
	Eraser	The Eraser tool removes pixels from almost all layers, leaving transparent pixels in their place. When applied to the Background layer, which does not have an alpha channel by default, this tool will replace pixels with the background color.
	Airbrush	The Airbrush tool works much like the Paintbrush tool, but the effect is softer.

Tool		Function
	Ink	The Ink tool is designed specifically for use with drawing tablets like those from Wacom. It responds to pressure and those tablets' tilt features.
	Clone	*Cloning* is the process of copying pixels from one region of a layer for use in another. To use the Clone tool, you must first press the CTRL key and click the mouse to choose the point that you wish to clone. With a source location set, you can clone pixels by using paint strokes.
	Convolve	A *convolution* either blurs or sharpens an image. The Convolve tool functions like the Paintbrush tool and allows you to paint over a layer to sharpen or blur the regions under the brush.
	Smudge	Imagine dragging your finger across wet paint on a canvas. This tool functions in the same way as you drag it in the image window. It's perfect for small touch ups.
	Dodge/ Burn	Similar to the Convolve tool, the Dodge/Burn tool can be used to lighten (Dodge) or darken (Burn) the region under the brush.

The Tool Options Dialog

The *Tool Options dialog* gives you access to the active tool's options and settings. The dialog begins at the bottom of the toolbox. Clicking the icon for a GIMP tool does two things: It activates the tool, and it displays the Tool Options dialog for that tool.

NOTE *In addition to a Tool Options dialog, many of the toolbox tools have dialogs that are associated with them. These dialogs give easy access to brushes, layers, colors, and more. Double-click a tool's toolbox icon to access that tool's dialog, or use the File menu to access it (File ▸ Dialogs).*

Color Swatches and Tool Previews

At the bottom of the toolbox you'll find the color swatches and the brush, pattern, and gradient previews. If you've enabled it in the Preferences dialog, you'll also see the active image preview.

The Tool Options dialog for the Rectangle Select tool

In the swatches box you'll find the current foreground color (upper-left box) and the current background color (lower-right box). The color swatches are referenced throughout this book. Double-clicking either of these will open a dialog in which you can adjust the current colors.

The curved, doubled-ended arrow in the upper-right corner of the swatches box swaps the current foreground and background colors. Clicking the smaller boxes in the lower-left corner resets the foreground color to black and the background color to white (pressing D while the canvas is selected does the same).

The (1) foreground and (2) background colors in the swatches box at the bottom of the toolbox

The Change Foreground Color dialog

Brush, Pattern, and Gradient Previews

The brush, pattern, and gradient previews reflect the selection that is currently active for the Brushes, Patterns, and Gradients dialogs. Click any of these previews to open the associated dialog and change the active selection.

A gradient is a change in color, often smoothed in a way that simulates lighting changes or curved surfaces when applied to a selection. The Blend tool is often used to apply gradients, but you can set that tool to use the current foreground or background colors instead.

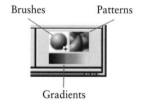

The brush, pattern, and gradient previews in the toolbox

Active Image Preview Window

As you'll soon discover, having several image windows open at once can get confusing. The active image preview window lets you quickly activate the window of your choice. This feature is not enabled by default, so if you want to use it, you must turn it on in the Preferences dialog. Choose File ▸ Preferences in the toolbox, and select the Toolbox entry on the left. Then check the box next to the words *Show active image*. The active image window is displayed at the bottom of the toolbox here.

Once you've enabled the active image preview in the Preferences dialog, the preview appears at the bottom of the toolbox.

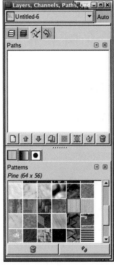

Docking windows saves screen space and reduces clutter.

Docking

A *dock* is a window that holds other windows. For example, the toolbox has a dock at its base. Any dialog can be made into a dock. To turn a dialog into a dock, drag one dialog title into another dialog to dock the two, resulting in a series of tabs. To detach a dialog from a dock, drag the tab to a new part of the screen.

Menus

You may notice that, somewhat confusingly, the GIMP has two menu bars, one for the toolbox and one for the active image window. The toolbox has three menus: File, Xtns, and Help. Most of the features in these menus can be accessed directly from image window menus or by using the toolbox icons, meaning that you won't be using this menu often.

The File menu includes Open, Acquire, Preferences, and Quit options. The File ▸ Open Recent command lists the files you've recently saved. The Acquire option accesses any scanners you might have configured. See Section 1.7 for more information about using the GIMP with scanners.

Notice that the File menu does not have a Save option. This is because each image window is saved directly from its own menu bar. You're better off memorizing the keyboard shortcut CTRL-S anyway.

The Xtns menu is primarily for software developers, but there is one option that will be of interest to end users: Script-Fu. The Script-Fu menu contains tools for creating predefined effects such as logos, buttons, and more. These tools won't be used in the tutorials described in this book; we'll focus on learning how to create personalized logos and such from scratch instead. But give Script-Fu's scripts a try. They're perfect when you're looking for instant gratification!

The Tool Options dialog for the Crop and Resize tool is an example of a window with a single dock.

The toolbox menus

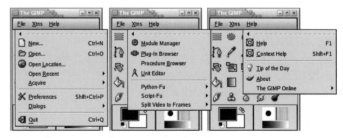

The toolbox menu's File, Xtns, and Help submenus

Even though it's beyond the scope of this book, you should know that you can create your own Xtns. If you're a programmer interested in creating scripts for the GIMP, I suggest you review the material on the GIMP Developers website (http://developer.gimp .org), specifically the Plug-In Development section.

The Image Window

In addition to the toolbox, the GIMP's other main window is the *image window*, or *canvas*, where your work is displayed. The GIMP allows you to have several image windows open at once, and this is helpful when copying from one window and pasting into another.

NOTE *Unless otherwise specified, all menu paths in this book's tutorials are relevant to the image window.*

Menus

Like the toolbox, the image window also has a menu bar, which you can also access by right-clicking the canvas. This menu includes File, Edit, Select, View, Image, Layer, Tools, Dialogs, Filters, and Script-Fu options. Linux users may also find a Python-Fu and/or a Video option, depending on how their distribution packaged the GIMP. Windows users are not likely to have either of these latter two options, however.

We'll be using features from the Edit, View, Image, Layer, and Filters menus throughout this book. The Select menu is also very useful, but you can use the mouse, the toolbox, and keyboard short-cuts to access most of its options. Don't forget to look at the File menu to familiarize yourself with its Save and Print options.

The image window menus

Menu	Feature
File	The File menu offers operations such as Open, Close, Print, and Save.
Edit	The Edit menu gives you access to the Cut, Copy, Paste, Fill, and Stroke operations. Some of these operations only apply to selections, but others apply to the entire active layer if no selection is present.
Select	The Select menu offers operations that complement the toolbox selection tools, including All, None, Invert, and Save to Channel. Selections can also be feathered, grown, shrunk, and sharpened from this menu. If you need to round the corners of a rectangular selection, use the Rounded Rectangle option.
View	Zoom is just one of the View menu's options. You can also use this menu toggle visibility of guides, layer boundaries, selections, and grids of dots. Forcing the image window to shrink wrap to the zoom level of the image helps make more room on the desktop when zooming out. Choose View ▶ Full Screen to switch to and from full-screen mode.
Image	Operations that apply to the composite image are found here, including rotation transforms, canvas sizing, and merging all layers into a single layer.
Layer	This menu offers operations that apply specifically to layers. This includes layer ordering, color management for the active layer, and layer transforms, masks, scaling, and alignment.
Tools	The Tools menu provides access to the toolbox tools, but you'll rarely use it unless you're in full-screen mode. Selecting an item from this menu makes that tool the active tool, just as if you had clicked its icon in the toolbox.
Dialogs	The dialog menu provides quick access to the GIMP's many dialogs, including the Layers, Channels, Paths, Brushes, Patterns, Gradients, and Document History dialogs.
Filters	As you follow along with the tutorials in this book, you'll become very familiar with the Filters menu. It offers the tools you'll need to manipulate images in creative ways, applying blurs, lighting effects, cloud renderings, and warping.
Script-Fu	This menu provides filters written in the Script-Fu language. They often do not have previews, but you can use them to quickly produce effective designs.

NOTE *You don't need to use the File menu to access these options. Try right-clicking instead. You'll bring up a fly-out menu, which contains all of these options. It's much faster!*

Additional Features

There are a few other image window features you should get to know. Each is labeled here and discussed briefly here.

Additional image window features

1. Use the Quick Mask to create and modify selections. It's discussed further in Section 1.4.

2. Use the rulers to pull out vertical and horizontal guides. Click one of the rulers and drag out to create a new guide, or create one more precisely by choosing Image ▸ Guides ▸ New Guide. Guides are invisible lines you can use to line up objects.

3. Panning around images is made easier with the navigation control. Click it while viewing a large image or while zoomed in on a small one, and you'll see it in action.

4. The pointer coordinates display the exact location of the cursor in the units (inches, pixels, etc.) you select from the drop-down menu on the right.

5. The zoom drop-down menu let you quickly change the view of your image, but you're usually better off using the keyboard shortcuts plus (+) and minus (–) to zoom in and out. Press 1 to view your image at 100 percent.

6. The status area shows you how much memory your project is using.

7. You can also use the right-pointing arrow (in the upper-left corner of the image window) to access the image window menu. Why are there two ways to do this? This allows you to access the File menu, even when you're working with a very small canvas. Right-clicking the canvas also opens this File menu.

8. The image window also includes a zoom button, which is shaped like an hourglass and located in the upper-right corner of the image window. Click this button and then drag the window corners to resize the image. The canvas will zoom in and out to fit the new window size.

The Preferences Dialog

The GIMP's user interface is extremely configurable. You can change the keyboard shortcuts used to access tools and filters or add shortcuts to features that don't already have them. In addition, you can change the default new image size, specify how your dialogs appear on startup, set your resource consumption preferences, and much more. These options and many others are accessible via the Preferences dialog (File ▸ Preferences).

Shortcuts

One of the best ways to save time while working in the GIMP is to use existing shortcuts. You can also map your own, if you like. Open the Preferences dialog (File ▸ Preferences), and click the Interface entry on the left. Clicking the Configure Keyboard Shortcuts button allows you to map commands individually. If, for example, you often have to blur images, you may want to map CTRL-SHIFT-B to the blur command you need to apply.

Enabling dynamic keyboard shortcuts in the Preferences dialog

Alternatively, you can map shortcuts interactively. Check the box next to the words *Use dynamic keyboard shortcuts* to enable this feature. Then click OK to save your Preferences.

Return to the File menu in the toolbox. Notice that the Preferences option does not have a keyboard shortcut listed to the right of it. To add a shortcut, place the cursor over the Preferences option but don't click it. Instead, press the CTRL, SHIFT, and P keys all at once. The Preferences dialog now how has a keyboard shortcut, so go ahead and give it a try. Press CTRL-SHIFT-P, and you should find yourself back in the Preferences dialog. To remove a dynamic shortcut, keep the mouse over the menu entry and press the backspace key. Shortcuts are a huge timesaver, and they're an easy way to personalize your GIMP experience.

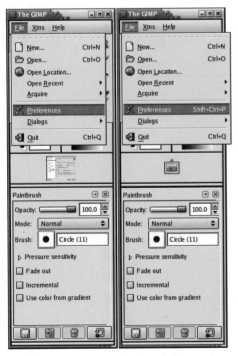

Before and after setting a keyboard shortcut for the Preferences dialog

Undo Levels and Other Environment Options

The Preferences dialog can also improve the performance of the GIMP. You can modify features such as the size of the image cache, the number of undo levels, the maximum memory that can be used for undo operations, and the maximum size that can be used for image thumbnails. If you've got the memory and the inclination, feel free to push up these values. The most often modified value is probably the Tile Cache Size. Smaller values reduce memory usage by the GIMP but slow processing of large images. If you have lots of memory and work on large images, try increasing the value from 128MB to 256MB. If you're low on memory, another option you might consider is reducing the undo levels. The default of 5 is already pretty low, however. If you reduce this value to save memory, remember to save your work often.

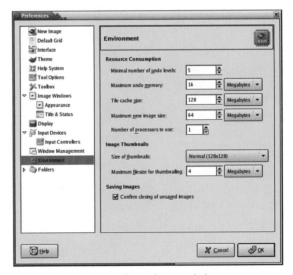

Environment settings in the Preferences dialog

Resource Folders

The Preferences dialog also allows you to configure the directories that hold files for your brushes, patterns, gradients, fonts, and so on. Click the arrow next to the Folders entry to expand all resource folders. If you want to create your own patterns or files, you can use the Preferences dialog to tell the GIMP where to save and look for those files.

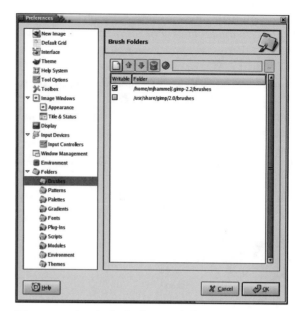

Directory settings in the Preferences dialog

1.1 DRAWING AND PAINTING

The GIMP can be used for drawing and painting, even if it's better known as a tool for editing images and photographs. The Pencil, Paintbrush, Airbrush, Eraser, and Ink tools are collectively referred to as the GIMP's paint tools. The tutorials Section 1.8 will help you get a grasp on these paint tools so you'll be prepared to experiment with them later in the book.

Paint Tools and Features

Before we discuss each of the paint tools in turn, let's discuss a few of the features they have in common.

Opacity   In the Tool Options dialog boxes for each of the paint tools, you can adjust the opacity of the brush stroke to be applied. Remember that opacity is the opposite of transparency, so a higher opacity value means the brush stroke will be less transparent.

Mode   Most of the paint tools also allow you to set the mode for the brush stroke. The blend mode defines how the stroke blends with the existing pixels in the layer upon which the stroke is applied. Different modes have different effects. Addition mode adds the brush's colors with those in the image, causing the image to lighten. Multiply mode causes the image to darken. Overlay mode can either lighten or darken the image, depending on the brush you use.

Setting the mode to Normal in the Paintbrush tool's Tool Options dialog

Modes are also used to composite layers. We'll cover modes in more detail in Section 1.2. Don't worry too much about them for now. While you experiment, stick with Normal mode.

Brushes   The global brush setting is set in the Brush preview in the Toolbox. You can also choose a brush for any of the paint tools from the Tool Options dialog. Except for the Ink tool, which uses its own brush, all of the paint tools require that you choose a specific brush. The paint tools even remember brushes; you can switch from one paint tool to another and back again without losing the settings you've chosen for either tool. The default configuration is for all paint tools to share the same brush, but this can be changed in the Preferences dialog under the Tool Options entry.

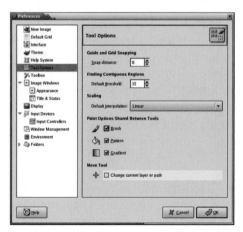

The Preferences dialog shows that brush settings are shared among all of the GIMP's paint tools (the box next to the word Brush is checked).

As you can see here, a paint tool's brush stroke can be set to fade as it is applied. The distance the stroke travels before the fade can also be adjusted in the Tool Options dialog. Just check the box next to the words *Fade out*, and then adjust the Length value to determine the length of the stroke before the fade. The Ink Tool is the only paint tool that does not offer this option.

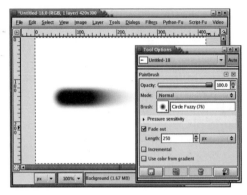

Specifying how to fade out of a brush stroke using the Paintbrush tool

Spacing　All brushes have a spacing setting. This value, which is measured in pixels, determines how far apart brush images are applied during a brush stroke. You can use the Tool Options dialog to change the default spacing for any brush. A higher spacing value allows you to create shapes like wire frames and tubing from ordinary brushes. (I'll show how to use this technique to make tubes and wires in Sections 6.3 and 6.4.)

Now that you're familiar with the basics, let's turn to the GIMP paint tools we'll use most often in this book's tutorials.

The Pencil Tool

The Pencil tool applies a hard edge, and that's important to remember. Making the most of the paint tools requires understanding the difference between hard and soft edges. When working with soft edges, levels of gray or fading color are considered partially transparent and are merged with the existing pixels in the canvas. This creates soft edges around the brush stroke.

When working with a hard edge, if a pixel in the brush stroke is more than 50 percent black (or more than 50 percent colored), the pixel in the brush stroke *replaces* the pixel on the canvas, rather than being *merged with* the existing pixel. If a pixel in the brush stroke is less than 50 percent black or colored, the pixel on the canvas is unchanged.

The difference is easy to see here, where both the Pencil tool and the Paintbrush tool are used in conjunction with the Circle (19) and Pepper brushes. The Pencil tool uses a hard edge, so it creates a jagged curved edge, whereas the Paintbrush tool (which applies a soft edge) creates smooth edges. For this reason, you won't usually make use of the Pencil when working with masks or editing photos.

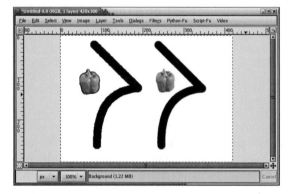

The Pencil tool (left) and Paintbrush tool (right) are used to draw lines with the Circle (19) and Pepper brushes.

The Paintbrush Tool

Throughout the tutorials, this is the paint tool we'll use most frequently. The Paintbrush tool is perfect for creating layer masks and creating selections by painting Quick Masks. In either case, the soft-edged nature of the paintbrush makes it ideal for closely matching curves.

The Paintbrush tool applies its brush only once over a given point. That is, if the Paintbrush tool is active and you hold the mouse button over the canvas and click, only one brush stroke is applied. More brush strokes are applied as you drag the cursor around the canvas.

The Airbrush Tool

The Airbrush tool is very similar to the Paintbrush tool, except that it applies a lighter or darker stroke, depending on the Rate and Pressure values set in the Tool Options dialog. It will also continue applying the brush to a single point if the cursor does not move. For these reasons, the Airbrush tool is useful for enhancing shading and lighting in images.

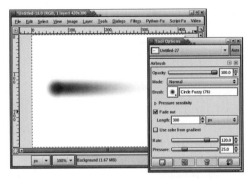

The Rate and Pressure values set in the Airbrush tool's Tool Options dialog determine how the brush stroke will look when the Airbrush tool is applied to the canvas.

The Eraser Tool

The Eraser tool is a soft-edged paint tool that removes pixels from a layer in the shape of the current brush. In all layers except the Background layer, the pixels are changed to transparent (or semi-transparent, depending on the brush used). In the Background layer, which by default does not support transparency, the erased pixels are changed to the background color in the toolbox.

The Eraser tool removes pixels from a layer.

The Eraser tool is a destructive tool; the pixels it changes are gone forever if you save the file and try to edit it again later. A better way to hide those pixels from view is with a layer mask, which is not destructive. (You'll learn a little more about layer masks when I discuss selections in Section 1.4.) You can edit a layer mask at any time in the future to adjust what is hidden. That just isn't possible with the Eraser tool, so we won't be using it very often.

The same effect is achieved using a layer mask, which leaves layer content intact so it can be reused later if necessary.

The Ink Tool

The Ink tool was specially designed for use with drawing tablets from manufacturers like Wacom. You can use the Ink tool's Tool Options dialog to adjust the shape of the brush tip, the amount of tilt applied to the brush stroke, the speed at which the brush is moved relative to the tablet pen, and much more.

These features are quite useful to users who do pen drawings, such as manga or similar artwork. Pen drawings are not the author's forte, as you can see, so we won't be using the Pen tool in any of our tutorials.

Brushes

The GIMP's stock brushes are fine for most projects, and we'll use them in tutorials throughout this book. But with a little effort you can greatly expand the selection of styles available. Creating new brushes is almost a no-brainer. Almost.

There are two types of GIMP brushes we'll discuss: ordinary and color brushes, and parametric brushes (which are scalable and must be created using the Brush Editor).

Even with the best tools, it's possible to create bad drawings.

Creating Ordinary and Colored Brushes

You can create your own GIMP brushes. The simplest brush to create is an ordinary or colored brush, which consists of an image that you either draw or import and save as a brush file by giving it a .gbr extension. Any image that can be opened in the GIMP can be saved as a brush, though some images work better than others. Very detailed images don't work well when saved as brushes, for example. In most cases the image should also be scaled down because the image will become the tip of the brush.

NOTE   *Colored brushes are just like ordinary brushes, except the former have color, while the latter are simply levels of gray.*

Ordinary brushes paint with the foreground color wherever there is black in the brush image. Where black fades to white in the brush, the foreground color is mixed with transparency before being mixed with the pixels in the canvas.

To create an ordinary or colored brush, just follow these steps.

1. Open a new image window by choosing **File ▸ New** from the toolbox. Set the size to **25 × 25 pixels**.

2. If you're creating a colored brush, you need to add an alpha channel to the background layer (Layer ▸ Transparency ▸ Add Alpha Channel). If you're creating an ordinary brush, don't add the alpha channel but instead convert the image to Grayscale (Image ▸ Mode ▸ Grayscale).

3. Use the Paintbrush tool and paint an *X* shape in the canvas. The *X* can be painted in color if you're creating a colored brush, or it will appear in grayscale if you converted the image to Grayscale in the previous step.

4. Once you've finished creating your image, give it the .gbr extension and save it to a brush directory. (Choose **File ▸ Preferences** to open the Preferences dialog, and then look under **Folders ▸ Brushes** for the correct path.)

NOTE   *To quickly turn a selection into a brush, choose Script-Fu ▸ Selection ▸ To Brush. This saves you from having to slog through directories.*

5. When the Save as Brush dialog appears, type a brush name into the Description field and set the Spacing value appropriately. A brush is like a stencil that is applied repeatedly during a brush stroke; its Spacing setting is the percentage of the width of the brush from the center of one application of the stencil to the next. For most purposes you can accept the default spacing.

6. Open the Brushes dialog (**File ▸ Dialogs ▸ Brushes**) and click the Refresh button to update the Brushes dialog. This will cause the GIMP to reread all available brush files, and it should find the one you just saved. Your new brush should appear in the palette along with the built-in brushes and any other brushes that you've defined. Your new brush is ready to use. Select it and start painting.

The Save as Brush dialog, showing a sample brush

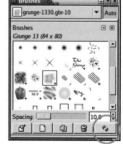

The refresh button in the Brushes dialog

NOTE *When using ordinary and colored brushes, it's not uncommon to create multiple versions of a particular brush at different sizes. The best way to do this is to create the largest brush first, then repeatedly scale down and save the image to create several smaller brushes.*

Creating Parametric Brushes

The *parametric brush* is easily modified; it can be configured to change in a number of ways as it is being used. Unlike ordinary and colored brushes, you can only create parametric brushes by using the Brush Editor. To open the Brush Editor, click the new icon in the Brushes dialog (it shows a blank sheet of paper). (If the Brushes dialog isn't active, choose File ▶ Dialog ▶ Brushes.)

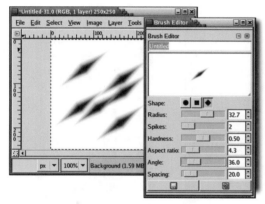

A parametric brush applied to the canvas several times (left) and shown in the Brush Editor window (right)

The Brush Editor window allows you to set a basic brush shape (oval, square, or diamond), and it allows you to adjust that shape in several ways several ways by entering values for a variety of options. The Radius is the size of the brush in pixels. The Spikes value is the number of lines that run from the center of the brush outward. These lines are obvious in the square and diamond shapes but are not visible immediately in the oval shape until you increase the Aspect Ratio, which exaggerates the effect of the spikes.

The last two options in the Brush Editor are Angle and Spacing. The Angle value is given in degrees and indicates how the spikes should be rotated around the brush center. As is true of other brushes, you can adjust the Spacing for parametric brushes.

The primary usefulness of parametric brushes is that they are easy to change as you work. It's also easy to tweak a particular brush shape to meet very specific needs. This can't be done with other brush types without opening the brush file in a canvas window, editing the brush manually, and saving it as a new brush.

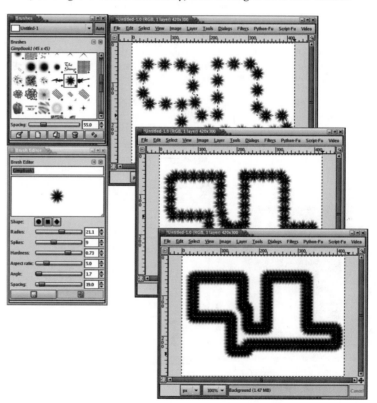

Using a parametric brush to stroke a selection allows you to achieve some interesting effects. In each example, the Spacing value is varied.

1.2 LAYERS AND MODES

Layers in the GIMP are like transparent sheets of paper piled one on top of another. Wherever a sheet is transparent, the sheets below it show through. If you lay several transparent sheets on an overhead projector and turn on the projector's light, the colors in each sheet combine to form new colors. That's exactly the way layers work. In the GIMP, the layers in the stack are combined to produce what you see in the canvas window. Changes made to layers are reflected on the canvas immediately.

Layers are the building blocks of GIMP projects because they allow you to build up an image a piece at a time, just as cartoons were created by hand before computers took over.

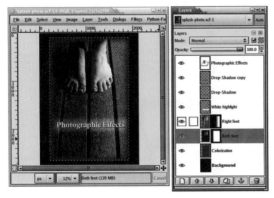

Layers in the Layers dialog and the combined image in the canvas window

The Layers Dialog

You can use either the Layer menu or the Layers dialog to manage layers. You can move a layer up or down in the layer stack by using the arrow buttons at the bottom of the Layers dialog, or you can

simply click the layer and drag it to its new position. The other buttons at the bottom of the Layers dialog include the new layer button (single page icon), the duplicate layer button (two page icon), the anchor layer button (anchor icon), and the delete button (trash can icon). Aside from the anchor layer button, the functions of these buttons are self-explanatory.

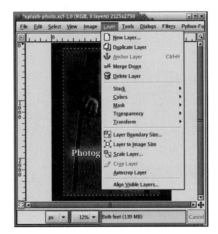

Accessing the Layer menu from the canvas window

The Layers dialog, with the button bar highlighted in red

When you copy and paste something onto the canvas, the GIMP creates a temporary layer called a *floating selection*. You can anchor this temporary layer to the current layer (the layer that was active before you pasted the new selection onto the canvas), or you make it a new layer. The anchor layer button is a shortcut for anchoring the floating selection to the current layer. Use the new layer button to make the floating selection a new layer instead. You can also use the new layer button to create a new layer from scratch.

Layers can have masks that hide parts of the layer from being used in the composite image displayed in the canvas. I'll discuss layer masks later in this section. All layers in the Layers dialog have a layer content preview. Layer masks are displayed in the Layers dialog as a second preview to the right of the layer content preview.

A layer can be visible or hidden, depending on the state of its visibility icon, which is the icon that looks like an eye in the Layers dialog and accompanies every layer. Clicking this icon toggles the layer's visibility. Somewhat counterintuitively, when a layer is not visible, the eye icon for that layer will not be displayed.

Here the Layers dialog shows a layer and its mask. The mask is indicated by the black-and-white preview to the right of the layer preview. The visibility icon appears on the far left. If the layer is hidden from view, the eye icon will not be visible either. Just click the spot where the icon should be to bring back the icon and make the layer visible again.

The Layers dialog, with a floating selection

Layers do not have to be the same size as the canvas. Layer boundaries can be outside the canvas boundary. If that is the case, any part of the layer that extends beyond the canvas is not shown

on the canvas. To expand a layer to match the canvas size, just right-click the layer in the Layers dialog and choose Layer to Image Size.

You can also use the Move tool to move layers around on the canvas. If you want to move more than one layer at a time, just anchor them together by clicking each layer's anchor icon, clicking the layers you want to anchor, and then clicking and dragging on the canvas.

You can make any layer partially opaque by choosing that layer and adjusting the Opacity slider in the Layers dialog. The setting you choose for this Opacity slider combines with any opacity changes that you may define with a layer mask.

The GIMP takes the transparent sheet metaphor a bit further, of course. You can use one of several methods to combine a layer with the layers below it. Each method is called a *layer mode*.

Modes are an important GIMP concept because besides being applicable to layers, they are also applicable to the paint tools. Let's start by looking at paint modes before we return to layer modes, though as you'll see, the two GIMP features are nearly identical.

The anchor layer icon links layers so they can be moved together.

Paint Modes

Paint modes are available for use with all paint tools, from the Blend tool to the Bucket Fill tool to the Paintbrush tool. A paint mode defines how the paint tool combines what it paints with the pixels already in the layer. This process of mixing the new with the old is known as *compositing*.

A paint mode is a mathematical method of combining colors and transparency in the GIMP. The idea is that for each color channel (red, green, and blue), two different pixels are composited in a specified manner using some combination of addition, subtraction, multiplication, and division.

An important paint mode concept is that color channels only have 256 possible values (0 through 255, where 0 is no color and 255 is full color in that channel). That is because the GIMP only uses 8 bits per color channel: 8 bits = 2^8 = 256 (you get the value by squaring the number of bits). And when you combine all three channels, you end up with 256^3 possible colors (not including the alpha [or transparency] channel) for any single pixel. With some modes, the process of adding, subtracting, and so forth can produce values outside of this range. In that case the mode either *clamps* (that is, forces) the value back to the minimum value (0) or maximum value (255), or it wraps around to the other side of the range.

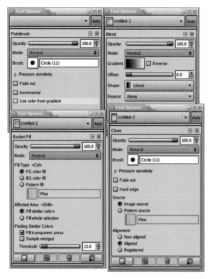

Paint modes (highlighted in red) are available for use with all paint tools.

NOTE *As part of an integration of the GEGL project and the GIMP project, the GIMP will get 16-bit color channels in an upcoming release. At this time, no date has been set for the release of this integrated product.*

Like paint modes, layer modes define how layers are composited. The difference between paint modes and layer modes is that paint modes are applied as painting operations occur, so paint modes changes are immediate and actually change the pixels in layers. A layer mode is used to tell the GIMP how to combine a layer with the layers below it, but this compositing does not actually change pixels. It only changes the way the canvas appears as the layers are composited internally and displayed in the GIMP.

There are 23 GIMP paint modes, of which 21 can also be used as layer modes (the Behind and Color Erase paint modes cannot be used by layers). The following table lists these modes and briefly describes how each of them work. In this table, the *existing pixel*

is the pixel (and its multiple color channels) in the current layer, while the *new pixel* is the one added by the paint tool. Operations performed on pixels affect each channel (red, green, and blue). When we discuss layer modes in the next section, remember that those modes apply in the same way, except that the existing pixel comes from the current layer and the new pixel comes from the layer below it.

Paint Modes and Functions

Mode	Function
Normal	Normal mode is the default paint mode. The color of the new pixel added by the paint tool replaces the color of the existing pixel in the layer.
Dissolve	Dissolve mode works just as Normal mode works, except that random blank areas are added to the stroke while painting. This is similar to dabbing paint on a canvas with just the tip of a brush.
Behind	In layers with transparency, this mode only paints the transparent areas. The result is that it looks as though the new pixels were applied behind the existing pixels.
Color Erase	Color Erase mode is similar to the Eraser tool, except that instead of erasing the complete brush shape it only erases pixels that are the foreground color.
Multiply	This mode multiplies the current pixel by the new pixel and then divides the result by white (255). It clamps the colors to 0. The result is usually a darker pixel.
Divide	This mode divides the new pixel by the existing pixel and then multiplies the result by white. It clamps the color to 255. The result is usually a lighter pixel.
Screen	Screen mode subtracts each pixel from white, multiplies the results together, subtracts that result from white again, and then divides by white. It clamps the color to 255. The resulting pixel is generally much lighter.
Overlay	Overlay mode is a mixture of Multiply and Screen modes. It makes dark areas darker and light areas lighter.
Dodge	This mode is similar to Screen mode. It subtracts the existing pixel from white, inverts the result, multiplies the result by the new pixel, and then multiplies by white. It clamps the color to 255. As is true of Screen mode, the result is a lighter image.
Burn	Burn mode subtracts the new pixel from white, multiplies the result by white, and then divides by the existing pixel. Then the result is subtracted from white again. The result tends to be a darker image.
Hard Light	Hard Light mode tests pixels to see if they are closer to black or white before it chooses which operations to perform. It's another mixture of Multiply and Screen modes, and the result is usually the opposite of what you'd get if you used Overlay mode.
Soft Light	Soft Light mode is another combination of Multiply and Screen modes that produces results that are similar to those of Overlay mode.

Mode	Function
Grain Extract	This mode subtracts the existing pixel from the new pixel and adds 128. In many images, the Grain Extract mode tends to produce what look like inverted colors.
Grain Merge	Grain Merge mode adds the existing pixel to the new pixel and then subtracts 128. In general, you'll find this produces richer colors in photographs.
Difference	This mode subtracts the existing pixel from the new pixel and takes the absolute value of the result. Because an absolute value is used, there is no clamping necessary, and the result can often appear similar to color negative film.
Addition	The Addition mode adds the two pixels together and clamps to 255.
Subtract	This mode subtracts the existing pixel from the new pixel and clamps to 0.
Darken Only	If the existing pixel is greater than the new pixel, Darken Only mode uses the new pixel.
Lighten Only	If the existing pixel is less than the new pixel, Lighten Only mode uses the new pixel.
Hue	Hue mode works on pixels by converting from RGB to HSV first, then pulling the Hue from the existing pixel and using the Saturation and Value from the new pixel.
Saturation	Saturation mode is similar to Hue mode, except that this mode pulls the Saturation from the existing pixel and uses the Hue and Value from the new pixel.
Color	Color mode is similar to Hue mode, except that when this mode is used, the Saturation and Hue come from the existing pixel, while the Value comes from the new pixel.
Value	Value mode is also similar to Hue mode, except that this mode pulls the Value from the existing pixel and uses the Saturation and Hue from the new pixel.

Layer Modes

Using paint tools to mix pixels is an inherently destructive process, as painting with any mode will change the pixels in the layer. That isn't always a bad thing, but what about those times when you need to restore the original pixel information? Using the GIMP to create art nearly always involves experimenting, which often means abandoning one set of changes, going back to the source image, and trying something different. What if tomorrow—after having saved and exited the GIMP—you want to edit the image differently? Those pixels will have lost their original settings forever.

To keep the original pixel settings, use layer modes instead. A layer mode works by blending the current layer with the pixels in the layers below it. The method of blending is the same as with paint modes, except that layer modes combine the pixel values as they are displayed on the canvas, without actually changing the pixels in the lower layers. For example, using the Bucket Fill tool

to apply a pattern and then switching to Hard Light layer mode doesn't change any of the pixels below the current layer. The current layer can therefore change in any way necessary—at any time—without worry that you'll lose pixel values for any other layer.

To set a layer mode, use the Layers dialog's Mode drop-down menu. Aside from the Behind and Color Erase modes, all of the modes that are available for use as paint modes are available for use as layer modes. And layer modes can be changed at any time. Because changing layer modes doesn't physically change the pixels (it only affects how the composite image is displayed on the canvas), doing so doesn't use up any additional memory or consume any of your undo levels.

The Layers dialog, with the Mode drop-down menu highlighted

NOTE   *The Undo command allows you to step back through your recent changes. You can step back as many times as you want until you've used the maximum amount of undo memory, as configured in the Environment section of the Preferences dialog. The default amount of undo memory is 16 megabytes, which is quite sufficient for small images destined for the web but may not be enough for poster-sized prints. You can step back through your recent changes by repeatedly pressing CTRL-Z or by choosing Edit ▸ Undo from the canvas window. You'll know you've reached the maximum undo memory allowed if pressing CTRL-Z stops undoing your steps. Instead of being surprised when you reach that point while working on a project, you may want to increase the minimum undo level right now. . . .*

Using a Layer Mode to Colorize an Image

We'll use layer modes in many tutorials throughout the book, but here's a minitutorial to introduce you to them. *Colorizing* an image adds color wherever the target area is not completely black. In this process, the image is *desaturated*—all color content is removed—leaving behind an image that is still in RGB mode but only contains shades of gray. Only at this point do we add color.

1.   Open any image and start by desaturating the original layer (**Layer ▸ Colors ▸ Desaturate**).

2. Add a new transparent layer above it by choosing **Layer ▸ New** and setting the Layer Fill Type to **Transparency**.

3. Click the foreground color in the toolbox to change the foreground color. Choose any color you like, and then drag the foreground color onto the canvas to fill the new layer with the chosen color.

4. Set the mode for this layer to **Color**.

Because the color is specifically chosen in the Change Foreground Color dialog, this colorization method provides more control than other methods. It also doesn't wash out the image as much as the Colorize tool does.

First desaturate your image. Then colorize the image by adding a layer above the original layer, filling the new layer with color, and setting the new layer's mode to Color.

Using a Layer Mask to Colorize an Image

Using layer modes you can selectively add color to your image using the same technique we just used combined with a layer mask. A *layer mask* prevents portions of a layer from showing through so that only certain parts of a layer appear in the composite image displayed in the canvas window. Wherever there is black in the mask, that part of the layer is not used in the composite image. Wherever there is white in the mask, that part is used.

1. Add a layer mask to the colored layer from the previous example (**Layer ▸ Mask ▸ Add Layer Mask**).

2. When prompted, click the radio button next to the words *White (full opacity)*.

3. With the canvas selected, press **D** to reset the default foreground and background colors. Then drag the foreground color (black) from the toolbox onto the canvas to fill the mask with black so that none of the colored layer is visible.

4. Make a selection on the canvas, and then drag the background color (white) into the selection. This will add white to the mask inside the selected area, allowing that part of the colored layer to be used in the composite image displayed in the canvas window.

A layer mask—visible to the right of the layer preview—lets us colorize only the lion. Click the mask in the Layers dialog to make the mask active. Then apply the paint tools to the mask to change the shape of the mask to suit your needs.

Layer and Layer Mode Tips

By now you should be familiar with the fundamentals of layers and modes. Here are some tips to keep in mind as you experiment.

- Screen and Addition layer modes brighten images. Multiply and Subtract modes darken them. But Overlay mode can do both!

- Remember that differencing white from red gives a different result than subtracting white from red. Subtracting one layer from another will clamp the result to black. Imagine that one layer contains a red value of 100 and a second layer contains a red value of 40. Subtracting the first layer from the second would result in −60, but Subtract mode can't read values below 0 (black). Difference mode will take the absolute value instead.

- For a cleaner effect, try using the Soft Light layer mode instead of the Color layer mode to colorize an image.

- Layer modes do not use up memory. Switching among layer modes will not affect the GIMP's overall performance, so go ahead and experiment! (You'll get plenty of practice with layer modes in the upcoming tutorials.)

- Be sure to give layers meaningful names. The default names are never descriptive enough, and it's easy to get lost when working with a dozen or more layers. Just click the layer name in the Layers dialog and type the new, more descriptive name. Press ENTER when you're finished making your changes.

- There are many ways to colorize an image. One way is to use the Colorize tool. This is the fastest method, and the results will be nearly as good as if you'd used a layer mode. Open any image, then desaturate it (Layers ▸ Colors ▸ Desaturate). Then open the Colorize tool (Layers ▸ Color ▸ Colorize) and adjust the Hue, Saturation, and Lightness sliders until the preview shows the desired result.

Here I've used the Colorize tool to colorize an image. Unlike the Color layer mode, the Colorize tool actually changes the pixel content. Be certain you really want to make the change before using this tool.

1.3 COLOR MODES

When working with images, the GIMP uses one of three color modes: RGB, Grayscale, or Indexed. Each mode represents a particular type of color model. Color is a very complex subject, but I'll try to summarize it for you.

A color model is way of representing colors with a set of numbers that define the color's component parts. Different color models can map to different color spaces. Imagine a color space graph inside which you could draw a triangle. The triangle would be the model where each vertex is one of the three primary colors: R, G, or B. According to this model, when R = 100, G = 100, and B = 100, you have dark gray. If you slide the triangle to the right in the graph (be careful to stay inside the graph) you still have a color model with three values at 100, but those values define a different color. To produce a particular color, you need both the color model (which is the set of colors you can display) and the color space (which defines the colors you see).

NOTE   *To be honest, it's much more complex than this. We won't get into the mathematics behind color theory here, but the general idea is important, as you'll see.*

There are many different color models and color spaces. At this time, however, the GIMP only works within the sRGB color space using the RGB, Grayscale, and Indexed color models. The RGB model is used for displaying work on the monitor because it is an additive model, according to which each component is added together to produce a color. The monitor starts with black (0/0/0), and as you increase the values of each component, the screen grows brighter. If the full amounts of each component is added, you get white.

Another well-known and popular color model is CMYK, which is used primarily for printing, and which the GIMP does not yet support. In contrast to RGB, CMYK is a subtractive model. If equal amounts of C, M, Y, and K are applied, you get black.

You can see why converting from one color model to another is a fairly complex task. You need to know a lot more than just the color of the pixel on your display.

NOTE   *Support for CMYK is expected in the next GIMP release, but this update is dependent upon another open source project that may not be completed in time, so I can't make any promises.*

RGB mode is the mode that's most commonly used for screen images, and it will be used throughout this book. The letters R, G, and B stand for *red*, *green*, and *blue* and represent the three color channels of an RGB image. Every pixel in an image is a composite of the pixels in each of the three color channels. Each channel uses 8 bits and can define a color by a set of integer numbers that range from 0 to 255. This gives you a respectable 16 million total colors with which to work.

The GIMP's image modes: RGB, Grayscale, and Indexed

Working in RGB mode (Image ▶ Mode ▶ RGB) means you can also use transparency. *Transparency* is a measure of how much light can pass through a given pixel. The color of a pixel that appears on the canvas is the result of combining that pixel's three channels and then mixing the color of the composited pixel with some percentage of the composited pixels beneath it in the layer stack. Transparency is also the opposite of opaqueness. If a pixel is 30 percent transparent, it is 70 percent opaque.

Default color channels for an RGB image

By default, transparent regions in a single layer are indicated by a checkered pattern. The pattern is configurable in the Preferences dialog.

If an RGB image has some transparency, that information is stored in a fourth channel, called an alpha channel. When you're asked to choose Alpha to Selection or Add Alpha Channel, you'll be working with an image or layer's transparency information.

Grayscale mode (Image ▶ Mode ▶ Grayscale), which is an image setting that uses a single channel with 256 levels of gray (no color), can be useful for some artistic projects, or when working with black-and-white photographs or scans. You can easily desaturate an image by switching to Grayscale mode.

Indexed mode (Image ▶ Mode ▶ Indexed) is useful when converting an RGB image to a GIF file destined for use on the Web. The GIF file format only allows for 256 colors in an image. Each image holds a table of index numbers and each index number represents a single color. One, but only one, of those index numbers can also be used to specify transparency. For example, if the index number that specifies blue is also set to specify transparency in a GIF file, when a program displays the image, it will display transparency instead of displaying blue. Indexed formats like GIF have only two levels of transparency: on and off. When using Indexed mode, there is no way to specify that a pixel should be semi-transparent.

Changing from RGB to Indexed mode will allow you to choose from one of several methods of *dithering*, which is a way of grouping similar colors into a single color, thus reducing the total number of colors to less than or equal to 256 (the maximum number of colors allowed in a GIF file). Dithering is required in the conversion from RGB mode to Indexed mode because RGB images can have up to 16 million colors, while Indexed images can't have more than 256 colors. The colors in the

Convert Image to Indexed Colors dialog

image can also be mapped to a particular color palette. Both the color palette and method of dithering are selected in the Convert Image to Indexed Colors dialog, which opens when you choose Image ▶ Mode ▶ Indexed.

The GIF format uses a single pixel for transparency, making it very difficult to blend round edges next to transparent areas with anything that might be behind them. The GIF format does not support alpha blending, a technique for mixing pixels along edges that requires multiple levels of transparency for individual pixels. In a GIF file, a pixel is either transparent or it isn't.

A good alternative to the GIF format is the PNG format, which supports multiple levels of transparency for individual pixels, comes with fewer licensing restrictions, and is also supported by the GIMP. For all of these reasons, GIF files are quickly being replaced by PNG files. I recommend converting Indexed images to RGB and saving them as PNG, TIFF, or JPEG files.

While many web designers are migrating from GIF to PNG files, the problem remains that not all versions of Internet Explorer properly display PNG files that contain varying levels of transparency. The GIMP can correctly save an RGB image with multiple levels of transparency (in other words, areas that are semi-transparent and intended to blend with whatever background the image is positioned over). The issue is that most recent versions of Internet Explorer interpret anything other than complete transparency incorrectly and display such an image with a solid color instead.

1.4 SELECTIONS

Want to make the most of your GIMP experience? Master the art of effectively creating selections. Nothing is more important. Nothing. The perfect selection can meld one image with another or map one image onto another. The perfect selection can turn day into night. There's not much you can do with an image editor without making selections, and this section focuses on learning how to select as accurately and efficiently as possible.

All GIMP selections are outlined by a set of moving dashes, known as *marching ants*. You can set the speed of the ants by choosing File ▸ Preferences from the toolbox menu and clicking the Image Windows entry. If you want to toggle the visibility of selections, choose View ▸ Show Selections.

Selection Constraints

It is possible to change the behavior of the GIMP's selection tools by holding down various keys on the keyboard. These keys are known as *keyboard modifiers* because they modify the behavior of the active tool. If a keyboard modifier is pressed when you click and drag on the canvas to create a selection, the modifier affects the selection constraint. A *selection constraint* defines the shape and size of a selection.

Pressing CTRL or SHIFT *while* using the Rectangle or Ellipse Select tool constrains the selection in such a way that the height and the width are always equal. This means rectangular selections are squares and elliptical selections are circles. But this is only true if you release the mouse button *before* you release the keyboard modifier. If you release the CTRL or SHIFT key first, the constraint is removed.

Another way to constrain a selection is by using the drop-down menu in the Tool Options dialogs for each of the selection

tools. This menu has three options: Free Select, Fixed Size, and Fixed Aspect Ratio. When you choose Fixed Size or Fixed Aspect Ratio, you must set values in the Width and Height fields below the drop-down menu. If you choose Fixed Size, dragging on the canvas creates a selection of the specified size. If you choose Fixed Aspect Ratio, the Width and Height values you enter define the preferred ratio and any selections you create are constrained to that ratio.

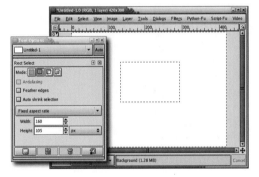

You can use keyboard modifiers to constrain selections. You can also use the Tool Options dialog for each selection tool.

Guides and layer boundaries can also serve as constraint tools.

Guides   A *guide* is a horizontal or vertical line that doesn't show up in your final image but can be used to align project elements such as layers and selections. You can drag out guides from the rulers, but you can only position them imprecisely that way. If you need to position guides at absolute pixel offsets (as we'll do in several of this book's tutorials), use one of the options available in the Image ▸ Guides menu.

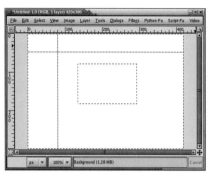

Pull horizontal guides from the top ruler, or pull vertical guides from the left ruler. Use the Move tool to drag them out of the window one at a time, or choose Image ▸ Guides ▸ Remove All Guides to remove all guides at once.

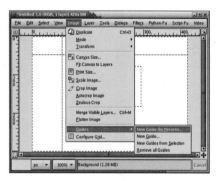

The Image ▸ Guides menu allows you to add guides by percent (New Guide (by Percent)) or by pixel offsets (New Guide). You can also wrap guides around an existing selection (New Guides from Selection).

Layer Boundaries Layer boundaries are indicated by yellow-and-black dashed lines. When a layer is selected, nothing can be drawn beyond its layer boundary. You can select a layer's corner without clicking it; just start inside the selection and drag through the corner you want to select and beyond the layer boundary. Only the portion of the selection inside the layer boundary will be selected.

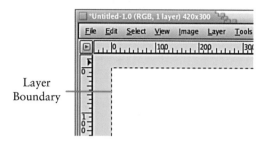

A yellow-and-black dashed line indicates the layer boundary.

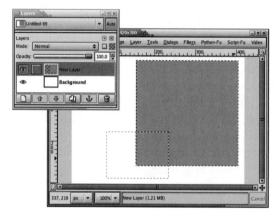

If part of a selection lies outside a layer's boundaries, that portion is not actually selected.

Selection Modes

While selection constraints set the size and shape of a selection, *selection modes* combine two or more selections, regardless of the constraints that have been applied to each. It's often necessary to make several selections and then combine them in different ways. Such merged selections are useful, for example, when selecting unusually shaped objects in a photograph or when outlining a shape before filling it with a color or pattern. We'll merge selections in Chapter 6 when we create each piece of a user interface design separately and then combine them in one image.

To combine selections, use the mode buttons in the selection tools' Tool Options dialogs. In order from left to right, Replace mode creates a new selection that replaces any existing selections, Add mode adds the new selection to the existing selection, Subtract mode subtracts from the existing selection wherever the new selection overlaps the existing selection, and Intersect mode creates a selection

Each selection tool's Tool Options dialog gives you access to four mode buttons: Replace, Add, Subtract, and Intersect.

a selection only where the new and existing selections overlap. If there is no existing selection, Replace and Add modes simply create the new selection by itself and Subtract and Intersect mode do nothing.

The mode buttons in the Tool Options dialog also map to keyboard modifiers. Holding down the SHIFT key while dragging activates the Add mode, while holding down the CTRL key while dragging activates the Subtract mode. Holding down both keys while dragging activates the Intersect mode. These keyboard modifiers apply to the Rectangle, Ellipse, and Free Select tools, as well as to the Select by Color tool. Note that when you hold down these keys, the associated mode button is selected in the Tool Options dialog until you release the keys.

You can use the ALT key to move selections. Hold down the ALT key and click and drag inside a selection on the canvas to move that selection. As with all of the keystrokes discussed here, be sure to hold these keys down before you start to work with a selection, otherwise you may end up setting a selection constraint instead of setting a selection mode.

When using the various selection tool modes, the cursor changes depending on which mode is active, as shown here. With experience,

The cursor changes, depending on which mode is active. In Add mode, the cursor does not have an icon to the upper right, as it does for the other modes.

you'll learn to recognize these cursors, but if you're new to the GIMP you'll want to keep an eye on the Tool Options dialog when working with selections. When working with keyboard modifiers, it's very easy to confuse the mode you're in with the constraint you may (or may not) be trying to apply to a new selection.

Free Selections

When working with photographs or any existing digital image, you seldom need a perfectly rectangular or oval selection. Instead, you need to outline odd shapes with odd selections. When these shapes have complicated edges, often your only option is to draw the selection by hand. In the GIMP, you use the Free Select tool for this.

To make a freehand selection, choose the Free Select tool from the toolbox, click the canvas, and drag around the shape you want to select. As you drag, a solid line appears, showing the edge of your selection. When you release the mouse button, the solid line is replaced by the familiar marching ants.

Using the Free Select tool to make a freehand selection

Dragging to create a closed loop around part of an image isn't always the easiest way to make a selection. Fortunately, the GIMP offers a wealth of alternatives. Let's experiment by using three different tools to create a selection.

The Fuzzy Select Tool

If the portion of the image you want to select is outlined by a solid color or other obvious edges, the toolbox provides the Fuzzy Select, Select by Color, and Scissors tools. The Fuzzy Select tool works best when a solid color surrounds the object of interest. The Select by Color tool is best at pulling a shape from an image based on groups of pixels that are not necessarily adjacent to each other. The Scissors tool is for when you need to get down and dirty; it finds the edges of an object by noting where color changes are dramatic near a line you draw with mouse clicks. The outline is solid, and anchor points appear wherever you click the image. The actual selection isn't created until you re-click the first anchor point to close the solid outline and then click inside the solid outline to convert it to the marching ants.

There are several alternatives to the Free Select tool, among them the Fuzzy Select, Select by Color, and Scissors tools.

The most important option in the Fuzzy Select tool's Tool Options dialog is the Threshold setting. Lower Threshold values mean fewer pixels are selected. Keep in mind that when you click the canvas using the Fuzzy Select tool, all pixels that are within the distance specified (a difference in color) and that are adjacent to each other are added to the selection. It's important to remember that the pixels must be adjacent. Notice that the Fuzzy Select tool will always create one large selection. It will be oddly shaped, but there will be just one. The Select by Color tool, on the other hand, creates many selections.

The Select by Color Tool

The Select by Color tool's Tool Options dialog also offers us a Threshold setting. It functions just as the Fuzzy Select tool's Threshold setting functions: The tool selects all pixels within the range of the threshold. When using the Select by Color tool, however, the pixels do not have to be adjacent. Because of this, the Select by Color tool has the potential to create thousands of small and independent selections. In this example, because the white background contrasts so much with the beans and their shadows, the Select by Color tool creates only one selection. Using a low Threshold setting and clicking the white background creates a selection that includes all the beans and nearly every pixel that contains even a hint of shadow.

The Fuzzy Select tool allows you to select the beans and their shadows by simply clicking the white area that surrounds them.

Because in this case we can simply choose a white pixel from the area around the beans, the Select by Color tool and the Fuzzy Select tool work similarly. The beans and their shadows contrast with the white background, so the Select by Color tool works quickly.

This example shows that both the Select by Color tool and the Fuzzy Select tool can make very precise selections as long as the contrast between the object of interest and the rest of the image is high. For situations where that isn't the case, you're better off using the Scissors tool.

Scissors could be used to outline the beans (sans the shadows) to make a finer grain selection, though for this particular image it would probably be easier to use Fuzzy Select and increase the Threshold setting.

The Scissors Tool

The Scissors tool works by outlining an object with a set of solid lines that are connected with anchor points. The anchor points are also referred to as *control points* or *nodes*, and the Scissors tool's anchor points are similar to the Paths tool's anchor points (see "Path Anchors" on page 58).

To create a selection with the Scissors tool, click the canvas to drop anchor points around the object of interest. As you drop anchors, the GIMP draws a solid line connecting each new anchor to the previous anchors. The GIMP computes these lines based on changes in color. In this example, the beans and their shadows have distinct color differences, so clicking near the edge of the bean creates an outline around just the bean, excluding the bean shadow. To close the outline, click the first anchor you dropped. Then click inside the outline to convert the area to a selection.

You can edit the outline before you convert it to a selection by clicking any existing anchor point and dragging it to a new location. You can even add new anchor points by clicking a line between any two existing anchor points. Adding new anchors and moving existing anchors lets you tweak your outline before you convert it to a selection. This might be necessary if you find that the GIMP's dividing line doesn't suit your needs.

Creating Masks from Selections

Sometimes a project requires you to isolate an object in an image in order to create a mask of that object. Often this object is not easy to select by itself, but the area around it is.

Look at this rose set against a white background. It's easy to isolate the white area with the Select by Color or Fuzzy Select tools. Once the selection is made, you can invert it (Select ▶ Invert) to create a selection that only includes the flower. Then all you need to do is create a black mask and fill it with white.

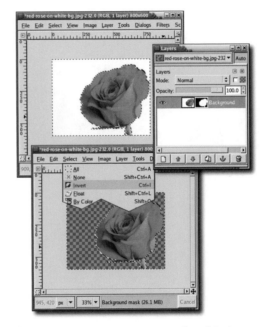

To create a mask of the rose, choose the solid white background, invert the selection, add a black layer mask, and fill the selection with white.

Feathering Selections

Creating a selection to isolate an object in a photograph sometimes requires a little more work. You may need to *feather* the selection. When creating a selection, the GIMP normally includes a pixel or doesn't include it; there are no partially selected pixels. This will usually give the selection hard edges, and you'll often notice that they have a stairstep appearance.

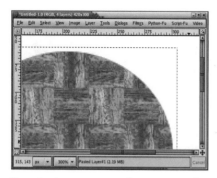

Zooming in on a pattern that was cut and pasted as an unfeathered selection reveals a jagged edge.

Feathering a selection softens the selection's edge by allowing pixels to be partially selected. This means that some pixels are actually partially transparent, and that means that when you copy and paste the selection, the selection's edge will blend more easily with its new surroundings.

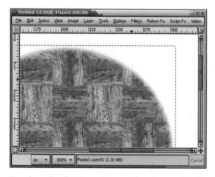

Feathered selections have soft edges, allowing them to blend into the background when copied and pasted into another image.

You can use the Feather Selection dialog (Select ▸ Feather) to feather a selection you've created. In the dialog shown and by default, the feathering depth is set in pixels, but you can choose several other units from the drop-down menu. The feathering application divides this depth in half. It leaves the innermost pixels fully opaque and makes the outermost pixels fully transparent.

The Feather Selection dialog lets you specify the feathering depth in one of several units.

As they are closer to the outermost edge, the pixels in between are increasingly transparent.

To see how feathering a selection can make a difference, let's look at how we'd use feathering with the rose image. Starting with a red rose on a white background, use the Fuzzy Select tool to create a selection of the white background, and then invert the selection to select the rose (**Select ▸ Invert**).

The Fuzzy Select Tool makes it easy to create a fairly accurate selection before feathering.

Before we feather the selection, let's take a look at what the selection would look like without feathering. The selection looks pretty good until you copy and paste it onto a black background as shown here. The edge of the rose has a white line that becomes clear only when you paste the selection onto a high-contrast background. With feathering we can make the edge of the rose blend into the black background much better. Let's get back to the selection of the rose.

The edge of the rose picked up some of the white background, making it difficult to blend it with the new black background.

1. Shrink the selection by **3 pixels** (**Selection ▸ Shrink**). Shrinking the selection allows us to move the selection past the alpha-blended pixels (pixels that are partly rose colored and partly background colored) on the edge of the rose in toward more solid rose-colored pixels.

2. Use the Feather Selection dialog (**Select ▸ Feather**) to feather the reduced selection by **3 pixels**. Since we shrank our selection, this will give us semi-transparent pixels at the edge of our selection that are mostly rose colored rather than the color of the background.

   The number of pixels by which we shrink and feather the selection is the same here, and the number is small. This is because the rose image's dimensions are only 1,024 × 768 pixels. For larger images the amounts would be increased. For images where the background color doesn't contrast with the selection as uniformly, the amount might also increase. There is no rule of thumb for the amount to shrink or feather. Experimentation is really your only guide.

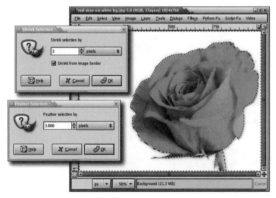

Shrinking changes the position of the selection, but feathering does not.

3. Once you've applied the feathering, copy the selection, and then paste it as a new layer by choosing **Edit ▸ Paste** and then choosing **Layer ▸ New**.

4. Add a new layer (**Layer ▸ New**) and fill it with black by dragging the foreground color from the toolbox into the selection.

5. Move this new layer below the copied layer in the layer stack (**Layer ▸ Stack ▸ Lower Layer**).

Feathering the rose selection allows it to blend more smoothly with the high-contrast background.

Zoom in on the edges to compare the unfeathered and feathered selections. The difference that feathering makes should be obvious. Without much more effort, the edge of the rose blends more smoothly with the black background. The rose on the left was not feathered, and the edges of that image are pixilated. The image on the right *was* feathered, and its appearance is improved.

Comparing unfeathered (left) and feathered (right) selections

Using the Quick Mask

The Fuzzy Select tool works well with images like the rose, where the subject appears against a solid background. But there is an even more intuitive way to make selections of oddly shaped objects, and it can be especially handy when the background isn't solid. *Quick Masks* allow you to paint over an image to create your selection.

To use the Quick Mask, click the Quick Mask button in the lower-left corner of the image window. Doing so gives the image a red tint. Choose any paint tool and any brush. Set the foreground color to white by pressing D and then X while the canvas is selected. Start painting with your chosen paint tool and brush, rubbing away the red in the Quick Mask. Click the Quick Mask button again when you've covered the area you want to select. Where you remove the Quick Mask, the area is converted into a selection. It doesn't get any easier than that!

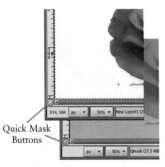

Quick Mask Buttons

The Quick Mask button is in the lower-left corner of the canvas window. When not in use, the button's icon is a square selection symbol. When you click the Quick Mask button, the icon becomes a red square.

The original yellow car is in the upper-left image. In the upper-right image, the Quick Mask is turned on and the image is tinted red. In the lower-left image, the yellow body of the car has been painted with white. Clicking the Quick Mask button again converts the painted area into a selection and allows us to change the color of the car's body.

Deselecting Selections

So what do you do after you're done with your selections? You can save a selection to a channel by choosing Select ▶ Save to Channel from any canvas menu, or you can discard the selection. Choosing Select ▶ None will discard the current selection. Alternatively, you can press CTRL-SHIFT-A.

Saving a selection to a channel allows you to retrieve the selection from the Channels dialog later (Dialogs ▶ Channels). Simply click the saved channel to make it active, then click the Channel to Selection button at the bottom of the dialog. We'll use this process a few times in various tutorials later in this book.

The Channel to Selection button is highlighted in red in the Channels dialog.

Working with Selections

Once you have a good selection, you can do just about anything with it. You can fill it with color by simply dragging the foreground or background colors from the toolbox into the selection. You can use any of the paint tools inside the selection without worrying about painting outside the selection area.

Drag the foreground or background colors from the toolbox into any selection to fill it with color.

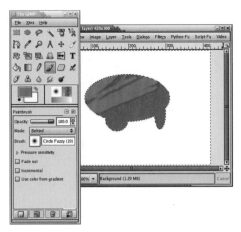

Paint in the selection without worrying about affecting anything beyond the selection.

You can also use selections to isolate regions where filters can be applied. For example, you can apply a motion blur to the rose selection without blurring anything that lies beyond it.

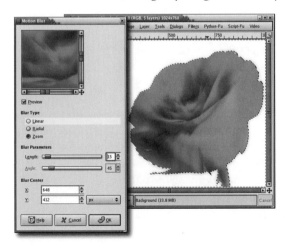

Blur the selection without worrying about blurring anything beyond the selection.

You can also use any paint tool in combination with the foreground color to trace a selection. Tracing a selection in this manner is known as *stroking* the selection, and the Stroke Selection menu is available by choosing Edit ▶ Stroke Selection.

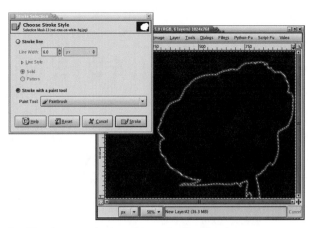

Stroking the rose selection with a soft-edged brush

Selection Tips

Keep these hints in mind as you practice working with selections:

- If you have trouble remembering how the SHIFT and CTRL keyboard modifiers work, remember that it's easier to use the mode buttons in the selection tools' Tool Options dialogs to specify how you want the new selection to interact with the existing selection. If you can remember that you can set the aspect ratio in the same dialog, you can just forget about the SHIFT and CTRL keys.

- You can combine Quick Masks with existing selections. Any existing selections will not have the red tint when you click the Quick Mask button for the first time. Paint as necessary, and then click the button again to combine the selections.

- It's not uncommon for users to find that they can't create a new selection, having forgotten that they chose Subtract or Intersect mode in a selection tool's Tool Options dialog. If this happens to you, just check the Tool Options dialog and make sure the mode is set to Replace. Using the mode buttons sets a selection tool to that mode until you change it manually. That's one reason why experienced users learn to use the keyboard modifiers. The modifiers only apply for the time it takes to make a new selection.

1.5 DRAWING BASIC SHAPES

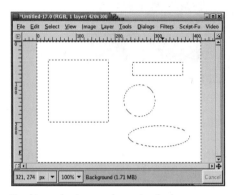

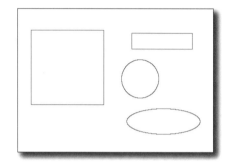

Stroking selections to draw simple shapes

The most common question new GIMP users ask is, "How do I create basic shapes?" In this section we'll consider two methods: stroking selections and using the Gfig plug-in.

Drawing Simple Shapes

If the shapes you need to draw are relatively simple, your best bet is to stroke selections.

1. Choose the **Rectangle Select** tool or the **Ellipse Select** tool from the toolbox, and then drag to create a selection. Press the SHIFT key as you drag to constrain the selection such that its width and height are equal (producing a perfect square or circle), and then release the SHIFT key create the selection.

2. Choose the **Circle (01)** brush from the Brushes dialog.

3. Choose **Select ▸ Stroke Selection** and in the Stroke Selection dialog click the radio button next to the words *Stroke with a paint tool*. Select **Paintbrush** from the Paint Tool drop-down menu. This gives the selection nice, clean edges.

4. Click **Stroke** to stroke the selection.

Triangles require a little special handling.

1. Drag two vertical and two horizontal guides from the rulers to outline a square to contain the triangle. Basic geometry tells us that any rectangle can be divided into two triangles by dissecting the rectangle diagonally between opposite vertices. We'll use this knowledge to draw our own triangle.

2. Choose the Paths tool from the toolbox, and then click any three intersections of the guides to mark the vertices of the triangle.

3. In the Paths dialog (choose **File ▸ Dialogs ▸ Paths** if it isn't already open) click the **Create Selection from Path** button. This will create a selection using the three points you chose and the vertices of a triangle.

4. Choose **Edit ▸ Stroke Selection** to draw the shape.

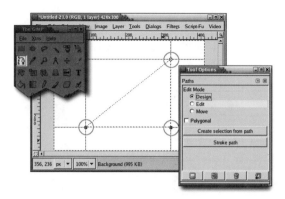

Using paths to draw a triangle

Drawing Irregular Shapes

Creating closed irregular shapes can be simple, or it can be complicated, depending on the project. The easy way to create such shapes is to subtract from and add to existing selections. For example, start by creating a rectangular selection. Then hold down the CTRL key to subtract from the existing selection, or hold down the SHIFT key to add to the existing selection. As an alternative, you could also use the selection tool's Tool Options dialog, clicking the appropriate mode buttons instead. Using the Tool Options dialog also lets you specify exact pixel amounts to subtract or add.

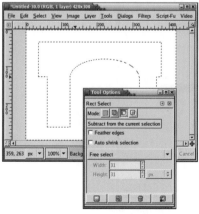

The mode buttons in the selection tools' Tool Options dialogs let you combine selections in various ways before stroking them.

Using the Paths tool to create irregular selections is more difficult than simply adding to and subtracting from selections, but it's also more accurate. Pull out horizontal and vertical guides that intersect where the vertices of your irregular shape should be, and then use the Paths tool to outline the shape. Stroke the path or convert it to a selection, and then fill as desired. This method works well when you need to isolate multiple buildings in a photo.

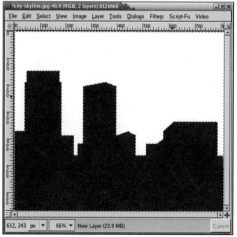

Outlining a shape with the Paths tool

Drawing Predefined Shapes

Gfig is a primitive vector drawing tool that offers a set of predefined shapes, including stars, spirals, curves, polygons, and arcs. For simple shapes like squares and triangles, it's faster to use the techniques we discussed earlier in this section, but Gfig can come in handy when you need to create something more complex. Let's experiment a bit with Gfig.

1. Add a new layer to the image (**Layer ▸ New Layer**).
2. Open Gfig (**Filters ▸ Render ▸ Gfig**).
3. Click the **Create Star** button on the button bar. Change the Sides setting to **5 sides**.
4. Click the middle of the preview and drag toward the lower-right corner of the preview. The star will be created using the brush that is currently selected.
5. If you need to move the star once it has been created, click the **Move an Object** button (three buttons to the right of the star), and then drag the star around the preview.
6. Modify the brush and fill options as necessary, and then click **Close** to render your shape on the canvas.

Before you render them on the canvas, the objects you create in Gfig are in vector format and have a stacking order. You can use Gfig to change this order, or you can render each shape on a new layer and change the stacking order later by moving around the layers in the Layers dialog.

You can use Gfig to edit shapes you've rendered to layers, even after you've applied effects to those layers. Those effects will be lost when you use Gfig to edit the shapes, however, so plan your workflow carefully.

The problem with Gfig is that it is a very simple vector editor. A regular polygon created with Gfig, for example, doesn't have editable points at its vertices. You can only move the center point or resize the polygon. Gfig isn't the most stable GIMP plug-in either. It has a tendency to crash if you try to create a lot of objects or edit objects repeatedly.

If you need real vector-editing capabilities, you're better off using a tool like Inkscape (http://www.inkscape.org). Just create the shape and then export it as a PNG for use in your GIMP project.

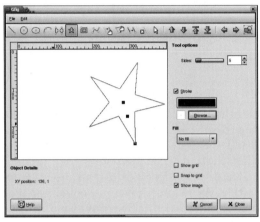

Creating a star with Gfig

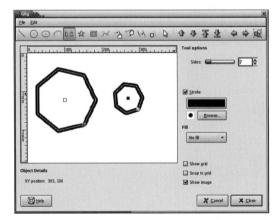

You can resize a Gfig polygon, but you can't edit its vertices individually.

Basic Shape Tips

Here are a few words of wisdom you should take away from this section.

- By default, selections *want* to attach to guides! As you've seen, this simplifies tasks like outlining a city skyline. But you can disable this behavior if necessary; just choose View ▶ Snap to Guides.

- Draw shapes in new, transparent layers instead of drawing over existing layer content. It's always easier to delete a layer later than it is to recover the pixels that have been overwritten. Be sure to turn off the Keep Transparency option for the transparent layer! If you don't, you won't be able to draw over the transparent parts of the image.

The Keep Transparency option is located in the Layers dialog. If the box is checked, you won't be able to make any changes to the transparent parts of the layer.

- Stroking with a brush that's 1 pixel wide (like the Circle (01) brush) and the default foreground color (black) will not produce a solid black outline because of the antialiasing of the brush stroke. Just repeat the process once or twice to get a darker line. Larger brushes don't have this problem.

- Want to rotate a shape? Draw it with paths in a new, transparent layer, then stroke the path and rotate the layer. Alternatively, you can use the Rotate tool, but this will produce a copy of the selection that appears as a floating layer. You'll need to convert the floating layer to a new layer before moving on.

- Don't forget that you can fill a selection with a pattern or solid color instead of stroking it. Use the Bucket Fill tool for patterns, or drag the foreground or background color from the toolbox into the selection to fill the selection with a solid color.

1.6 PATTERNS AND GRADIENTS

Patterns are image files that you can use to fill selections or layers. Patterns are most commonly used to create textures for three-dimensional objects like the walls of a castle or the skin of a scaly creature. Gradients are formed when two or more colors blend together. You can use gradients for a variety of purposes, from simulating tubes, pipes, and poles to applying wave distortions to cloth or water.

The GIMP does provide a wide range of stock patterns and gradients. Most of the stock patterns are suitable for web images but are probably too small for larger print projects. The stock gradients are plentiful, and we'll use several of them in tutorials later in this book.

This section is an introduction to creating your own patterns and gradients. We won't be creating any of our own for use in this book's tutorials, but learning how to create your own is useful for when you strike out on your own.

Patterns

Patterns, like brushes, can be made from any image. A pattern that is designed correctly is *tileable*—many copies of the pattern blend together seamlessly. Tiled patterns are often used as background images for web pages and textures for three-dimensional projects.

You can access the Patterns dialog and see all of the patterns that are available to you by choosing File ▸ Dialogs ▸ Patterns from the toolbox menu. Any image can be saved as a pattern, and a pattern can be any size. Patterns can be saved in any file format. The GIMP-specific extension is *.pat*, but there is no advantage to using one file format over another.

If you want to access a pattern file through the Patterns dialog, it must be saved in one of the GIMP's pattern directories

(choose File ▸ Preferences and select the Folders ▸ Patterns entry on the left).

If a pattern is large, the Patterns dialog will only display a thumbnail of the image. Click the pattern and hold down the left mouse button to view the pattern at its full size.

New GIMP users often underestimate the usefulness of patterns. And to be honest, the built-in patterns *are* a little boring. But it isn't difficult to create reusable patterns that simulate the textures of concrete and cloth. It just takes a little imagination.

NOTE   *Patterns don't have to come from the Pattern dialog. The GIMP's render filters (Filter ▸ Render) also make very good patterns, and you can save the resulting images as pattern files for use in project after project. The tutorials in this book often ask you to generate patterns on the fly, but it's good to know that there are so many options.*

The Patterns dialog displays thumbnails of uniform size, but if you click a thumbnail and hold down the left mouse button, the thumbnail will enlarge.

Concrete Texture

One of the easiest textures to create is a simple concrete background. Such textures can be used to turn a basic box into a cement block, or to turn any flat surface into a sidewalk or road. Let me walk you through the steps.

1.   Open a new white canvas window by choosing **File ▸ New** from the toolbox menu.

2. Add a new layer and use the Plasma filter to fill it with colored clouds (**Filters ▸ Render ▸ Clouds ▸ Plasma**). The default settings should be sufficient for this texture. Click **OK** to apply the filter.

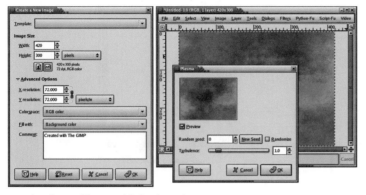

Use the Plasma filter to add clouds to the canvas.

3. Choose **Filters ▸ Noise ▸ Scatter RGB** from the canvas menu to use the Scatter RGB filter to apply some noise to this image. Make sure the boxes next to the words *Correlated noise* and *Independent RGB* are not checked. Set the Red, Green, and Blue sliders to **0.20** to apply a visible but not overwhelming amount of noise to the layer. Click **OK** to apply the filter.

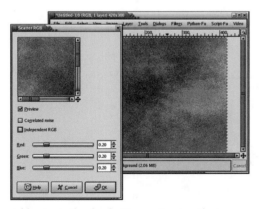

Add noise to the clouds. More noise gives the image a rougher texture.

4. Desaturate the layer (**Layer ▸ Colors ▸ Desaturate**). This removes the color content and makes the image look more like concrete.

5. To give the texture some depth, open the Bump Map filter (**Filters ▸ Map ▸ Bump Map**). Keep an eye on the preview window as you play with the Azimuth, Elevation, and Depth values. Pan around the preview to see how each adjustment affects the image. Choosing Linear, Spherical, or Sinusoidal from the Map Type drop-down menu also alters the effect, but this setting is less important than the others. Click **OK** to apply the filter to the desaturated layer.

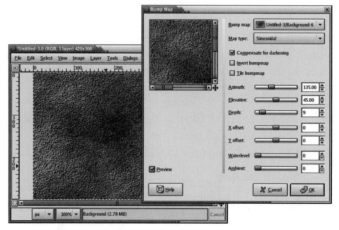

The concrete texture gets some depth from the Bump Map filter.

NOTE *Variations on this technique include using different noise filters and increasing the Turbulence setting in the Plasma filter's Tool Options dialog.*

6. While the result is a fairly realistic concrete texture, adjustments to the contrast and brightness (**Layer ▸ Colors ▸ Brightness-Contrast**) can soften the effect and give you a jumping-off point for even more complex textures like skin.

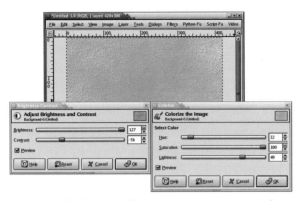

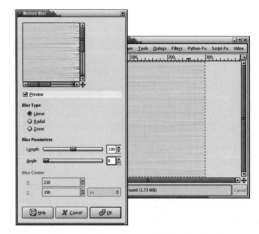

Contrast and colorization changes can turn concrete into skin.

Simulated Cloth

Creating a cloth texture starts with noise. Start with a new white canvas window that is **300 × 300 pixels**. Because we'll be rotating one of the layers in a moment, a square image works best.

1. Open the Scatter RGB filter again (**Filters ▸ Noise ▸ Scatter RGB**), but this time increase the Red, Green, and Blue values to **0.90**. Click **OK** to apply this filter.

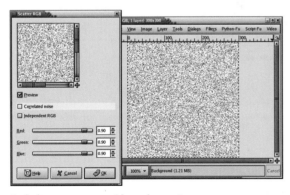

A cloth texture starts with random noise.

2. Open the Motion Blur filter (**Filters ▸ Blur ▸ Motion Blur**). Set the Blur Type to **Linear**, set the Length to **130 pixels** or more, and set the Angle to **0 degrees**. Click **OK** to apply this filter layer.

3. Repeat steps 1 through 2, this time setting the Angle to **180 degrees**. This will clean up the edges of the layer.

Motion blurred noise makes soft lines in the image.

4. Duplicate the Background layer (**Layer ▸ Duplicate**). The duplicate layer will become the new active layer.

5. In the Layers dialog (**Dialogs ▸ Layers**) change the duplicate layer's mode to **Multiply**. This composites the two layers in such a way that the image appears darker.

6. Rotate the duplicate layer by 90 degrees (**Layer ▸ Transform ▸ Rotate 90 degrees CW**).

7. You can now flatten the image (**Image ▸ Flatten Image**), and colorize it as you like.

The cloth has a cross-weave texture.

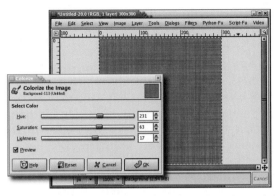

Adding color to the cloth is made easy with the Colorize dialog.

Creating Tileable Patterns

To create a tileable pattern, offset an image by one-half of its width and height by choosing Layer ▸ Transform ▸ Offset and clicking the Offset by x/2, y/2 button. Use the Clone tool to patch the seams as shown here. To use the Clone tool, you must first press the CTRL key, and then click the source location (which can be in any layer). The Clone tool works by taking a source copy of the image at one point (where you've clicked while pressing the CTRL key) and copying it to some other destination location in the image. The copy is in the shape of the active brush. When you click a destination location, hold down the left mouse button, and drag, the source is copied to the destination. Additionally, the angle and distance between the destination and source remains constant, which means the source location changes as you drag. Take a moment to play with the Clone tool, as it's one of the most powerful GIMP tools.

You don't have to use the Clone tool to create tileable patterns. The Tileable Blur filter (Filters ▸ Blur ▸ Tileable Blur) and the Make Seamless filter (Filters ▸ Map ▸ Make Seamless) work more quickly but give you less precise results.

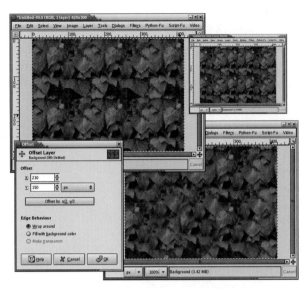

The Offset dialog allows you to automatically offset the layer by one-half of its width and height.

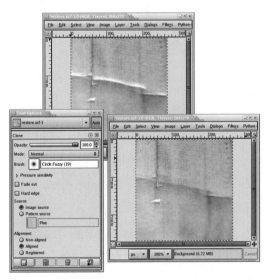

The Clone tool's default settings are shown in the Tool Options dialog. The Clone tool can be used to remove a tear in an old photo.

Creating Script-Fu Patterns

Most patterns are created for specific purposes. You may find you need to simulate the texture of a concrete wall or the skin of a dinosaur. The GIMP's built-in patterns usually don't suffice in those cases. But what if you need a surface for your new computer game or a low-contrast background for a website? When you need a general-purpose, ready-made texture, you can use the Script-Fu pattern generators to create it. Just choose Xtns ▸ Script Fu ▸ Patterns from the toolbox menu.

Because these scripts lack previews, you'll need to spend time experimenting to find the right settings.

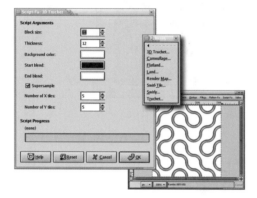

Two different Script-Fu pattern generators can create the Truchet pattern, as you can see from the menu shown.

Gradients

Gradient files are different than pattern and brush files in that they do not contain image data. Instead, they are text files that describe how color should be applied across a range of pixels. The gradient preview in the Gradients dialog (Dialogs ▸ Gradients) shows you how the colors would be blended if you chose a linear shape,

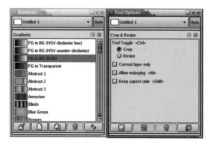

The Gradients dialog and the Tool Options dialog for the Blend tool. Choosing a different gradient updates both dialogs at the same time.

but the preview shows only the definition of the gradient. You can use the Blend tool to apply the gradient in many different ways.

NOTE *Keep in mind that the terms* gradient *and* blend *are often used interchangeably.*

The Blend tool's Tool Options dialog includes two important features: the Shape and Repeat settings. The Shape drop-down menu allows you to define the direction and shape the gradient will take when you apply it to a layer, mask, or selection. We'll use Linear, Bi-Linear, and Radial in this book's tutorials. Choosing Linear applies a smooth gradient that starts where you press the left mouse button and begin dragging and ends where you release the mouse button. The Bi-Linear effect is similar, but imagine applying two brushes at the same time, each of which moves in the opposite direction. Choosing Radial applies the color on the left side of the gradient at the start point and radiates the color out to the point where you stop dragging and release the mouse button.

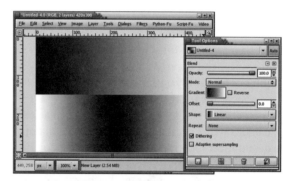

Choosing Linear (top), Bi-Linear (middle), and Radial (bottom) from the Shape drop-down menu produces very different results, even when we apply the same FG to BG gradient.

A gradient is a color transition. Most of the gradients we use in this book are made up of smooth, gradual color transitions. But the transition doesn't have to be slow and smooth. It can be abrupt. Consider the Radial Eyeball Blue gradient. When you choose Linear from the Shape drop-down menu and apply this gradient, the effect is an abrupt change from white to blue to black. But when you choose Radial and apply the same gradient, the result looks like an eyeball.

Experimenting is the only way to discover all of the ways your projects can benefit from gradients. You can choose Radial from the Shape drop-down menu and use the FG to BG (RGB) gradient to create balls or spheres. Choosing Linear and using the Blinds or Crown Molding gradients can simulate undulating waves when used in layers below a color layer. We use this very trick in Section 4.11.

Selecting gradients directly from the Gradient menu in the Tool Options dialog for the Blend tool

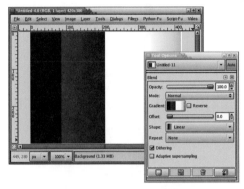

The Radial Eyeball Blue gradient applied with a Linear shape

Here the Radial Eyeball Blue gradient is applied with a Radial shape over a black background. Now we know how this gradient got its name!

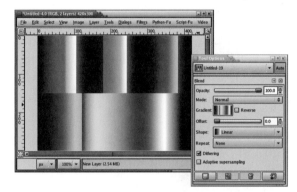

Applying the Blinds (top) and Crown Molding (bottom) gradients directly to a layer without blending them with other layers

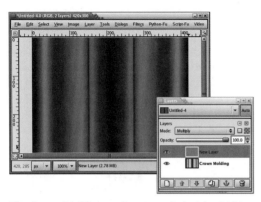

The Crown Molding gradient is applied with a Bi-Linear shape in a layer beneath a colored layer. The layer's mode is set to Multiply. The result looks a bit like folded satin.

So why use gradients? In this book we use them primarily for two reasons: to create layer masks and to apply textures to other layers. Applying a gradient to a layer mask can create a smooth transition from the image in one layer to the image in the layer below it. After applying a gradient in a layer by itself, you can also use one of the layer modes to blend it with another layer. This latter method is used when creating wave patterns, though you can also use it to blend colors in a pattern.

Blending two images together by applying a gradient to a layer mask

The Gradient Editor

While we won't need to do so for any of the tutorials in this book, it is possible to create your own gradients. At the bottom of the Gradients dialog there is a set of icons. Click the second icon from the left to open the Gradient editor and create a new gradient.

The Gradient Editor allows you to edit existing gradients, such as the Caribbean Blues gradient shown here. Use the Edit button in the Gradients dialog to open the Gradient Editor.

Below the preview window in the Gradient Editor window is a set of triangles. These are handle bars. There are two black handles on either end of a segment and a white handles between them. Initially there is only one segment in the preview. Right-click this segment to open the Gradient Editor menu. In this menu you can set the colors for each side of a segment (Right and Left endpoint colors), add new segments (Split and Replicate menu options), and adjust the way color flows across the segment (Blending menu options).

The Gradient Editor's default settings are shown here. Note the segment with two black handles and one white handle.

Right-click the segment to open
the Gradient Editor menu.

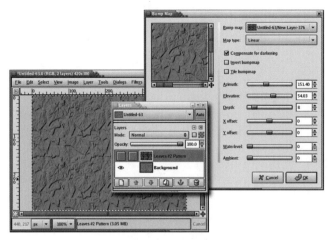

*Creating a new gradient
with the Gradient Editor*

I'll leave you to play around with creating gradients for your own projects. Just remember that you can create as many gradients as you like and then use the Gradients dialog to delete them when you don't need them anymore. Go ahead and experiment. You've got nothing to lose!

Pattern and Gradient Design Tips

Think you've got a handle on patterns and gradients? Here are some tips that are sure to come in handy.

- You can use patterns to stroke selections. Make a selection, choose Edit ▶ Stroke Selection, and then choose the pattern option in the Stroke Selection dialog.

- Besides using patterns to fill your layers and selections, you can use them as the source image for a bump map. Fill one layer with the pattern, then apply the Bump Map filter (Filters ▶ Map ▶ Bump Map) to another layer by using the first layer as the bump map image.

- Sometimes a pattern is very small when compared to a canvas. Applying the texture to the canvas gives you a bunch of tiled versions of the pattern. Want to scale a pattern to fit the canvas

without tiling it over an entire layer? Make a small selection, fill it with the pattern, copy and paste the selection as a new layer, and then scale the layer to the size of the image.

Using a pattern as the source image for a bump map

- You can use the Bucket Fill tool's modes to blend patterns with existing layer content. But an even better, nondestructive method is to fill a layer directly above the target layer with the pattern and then set the layer blend mode accordingly. (See Section 1.2 to learn more.)

- As we'll see in later chapters when we make balls and buttons, gradients are often used to simulate lighting because they can represent gradual changes from dark to light. However, the appearance of a smooth gradient can be lost if you save it in the wrong file format. GIF files, for example, are not well suited for images with gradients, because the GIF format will reduce the number of colors and can cause banding (streaks of colors). If you're saving your gradient image for use on the web, try using the JPEG format instead, and use little to no compression.

When using gradients to create spheres, always have the gradient flow from a lighter color on the left to a darker one on the right. In the Tool Options dialog for the Blend tool, check to make sure the Gradient option shows it this way. If this isn't the case, try clicking the Reverse button just to the right of the Gradient option.

1.7 WORKING WITH SCANNERS

In the good old days of color film, slides, and paper prints, many graphic artists spent hours using scanners to import images into their computers. This process was always less than ideal for photographs, as dust and muck on the scanner glass or the source slide could lead to immeasurable frustration.

But then along came the digital camera. Now photographers just upload images—which are already in digital format—directly to the computer. No muss. No fuss. Who needs scanners now, right? Everyone!

Scanners still do the heavy lifting when it comes to transferring drawings, archival photos, and even textures to computers. Initial line drawings often serve as templates for cartoons and background images for movies. You might even need to scan something as mundane as a map to school or work. It should be obvious that scanners still fill an important need for GIMP users. This section shows you some simple tricks for getting the most out of your scanner.

Scanning an Image

The GIMP doesn't scan by itself. You need an external program for that. The big kahuna here is Scanner Access Now Easy (SANE), a project that provides drivers for various scanners and applications that can talk to those drivers. The SANE drivers also include support for network-attached scanners, allowing you to share a scanner among multiple users across a network. SANE's primary desktop tool is called XSane, and it's a freestanding application that can also be linked with the GIMP plug-ins folder to work as a plug-in. (See http://www.sane-project.org or http://www.xsane.org for more information.)

The XSane plug-in, running in the GIMP

The XSane application is available for most Linux distributions. If you don't already have XSane, try using an install tool like yum, Advanced Packaging Tool (APT), or Synaptic. XSane is also available for the Windows and OS/2 platforms. SANE has a separate TWAIN interface (which is unrelated to Xsane), and it is suitable for Mac OS X users.

1. Once you've installed XSane, choose **File ▶ Acquire** from the toolbox.
2. You'll have several options, depending on your SANE backend configuration. Choose the option for your specific scanner. In this example, a scanner that uses the Plustek backend driver is attached as a USB device, so the last option in the Acquire menu is selected.

3. When the XSane dialog opens, click the **Acquire Preview** button (1), drag an outline around the area of interest, and then set the scan resolution (2).

4. Click the **Scan** button (3) when you're ready to scan.

Launch the scanner interface by choosing File ▸ Acquire.

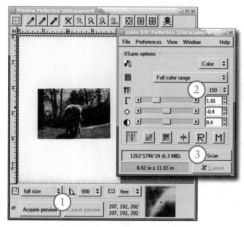

The XSane interface is easy to use and allows you to adjust the scan settings to suit your needs.

Sharpening a Scan

Nearly all scans are a little blurry. You can use either the Sharpen filter (Filters ▸ Enhance ▸ Sharpen) or the Unsharp Mask filter (Filters ▸ Enhance ▸ Unsharp Mask) to fix this. Both filters work to increase the contrast between light and dark pixels (which we perceive as edges) in the image. Unfortunately, the Sharpen filter also emphasizes scratches and dust. It works best on very clean scans or scans of drawings that have been done on white paper with a dark pen or pencil.

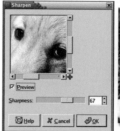

The Sharpen filter can improve an initial scan. The amount to sharpen depends mostly on personal taste.

The Unsharp Mask filter functions as a digital adaptation of a darkroom a technique that has long been used with film. In the darkroom, the photographer filters light first through a blurred copy of the original color negative and then through the original and onto photographic paper. In addition to masking what was "unsharp," this has the effect of minimizing scratches and dust. The Unsharp Mask filter is better than the Sharpen tool for most photographs. By making some minor adjustments to the Radius and Amount sliders, you can also use the Unsharp Mask filter to clean up scanned diagrams and drawings.

Before using the Unsharp Mask filter (left) and after applying it (right)

Reducing Distortions

Scanning from slide film produces the best digital image because the colors are of a continuous tone—there are no dots of ink on the film. Scanning a photograph or, worse, printed material from a book or magazine can lead to distortions.

1. To reduce these distortions from scans of printed material (as opposed to scanning from slide film), first scan the image at up to four times the resolution needed. For example, if you ultimately need a 72 dpi web image, scan it at 280 dpi or more.

2. Apply the Despeckle filter (**Filters ▸ Enhance ▸ Despeckle**) and/or the Gaussian Blur filter (**Filters ▸ Blur ▸ Gaussian Blur**), using low values for both.

Here's a scanned image in need of help.

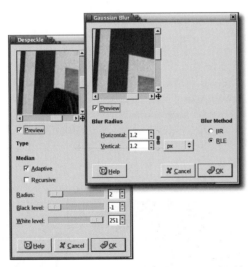

You can also use the Despeckle and Gaussian Blur filters to clean up scans.

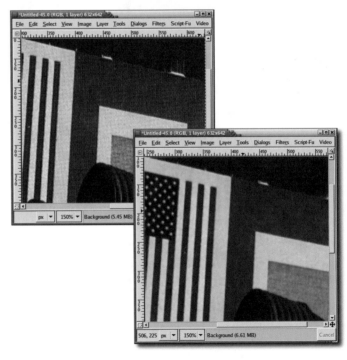

The Despeckle filter cleans up some of the moiré patterns.

3. Apply the **Unsharp Mask** filter to the resulting image.

4. Then—and here's the real trick—scale down both the resolution and the physical size of the image as necessary.

5. Apply the **Sharpen** filter if necessary.

Applying the Sharpen filter brings back some detail that was lost when we used the Despeckle filter.

Fixing Alignment Issues

The edges of a scanner bed can help make sure that a vertical image scans, well, vertically. But if multiple images are laid out on the glass, their alignment may not match. Or, if the image itself is not aligned, the scan won't be either. Imagine a photograph where the subject is tilted a few degrees to the left. What if you'd prefer the subject to be upright? The GIMP makes it easy to solve problems like these. The Measure and Rotate tools are all you need.

NOTE   *Always scan more area than you will need in the final image. Once you've fixed the alignment issue, you can crop the image to the proper size.*

1. After scanning the image, add a new vertical guide at 50 percent by choosing **Image ▸ Guides ▸ New Guide (By Percent)**.

2. Find a straight line in the image that is tilted and needs to be made completely horizontal (or something that's positioned perpendicular to whatever needs to be completely vertical). This is your reference line (shown in red). The trick with aligning scans is to measure from the center point of the reference line to the right endpoint. The rotation will occur around the center of the image, so the angle must be measured from the image's vertical center.

A horizontal reference line makes it easy to adjust alignment.

3. Drag down from the top ruler a horizontal guide that intersects with both the vertical guide you added earlier and the reference line. Drag down another horizontal guide to intersect with the right endpoint of the reference line. Drag out from the left ruler to add a new vertical guide that also intersects with the right endpoint of the reference line and passing along the right edge of the subject.

Add a new horizontal guide that intersects with the reference line and the right edge of the subject.

4. Choose the **Measure** tool from the toolbox. Click the point where the centered vertical guide and the reference line intersect, and then drag toward the reference line's right endpoint. The guides should make it easy to hit both marks exactly.

5. The status bar shows the angle to rotate. Write down the angle value so you can use it when you put the Rotate tool to work (it won't be available once the active tool has been changed).

When using the Measure tool, this value is always displayed as a positive number. If the center point is higher up in the image than the endpoint of the reference line, however, the angle entered in the Rotation Information dialog will actually be a negative value.

6. Choose the **Rotate** tool from the toolbox. Click in the image window to open the Rotation Information dialog. In the **Angle** field enter the angle displayed previously by the Measure tool. Make sure to enter a negative value if necessary. Click **Rotate** to apply the rotation.

Measure the angle from the center of the reference line to either edge. The status bar shows the angle.

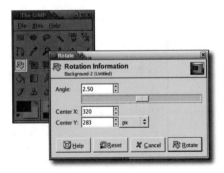

The Rotation Information dialog allows you to set precise rotation angles. Positive values rotate clockwise, while negative values rotate counterclockwise.

7. Rotating the image will blur it slightly. Apply the **Unsharp Mask** filter to clean up the image.

8. Rotations can also cause white space or transparency to show through in the rotated layer. If that happens, cropping is necessary. Drag out guides to frame the image. Choose the **Crop** tool from the toolbox and use the intersections of the guides to crop the image to suit your needs. Click the **Crop** button to complete the process.

Rotating a layer can cause white or transparent areas to appear in the image after rotation. Use the Crop tool to get rid of these.

After rotating and cropping the image, the upper edge of the monitor is horizontal.

Scanning Tips

These tips will help you make the most of your scanner and the GIMP:

- Keep the scanner glass clean! Wipe it with a dust-free cloth before using it to scan. Use a glass cleaner to get rid of smudges if necessary.

- Most photographs work well with balanced white and black levels—just use the Autolevel option when scanning to adjust this automatically.

- Don't use the Brightness-Contrast tool on scans! Instead of enhancing a range of colors, this tool affects global appearance. The best adjustments for photographic scans always work on tonal ranges. Use the Levels dialog and play with the input and output values. If you need to make a contrast adjustment, try using the Stretch Contrast command (Layer ▸ Colors ▸ Auto ▸ Stretch Contrast).

- Actually, there is an appropriate use for the Brightness-Contrast after all: If you've applied the Autolevel option to a hand drawing and the drawing still appears smudged, increase the brightness and contrast.

- It is possible to clean up blurred text by adjusting the individual color channels in the Curves dialog.

- When fixing a misaligned scan, you can drag the Measure tool to the left endpoint instead. A lower left endpoint means a positive angle value, whereas a higher left endpoint means a negative angle value. This is opposite of dragging to measure to the right endpoint.

- Don't try dragging through the image window to perform the rotation. The interactive feedback is nice, but it is unlikely that you'll get the exact angle you want.

- Can't find a horizontal reference line? If there is a distinct central subject (a person who needs to be centered in the image, for example), use guides to mark the subject's horizontal center point, measure the angle from the subject's horizontal center point to the middle of the top of the subject, and then subtract this value from 90 degrees to get the rotation angle. If the drag goes to the right, the rotation angle will be a negative value. If the drag goes to the left, it will be positive.

Using a subject's horizontal center point to rotating an image.

1.8 BASIC TUTORIALS

If you're new to the GIMP, the best way to get started is to familiarize yourself with some very common processes—those that you can apply to many different design projects. These tutorials aren't as flashy as the ones you'll find in the rest of the book, but they will help you master common techniques that are applicable to all kinds of designs.

Clouds

Some of the most artistic GIMP effects involve merging layers in random ways. A grunge image, for example, might mix several textured layers like a collage of torn pages. Creating the texture in each layer is an artistic experiment in itself. But how do you then tear the layers? It's easier than you might think. You just apply a layer mask filled with random shapes to each layer. The layer masks block out sections of the layers, making it look as though those sections have been torn away.

What kind of random shapes work well as layer masks? You can use brushes to draw in a layer mask and produce a customized result. But the process is often time consuming, and it's difficult to achieve random shapes with similar brush strokes. What we need is something that is fast and gives us more randomness than hand-brushed strokes ever would. What we need are clouds.

Clouds are very effective graphic design tools. While creating grungy textures might not be your thing, you can simulate an increased depth of field in any design project by applying a cloud as a layer mask and then using it to create selective blurs. As you've already seen, you can also use clouds as the starting point for various textures, including skin and cloth. And, of course, clouds can be used simply as clouds, to create everything from wispy cigarette smoke to light steam rising over a cup of coffee to those big white balls of cotton in the sky.

The GIMP provides two filters that we can use to create clouds: the Plasma and Solid Noise filters. While you can use each filter on its own to create interesting cloud shapes, you may find that a combination of the two results in more realistic effects.

The Plasma Filter

The Plasma filter (Filters ▸ Render ▸ Clouds ▸ Plasma) produces a colored-smoke screen. Most of the tutorials in this book that use clouds use the Plasma filter, precisely because it provides random noise. In many of those tutorials, we'll be applying the Plasma filter to a layer mask.

The initial result won't resemble a cloud, however.

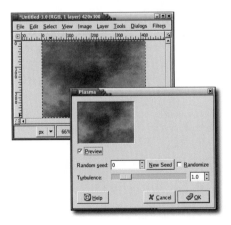

The Plasma filter's options (right) and the colored cloud the Plasma filter renders (left)

1. To remedy this, first desaturate the layer (**Layer ▶ Colors ▶ Desaturate**).

2. Adjust the curves to increase the black space (**Layer ▶ Colors ▶ Curves**). The curves adjustment is a curve that initially is shown as a diagonal line. Click the line near its middle and drag down to increase the layer's black content. Youcan go on to click other sections of the line, dragging down for more black or dragging up for more white. In this example, one section of the line (left of center) was dragged down, while another section (right of center) was dragged up.

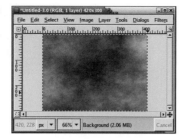

At this point, the desaturated plasma cloud looks a bit like fog at night.

3. Fill the Background layer with sky blue and then change the layer mode to **Screen**. This creates wispy clouds that can be manipulated for other cloud effects.

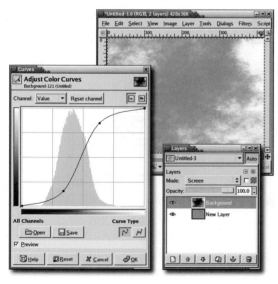

Adjust the Curves dialog at two points. Dragging the curve down makes dark gray look more black, while dragging the curve up makes the clouds look less like fog.

Lowering the Plasma filter's Turbulence setting produces more uniform cloud coverage, resulting in something that looks more like fog than clouds in the sky. Increasing the Turbulence setting is useful for achieving more complex effects, like simulating fire (see Chapter 4.13).

The Solid Noise Filter

Clouds in the sky often have a little more puff to them, like cotton balls. The Solid Noise filter does a good job of creating more substantial clouds.

To see an example, start with a sky-blue Background layer. Add a new layer and apply the Solid Noise filter (**Filters ▶ Render ▶ Clouds ▶ Solid Noise**), using a low X Size value (about 1.0) and higher Y Size value (about 4.0) to stretch the clouds horizontally. Adjust the curves to increase the black area of the cloud layer. Set this layer's blend mode to **Screen**. Duplicate the layer to emphasize the effect.

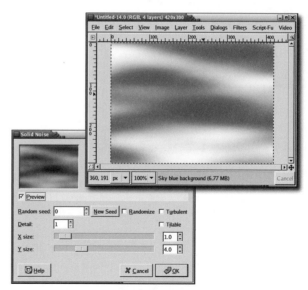

The Solid Noise filter produces wispy clouds.

Combining the Filters

While this effect is good, it could be better.

1. Add a plasma cloud layer above these layers to add some random wisps to the clouds. Force the wisps to align with the Solid Noise patterns.

2. Add a layer mask to the plasma layer, and fill the layer mask with a copy of the Solid Noise layer by choosing **Edit ▸ Copy**, choosing **Edit ▸ Paste**, and then choosing **Layer ▸ Anchor**.

3. Adjust the layer mask's curves to increase the white content. As a result, the cloud patterns should appear fluffier.

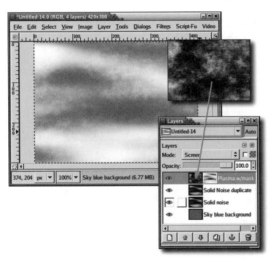

Apply the Plasma filter in addition to the Solid Noise filter to give clouds that are otherwise smooth a cotton-like appearance.

Creating a Steam Effect

To create steam such as might rise from a cup of coffee, first use the Solid Noise Filter to create puffy vertical clouds.

1. Choose **Filters ▸ Render ▸ Clouds ▸ Solid Noise**, set the Y Size to **1.0** and the X Size to **4.0**, and click **OK** to apply the filter.

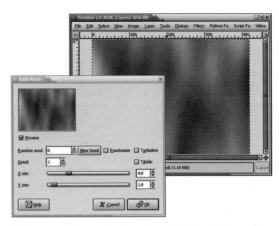

Adding vertical clouds of smoke with the Solid Noise filter

2. Add a layer mask to the cloud layer (**Layer ▸ Mask ▸ Add Layer Mask**).

3. Choose the **Blend** tool from the toolbox. In the Tool Options dialog set the Shape to **Bi-Linear**, set the mode to **Multiply**, and then drag through the layer mask a few times.

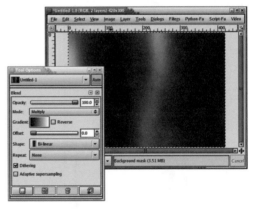

Using a Bi-Linear gradient in the layer mask to isolate just a few clouds

4. Use the **Move** tool to position the wisps of steam over the coffee cup.

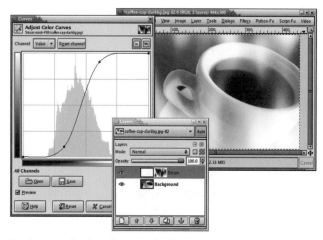

Applying the steam layer over the cup of coffee

Rendering a cloud in a layer mask allows you to use the Curves dialog to increase or decrease the amount of steam.

As an alternative, you could render the same cloud in the layer mask of a layer that has been filled with white.

1. Start with the original coffee cup image as the Background layer.

2. Add a new white layer above the Background layer (**Layer ▸ New**).

3. Add a layer mask (**Layer ▸ Mask ▸ Add Layer Mask**). Fill the layer mask with a cloud that has been rendered by using the Solid Noise filter (**Filters ▸ Render ▸ Clouds ▸ Solid Noise**).

4. Use the Curves dialog (**Tools ▸ Color Tools ▸ Curves**) to increase the contrast in the layer mask, as shown.

Use the Bucket Fill tool or one of the other paint tools to carve out the steam pattern in the layer mask. Because the majority of the layer mask is black (as shown in the small window), the composite image only shows the steam for this layer.

Isolating the steam in the layer mask with paint tools

Cloud Tips

These suggestions will help you take your cloud effects to the next level:

- You can use the IWarp filter (**Filters ▸ Distorts ▸ IWarp**) to add swirls to your smoke and clouds. The IWarp filter provides more control than the Whirl and Pinch filter (**Filters ▸ Distorts ▸ Whirl and Pinch**).

- When the wisps of smoke you've created are drowned out by light or busy backgrounds, duplicate the smoke layers. Then just set the layer modes for those layers to Screen or Addition.

- You can apply most GIMP filters to both layers and layer masks. Before rendering a cloud, make sure to click the appropriate thumbnail in the Layers dialog!

Rips and Cracks

Rip effects are popular, but they're often difficult for new GIMP users to reproduce. The technique is actually very simple and amounts to nothing more than clever but judicious use of layer masks and selections. A similar process adds cracks (or other patterns) to an image. Again, layer masks make it all possible.

Ripping an Image's Edges

Let's start by creating the colored background layer that will show through the ripped edges. Open the image you want to use to practice ripping (this tutorial uses a colorful beach photograph). The process described here works for images of any size, but let's start by practicing on a rather small image, one that's no larger than 500 × 800 pixels.

1. Add an alpha channel to the background layer (**Layer ▸ Transparency ▸ Add Alpha Channel**).

2. Add a new layer (**Layer ▸ New Layer**), fill the new layer with a contrasting color, and then move the colored layer below the background layer in the Layers dialog.

Move the colored layer below the layer that contains the photograph. The color will show through where the edges of the photograph are ripped.

3. Add a white layer mask to the original image layer (**Layer ▸ Mask ▸ Add New Layer Mask**).

4. Create a rectangular selection of the entire photograph layer by choosing **Layer ▸ Transparency ▸ Alpha to Selection**. Choosing Alpha to Selection tells the GIMP to select all of the opaque pixels in the image. Because this image is entirely opaque, this operation selects the whole image. Pressing CTRL-A also works.

5. Shrink your selection by **35 pixels** (**Selection ▸ Shrink**) and then round the corners of the selection by **35 percent** (**Select ▸ Rounded Rectangle**). This creates a boundary, marking off an area of the photograph that remains unchanged when we create the layer mask.

6. Feather the selection by **8 pixels** (**Select ▸ Feather**). Feathering the selection will allow the rips to meld with the image. The number of pixels to shrink and feather the selection should be larger if your image is larger than the one in this example.

7. Invert the selection (**Select ▸ Invert**) to isolate the area where the rips will be applied.

The Shrink Selection dialog (top), the Rounded Rectangle dialog (center), and the Feather Selection dialog (bottom)

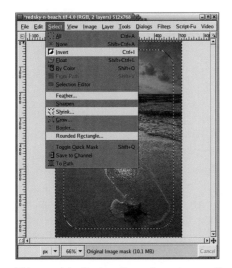

This tutorial relies heavily on the options available in the Select menu.

8. Click the layer mask in the Layers dialog to make sure that it is active. Use a brush to paint with black in the layer mask. (The Galaxy (AP) brush works well—move the Spacing slider to 40.0 pixels for an image of this size.) Paint with horizontal strokes along the left and right sides of the selection, and then paint with vertical strokes along the top and bottom of the selection, paying more attention to the edges of the image than the inside edges of the selection.

Because you are working on a layer mask and not modifying the actual image, feel free to experiment. Try using a different brush along the outer edges of the layer mask to change the shape of the ripped edge.

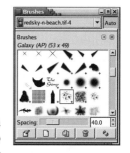

Choose a brush that contains random patterns, and then use that brush to paint in the layer mask.

It looks as though the edges of the original photograph have been ripped.

Creating Cracked Text

Adding cracks to text (or any other image) is even easier. Open a new canvas and fill it with any color. Choose the **Text** tool from the Toolbox. In the Tool Options dialog, choose a font with thick strokes, such as a Sans Bold font, to make the effect more visible. This example uses a font called RyndersBlack. Click the canvas to add a text layer. Type the word **Cracked** in the Text Editor.

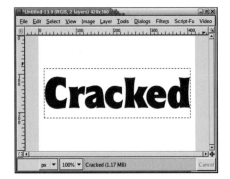

A font with thick strokes works best because it gives us characters with more surface area to showcase the cracked text effect.

1. Add a white layer mask to the text layer (**Layers ▸ Mask ▸ Add Layer Mask**).

2. Click the layer mask in the Layers dialog to make it active. Press CTRL-A to select the entire layer mask.

3. Choose the **Dried Mud** pattern from the Patterns dialog. Drag the pattern thumbnail from the toolbox into the image window to fill the layer mask with the pattern and give the text a cracked texture.

4. Use the Curves dialog (**Layer ▸ Colors ▸ Curves**) to make the cracks in the layer mask more distinct. You can even add a drop shadow to enhance the effect, as I've done here.

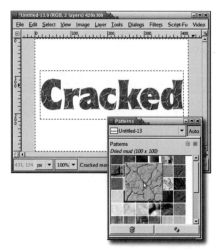

Filling the layer mask with the Dried Mud pattern makes it easy to achieve the cracked text effect.

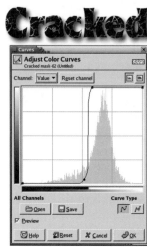

Giving the layer mask an exaggerated curve causes the cracked text to stand out from the background.

This section has introduced you to a couple of the text effects that are possible when working in the GIMP. The text-based tutorials in Chapter 5 will take you beyond these basics.

Ripping and Cracking Tips

Think rips and cracks might be just what your project needs? Here are a few more tips:

- To get the right effect, you need the right brush. If the GIMP's stock brushes don't suit your needs, consider creating a few new ones. The process is described in Section 1.1.

- Want to use layer masks to create text effects? Here's the quickest way to do it. Choose Layer ▸ Transparency ▸ Alpha to Selection to select the area around the text for use as a layer mask region. Fill the layer mask with a grungy, scratched texture. Then invert the text selection and fill it with white. This will only apply the effects inside the text area.

Tweaking Text

The GIMP is not primarily designed for working with text, but you can use it to achieve quite a few text effects. As you'll see in Chapter 5, most of the fun happens after the text is rendered to a layer, and most of the processes focus on adding, removing, or modifying the color in the image's pixels.

But what about changing the shape of text? There are two ways to do this in the GIMP. The first method modifies rendered text (i.e., the rasterized text as it is drawn in a layer). Those changes don't actually change the text, but rather change the pixels in the layer. Later in this section you'll be introduced to a couple of layer-based tools for curving text.

Before using layer-based tools, however, let's explore the second method, which involves using paths to change the shape of text.

Creating a Text Path

A path is a vector element in the GIMP, one that isn't rendered until it is stroked. Because it is a vector element, you can edit it over and over again without sacrificing definition. Paths exist completely separate from image layers, and you can apply paths to any layer at any time. But you'd never know any of this unless you opened the Paths dialog (File ▸ Dialogs ▸ Paths).

1. Open a new canvas.

2. Choose the **Text** tool from the toolbox. Click the canvas to open the Text Editor. Type some text, and then close the window. In the Tool Options dialog choose a font and size as shown here.

3. Use the **Move** tool to drag the text layer to an appropriate location.

4. Click the **Text** tool to make that tool active again, and then click the canvas. At the bottom of the Tool Options dialog you should now see a button labeled with the words *Create path from text*. Click this button to convert the rasterized text into a vector path, and then delete the text layer.

Use the Tool Options dialog for the Text tool to convert the text to a path.

5. The path won't be visible at this point, but it is saved as a layer in the Paths dialog. Open the Paths dialog now by choosing **File ▸ Dialogs ▸ Paths** in the toolbox. You'll see that a single path is displayed, and you'll notice that by default the new path layer is named according to the text it outlines.

6. Click the path layer to make it active. Click the leftmost box to toggle visibility for this layer. An eye icon appears here when visibility is active, but otherwise the box is empty. To activate visibility, click in the dialog's leftmost column, and the eye icon will appear.

7. With visibility active, the path appears in the image window. Zoom in on the path (SHIFT-plus), and then choose the **Paths** tool from the toolbox and click one of the lines in the path. The path anchors will appear, indicating where the path can be edited by dragging the anchors or lines.

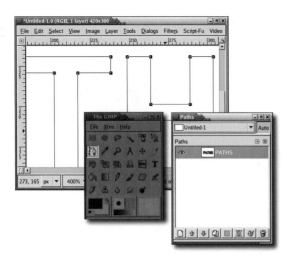

Zoom in on the path to see the path anchors more easily.

Disconnected paths move independently.

Path Groupings

Text paths are grouped in two ways. First, the path exists as a whole, including all of its anchors. To see this for yourself, choose the Move option in the Paths dialog, click any point on the canvas that isn't on a line in the path, and then drag the mouse. The entire text path will move. Secondly, all of the anchors on each line are connected. Click any line and drag; you'll see that the whole letter moves. Notice that when you do this with an *e* or *a,* the internal portions of those letter do not move. Disconnected paths are not grouped when text is converted to paths.

Path Anchors

The Tool Options dialog for the Paths tool provides three path edit modes: Design, Edit, and Move. Use Design mode to move or delete existing anchors and add new anchors. Use Edit mode to modify the handles (i.e., the curve between two anchors). Use Move mode to reposition entire paths. While in Design mode, you can group anchors in disconnected paths by holding the SHIFT key down and clicking each of the anchors in each of the paths.

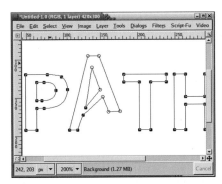

Having grouped the disconnected paths, it's possible to move them as a unit.

The Stroke Path button renders the text outline to the current layer.

The Stroke Path dialog with the Paintbrush tool selected

Rendering Paths

You've edited the path as necessary, but you still need to render the path back in a GIMP layer for use in your designs.

1. Start by creating a new layer (**Layer ▸ New**).

2. Return to the Paths dialog and click the **Stroke Path** button highlighted in red here. Doing so uses the current foreground color to render the outline of the path in the current layer.

3. Filling in the outline is as easy as using the **Fuzzy Select** tool to make a selection and then dragging the foreground color into the selection to fill it with that color.

Tweaking Text Tips

Before you strike out on your own, keep these tips in mind:

- While it's possible to edit text with paths, this technique should probably be reserved for the smallest of edits. Most professional graphic artists prefer editing text in a vector program and then exporting that text to a format the GIMP can use (such as JPEG, TIFF, or PNG).

- Check out Inkscape for all your vector-drawing needs.

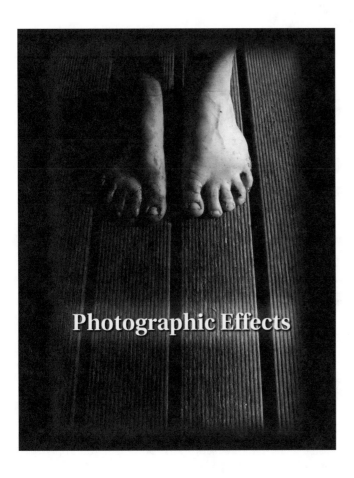

Photographic Effects

2
PHOTOGRAPHIC
EFFECTS

As a raster image editor, the GIMP loves to play with points of color, both individually and in blocks and blobs grouped together in selections. This makes the program perfect for working with photographs. Digital photos and the GIMP were made for each other. Because both the digital camera and the software work with pixels, no real conversion is required (though the format of the files that hold those pixels is another story). Photographs on film are continuous-tone images, meaning there are no dots of color. (Dots are used in photographic prints, but that's also another story.) Whether printed or on slides, photographs that originated on film need to be scanned at some point to convert them to digital images for use with the GIMP. (See Section 1.7 for an introduction to the open source scanning software XSane and tips for handling common scanning problems.)

Once you have the images in digital format, there is no end to the magic you can perform. Going from average photos to studio-quality productions requires only a few techniques that anyone can learn to use. Many techniques are based upon simple color corrections such as those provided by the Curves, Levels, and Color Balance tools.

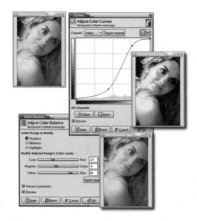

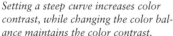

Setting a steep curve increases color contrast, while changing the color balance maintains the color contrast.

This levels histogram shows that the blackest pixels are not completely black. Moving the left and right sliders toward the middle produces the dramatic lighting change shown in the figure on the left.

In addition, you can use various GIMP filters to enhance photographs. The Retinex filter, for example, normalizes colors in order to enhance focus. Originally produced by NASA's Langley Research Center to enhance images taken through smoke and haze, this filter has interesting possibilities for enhancing portraits.

The following tutorials describe techniques that photographers will find useful. Along the way you'll create vignettes, add focal blurs, adjust color, insert lighting, simulate depth of field and motion, and use cloning methods to clean up damaged photos. Unlike previous tutorials, these won't start with a blank canvas at the default dimensions and walk you step by step through a process you can repeat. Instead, I'll start with specific base images and apply standard processes that you can use with your own images. My goal is to show you basic rules for working with images. Your goal should be to reproduce similar effects starting with your own base images.

The Retinex filter produces an image that is sharper than the desaturated original (upper left). Applying the Colorize tool and the Filter Pack filter produces the other two images.

We're not all professional photographers or graphic artists. We may not have $5,000 digital cameras or fancy studios, but we do have access to many of the same digital effects professionals use: selections, blurs, masks, and layer modes. Taken by themselves, these don't seem like powerful tools. But when you apply them to your own photographic masterpieces, they become the tools of a new graphic artist—you.

2.1 SOFTENING EDGES

In film photography, the technique of airbrushing has long been used to soften the hard edges between shadows and light, allowing a foreground image to fade into the background. This is especially true for studio portraits, where backgrounds are often no more than painted canvas images. But airbrushing is a time-consuming and inaccurate art, and it's far messier than pointing and clicking on your laptop.

Fortunately for photographers, airbrushing is a technique that is fading away. Raster-based programs such as the GIMP now provide the option of softening images using very common processes such as feathering and blurring.

This tutorial will show you how to soften the focus of a fine studio portrait. Techniques like this require only modest talent with selections combined with the use of the Gaussian Blur filter.

A soft focus draws the eye to the subject.

Getting Started

Start with a black-and-white portrait. The one I've chosen comes from Stock.xchng, an online collection of stock images available at http://www.sxc.hu. The portrait looks fine as it is, but it could look even better—moodier and more evocative—with a few softened edges. Its best feature is the high contrast that exists between the dark background and the well-lit model; be sure to find an image with similar contrast.

The original image is well executed, but we can improve it by softening the focus.

Adding Color

The first step is to colorize the image. The GIMP provides several ways to do this, including the Bucket Fill tool and the Colorize tool. Colorizing the image isn't the focus of this tutorial, so we'll just use the Bucket Fill tool.

1. Click the foreground color box in the toolbox, and in the Change Foreground Color dialog, set the RGB values to **16/130/35** to match the green tint shown here. Click **OK** to close the dialog.

2. Select the **Bucket Fill** tool from the toolbox. In the Tool Options dialog, set the layer mode to **Overlay** and the Affected Area (not shown in this image) to **Fill Whole Selection**. Click the canvas to color the image.

Tint the image with a simple Bucket Fill operation.

Isolating the Image and Adding Depth

1. Use the **Fuzzy Select** tool to separate the subject from the background. For my image, I set the Threshold to 25 pixels and clicked in the canvas three times—once in the light region on the right, once in the dark region on the left, and once in a region on the right that hadn't been selected by the first click. This left just two small blobs of background that still weren't selected; I added these to the selection using the Free Select tool.

2. Once you've completed the selection, invert it (**Select ▸ Invert**) and feather the result by **10 pixels** (**Select ▸ Feather**).

3. Copy the selection and paste it as a new layer (**Layer ▸ New**). Give the new layer a name that will distinguish it from others you'll create; mine is named *Girl*.

Isolating the model takes a little effort. If the Fuzzy Select tool doesn't work well for you, try using the Quick Mask (see Section 1.4).

4. To add a little depth to the image, we can add a drop shadow to the model. Click the **Girl** layer in the Layers dialog to make that layer active.

5. Open the Drop Shadow filter (**Script-Fu ▸ Shadows ▸ Drop Shadow**). To start, set the Offset X and Offset Y fields to **15 pixels**, set the Blur Radius to **40 pixels**, and uncheck the **Allow Resizing** box. (Drop shadows are always offset from their source images. If enabled, the Allow Resizing option will resize your canvas to fit a drop shadow that overflows the bounds of the canvas. Because our model is left-justified with plenty of canvas space to hold the drop shadow, we don't need to resize the canvas.)

6. If the shadow isn't as easy to see as you'd like, duplicate it (**Layer ▸ Duplicate**) and blur it a bit (**Filters ▸ Blur ▸ Gaussian Blur**).

In a portrait like this one, a drop shadow separates the subject from the backdrop.

Adding random noise to the background is the first step in removing all noise from the background; it allows us to eliminate any patterned noise that existed in the original image.

Getting Rid of Background Noise

Zooming in on the background of my image, you can detect graininess, which is a result of shooting in low light. If your image has similar contrast, you may also detect some graininess. Our next step is to clean up the background.

1. Click the **Background** layer to make it active.
2. Open the Scatter RGB filter (**Filters ▶ Noise ▶ Scatter RGB**).
3. Disable the **Correlated Noise** and **Independent RGB** options, and set the Red slider to **0.14**. (Enabling the Independent RGB option would allow independent changes to each RGB channel slider, but we want uniform distribution for each channel. Enabling the Correlated Noise option guarantees that the same amount of each channel is applied to each speck of noise applied to the layer.) Click **OK** to apply these settings to the Background layer.

Adding Motion Blurring and Vignetting

1. To soften the image a bit, first click the **Girl** layer.
2. Create a selection from that layer (**Layer ▶ Transparency ▶ Alpha to Selection**). Grow the selection by **2 pixels** (**Select ▶ Grow**).
3. Invert the selection (**Select ▶ Invert**), and then click the **Background** layer again.
4. Copy and paste the selection as a new layer (**Layer ▶ New**) named *BG Blur*. Move the layer to just above the Background layer in the Layers dialog.
5. Open the Motion Blur filter (**Filters ▶ Blur ▶ Motion Blur**). Set the Blur Type to **Linear**, the Length to **35 pixels**, and the Angle to **135 degrees**. Your image might work better with a different Length, though the Blur Type and Angle can be the same. Click **OK** to apply these settings to the Background layer.

   We could stop now that we've softened the outline of the subject's hair, but the image will be even more interesting if we add vignetting. This will have the effect of bringing the subject out of the background.

The motion blur streaks all noise into a more uniform pattern. If the streaks bother you, try adding a Gaussian Blur on top of the motion blur.

6. Add a new layer named *Vignette*.

7. Select the **Ellipse Select** tool, and then drag to create an oval on the canvas about the height and width of the subject.

8. If your subject's overall axis isn't perfectly vertical, you should rotate the oval to match the subject. Select the **Rotate** tool. In the Tool Options dialog, choose **Transform Selection** mode. Click the canvas and rotate the selection to match the subject's axis; in this case I've rotated it slightly clockwise.

9. The position of the oval may need to be adjusted at this point. If so, click the **Rectangle Select** tool in the toolbox. Holding down the SHIFT key, click inside the rotated oval and drag across the canvas to position the selection so that it overlaps but doesn't completely encompass the subject. Depending on how your desktop is configured, you may also need to hold down the ALT key while you do this.

10. Now it's time to turn the selection into the vignette. Feather the selection by **50 pixels**. This is what gives the vignette its soft edges.

A vignette is just a semi-transparent, colored oval with very soft (i.e., heavily blurred) edges. I'm rotating this one slightly to match the tilt of the model's head.

11. Click the foreground color box, and in the Change Foreground Color dialog, set the RGB values to **271/214/0** if you want to match my dark yellow. Drag the foreground color into the selection.

The vignette is colored, but it is behind the model.

12. Set the layer mode for the Vignette layer to **Grain Merge**.

13. Duplicate the Vignette layer and call it *Vignette Copy* (**Layer ▸ Duplicate**). Move the new **Vignette Copy** layer to the top of the stack (**Layer ▸ Stack ▸ Layer to Top**).

14. Open the Gaussian Blur filter (**Filters ▸ Blur ▸ Gaussian Blur**). Set the Blur Radius to **120 pixels** for both the Horizontal and Vertical fields. Apply this filter to the Vignette Copy layer.

Placing vignette layers behind and in front of the model completes this step.

Applying the Finishing Touches

1. Create a selection from the Vignette layer (**Layer ▸ Transparency ▸ Alpha to Selection**).

2. Grow this selection a bit (**Select ▸ Grow**); in this tutorial I've grown it by 25 pixels.

3. Select the **Girl** layer again and invert the selection (**Select ▸ Invert**). Feather the selection by **25 pixels** (**Select ▸ Feather**).

4. Copy and paste the selection as a new layer named *Girl Softened*. Make sure the **Keep Transparency** box for this layer is unchecked in the Layers dialog.

5. Open the Gaussian Blur filter (**Filters ▸ Blur ▸ Gaussian Blur**) and set the Blur Radius to **7 pixels** for both the Horizontal and Vertical fields, then apply it to the new layer. Move this layer below the Vignette Copy layer.

Softening the model's hair and body leaves just her face and hand in focus.

Further Exploration

The final step in this tutorial copied and blurred a fraction of the subject in order to simulate an increased depth of field. You'll learn more about how to simulate this effect in Section 2.5.

2.2 PHOTO TO SKETCH

This next technique is for all the would-be artists among us. What we can't do with a pen and pencil, we can now do with a camera and the GIMP. And although an inkjet print on textured paper isn't quite the same as a fine hand-drawn sketch, it's close enough for the digital crowd.

Converting a photo to a sketch basically means detecting the edges in an image and applying a slightly irregular line, one that looks like it might have been drawn by a pen. This process isn't exact—you might substitute a different edge-detect filter or use the Curves or Levels tools to adjust the desaturated layers before applying filters. But these basic steps will get you started.

Is it pen or pencil? Actually, it's just a little GIMP magic.

Getting Started

The original image you choose for this effect shouldn't be too busy—lots of soft lines are useful, but really intricate patterns such as paisley would be problematic. Although I chose a still-life image for this example, the trick also works well with formal portraits and other pictures of people.

The subject of this image is a room that has lots of lines and shapes but few odd patterns.

Converting the Image to a Sketch

1. First desaturate the image (**Layer ▸ Colors ▸ Desaturate**).
2. Duplicate the layer twice (**Layer ▸ Duplicate**). Name the first layer *Burn* and the second layer *Hard Light*. Turn off the visibility of the two duplicate layers by clicking the eye icon for each layer in the Layers dialog. Then select the Background layer again.

Blend the duplicate layer with outlines created on the desaturated original layer.

3. Open the Sobel filter (**Filters ▸ Edge Detect ▸ Sobel**). Keep the default settings and click **OK** to apply them to the Background layer. The Sobel filter is an edge-detect filter that looks for nearly horizontal and vertical lines in the layer and keeps those in the resulting image. The default settings for this filter, as opposed to the other edge-detect filters available in the GIMP, will work best with this image because they will produce more solid and distinct lines that appear hand-drawn. However, you may get better results using one of those other edge-detect filters—give them a try if your image doesn't look quite right after applying the Sobel filter.

4. Invert the colors (**Layer ▸ Colors ▸ Invert**) for this layer to produce black lines on a white background.

Adding Depth to the Sketch

1. Click the **Burn** layer in the Layers dialog to make it active, and click its eye icon to make the layer visible once again.

2. Open the Gaussian Blur filter (**Filters ▸ Blur ▸ Gaussian Blur**). Set the Horizontal and Vertical Blur Radius to **10 pixels** and apply this filter to the layer. Set the layer mode to **Burn**. Burn mode makes dark areas in the background even darker, so the hand-drawn appearance looks as if it was achieved with a dark pencil.

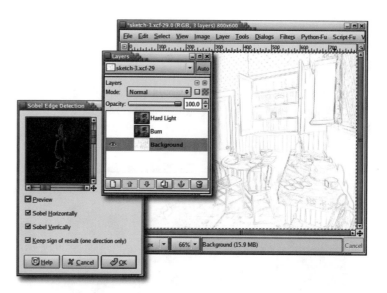

The Sobel filter creates nice outlines of the important shapes in the image. Other edge-detect filters might work better for your image, so you should experiment.

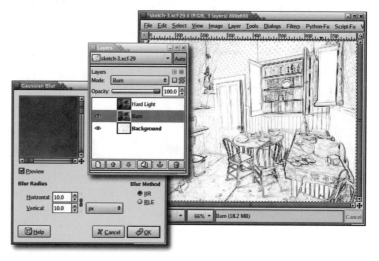

Blending with a blurred original using the Burn mode darkens the outlines created by the edge-detect filter.

3. In the Layers dialog, click the **Hard Light** layer to make it active, and then click its eye icon to make it visible.

4. Again, open the Gaussian Blur filter (**Filters ▸ Blur ▸ Gaussian Blur**). This time, set the Horizontal and Vertical Blur Radius to **15 pixels**. Click **OK** to apply these settings to the layer.

5. Set the layer mode to **Hard Light**. This layer mode will simulate the smudged charcoal appearance you get when you rub your finger over a pencil mark on paper.

Applying the Hard Light mode lends the image a smudged charcoal appearance, just like the one that is achieved when you smear a pencil mark with your finger.

Adding the Finishing Touches

1. The results here are good, but we can take this particular image a little further. Start by duplicating the original layer (**Layer ▸ Duplicate**).

2. Set the layer mode of this duplicate layer to **Multiply**.

3. Set the Opacity to **50 percent**. This brings out the image's lines even more without making the drawing look artificial.

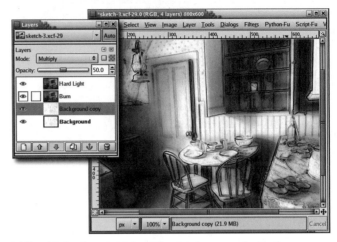

Adding this last layer is optional, but it helps to emphasize the lines in this particular image.

Further Exploration

This simple technique has numerous variations, including hand-smudging the charcoal layer using the Smudge tool and manually tinting the strokes with the Colorize tool to simulate drawing with colored pencils. You can also use the Oilify filter (Filters ▸ Artistic ▸ Oilify) to produce impressionistic images, or you can use the Curves, Levels, or Posterize tools to produce images that look more like line drawings.

2.3 ANTIQUING WITH SEPIA TONES

Antique photos come in two flavors: black-and-white or tinted. Coloring black-and-white photos is easy with the GIMP: you simply choose a color, pick a layer mode, and apply a Bucket Fill. There's nothing to it. The tricky part is making it look right—adjusting the contrast in the grayscale image appropriately and then choosing the right layer mode.

Most people associate tinted pictures, rather than plain black-and-white ones, with antique photos. This may be because more old sepia-toned photos have survived. The processing chemistry for sepia prints converts the silver metal, which forms the image in black-and-white prints, into silver sulfide. Silver sulfide is more stable than silver metal. Thus, converting the silver to sulfide gives the photographs a much longer shelf life.

Sepia prints get their name from the range of brown tints produced by the development process, which resemble the ink of the cuttlefish (*sepia* in Latin). Recreating true sepia tones digitally therefore limits us to a small set of dark brown colors, some with a slight tint of red. Similar processes could be applied using colors other than shades of brown, though the resulting images would not mimic true sepia prints.

In this tutorial you'll try out some of the variations possible as you produce sepia-toned images using different combinations of colors, contrast, and layer modes.

Getting Started

This tutorial's original image comes from an online image archive (it's available with Creative Commons license from PDPhoto.org in the Bodie collection) and has been desaturated (Layer ▸ Colors ▸ Desaturate). An alternative to using the Desaturate command is

Converting an image from full color to sepia is a fairly simple process.

to convert the image to grayscale (Image ▸ Mode ▸ Grayscale) and then back to RGB (Image ▸ Mode ▸ RGB). The only difference between these two methods is that the Desaturate command only works in the current layer. If your image has more than one layer, the Desaturate command won't convert all of those layers. In that case, it would be more appropriate to convert the image to grayscale and then back to RGB.

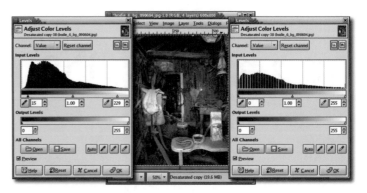

Desaturate the original image.

There is a wide tonal range in this image, which with a slight levels adjustment makes it an excellent candidate for application of sepia tones.

Reducing the contrast and brightness will add more gray areas, making the image appear more aged when the sepia tones are applied.

Increasing the Middle Grays

Sepia toning works primarily in the gray region of the desaturated image. Dark pixels are relatively unaffected, and lighter pixels just get a bit lighter. My image has some middle grays but needs to be a little lighter overall.

1. The first step in getting more gray into the image is to flatten the Levels histogram (**Layer ▸ Colors ▸ Levels**). Move the black slider to the right and the white slider to the left, each to the point where the histogram starts to show measurable levels. This divides the range of grayscale values actually present in the image into the 256 values available in an 8-bit channel, so that your darkest gray is assigned a value of 0 and your brightest white a value of 255. With more room to spread out, the histogram flattens when you apply the change, and the darker areas of the image lighten up.

2. As an additional measure, you can also reduce the contrast in the image (**Layers ▸ Colors ▸ Brightness-Contrast**). In this example, moving both the Contrast and the Brightness sliders to the left gives the result shown here.

Adding the Sepia Tone

The image is now ready for a sepia tone. Sepia is a brown color with a slightly reddish tint, varying from light to dark shades. You can use many RGB value sets to achieve a sepia tone, and an Internet search will help you find them. To show you what they might look like, I've used the RGB values of 135/96/40 (left), 178/30/96 (middle), and 91/56/17 (right). I'll use 135/96/40 in the final step of this project. The final step is to combine a colored layer with the original.

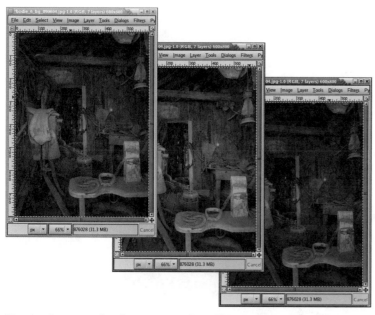

Here are three examples of sepia tones, achieved by using three different RGB value sets. Lighter tones and colors with less red are also common.

1. Duplicate the original layer (**Layer ▸ Duplicate Layer**) and position it above the desaturated layer.

2. The next step is to fill the new layer with the appropriate sepia tone. To do this, first click the foreground color box to open the Change Foreground Color dialog. Enter your RGB values in the appropriate fields, and then click **OK**. In this example I used the RGB values of 135/96/40 for the sepia tone.

3. Select the **Bucket Fill** tool, and in the Tool Options dialog set the mode to **Color** and the Affected Area to **Fill Whole Selection**. Click in the duplicate layer to colorize the layer with the sepia tone.

4. To combine this new layer with the original, set the mode for this colored layer to **Overlay**, **Color**, or **Soft Light**. Any of these should work well, but the final choice is yours. You can see that I chose the Color layer mode. Notice, too, that I have

saved each step of this process in a different layer, making it far easier to experiment and find just the right combination of steps.

In the Layers dialog you can see a different sepia tone layer for each of the three example tones shown earlier. Having a different layer for each tone lets you experiment to find the tone that works best for your project.

Further Exploration

This process lends itself well to experimentation. Use multiple layers with different processes applied and then flash back and forth between them using the eye icon in the Layers dialog to compare the results.

Remember too that using layer modes to blend a solid-colored layer with an image layer can provide slightly different results than simply colorizing a layer by using the Bucket Fill tool with its mode set to something other than Normal. Filling a layer with a solid color and blending it with a desaturated layer is usually preferable (it makes it easier to change the sepia tone without altering the original image, and the result is truer to the faded colors in old photographs). But you might still experiment with using the Bucket Fill tool directly on the desaturated original layer, as I did here, in order to give your final image a richer color.

2.4 COLOR SWAP

Photographers are often asked to change the color of one or more elements in an image. How easy this process is depends entirely on how easy it is to isolate the objects that need to be updated.

This tutorial looks at two examples of color swap. The first is the easy case, an image in which the color change doesn't require difficult selections. The second image requires a more delicate hand.

Successful color swaps are all a matter of good selections. This image is fairly easy to work with because the items we want to change are easy to isolate.

Color swapping is more complicated when the object you want to change is difficult to select. This project uses the Quick Mask to change the color of the vase.

A Simple Color Swap

The first example is a collection of boats on a beach. There is a plethora of color here. Let's imagine we need to change the yellow trim on some of these boats to a light blue.

It's easy enough to swap the yellow with blue on all the wood in the bottom half of the original image.

Isolating the Object

To change the color of only certain objects in an image, we need to isolate those objects from objects of a similar color elsewhere in the image. It's obvious that some of the boats are yellow. Yellow isn't so apparent in the rocks and trees in the background, but there is plenty of yellow there too. To isolate the boats, use the **Rectangle Select** tool to make a simple selection that encompasses the majority of the boats, and then add smaller rectangular selections to squeeze in the highest prow without selecting the rocks around it. Here the selected region is made lighter so that you can more easily see what has been selected.

We don't need to isolate the yellow elements from their immediate surroundings; we just need to isolate the lower half of the image. If we include the upper half of the image, the yellow in the trees will be also be changed to blue when we swap colors.

Choosing the Destination Color

1. Open the Hue-Saturation dialog (**Layer ▸ Colors ▸ Hue-Saturation**). You can use this dialog to edit multiple channels, including the familiar red, green, and blue channels and their counterparts in the world of digital printing: cyan, magenta, and yellow.

2. Choose the yellow channel and adjust the **Hue, Lightness,** and **Saturation** sliders until a soft blue replaces the yellow.

This process works because the color to be replaced—yellow—is not a part of the other colors contained within the selection. An exact selection isn't necessary to swap the color yellow with the color blue. The only place that might be a problem is the log on the beach. Brown contains some yellow, so after the Hue-Saturation changes are applied, the log has a blue tint to it. This is easily fixed by removing the log from the selection using any of the selection tools, including the Quick Mask. The sawhorse on the

beach near the middle of the picture also has heavy yellow content and needs to be handled in a similar manner (unless you want it painted blue as well).

Use the Hue-Saturation tool to swap yellow with blue.

A More Complex Color Swap

The same trick doesn't work on the next image. Let's say we want to change the color of the vase to a shade of yellow. The problem is that although the vase's reddish brown color contains a lot of red, red also appears throughout the rest of the image. In fact, if we made the same change to this image's red channel as we did to the boat image's yellow channel, we'd change the color of the background chair, the berries, and the table.

Creating a Complex Selection

1. This image requires a complex selection. Start by using the **Fuzzy Select** tool with the Threshold set to **40**. Clicking the lightest part of the vase creates an initial selection.

2. To finish off the selection, use the **Quick Mask** and some soft-edged brushes. The problem with using the default Quick Mask in this situation is that it uses a red tint to highlight what is not selected, but we're trying to select objects that have lots of red in them. This makes the selections created with the Fuzzy Select tool difficult to see when converted to the Quick Mask.

The previous technique doesn't work here because the color we want to change appears throughout the entire image.

The default Quick Mask is red, making it difficult to see the reddish selections.

Changing the Quick Mask Color

1. This problem is easily fixed. Right-click the **Quick Mask** button in the lower-left corner of the canvas window. A menu opens, as shown here.

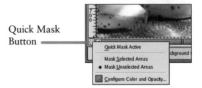

Quick Mask Button

Access the Edit Quick Mask Attributes window to change the Quick Mask color.

2. Keeping the right mouse button held down, drag to the bottom of the menu to select **Configure Color and Opacity.**

3. In the Quick Mask Attributes window, click the preview window (it shows the color and transparency of the mask) to open the Edit Quick Mask Color dialog.

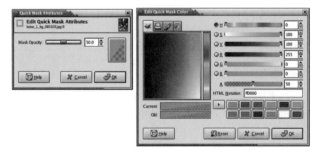

Click the preview window in the Edit Quick Mask Attributes window to access the Edit Quick Mask Color dialog.

4. Here you can change the RGB values used for the Quick Mask as well as the opacity for the mask (by adjusting the A slider below the B slider). Choose a color for the Quick Mask that contrasts with the colors in the object to be selected. A higher opacity value will make it easier to see what has already been selected, but it will also make it more difficult to see what needs to be selected. Here I've chosen a cyan mask with an opacity of 70 percent instead of the default 50 percent. The result is that the selected parts of the vase are much easier to see, while the parts of the vase that need to be selected are still visible.

Cyan is a high-contrast color for this image, which makes working with the Quick Mask much easier.

Painting the Selection

You learned in Section 1.4 that using the Quick Mask is the most effective way to select oddly-shaped objects. Here's a chance to try it out.

1. Zoom in on the vase by pressing the **+** key.

2. Draw straight lines in the Quick Mask with the **Paintbrush** tool's small, hard-edged brushes by clicking at one endpoint of the line, holding down the SHIFT key, and then clicking at the other end of the line. When painting (or drawing) with the Quick Mask, you must paint with black and white. Set the foreground color to white to paint over what should be included in the selection, and set the foreground color to black to paint over what shouldn't be in the selection. When you're finished, click the Quick Mask button again to convert the mask to a selection.

3. Grow the selection by **1 pixel** (**Select ▸ Grow**), and then feather it by **2 pixels** (**Select ▸ Feather**). Save the selection to a channel (**Select ▸ Save to Channel**) in case you decide to undo your color change later and need the selection again.

Select the vase by painting carefully in the Quick Mask. Remember that whatever you paint with white in the mask will be included when you convert the Quick Mask to a selection.

Working in a Duplicate Layer

Working in a duplicate layer saves you the headache of making mistakes in the original layer. If you don't like your changes in the duplicate layer, just try again.

1. After saving your selection, click the **Background** layer to make it active again.

2. Copy the selection and paste it as a new layer (**Layer ▸ New**). Name this layer *Vase* and make sure it's the active layer.

3. At this point we could use the Colorize tool (Layer ▸ Colors ▸ Colorize) to change the color of the vase, but the vase has varying shades of red and yellow in it, and the Colorize tool will completely wash out those variations. Instead, let's use the Hue-Saturation tool again. Open the Hue-Saturation dialog (**Layer ▸ Colors ▸ Hue-Saturation**).

4. Choose the red channel and move the Hue slider to the right to change the red content of the vase to a more yellow color. Then click the yellow channel and do the same. Be sure to

make both changes before clicking **OK**. The results will be much greener if you adjust the red channel first, click OK, reopen the dialog, and then adjust the yellow channel.

5. Deselect all (**Select ▸ None**) when all color changes are completed.

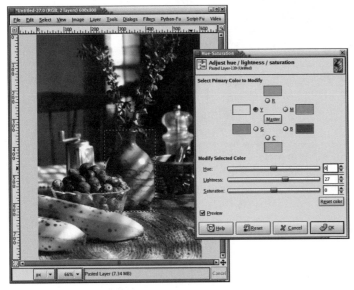

The vase's color can be changed using the Hue-Saturation tool once the color has been isolated with the Quick Mask selection.

Further Exploration

Swapping the color of objects in stock photos is a very common practice. Objects that have colors not found in the rest of the image are the easiest to change, as we saw with the image of boats on a beach. Changing the color of a vase or shirt or some other oddly-shaped subject requires complex selections created using the Fuzzy Select tool, the Quick Mask, and other GIMP selection tools. These selections are more difficult to create, but they're not impossible to master.

Mastery of the Quick Mask tool will help in the next tutorial, one in which we use a set of complex selections to add depth to a photograph.

2.5 CHANGING DEPTH OF FIELD

Take a look at any of your personal photos. If you've used a consumer-grade camera, you'll notice that the photo has a deep depth of field. That is, assuming your subject is more than a few yards away, most of the photo is in focus. Changing the depth of field can alter the feeling an image conveys. If your intended subject is not centered in the frame or not completely obvious, a depth-of-field change can draw attention to the subject and expose the true meaning of the photo.

Changing the depth of field can also mimic the effect of a macro lens, making a normal scene appear as if it was a miniature.

In reality, our computer-aided depth-of-field trickery is no more than a selective blur. You've probably seen this trick used in automobile advertisements, where the car is in focus but the background is blurred beyond recognition. In this tutorial we'll pull a building to the forefront of a photo using modest depth of field changes.

Changing a photograph's depth of field is a simple process of selecting and blurring. As is often the case in photography, the trick is making a good selection.

Getting Started

This tutorial begins with an image that has a relatively flat depth of field and is completely in focus. The solid blue sky will allow you to create selections of the buildings easily. You'll still have to make some manual selections, but the solid blue sky will save some time.

NOTE   *The image used in this tutorial is in the public domain and is available from PDPhoto.org.*

A solid blue sky makes the initial selections easy.

Isolating the Foreground

The original image is in focus and has an obvious foreground object—the outhouse. Let's start by creating a selection that includes the outhouse and some of the grasses in front of it.

1. Choose the **Fuzzy Select** tool. Click the blue sky to create an initial selection. If one click doesn't select the entire sky, click somewhere in the unselected area while holding down the SHIFT key.

Because the sky is a solid color and contrasts so dramatically with the land, you should be able to select the sky using the Fuzzy Select tool in just three clicks.

2. Invert the selection (**Select ▸ Invert**), and then click the **Quick Mask** button. As you've seen, unselected areas are tinted red when the default Quick Mask properties are in use (Section 2.4 showed you how to change the default color).

3. Select the **Paintbrush** tool and press **D** to reset the default foreground and background colors, making the foreground black.

4. Paint over the house on the left, some of the background grasses, and the rocky hill on the right. Use smaller brushes until the Quick Mask looks similar to that shown. Everything you paint over will be excluded from the selection.

5. Click the **Quick Mask** button again to convert the mask back into a selection.

6. Save the selection to a channel (**Select ▸ Save to Channel**). Then click the channel name in the **Channels** dialog and change the name to *Outhouse Selection*. Saving selections

The outhouse and foreground grasses are isolated with the Quick Mask.

to a channel allows you to easily recall them for further editing should you decide the original selection just wasn't sufficient for your project. Later in this tutorial you will retrieve the saved selections and invert them for use with areas outside the original selection.

7. Select the **Background** layer in the **Layers** dialog. Feather the selection by **10 pixels** (**Select ▸ Feather**), and then copy the selection and paste it as a new layer (**Layer ▸ New**). Click the layer name and change it to *Outhouse*.

The outhouse and foreground grasses are copied to their own layer so that blur operations we perform later won't affect them.

8. In the **Channels** dialog, click the **Outhouse Selection** channel, and then click the **Channel to Selection** button.

9. Select the **Background** layer in the **Layers** dialog to make that layer active. Invert the selection to select everything except the original outhouse and foreground landscape.

10. Click **Select by Color** in the toolbox. Adjust the **Threshold** level in the Tool Options dialog as necessary (I set it to 50 for this image).

11. Hold down the CTRL key and click in the blue sky to remove the sky from the selection, leaving just the background grasses, the house, and the hill. Use **Quick Mask** to remove the house and hill from the selection, leaving some of the grasses. Click the **Quick Mask** button once more to convert the mask to a selection. Save the selection to a channel named *Grasses Selection* (**Select ▸ Save to Channel**).

The grasses between the foreground outhouse and the background roof are selected in this step. This allows us to blur the middle (grasses) and background (roof) subjects to different degrees, exaggerating the depth of field.

12. Select the **Background** layer to make it active again. Feather the selection by **10 pixels** (**Select ▸ Feather**), and then copy and paste the selection as a new layer. Name this layer *Grasses* and move it below the Outhouse layer. This process has created a secondary focal point that is not in the foreground but not completely in the background.

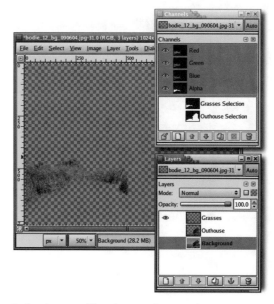

Isolated grasses fill in the space between the outhouse and the roof in the background.

Adding Depth of Field

1. Now let's increase the depth of field. Select the **Background** layer.

2. Open the Gaussian Blur filter (**Filters ▸ Blur ▸ Gaussian Blur**). Apply a blur of **20 pixels** to the **Background** layer. Then select the **Grasses** layer and apply a blur of **5 to 10 pixels**.

3. Adjust the levels (**Tools ▸ Color Tools ▸ Levels**) for the Grasses and Background layers to darken them slightly and add to the photo's sense of depth.

Further Exploration

This process works well on this image because making the initial selection was easy: The sky contrasts dramatically with the outhouse and grasses. This process is often applied to outdoor portraits, and those projects work just like this one, though selecting the foreground object (the bride in a wedding photo, for example) is more difficult. Again, the Quick Mask will be a big help.

The grasses behind the outhouse are blurred slightly, and the roof behind those grasses is blurred even more.

2.6 MOTION EFFECTS

Adding motion to a still photograph is another technique professionals often use. The real trick is in separating the subject from the background so the effect can be applied only to that object.

It's important to note that techniques like this one work well with nonlinear and distant backgrounds, like mountains. If edges need to line up exactly, however, the cloning process I show here won't fill in the hole left after the subject has been pulled from the background. If that happens, you'll simply have to find a more suitable photograph.

Much of the work you'll perform in this tutorial will be of the trial-and-error variety as you try to find good patches to fill that hole. It can help to experiment on a smaller version of your photograph before applying this effect to the full-size image.

It looks like this plane is speeding just above the ground, but it didn't start out that way.

Getting Started

The original image actually shows a plane that has just taken off. I took this photograph, but similar images can be found in any online image archive—just search for *air show*. The plane is also slightly off center in this photo. To improve this image, I've decided to take artistic license and position the plane low over the ground, wheels up, centered in the frame. Let's also remove the two runway lights so they don't distract from the image of the plane in flight.

In the original image, the plane is taking off from the runway.

Isolating the Subject

1. Grabbing the plane is the easy part. Use the **Free Select** tool to draw a selection around the plane.

2. Click the **Quick Mask** button. Use soft-edged brushes to outline the plane more precisely, zooming in and using smaller brushes where necessary. Remember that painting with white

on the Quick Mask adds to a selection, while painting in black subtracts from it, so be sure to appropriately set the foreground color box in the toolbox before you start to paint in the Quick Mask. Notice that in this example the wheels have not been selected. Click the **Quick Mask** button again to return to the selection.

The plane is selected by painting over it with white paint while in Quick Mask mode. In this example, the wheels have not been included in the selection.

3. Feather the selection by **3 pixels** (**Select ▸ Feather**). Cut and paste the plane into a new layer (**Layer ▸ New**). Double-click the layer name and change it to *Plane*. Keep this layer on top of all other layers as you work.

The plane is copied and then pasted to its own layer.

Replacing the Subject in the Background

The next trick is replacing the plane in the background. The problem is that once the plane is cut out, a hole is left in the image. We need to patch this hole with copies of other parts of the image. This can be done by using the Rectangle, Ellipse, and Free Select tools to create selections of various shapes from elsewhere in the image.

The plane is cut out from the background so it can be replaced with cloned patches. Notice that the area where the plane used to be is filled by a checkered pattern that indicates transparency. Where you see that pattern, there is no image data in any visible layer.

1. Feather the selections by **20 pixels** and then copy and paste each one over some part of the hole. Use layer masks to blend these patches into one another.

2. When the hole is filled by a series of layered patches, merge all the patches into a single layer, and then merge the patch layer into the Background layer where the plane was cut out (**Layer ▸ Merge Down**). Remember to always keep the Plane layer above the patch layer. It helps to turn off the visibility of the Plane layer while patching the hole in the Background layer. The patching won't be exact.

3. After merging the patches with the Background layer, use the **Clone** tool to clean up the patches even further. If you're not familiar with how to use the Clone tool, take a look at Section 2.10.

NOTE *Merging is a fundamental technique in digital image editing. You'll get many chances throughout the book to practice it, particularly in Section 3.5.*

By cloning irregularly shaped patches of the background mountains and foreground grasses, I was able to cover the hole left by the plane cutout and remove the runway lights.

Here you can see the composite patch by itself and when it is merged with the background image with the plane cutout. It's pretty easy to see where large pieces of the background have been duplicated (one duplicated piece is circled in red), but because the moving plane will cover most of the patch, it will be difficult to spot these duplications in the final image.

Motion-Blurring the Background

1. Click the **Background** layer.
2. Open the Gaussian Blur filter (**Filters ▸ Blur ▸ Gaussian Blur**). Set the Horizontal and Vertical fields to **7 pixels** and apply this filter to the Background layer.
3. Open the Motion Blur filter (**Filters ▸ Blur ▸ Motion**). Set the Blur Type to **Linear**, the Length to **30 pixels**, and the Angle to **0 degrees**, and apply this filter to the Background layer.

Large patches can be easy to spot when you look closely, but in this case the patch is partially obscured by another object (the speeding plane).

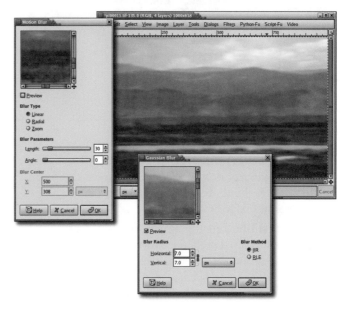

Motion-blurring the Background layer gives the illusion of movement while merging the edges of the patches with the original background.

Placing the Subject

1. Select the **Rotate** tool from the toolbox. In the Tool Options dialog, make sure the Affect is set to **Transform Layer**. There are three buttons next to the word Affect. The button on the left is the Transform Layer button, and clicking this button applies the rotation to the current layer.

2. Select the **Plane** layer in the **Layers** dialog, and click the canvas. Rotate the Plane layer so the midline of the plane's body is horizontal.

3. Center the Plane layer manually using the **Move** tool.

Rotating the plane moves it into an in-flight position.

Motion-Blurring the Subject

1. Duplicate the Plane layer (**Layer ▸ Duplicate**). Make sure the **Keep Transparency** box is unchecked. Name this layer *Plane Motion*. Set the layer boundary size to the image size (**Layer ▸ Layer to Image Size**).

2. Open the **Motion Blur** filter. Set the Length to **45 pixels** and the Angle to **0 degrees**. The Plane Motion layer should be above the Plane layer.

3. Add a white layer mask to the Plane Motion layer (**Layer ▸ Add Layer Mask**). Mask out the areas around the cockpit along with the edges of the tail fin, wing, and propeller by painting black in the mask with the **Paintbrush** tool and any round brush.

The result is the original layer showing through the Motion Blur layer, with sharp detail remaining from the original plane.

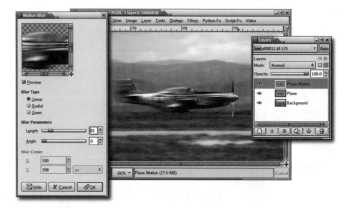

Motion-blurring the plane adds to the illusion that this photo was taken while the plane was in flight.

Masking out the blurred pilot gives the image a focal point. If everything was blurred, it would just look like a really bad photograph.

Further Exploration

The pilot and propeller would be blurred if this photograph had been taken while the plane was in mid-flight, but digital tools allow us to emphasize those two areas by leaving them in focus. You might want to experiment with creating focal points in other motion effect images.

2.7 REFLECTIONS ON GLASS

Simulating the reflection of an object on a glassy surface is actually pretty simple. In this example I'll use a yellow rose. An object that can stand upright in the image, such as a cellular phone photographed head on or a car seen directly from the side, will give you the best results if you want the object to be recognizable in the reflection.

Using the Fuzzy Select tool and the Quick Mask is the fastest way to accurately select the rose.

Preparing the Image

1. Using the **Fuzzy Select** tool and the **Quick Mask** in combination, make a selection around the rose.

2. Feather the selection (**Select ▸ Feather**) by **3 pixels**. Copy the selection, paste it to its own layer, and name the layer *Rose*. Delete the original layer.

3. Add a new layer (**Layer ▸ New**) with a black background and call it *Black Background*. Move it below the Rose layer.

4. The rose doesn't leave enough space on the canvas for a full reflection, so it needs to be scaled down. Select the **Rose** layer to make it active. Choose the **Scale** tool from the toolbox, make sure that the **Keep Aspect** option in the Tool Options dialog is selected, and then click the canvas. Drag in the canvas to scale the rose to about half its original size.

You can achieve this rosy reflection in five easy steps.

Getting Started

In the original image, a yellow rose is set against a red background. This image offers high contrast around the edges. When working to create reflections using images like this one, it's best to remove the darker edges and leave the lighter color of the object. This allows you to place the selection on just about any background.

NOTE *The image used in this tutorial is available at PDPhoto.org.*

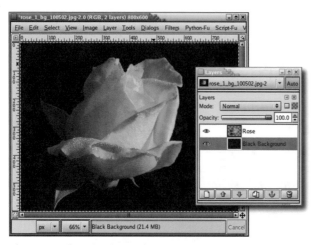

The rose is selected and copied to its own layer. The Black
Background layer replaces the original image layer.

5. Using the **Move** tool, position the Rose layer in the upper
half of the window.

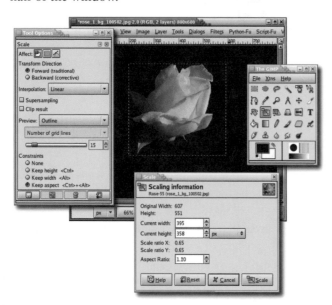

Scale down the rose to about half the size of the canvas to make
room for its reflection.

Creating the Reflection

1. Duplicate the Rose layer (**Layer ▸ Duplicate**) and name the
duplicate layer *Rose Reflection*.

2. Enlarge the layer boundary (**Layer ▸ Layer Boundary Size**) by
20 percent—just choose **Percent** from the drop-down menu
next to the Current Height field—and click the **Center** button
in the Layer Boundary Size dialog.

3. Make sure the **Keep Transparency** box is unchecked for the
Rose Reflection layer (the Keep Transparency box is in the
upper-right corner of the Layers dialog).

4. Open the Gaussian Blur filter (**Filters ▸ Blur ▸ Gaussian Blur**)
and blur the Rose Reflection layer by **8 to 10 pixels**.

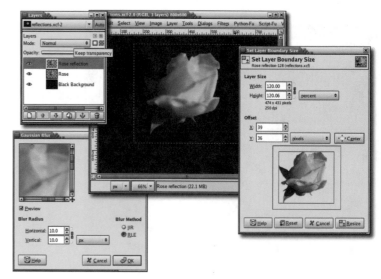

Increasing the layer boundary size of the Rose Reflection layer gives us some extra
room for blurring. If we didn't resize, the blur might bump up against the edge of
the original rose.

Adding a Surface for the Reflection

1. Next let's add a visible surface. Add a new transparent layer (**Layer ▸ New**) and name it *Aqua Gradient*.

2. Press **D** then **X** in the toolbox to set the background to black.

3. Double-click the foreground color box to open the Change Foreground Color dialog. For the aqua color shown here, set the RGB values to **0/179/152** and click **OK**. I've chosen this color for its aesthetic value as well as its contrast with the color of the rose. Using a high-contrast color for the surface will emphasize the reflection all the more.

4. To create the gradient effect shown, select the **Blend** tool from the toolbox. Then drag from the bottom of the canvas to three-fourths of the way up to apply the aqua-to-black gradient to the Aqua Gradient layer.

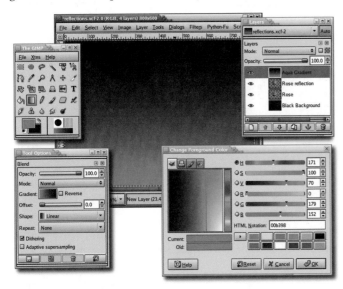

The rose is reflected on the surface created by the aqua-to-black gradient.

5. The next step is to add variation to the surface by slightly changing the flow of the gradient across the width of the canvas window. With the toolbox selected, press **X** to swap colors.

6. In the Tool Options dialog, set the Opacity to **48 percent**, choose **Multiply** from the Mode drop-down menu, and set the Gradient to **FG to Transparent**. Then drag from the top to the middle of the canvas at a slight right-to-left angle to offset the black gradient.

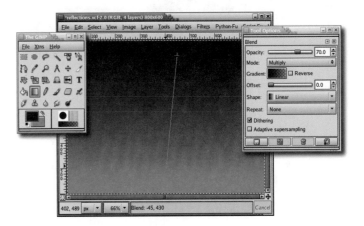

Offsetting the black gradient at an angle makes the surface less uniform as it recedes into the distance.

7. The surface created by the gradient is too large for our purposes and needs to be scaled down so it looks more like a reflective tabletop. To make this adjustment, first open the Scale Layer dialog (**Layer ▸ Scale Layer**).

8. Click the chain connecting the Width and Height fields to disregard the original aspect ratio. Reduce the height by **65 percent**. Turn off visibility of the Rose layer and the Rose Reflection layer.

9. Align the Aqua Gradient layer with the Black Background layer (**Layer ▸ Align Visible Layers**) by setting the Vertical Style to **Collect** and the Vertical Base to **Bottom Edge** and checking the box next to the words *Use the (invisible) bottom layer as the base*. Move the Aqua Gradient layer to just above the Black Background layer (use **Layer ▸ Stack ▸ Lower Layer** twice).

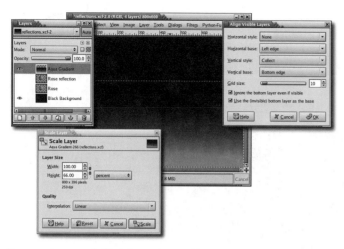

Because the upper half of the gradient is black, the top of the resized Aqua Gradient layer is not visible against the Black Background layer.

The reflection effect is nearly complete, but a real reflection would include a shadow cast by the reflected object.

Placing the Reflection on the Surface

1. Click the **Rose Reflection** layer in the **Layers** dialog to make that layer active.

2. Select the **Flip** tool from the toolbox. In the Tool Options dialog select **Vertical** for the Flip Type, and then click the canvas to flip this layer.

3. Use the **Move** tool to position the Rose Reflection layer beneath the Rose layer.

4. Reduce the Opacity of the Rose Reflection layer to **50 percent** and lower this layer between the Rose layer and the Aqua Gradient layer.

Adding a Shadow

Because the rose would block any light shining directly overhead, we must add a shadow to the surface. And because light would shine in multiple directions above the rose, more than one shadow would be cast. Next we will create these shadows.

1. Add a new layer named *Shadow 1*.

2. Choose the **Ellipse Select** tool from the toolbox and create an oval selection just below the rose.

3. Feather the selection by **10 pixels** (Select ▸ Feather) and fill it with black. Deselect the oval (Select ▸ None).

4. Open the Gaussian Blur filter (**Filters ▸ Blur ▸ Gaussian Blur**) and apply a blur of **45 pixels** to the Shadow 1 layer, and then set the layer's Opacity to **65 percent**. Move this layer to just above the Rose Reflection layer.

5. Duplicate the Rose layer, name the duplicate layer *Shadow 2*, and increase the layer boundary size by **10 percent** (**Layer ▸ Layer Boundary Size**).

6. Create a selection of the rose (**Layer ▸ Transparency ▸ Alpha to Selection**), and then grow the selection by **2 pixels** (Select ▸ Grow).

7. Press **D** and then **X** in the canvas to reset the foreground color to black, and then fill the selection with black by dragging the foreground color box from the toolbox into the selection. Deselect all (SHIFT-CTRL-A).

8. Open the **Gaussian Blur** filter and apply a blur of **45 pixels** to the Shadow 2 layer.

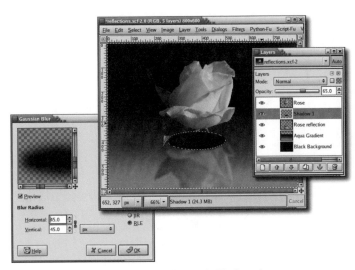

Blurring and reducing the opacity of a simple black oval creates an initial shadow.

The shaped shadow merges with the oval shadow, making the area directly beneath the rose darkest but also allowing the shadow to mimic the shape of the rose.

9. Use the **Flip** tool to flip the layer vertically, and then use the **Scale** tool to reduce the height of the layer by half.

10. Move the Shadow 2 layer beneath the Rose layer (**Layer ▸ Stack ▸ Lower Layer**), and then position it using the **Move** tool so the shadow appears below the yellow rose.

11. Reduce the Opacity of the Shadow 2 layer to **35 percent**.

Further Exploration

This technique for creating reflections on glassy surfaces can be extended to surfaces that aren't quite as flat or reflective. You can also add texture to the surface to distort the reflected shape or change the direction, color, and lighting to make the reflection less distinct. In the next tutorial I'll show you how to add waves to the surface of the reflection to create a lake effect.

2.8 LAKE REFLECTION

Section 2.7 showed you how to create reflections on glass, but much more can be done with the technique we discussed. That section's tutorial made slight modifications to the object being reflected (a rose). But what about adding texture to the reflective surface? How can we create a reflection on a surface that isn't perfectly flat—a surface like water?

An easy way to add surface texture is to grab it from another image. A photo that shows the surface of a lake or ocean will work well for this tutorial. Once the sampled image is desaturated and blended with the reflection, it turns a glassy surface into a realistic reflection.

This tutorial turns a lawn into an undulating lake. In the real world, creating exactly the image you want usually requires the application of more than one effect, so let's start by enhancing the colors in the original photo.

The lake looks real, but it has been added digitally using the GIMP.

Getting Started

The image we'll use in this tutorial is perfect for this kind of project. The building makes a dramatic focal point, and the grassy area in front is large enough to provide space for the lake. The color of the bricks could be more intense, however, so I'll increase the color saturation before reflecting the image of the building. If the image you choose needs any similar tweaks, it's best to handle them now.

First, open the Hue-Saturation dialog (**Layer ▸ Colors ▸ Hue-Saturation**). Then increase the saturation and reduce the lightness of the red channel to bring out the details in the building.

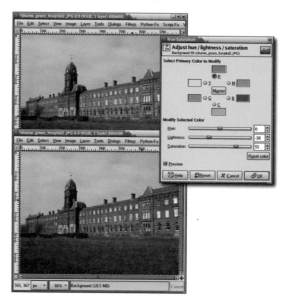

Adjust the saturation and lightness of the image to make the building's colors more vivid.

Creating the Initial Reflection

1. Make a square selection around the subject—in this case, the building. Let's also include some of the grassy area in front of the building. Copy the selection and paste it into a new layer, and then click the layer name and change it to *Reflection*.

2. Select the **Flip** tool from the toolbox. In the Tool Options dialog set the Flip Type to **Vertical** and click the canvas to flip the layer.

3. Use the **Move** tool to drag the Reflection layer down on the canvas. If the Reflection layer does not span the width of the canvas, select the **Scale** tool and then click the canvas to scale the layer manually.

A simple rectangular selection includes the building and some of the grassy area. This selection is copied and pasted to a new layer, and the layer is then flipped vertically. Finally, the new layer is dragged down on the canvas until it is positioned as shown here.

Adding Ripples

1. To look realistic, the reflected image should be more blurred and less saturated than the original. Open the Hue-Saturation dialog (**Layer ▸ Colors ▸ Hue-Saturation**) and make sure the **Master** button is selected. Reduce the Saturation level to **–45** for this image (your project may require different settings).

2. Open the Ripple filter (**Filters ▸ Distorts ▸ Ripple**). Set the Orientation to **Horizontal**, the Edges to **Smear**, the Period to **7**, and the Amplitude to **1**, and then apply this filter to the Reflection layer. Repeat this process with the Ripple filter once more, this time setting the Orientation to **Vertical**, the Period to **60**, and Amplitude to **2**. Applying the Ripple filter twice applies ripples to ripples, just as waves in water cause interference patterns.

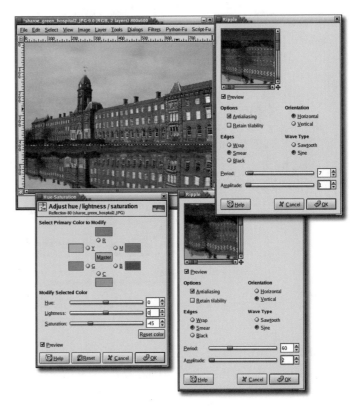

The Ripple filter lends an undulating effect to the reflection, though we'll improve upon this shortly.

3. Open the Gaussian Blur filter (**Filters ▸ Blur ▸ Gaussian Blur**). Set both the Horizontal and Vertical Blur Radius to **3 pixels** and apply the blur to the Reflection layer.

4. Duplicate the layer (**Layer ▸ Duplicate**).

5. Click the foreground color box to open the Change Foreground Color dialog. For the dark blue shown here, set the RGB values to **5/24/83** and click **OK**. Then drag the foreground color into the layer. Finally, move the layer below the original Reflection layer and reduce the Opacity of the Reflection layer to **60 percent**.

Waves are copied and pasted into the project image to make the lake look even more realistic.

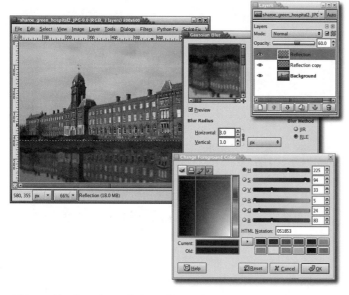

Adding a blue layer beneath the Reflection layer makes the reflection look more like a lake.

Adding Waves

The Ripple filter makes the lake's surface somewhat more realistic, but adding waves would improve the texture even more. To add waves, you can grab a selection from another photo.

1. Copy the blue layer and paste it into a new layer named *Water*, and then use the **Scale** tool to scale the layer.

2. Desaturate the Water layer (**Layer ▸ Colors ▸ Desaturate**).

3. I've reduced the opacity of the Water layer to 50 percent and set the layer mode to Overlay, but the appropriate opacity and layer mode will depend on the image you choose to sample. A brighter image might require more opacity, while a more uniformly dark image might work better with the layer mode set to Screen. Desaturating the layer allows it to be blended with the Reflection layer without modifying that layer's color content. Once these adjustments have been made, merge the Water layer, the Reflection layer, and the waves layer (**Layer ▸ Merge Down**).

4. Add a white layer mask to this merged layer.

5. With the toolbox selected, press **D** to revert to the default foreground and background colors. Use the **Airbrush** tool to paint portions of the top half of the layer so that layer blends more smoothly into the background.

In this version, a small peninsula extends into the lake, showing how the mask can be used to create a wide variety of images.

Further Exploration

This particular image lends itself well to further enhancement. The high contrast between the building and the sky allows you to make changes to the weather, perhaps even changing a sunny day into a starlit evening. Try converting this image to a nighttime scene. The Fuzzy Select tool can be used to capture most of the sky, and what is missed can be picked up easily using the Quick Mask. But be warned: The lake reflection will need to be changed too!

2.9 SCREENING TYPE

It's easy enough to place type over a photograph, but making sure the type can be read often requires a few additional steps. You need enough contrast between the type and the image to make the type stand out. Without some contrast, your message may be ignored. Adding contrast to an image so the type placed over it stands out is called *screening*. The process involves positioning a colored and/or semi-transparent layer—known as a *screen*—between the type and the image. Additional enhancements might include shadows or borders around the type and screen.

In this tutorial a stock image is used as the basis for a simple flier. A screen is added so that the text message can be viewed easily over the busy background.

A text screen is one of the easiest effects to achieve.

Getting Started

A stock image of some tennis balls and a tennis racket provides the starting point for a tennis tournament flier, and we want to add our message in white text over this image. The image has a mix of light and dark areas, so we need to screen a region, darken it, and position the text over it.

Because the stock image is of such high quality, we don't need to enhance it before going forward. No levels adjustments are needed. When choosing a background image for your own screening project, look for images with open space for your text. This image has more open space at the bottom than at the top, so that's where we'll position the text. This open space allows the screen to be used without blocking out the most important features of the background image, in this case the tennis balls and tennis racket.

For a project like this one, start with a high-quality stock photo that has enough open space for your text.

Creating a Text Screen

1. Drag a horizontal guide from the ruler at the top of the window down to just below the middle of the image.

2. Choose the **Rectangle Select** tool from the toolbox. Using the guide as the uppermost side, make a rectangular selection in the bottom half of the image, where we've decided to place our text. If necessary, combine two selections to span the entire width of the image.

3. Copy the selection and paste it as a new layer (**Layer ▸ New Layer**), and then click the layer name and change it to *Screen*.

Desaturate the Screen layer, and then reduce its brightness and contrast as shown here.

Copy the area where the text will be placed and paste that copy into its own layer.

4. To make the screen an effective background for the text, we need to desaturate and darken the screen. First, desaturate the Screen layer (**Layer ▸ Colors ▸ Desaturate**). Then open the Brightness-Contrast dialog (**Layer ▸ Colors ▸ Brightness-Contrast**) and set both the Brightness and Contrast sliders to **–65**.

5. Click the foreground color box to open the Change Foreground Color dialog. Set the RGB values in this dialog to **17/4/143**.

6. Select the **Bucket Fill** tool from the toolbox. In the Tool Options dialog, set the layer mode to **Multiply**, the Opacity to **50 percent**, and the Affected Area to **Fill Whole Selection**.

7. Click the canvas to colorize the Screen layer. Multiply mode will darken the screened region, making it easier for light text to show up.

We might also have desaturated the selected part of the original layer, filled the new layer with solid blue, and changed its layer mode to Color, Grain Merge, or Multiply. Feel free to experiment and decide which method you prefer. I prefer to work with desaturated copies of the original content, which means making a copy of the original layer so I don't change the original layer's content. Remember: Always keep the original safe so you can return to it if your experiments don't pan out!

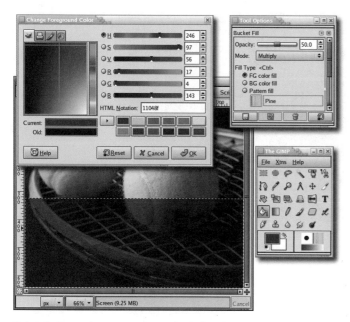

Color the Screen layer using the Bucket Fill tool.

Be sure to drag from the top of the Screen layer to fill your mask. Don't start at the top of the canvas! By starting at the top of the Screen layer you create a black edge that allows the layer to merge seamlessly with the original image.

Blending the Screen with the Background

1. In the Layers dialog, reduce the Screen layer's opacity to **80 percent.**

2. Add a white layer mask (**Layer ▸ Mask ▸ Add Layer Mask**).

3. Select the **Blend** tool and press **D** while the canvas window is selected to reset the foreground and background colors. In the Tool Options dialog make sure the Opacity is set to **100 percent,** the mode is set to **Normal,** the Gradient is set to black to white, and the Reverse option is not set.

4. In the Screen layer, drag down from the top of the layer to create a soft blend between the Screen layer and the background. Turn off guides (**View ▸ Show Guides**) and Layer Boundary visibility (**View ▸ Show Layer Boundary**) to make it easier to see the blended layers.

Adding the Type

1. With the toolbox selected, press **X** to swap the foreground and background colors.

2. Select the **Text** tool, choose an appropriate font and size in the Tool Options dialog, and type your text. I've used XBAND Rough for the heading in this tutorial to emphasize the hard-hitting sports competition being advertised. Because the original image and the text screen are rather dark, I've used white text. If the image had been light, I would have used dark text instead.

3. If the text layer is not active in the Layers dialog, click it to make it active. Open the Drop Shadow filter (**Script-Fu ▸ Shadow ▸ Drop Shadow**). Set the Offset X and Offset Y fields to **4 pixels** and the Blur Radius to **4 pixels,** and then make sure that the box next to the words *Allow Resizing* is not checked. Click **OK** to apply these settings to the Text layer.

The more contrast there is between your text and text screen, the easier it is to read the text.

A drop shadow causes the text to stand out against the background image.

The use of a text screen makes quite a difference. For comparison, see how the same flier appears with and without the screen. The added contrast makes the text much easier to read.

Without a screen, the text is much more difficult to read.

Further Exploration

When planning your designs, be sure to keep print costs in mind. If you're trying to keep costs down, blending the screen with the background can be an expensive proposition because it requires a four-color print process. Using a solid screen with high-contrast edges is an inexpensive alternative if you can only afford to print in two colors.

Text screening is one of the easiest techniques to master, so nonprofessionals often use it. In the next tutorial we'll look at a much more professional project: photo restoration.

2.10 PHOTO RESTORATION

Photo restoration and retouching—the art of preserving and enhancing old photographs that are folded from misuse or cracked and faded with age—is a form of digital image manipulation that is often overlooked. As you'll see in this tutorial, the GIMP's tools enable you to achieve high-quality photo restoration.

A number of tricks can be used to restore damaged photos, but the most common technique involves simply cloning similar areas and using those clones to replace damaged areas. The GIMP's Clone tool allows us to use brush strokes of any shape to copy and paste areas. This method is only appropriate for minor cleanup work such as removing a speck of dust or hiding a thin, short scratch, however. This method is also destructive because the cloning occurs in the layer where the damage exists. If the patches are not to your liking, you may not be able to reverse them easily.

A better strategy for correcting larger blemishes is to make a selection, copy and paste the selection as a patch layer, and then blend this patch layer into the original layer using the Airbrush tool in a layer mask. This approach has the advantage of allowing additional changes to be made later, by either modifying the layer mask or replacing the patch layer completely.

In this tutorial we'll look at the copy-and-paste method of fixing heavily damaged images. We'll also discuss when to use large selections to patch large areas and when to divide a blemish into pieces and patch them individually.

What was once old is new again.

Getting Started

This image was scanned from a 60-year-old photo that had been creased several times, with one crease actually leaving a slight tear along the subject's midsection. There are several problems to fix here: We need to correct the black-and-white points in the faded image, we need to remove the creases, and we need to clean up the background.

Your candidate for restoration is likely to have many of the same problems, but they may occur in different areas of the image, presenting different challenges. Scanning the original image at a high resolution, such as 250 dpi, will allow you to create a high-quality print once your image has been restored.

The restoration will improve tonal qualities and fix blemishes.

Enhancing the Scanned Image

1. Let's start with some basic image enhancement. To correct the white and black points, use the Autolevel option in the Levels dialog (**Layer ▸ Colors ▸ Levels**). Clicking the **Autolevel** button automatically moves the left slider (black) to the first entry on that end of the histogram, and it moves the right slider (white) to the first entry on that end. This has the effect of increasing the image's contrast so the darkest pixels become black and the lightest pixels become white, making the image clearer overall.

2. We also note that the image has taken on a brown tint as it has aged. Fix this by desaturating the image (**Layer ▸ Colors ▸ Desaturate**).

3. As is the case with most scanned images, some sharpening is required (**Filters ▸ Enhance ▸ Sharpen**). The Unsharp Mask filter (Filters ▸ Enhance ▸ Unsharp Mask) could also be used, although that's not the best choice for this image because there are very few straight lines.

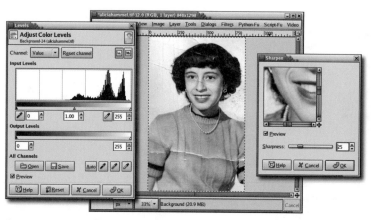

Sharpen the scan and adjust the levels before you start to patch the blemishes. If you make these changes after the patches are in place, the edges of your patches may be visible.

Correcting with a Single Patch

The big scratch across the woman's sweater is an example of the kind of damage you can fix with a simple copy-and-paste correction that consists of a single patch. There is enough undamaged sweater in the photo to allow us to use this technique.

1. Choose the **Free Select** tool and draw a selection around part of the scratch that traverses the woman's midsection. This will give you the size of the area that must be patched.

2. Hold down the ALT key (along with the SHIFT key in some Linux desktop configurations) and drag the mouse to move the selection to an unblemished area near the scratch.

3. Feather the selection by **10 pixels** (**Selection ▸ Feather**).

4. Copy the selection and paste it in a new layer (**Layer ▸ New**), and then position the new layer over the scratch. In this case, the sweater's pleats help us align the patch, but your images will probably provide similar guides. (To show where the patch has been applied, the original image is tinted red.)

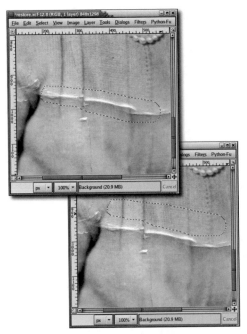

The Free Select tool is used first, and then the selection is moved to a nearby unblemished area to create a patch.

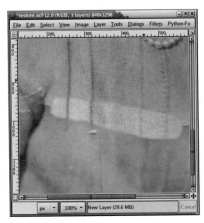

This patch covers the blemish quite well because it was taken from a nearby part of the image. The farther away you go from the blemish, the less likely the patch will fit as cleanly.

5. In this example, the pleats do not align perfectly, but this can be fixed by using the IWarp filter (**Filters ▸ Distorts ▸ IWarp**) to make minor adjustments. If the patch doesn't align with the original layer along the edges of the patch, add a layer mask (**Layer ▸ Add Layer**) and use the **Airbrush** tool to spray black in the mask along the edges of the patch.

6. If the patch's tonal qualities don't match those of the damaged area, you can use the Curves tool (**Layer ▸ Colors ▸ Curves**). Make sure the patch layer (and not its mask) is active by clicking the layer preview in the Layers dialog. To see if the patch lines up well with the original image, turn the layer visibility for the patch on and off quickly (using the eye icon in the Layers dialog). As you do this, it should appear that the pleats (or other guides) are in place and only the scratch is removed.

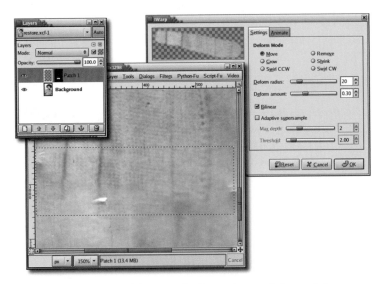

Flash the patch layer's visibility on and off to see how well the patch fits.

Correcting with Multiple Patches

The scratches across both of the woman's sleeves pose a more difficult problem. There is no single unblemished area large enough to cover these scratches, so they require several smaller patches. I used seven small patches to fix the scratch on the left sleeve, each patch created just as the large patch was created.

1. Simply use the **Free Select** tool to select part of the scratch, move the selection over a nearby unblemished region, copy and paste the selection as a new layer, and move that layer over the scratch. If necessary, use a layer mask on the patch to blend it with the surrounding areas.

2. In this photo, the dark area between the woman's sleeve and midsection has a very complex pattern. The patch requires use of the Curves tool (**Layer ▸ Colors ▸ Curves**) because the patch was taken from a region that had different tonal qualities. A simple blend with a layer mask is not sufficient to meld the patch over the scratch. The Curves adjustment modifies the tonal qualities so the patch blends seamlessly when combined with the mask.

3. After all the sleeve patches are created and blended, merge them (**Layer ▸ Merge Down**) one at a time into a single patch.

NOTE *See Section 3.5 for more practice with merging layers.*

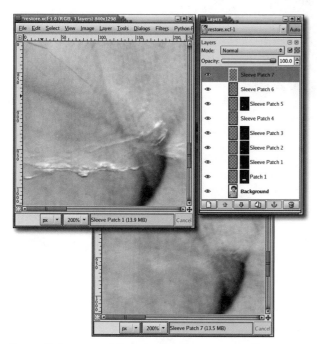

For small disconnected blemishes like this one, especially in high-contrast areas, use a series of small patches.

Correcting Facial Blemishes

Scratches on a subject's face are more difficult to fix than those on clothing. It's easier to spot differences between the patch and the surrounding face than it is to spot those between the sweater and its patches. Even so, facial scratches are best handled by using the Free Select tool as we've done so far. The main difference is that you must make even smaller selections, bounded by high-contrast lines. Areas between the face and the hairline or between the bridge of the nose and the shadowed sides of the nose work especially well. The woman's eye poses a particular challenge because that part of the image is so complex.

1. Make a selection of the eye, and copy and paste it to a new layer as a patch (**Layer ▸ New**).

2. Use the **Clone** tool to manually paint out the scratch. In this case it's safe to use the Clone tool because we're working on a copy of the original, blemished subject.

3. Using the Clone tool is a two-step process. First, specify a clone source location by holding down the CTRL key and clicking the image. The click point indicates the region that will be copied from, so make sure it is a reasonable match to the region you're patching. Once the clone source is established, choose the clone destination. Click and drag the mouse over the scratch. The source is copied over the destination as you drag.

When you use the Clone tool, the length and direction of the line between the clone source and the initial clone destination (where you first click when you start to clone the image) always remains uniform. When you drag a line over the scratch, that same line is cloned, positioned to start at the clone source location. This means that if you drag far enough from the initial clone destination, you can cause the clone source to fall over another blemish. The trick is to keep your brush strokes small and reset your clone source point frequently.

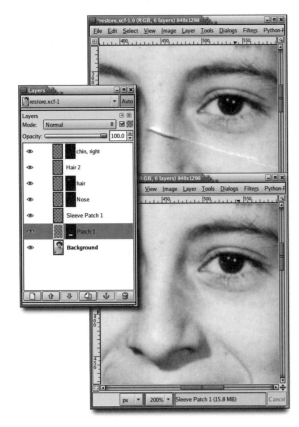

It's more difficult to fix blemishes on faces than on clothing. The process is the same, but make careful Curves adjustments and blend your patches using layer masks.

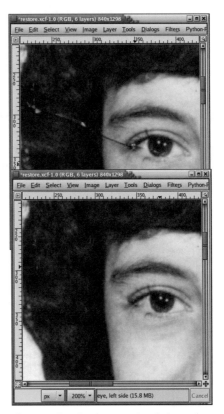

This scratch is fixed using several cloning operations, so more than one clone source is used. In fact, each clone source is used for a very small part of the scratch. This allows the cloned areas to blend seamlessly into the rest of the image.

Cleaning Up the Background

Cleaning up the background is a no-brainer.

1. Make a selection using the **Quick Mask** and an appropriate brush. Paint inside locks of hair where the background shows through. The painted areas (which are no longer tinted red) will become the selected area when you click the **Quick Mask to Selection** button in the lower-left corner of the canvas window.

2. Feather the selection by **3 pixels** or more (**Select ▸ Feather**). In previous tutorials the feather values were only 1 or 2 pixels, but higher feather values should be used when your image resolution is higher, as it is when restoring a photograph.

3. Use the **Color Picker** tool to select a color from the existing background inside the selection. Drag the foreground color into the selection to fill it with this color. This takes care of all problems in the background.

The background is selected using the Quick Mask instead of the Fuzzy Select tool because there is too much variation in the background and the background has faded so much that parts of it match the hair's outside edges.

All of the other large blemishes can be fixed using the same processes used for the sweater and face. In this case, the final results are dramatic. When the original image is scanned at a high resolution, an image restored using the GIMP's tools should produce a high-quality print. The results won't always be so dramatic, but with practice some people are able to make a living doing this kind of work.

A single pixel is chosen from the background and used to fill the selection.

Further Exploration

Professional image restoration depends upon the proper use of selections and layer masks, but it also relies heavily upon other tools in the GIMP arsenal, including the IWarp filter, Feather command, Curves tool, and Clone tool. As a process, image restoration doesn't lend itself to automation, so designers who understand how to make the most of these techniques will always be in high demand.

Restoring old photographs is a time-consuming but rewarding process. In the next section, we'll discuss a technique that requires far less time but is just as rewarding.

2.11 CASTING LIGHT THROUGH A WINDOW

Adding a light source to a photograph can increase the photograph's dramatic impact—especially when the light is shining through a paned window. Actually setting up a shot like the one shown here can be time consuming and usually requires a specific location. It would be easier if we could use software to add the light source to any image.

Fortunately, we can. The GIMP allows us to merge multiple shots to achieve this effect. Start with any stock photograph and use an image of a window as a stencil for the shadow. The process is so simple, in fact, that you'll probably have more trouble finding suitable stock images than you will producing the effect in the GIMP.

It would be difficult to set up a shot like this one, but the GIMP makes it easy to merge two stock photographs and achieve a dramatic effect.

Getting Started

This shot was created from two stock photographs. The first photo shows a model posing against a wall. Let's call this layer

Source. The second image shows light shining through an oddly shaped window. Let's call the second image the *Shadow mask*. You can certainly create a mask in whatever shape you like, but you'll save time if you can find a suitable stock photo.

Two source images are used in this project. The window provides the shadow mask for the light we'll cast on the model.

Setting Up the Shadow Mask

We'll start by opening up a source image and an image to use as the Shadow mask, both from their respective stock image files. If the Shadow mask image is intended to cover only a portion of the source image, make a selection around that part of the Shadow mask image and paste it into source image as a new layer. This example doesn't require a selection at all because we want to use the entire Shadow mask image, so we can just copy and paste the entire Shadow mask into a new layer in the Source image.

1. Copy the Shadow mask and paste it into the Source image as a new layer (**Layer ▸ New**) as shown here.

2. Reduce the Opacity of the Shadow mask layer to **65 percent**, then use the **Move** tool to position the window over the subject.

Copy and paste the Shadow mask into the Source layer.

3. To make the window look more like a shadow, we need to desaturate and blur it. Desaturate the Shadow mask layer (**Layer ▸ Colors ▸ Desaturate**), and then open the Gaussian Blur filter (**Filters ▸ Blur ▸ Gaussian Blur**). The Blur Radius should be set according to the image size. In this example, the source image is 800 pixels wide, so the Blur Radius is set to 25 pixels. That gives a 32:1 ratio, though you may find that a smaller ratio is more appropriate for smaller images.

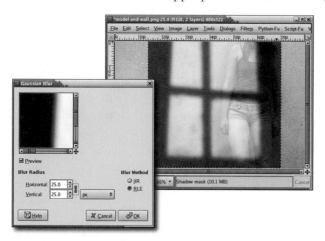

A blur softens the light areas of the Shadow mask, making it look as though light is being cast through a paned window.

4. Expand the Shadow mask layer to fit the full image (**Layer ▸ Layer to Image Size**). While the Shadow mask layer is selected, uncheck the **Keep Transparency** box in the Layers dialog.

5. Using the **Fuzzy Select** tool, click the transparent regions of the layer to the left and right of the window image. This may require multiple clicks with the SHIFT key held down.

6. With the canvas selected, press **D** to reset the foreground and background colors. Then drag the foreground color (black) into the selection to extend the shadow cast by the wall in which the window is set.

After resizing the Shadow mask layer to fit the canvas, fill the transparent areas with black. This works here because the area around the window is black. For other images, you may need to make some levels adjustments to the Shadow mask layer first.

7. Deselect all (**Select ▸ None**).

8. Set the Shadow mask layer mode to **Multiply**. In this example, the result is good, but more contrast would help. Use the **Fuzzy Select** tool and click in the darker areas of the Shadow mask. Invert this selection (**Select ▸ Invert**). Shrink (**Select ▸ Shrink**) the selection a bit (in this case, I shrank the selection by 10 pixels).

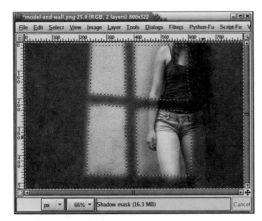

Select the illuminated regions of the Shadow mask.

Increasing the Light

1. Create a new transparent layer (**Layer ▸ New**) and call it *Light*.

2. Drag the background color (white) into the selection.

3. Deselect all (**Select ▸ None**).

4. Open the Gaussian Blur filter (**Filters ▸ Blur ▸ Gaussian Blur**) and set the Blur Radius to **50 pixels**.

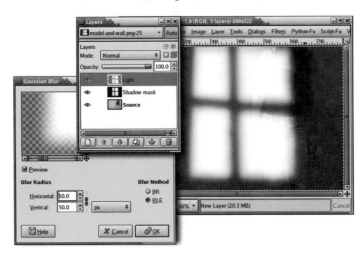

Fill the selection with white in a new layer.

5. Setting the Light layer's mode to **Overlay** completes the effect. Adding a layer mask (**Layer ▸ Mask ▸ Add Layer Mask**) to the Light layer and applying a black-to-white gradient using the Blend tool softens the lower edge. It may also be necessary to apply a black-to-white gradient to the Shadow mask layer, with the layer mode set to Multiply.

The additional light layer increases the contrast between the shadowed and illuminated areas on the wall and model.

Further Exploration

To take this tutorial further, you might add shadows that are cast by objects outside the window. Imagine a tree, for example. Its shadow would also be cast through the window and onto the source image. The process for adding the tree's shadow would be the same except that you would be taking light away wherever the shadow fell.

2.12 LIGHTNING

Lightning is difficult for the amateur photographer to capture, but it's one of the more dramatic elements that can be added to nature photography. While timed exposures help to capture real lightning, adding lightning digitally is not as difficult as you might think—and it's not nearly as dangerous as the real thing.

I spent a long time trying to find a method for creating realistic lightning. I even searched math texts for formulas that I could use to write my own lightning plug-in. But there was very little information to be found. Then the holy grail fell into my lap. I discovered a Photoshop technique that is easily reproduced with the GIMP. There are only a few steps, and the variations you can produce are endless. Additionally, once you've created one bolt of lightning, saved your Curves settings, and noted values for settings that can't be saved, it's easy to reproduce the same lightning bolt.

Don't be discouraged if your first attempt looks less like lightning and more like an explosion. Experimentation is crucial with this technique, and once you understand the process, most of the work will be in the form of minor adjustments.

Unlike many of the other tutorials in this chapter, this section's tutorial is definitely a recipe. Follow the steps exactly, and you should be able to create a realistic lightning bolt.

Getting Started

Start with a photo of the sky that includes an ominous cloud. Make a selection where the first bolt of lightning should appear. Copy and paste this selection into a new layer (**Layer ▸ New**). Name this new layer *Bolt 1*. (For very large images it is often less memory intensive to work with layers that are not the full canvas size.)

It's easy to create lightning, but it's more difficult to reproduce the same shape each time.

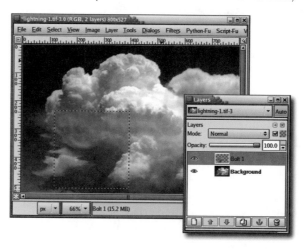

Make a copy of the area where you want to create the first lightning bolt.

Creating a Lightning Bolt

1. First let's use a gradient to create the lightning bolt. With the **Bolt 1** layer selected, select the **Blend** tool. In the Tool Options dialog, set the Opacity to **100 percent**, the layer mode to **Normal**, and the Shape to **Linear**. Choose **FG to BG (RGB)** from the Gradient drop-down menu.

2. Drag from left to right in the Bolt 1 layer, at a slight upward angle. For this image, which is 800 pixels wide, the gradient is 100 pixels long and at an angle of –10 degrees (see the status bar in this image). Note that the lightning will appear along a straighter line if the gradient is shorter—in other words, if there is less gray between the black and white.

Fill the new layer with a linear black-to-white gradient that is slightly angled.

3. Duplicate the gradient layer (**Layer ▸ Duplicate**).

4. Open the Plasma filter (**Filters ▸ Render ▸ Clouds ▸ Plasma**). Set the Random Seed to **0** and the Turbulence to **0.8**. Small turbulence values will create smooth lightning strikes, while high values produce rough edges on either side of the bolt.

5. Desaturate the layer (**Layer ▸ Colors ▸ Desaturate**).

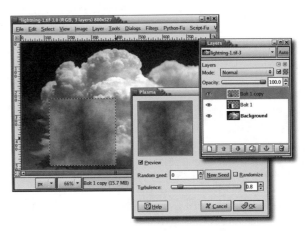

Duplicate the gradient layer and then apply the Plasma filter. Be sure to desaturate this new layer.

6. Set the duplicate layer's mode to **Difference**. Merge this layer with the Bolt 1 layer (**Layer ▸ Merge Down**).

7. Launch the Curves tool (**Layer ▸ Colors ▸ Curves**). Set the Value curve to resemble that shown here and click **OK**.

8. Invert the colors in the layer (**Layer ▸ Colors ▸ Invert**).

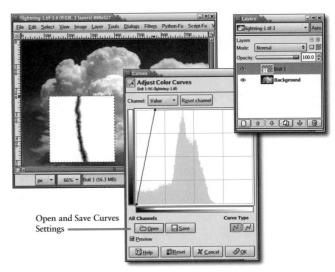

Difference mode combines the plasma layer and the gradient layer in a way that removes all but a jagged sliver of black.

9. Launch the Brightness-Contrast tool (**Layer ▸ Colors ▸ Brightness-Contrast**). Reduce the contrast to **–70** to smooth out some of the bolt's rough edges.

10. Final cleanup is done using the Curves tool once again (**Layer ▸ Colors ▸ Curves**). Set the Value curve to resemble that shown here. Your setting won't match this one exactly due to variations in the gradient and plasma layers you created earlier. You may need to move the curve to the right a bit if your bolt looks too gray. Don't forget to save these Curves settings for future use!

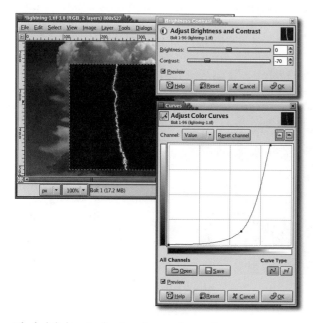

The bolt lights up after its colors are inverted.

Blending the Lightning Bolt with the Original Image

1. Continue working in the Bolt 1 layer, and open the Gaussian Blur filter (**Filters ▸ Blur ▸ Gaussian Blur**). Set both the X and Y Blur Radius to **2 pixels** and apply this filter to the Bolt 1 layer.

2. Duplicate this layer (**Layer ▸ Duplicate**). Set the duplicate layer's mode to **Hard Light,** and then merge the duplicate layer with the Bolt 1 layer (**Layer ▸ Merge Down**).

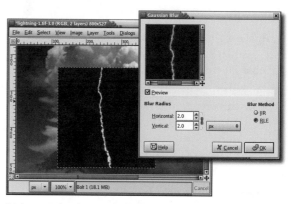

Lightning often has a soft glow around it, which is added by using the Gaussian Blur filter. A duplicate of this layer is merged with the original to bring back the brightness the bolt loses when the blur is applied.

3. Set the Bolt 1 layer's mode to **Screen**. This allows the bolt to continue to show and hides the black background.

4. Most lightning is tinted blue or purple, so let's add some color. Launch the Colorize tool (**Layer ▸ Colors ▸ Colorize**). Set the Hue to **282** and the Saturation to **68**, and apply these settings to the Bolt 1 layer.

5. Add a white layer mask (**Layer ▸ Mask ▸ Add Layer Mask**) and manually paint it black to blend the top of the bolt with the clouds.

The first bolt takes its place among the clouds!

Adding Flashes of Light

1. A realistic lightning bolt also lights up the clouds and sky around it, so let's add some flashes of light. Click the Background layer to select it, and then make a small rectangular selection around the top of the lightning bolt.

2. Copy and paste this selection as a new layer (**Layer ▸ New**), and name this layer *Cloud Flash*. Move the Cloud Flash layer directly below the Bolt 1 layer.

3. With the toolbox selected, press **D** and then **X** to set the foreground color to white.

4. Select the **Airbrush** tool. In the Tool Options dialog set the layer mode to **Grain Merge** and the Opacity to **40 percent**.

5. In the Cloud Flash layer, draw along the line of the lightning bolt and around the bolt's top to add cloud flashes where the bolt and cloud would touch.

The cloud lights up where the bolt meets it.

Forking the Lightning Bolt and Adding a Glow

1. To make the image look more realistic, we can fork the lightning bolt and add a glow effect around the bolt and in the cloud. To add fingers of light that fork off from the main bolt, select the **Bolt 1** layer (make sure the layer and not the layer mask is active by clicking the layer preview).

2. Make a selection around part of the bolt, and then copy and paste that selection as a new layer. Call this layer *Finger 1* and set the layer mode to **Screen**.

3. Rotate and scale the layer as needed using the **Rotate and Scale** tools, and then position the layer so it just touches the Bolt 1 layer. Make sure the Finger 1 layer's mode is also set to **Screen**.

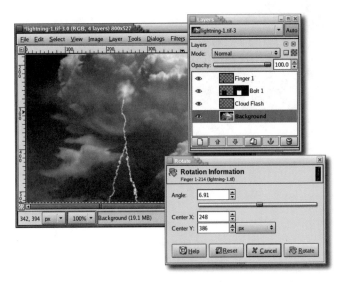

Adding fingers of lightning to the main bolt is just a matter of copying a part of the main bolt and positioning it appropriately.

4. To add a glow effect around the lightning bolts, add a new layer and call it *Glow*. The layer should be the size of the entire canvas.

5. Use the **Free Select** tool to select all the bolts. Feather this selection by **5 pixels** and fill it with white.

6. Deselect all (**Select ▸ None**).

7. Open the Gaussian Blur filter and blur this layer by **25 pixels** or more (**Filters ▸ Blur ▸ Gaussian Blur**).

8. Launch the Colorize tool (**Layer ▸ Colors ▸ Colorize**) and once more set the Hue to **282** and the Saturation to **68**. This time, however, also reduce the Lightness to **–20**.

9. Set the layer mode to **Screen** and reduce the Opacity to **48 percent**.

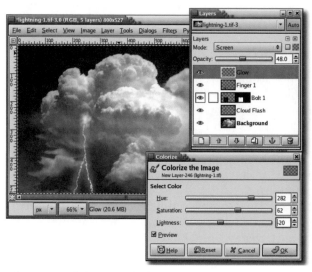

When creating lightning in the distance, add additional glow to the collection of bolts.

Further Exploration

The color of your lightning bolt is probably a personal choice. Bolts of light blue, cyan, and even red are possible. Imagine a bolt of lighting extending from a solitary thunderhead while the sun sets in the distance, casting a red glow on the early evening.

The nearly vertical shape of this particular bolt can be changed using the IWarp, Whirl and Pinch, or Waves filters. When experimenting with the shape of your bolt, try applying the distortions to the bolt itself as well as to the gradient created before merging with the plasma layer.

TIPS FOR PHOTOGRAPHIC EFFECTS

Now that you've practiced the basic techniques for working with photographs in the GIMP, you're probably eager to get started on your own photo projects. When you do, keep the following suggestions in mind.

Autolevel Option

Autolevel all scanned images using the Levels tool (Layer ▶ Colors ▶ Levels). This flattens the color histogram and automatically makes the darkest pixels black and the lightest pixels white.

Sharp Scans

Nearly all scanned photos can benefit from a little sharpening. Digital images don't normally need to be sharpened, but scanned photos usually do. The Unsharp Mask filter (Filters ▶ Enhance ▶ Unsharp Mask) works best for photos, though you can also get good results using the Sharpen filter (Filters ▶ Enhance ▶ Sharpen).

Selections, Selections, Selections

Learn to love 'em (and make them effectively, as described in Section 1.4). When you're working with photographs, you can't do much without them.

Soft Light and Overlay Modes

Add mood to your photos. Fill layers with any color on the color wheel and blend them using the Soft Light or Overlay layer modes.

Sepia Means Brown

Sepia tones are shades of brown, and they can lend your images an antique quality. Try applying RGB value sets like 124/81/61, 140/89/51, or 181/145/124 to your photographs.

The Color of Kelvin

Are you using ordinary halogen lamps for indoor shoots? Lighting color is measured in degrees Kelvin, with the sun at sunrise being about 2,500 degrees and the sun at noon being about 5,000 degrees (a bright white). A typical halogen lamp might be around 3,000 degrees, making its light a bit more yellow. Many photographers add a color-correction gel—which can be ordered from various online sources—to change the color of halogen bulbs.

If you can't fix a shot with proper lighting, you can try to digitally remove yellow tints from your photos using the Color Balance tool (Layer ▶ Colors ▶ Color Balance) or the Hue-Saturation tool (Layer ▶ Colors ▶ Hue-Saturation).

Experimentation

It can take a long time to make color adjustments to an entire image using tools from the toolbox. To experiment first, select a small part of the image and preview the color adjustments on that selection. When you've decided on the optimal values, undo the operation and adjust the entire image. Alternatively, try duplicating the image, scaling it down, and then experimenting with color adjustments on the smaller image.

3

WEB DESIGN

Graphic designers see the Web as one more medium in which to present their work. Consumers see it as a place to buy music and sell used cameras and lawn mowers. Big business sees it as a platform on which to develop new kinds of applications.

Any way you look at it, the Web is changing the world of graphic design. In the earliest days of the Internet, content was king, plain old HTML got the job done, and website design was, at best, a hack. These days, the best website designs utilize *Cascading Style Sheets (CSS)*. CSS is a relatively new stylesheet language that separates layout from content. This separation allows the designer to create visual consistency while somebody else works to create compelling content. CSS designs also make effective use of graphics, and that's where the GIMP comes in. It provides designers with the raster images required by the Web. (Modern web browsers only directly support raster images because the World Wide Web Consortium (W3C) has not yet finalized the protocol for handling vector images. Vector flash animations *are* supported, but only through plug-ins.)

NOTE   *css Zen Garden (http://www.csszengarden.com) has some excellent examples of CSS in action and shows you how the same content might look in several different designs.*

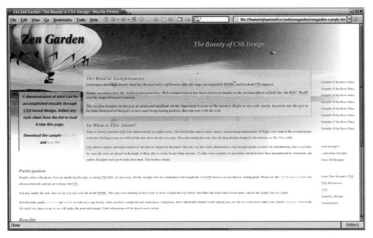

The best modern website designs utilize CSS.

One traditional limitation of the Web, at least from the designer's point of view, has been its static nature. Animated GIF images were an early hack, but they didn't provide real inter-activity. Today Adobe Flash works well with raster images, but it also offers web designers a wealth of vector support. The GIMP isn't the best tool for vector work, but if your web designs use raster images, Flash and the GIMP make a great team.

NOTE *If you're interested in vector design you can try Inkscape (http://www.inkscape.org), another open source graphics tool.*

Working in a Native Medium

Most of the previous tutorials have started with the default canvas size of 420 × 300 pixels. This has made it easy to re-create the tutorial image quickly, but you'd need to work with larger canvas sizes to make those images suitable for print or other media formats.

Well, that all changes now. Throughout this chapter, the image resolution of your desktop (72 dpi for most CRT displays or 98 dpi for LCD displays) will also be the image resolution of the medium.

That means the images created in this chapter won't need to be re-created at larger sizes. In fact, some will probably need to be scaled down (or re-created at a smaller scale) to be useful on the Web.

The focus of these tutorials will be the creation of simple graphics for the Web, specifically navigational aides, backdrops, and logos. To find techniques for achieving more sophisticated photographic effects that you could then incorporate into Flash or complex CSS designs, see Chapters 2 and 4.

GIMP Tools for Web Design

When working on the Web, you'll find yourself using a variety of the GIMP's tools and filters. Two of the tools you'll use for nearly every project are the Text tool and Blend tool.

Most web pages are made up of text and images. The text is often composed in WordPad, OpenOffice.org Writer, or vi, and web developers assume that the reader's browser will have access to the fonts required to display the text. The web designer can request a particular font, but if the browser doesn't have it, the browser gets to choose which font it will use instead. Because the various desktop platforms (Windows, Macs, and Unix/Linux) don't have all of the same fonts, you can't guarantee that readers will see your web pages exactly the way you do. In short, because the Web still doesn't support cross-platform font management very well, you can never be 100 percent certain that the font you request will be available on the system running the web browser.

One solution to this problem is to use rasterized text for some text elements. Using the GIMP to render text into an image guarantees that everyone who sees the image will see it as you saw it. This little trick is only suitable for titles and small captions, however. It makes little sense to render entire paragraphs into an image because image files are much larger than text files, and editing the text would require working with graphics programs that aren't as well-suited to text editing as HTML editors. Despite this, it is quite common to render text for headers, buttons, and title bars into images in order to guarantee that those elements will look the way the designer wants them to look.

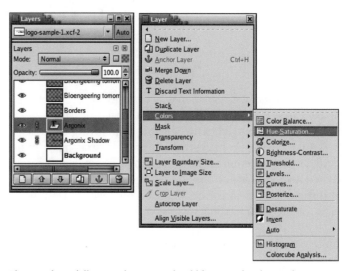

All of your web design projects will use multiple layers. In addition to the familiar Layers dialog and Layer menu, the Layer Colors menu (Layer ▸ Colors) will play a big role as well.

Creating a text logo in the GIMP ensures that all of the website's visitors see the same logo, no matter which browser is used.

The Blend tool and the Bucket Fill tool make it easy to colorize images and clipart. Sometimes adding a splash of color is the best way to give your client's ordinary image a unique identity.

If you've been following along, you should be quite familiar with layers by this point, but I'll continue guiding you through the menu selections where appropriate.

Finally, when designing web interface elements such as navigation aides, effective use of selections is crucial (see Section 1.4 if you need a refresher).

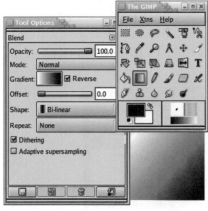

Gradients are easy to create, but be careful when using them: They don't work well in GIF images! If you use them, save your image as a JPEG instead.

3.1 GEL BUTTONS

Website buttons come in many shapes, sizes, and colors. Not every button makes sense in every design. Rectangular buttons are popular because they can be changed easily without you having to worry about how they blend into background pages. Gel buttons, on the other hand, generally require a lot of page space. Their nonrectangular shape also requires antialiasing the background color and makes it difficult to switch the background on a whim. Despite these shortcomings, many clients want their websites to have gel buttons.

Should you decide to use gel buttons in a web design, you're in luck. They're easy to create with the GIMP. As is true of most 3D effects, the trick is to play with light and dark regions to simulate depth and reflection.

This tutorial will walk you through the creation of a simple gel button. The technique is essentially the same for any type of gel effect. The tutorial in Section 5.3 shows a similar effect applied to text. Here you'll see a more general version of the process, but the possibilities are endless. It's not hard to imagine extending this effect to an oozing tube of toothpaste, for example. Just cycle the results through a wave filter.

A simple gel button

Getting Started

1. Start by opening a new white canvas window, set to the default width and height (420 × 300 pixels).

2. Create a new transparent layer in this canvas by choosing **Layer ▸ New** and setting the Layer Fill Type to **Transparency**, and then call the new layer *Light Pill*.

3. Add vertical guides at **10 percent** and **90 percent** (**Image ▸ Guides ▸ New Guide (by Percent)**). Add horizontal guides at **35 percent** and **65 percent**.

4. Select the **Rectangle Select** tool and use it to create a selection in the center rectangle that is outlined by these guides. Round off the edges of that selection by opening the Rounded Rectangle dialog (**Select ▸ Rounded Rectangle**) and setting the Radius to **90 percent** to provide a high level of arc on the ends of the selection. (The Radius specified is actually a percentage of half the width or height of the selection, whichever is smaller.)

5. Remove all guides (**Image ▸ Guides ▸ Remove All Guides**).

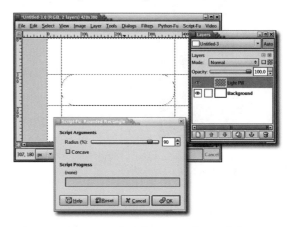

When creating rectangular selections with rounded corners, Radius values greater than 90 percent can distort the shape of the selection.

Adding Colored Layers

1. With the canvas selected, press **D** to reset the foreground and background colors.

2. Click the foreground color icon to open the Change Foreground Color dialog. Set the RGB values to **17/95/239** for the bright blue shown here, and then click **OK** to close the dialog.

3. Drag the foreground color icon from the toolbox into the selection to fill it with this color.

4. Shrink the selection by **20 pixels** (**Select ▸ Shrink**) and save it to a channel (**Select ▸ Save to Channel**). You can keep the default name, *Selection Mask copy*.

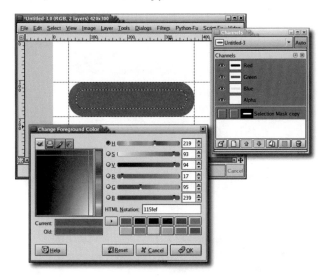

You can use any name you'd like for the selection. You don't even have to change the default name since this is the only saved selection in this tutorial.

5. Return to the Layers dialog and click the **Light Pill** layer to make it active.

6. Clear the selection (CTRL-SHIFT-A).

7. Duplicate the Light Pill layer (**Layer ▸ Duplicate**). Name the new layer *Dark Pill*.

8. In the Layers dialog, check the **Keep Transparency** box next to the Mode drop-down menu. Click the foreground color icon

to open the Change Foreground Color dialog. Set the RGB values to **11/0/97** for the dark blue shown here, and then click **OK**.

9. Drag the foreground color icon from the toolbox into the Dark Pill layer. Because the Keep Transparency option is selected, only the pill should be filled with the new color.

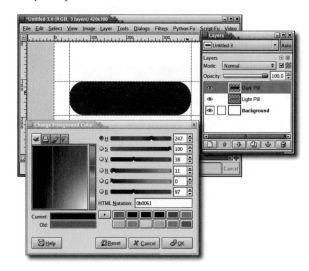

A layer mask is later used to allow the lighter layer to show through the darker one.

Adding a Lower Highlight

1. Create a new transparent layer by choosing **Layer ▸ New** and setting the Layer Fill Type to **Transparency**. Name the new layer *Lower Highlight*.

2. In the Channels dialog, choose the **Selection Mask Copy** channel, and then click the **Channel to Selection** button (highlighted in blue in the image on the next page).

3. Return to the Layers dialog and select the **Lower Highlight** layer to make it active.

4. Feather the selection by **20 pixels** (**Select ▸ Feather**).

5. With the canvas selected, press **D** and then **X** to set the foreground color to white, and then drag the foreground color icon into the selection. Clear the selection (CTRL-SHIFT-A).

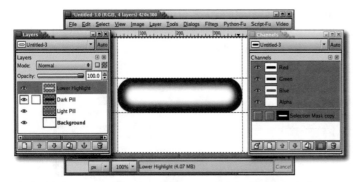

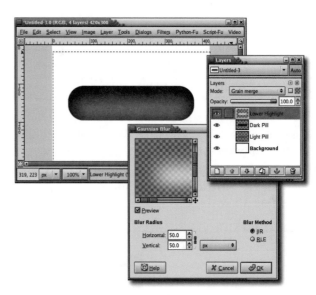

The highlight is made from the selection saved in the Channels dialog.

6. Open the Gaussian Blur filter (**Filters ▸ Blur ▸ Gaussian Blur**), and apply a blur of **50 pixels** to the Lower Highlight layer.

7. With the canvas selected, press **M** to activate the Move tool, and then drag the Lower Highlight layer down so its lower white edge just touches the Dark Pill layer's lower edge. Set the layer mode for the Lower Highlight layer to **Grain Merge**.

8. Click the **Dark Pill** layer. Select the nontransparent region (**Layer ▸ Transparency ▸ Alpha to Selection**), and then invert the selection (**Select ▸ Invert**).

9. Click the **Lower Highlight** layer to make it active. Press CTRL-X to cut off any bits of the highlight that may overflow the bounds of the button when it is moved down.

    We're beginning to see the 3D effect, but we still need to bring out the highlights from the Light Pill layer showing through the Dark Pill layer. Let's do that with a layer mask on the Dark Pill layer. As a result, there will be more reflection of light on the front of the pill and less reflection along its sides.

10. In the Channels dialog, choose the **Selection Mask Copy** channel, and then click the **Channel to Selection** button.

11. Click the **Dark Pill** layer in the Layers dialog. Add a white layer mask (**Layer ▸ Mask ▸ Add Layer Mask**), and then feather the selection by **50 pixels** (**Select ▸ Feather**).

The button starts to take on depth when soft lighting (the Lower Highlight layer) is added.

12. Press **D** to reset the foreground and background colors.

13. Fill the selection with black.

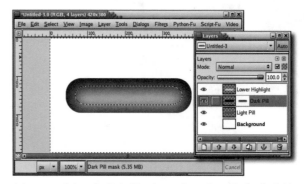

A layer mask lets the light blue layer show through the dark blue layer and blends in with the blurred Lower Highlight layer.

Adding an Upper Highlight

1. Add a new transparent layer by choosing **Layer ▸ New** and setting the Fill Type to **Transparency**. Call the new layer *Top Highlight*. If this new layer is not at the top of the layer stack, move it there by clicking it and dragging it up in the Layers dialog.

2. With the selection still active and the canvas selected, press **M** to activate the Move tool. In the Tool Options dialog, click the **Transform Selection Affect** button. Drag the selection up until its upper edge meets the pill's upper edge. Be sure to reset the Affect to **Transform Layer** when you're done, just to avoid confusion the next time you use the Move tool.

3. With the canvas window selected, press **L** to choose the Blend tool from the toolbox. In the Tool Options dialog, choose the **FG to Transparent** gradient.

4. Press **D** and then **X** to set the foreground color to white. Drag from the top of the selection to the bottom.

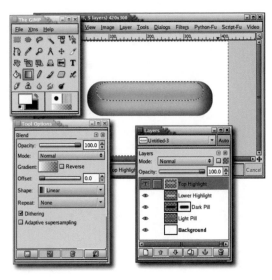

The highlight comes from a gradient this time, so it blends with the Lower Highlight and Background layers more easily.

Stretching the Upper Highlight

Reflections of light off of a shape such as this one are not always uniform. To make this design more realistic, we need to stretch the upper highlight so it's a little wider at the bottom. Let's do this with the Perspective tool. The Perspective tool changes the angle between the sides of a rectangular selection while keeping the sides straight. For the oval selection, imagine that the selection is tied to the sides of a box that bounds the selection. When the bounding box is stretched, the oval selection is stretched to keep it proportionally distanced from the sides of the bounding box.

1. Choose the **Perspective** tool. In the Tool Options dialog, set the Affect to **Transform Layer**.

2. Click the selection in the canvas. Drag the bottom handles horizontally until the highlight touches the left and right sides of the canvas window.

3. Click the **Transform** button. Anchor the layer (**Layer ▸ Anchor Layer**).

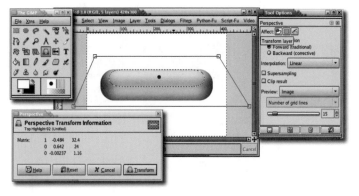

The Perspective tool (highlighted in the toolbox) is used to stretch the bottom of the layer.

Adding Text to the Button

Now let's add some text to the button. Be sure to choose a legible font. I've used Utopia, set to 65 pixels and colored black. (If your website will have multiple gel buttons, you should size the font so that the longest piece of button text will fit comfortably.)

1. Use the **Move** tool to center the text on the pill.

2. Add a drop shadow (**Script-Fu ▸ Shadow ▸ Drop Shadow**).

3. In the Drop Shadow dialog, set the Offset X and Offset Y fields to **2 pixels,** the Blur Radius to **3 pixels,** and the Opacity to **80 percent.** Make sure the box next to the words *Allow Resizing* is not checked.

Add a text layer so the button can be used to navigate a website.

Further Exploration

More realistic effects can be created by playing with the Lower and Top Highlight layers. Remember that reflected light is seldom uniform across an object, even when the object is perfectly shaped. This is what gives brushed metal its appearance and why gel buttons don't look like metal tubes. To achieve an even more realistic look, try adding nearly transparent shadow layers in addition to the highlight layers.

3.2 METAL BUTTONS

The gel button technique is easy to master, but it's even easier to generate metallic buttons. This technique is very generic and simple to reproduce, with the only variation coming from how you colorize the button in the last step.

In this tutorial, we'll create buttons that fill the 420 × 300 pixel canvas. In a real application, you'd probably scale down everything to create smaller buttons. Alternatively, if creating buttons at such a small size is difficult, you can create them at the default size and then scale them down to fit your website. If you choose to scale down the buttons, be sure to apply a little sharpening to bring out the reflective detail.

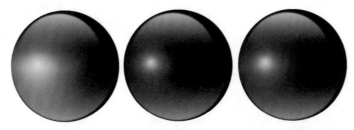

One simple process can be used to produce metal buttons of many colors.

Getting Started

1. Open a new canvas at the default size (420 × 300 pixels).

2. Add a new transparent layer by choosing **Layer ▸ New** and setting the Layer Fill Type to **Transparency**. Name the new layer *Button*.

3. Choose the **Ellipse Select** tool from the toolbox. In the canvas, hold down the SHIFT key and drag from the upper-left corner down toward the bottom-right until your circular selection is

as tall as the canvas window. Make sure the selection is completely inside the canvas boundaries.

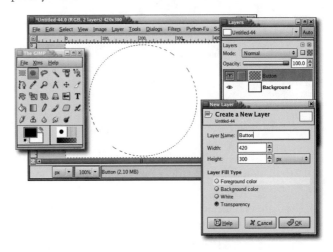

If the circular selection isn't perfectly centered on the canvas, you can center it by selecting the Move tool, setting the Affect to Transform Selection, and then dragging the selection to the center of the canvas.

4. With the canvas selected, press **D** and then **X** to set the foreground color to white.

5. Press **L** to select the Blend tool from the toolbox. In the Tool Options dialog, set the Gradient to **FG to BG (RGB)** and the Shape to **Radial**.

6. Click inside the selection, about one-fourth of the width from the left side of the selection, and drag across the width of the selection. This creates the basic reflective highlight, but the

reflection is a bit too perfect. (Recall from Section 3.1 that light reflects unevenly off of most surfaces.) The next step is to add some variance to this perfectly reflecting sphere.

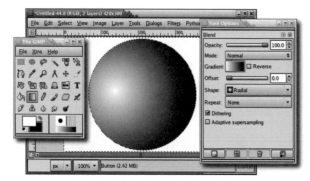

When you click just left of the circle's center and drag to the far side of the selection using a Radial gradient, it's easy to achieve this 3D effect.

Adding More Reflections

1. Add a new transparent layer by choosing **Layer ▸ New** and setting the Layer Fill Type to **Transparency**. Name the new layer *Darken*.

2. With the canvas selected, press **X** to set the foreground color to black.

3. With the Blend tool still active, set the Gradient to **FG to Transparent** and the Shape to **Linear** in the Tool Options dialog. On the canvas, click the top of the selection and drag down to its midpoint.

4. Add a new transparent layer by choosing **Layer ▸ New** and setting the Layer Fill Type to **Transparency**. Name the new layer *Top Reflection*.

5. With the canvas selected, press **X** to set the foreground color to white.

6. The selection should still be active, so shrink it by **10 pixels** (**Select ▸ Shrink**).

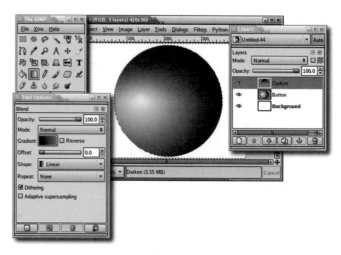

Adding a shaded area on top of the button increases the button's shiny appearance.

7. The Blend tool should also still be active. Click the top of the selection and drag to its midpoint. Deselect all (CTRL-SHIFT-A).

8. In the Layers dialog, set the Top Reflection layer's Opacity to **75 percent**. The light now reflects differently around the sphere, providing visual texture and giving the appearance of a smooth, glassy surface.

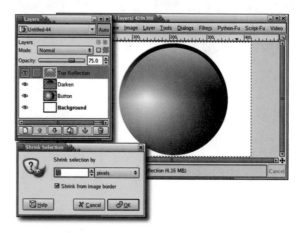

The Top Reflection layer sits above the Darken layer.

9. Duplicate the Top Reflection layer (**Layer ▸ Duplicate**) and name the new layer *Bottom Reflection*.

10. Use the **Flip** tool to flip this layer vertically.

11. Using the **Move** tool, drag this layer so that its bottom white edge is just above the button's bottom edge.

12. Open the Gaussian Blur filter (**Filters ▸ Blur ▸ Gaussian Blur**). Set the Blur Radius to **5 pixels** and the Opacity to **60 percent**. Click **OK** to apply the blur.

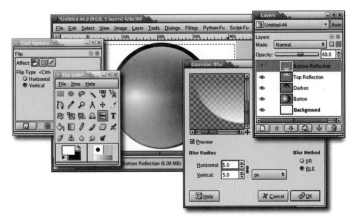

The Bottom Reflection layer is positioned to give the button a shape that is less than spherical. When this reflective layer is applied, the button appears to flatten out on the bottom.

13. Click the **Top Reflection** layer to make that layer active.

14. With the canvas selected, press SHIFT-T to activate the Scale tool. In the Scaling Information dialog, choose **% (percent)** from the measurement unit drop-down menu to the right of the Current Height field. Then change both the Current Width and the Current Height to **85 pixels** and click the **Scale** button.

15. Use the **Move** tool to realign the layer as shown.

16. Open the Gaussian Blur filter (**Filters ▸ Blur ▸ Gaussian Blur**) and set the Blur Radius to **5 pixels**. Apply this blur to the Top Reflection layer.

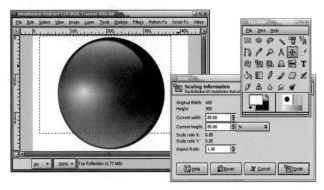

Though we don't do it in this tutorial, duplicating the Bottom Reflection layer increases the contrast between light and dark areas and can enhance the flattened appearance of the bottom of the button.

Adding Color

1. Click the **Button** layer in the Layers dialog to make that layer active.

2. Open the Colorize dialog (**Layer ▸ Colors ▸ Colorize**).

3. Set the Hue to **35** and the Saturation to **90**. You can create countless variations on this basic button simply by modifying the Hue and Saturation settings for this layer.

NOTE   *We use the Colorize dialog in this tutorial, but color can be added in a number of ways. You could add a new layer that is filled with color and set its layer mode to Soft Light or Color. You could also use the Bucket Fill tool on the Button layer and choose either of those same layer modes.*

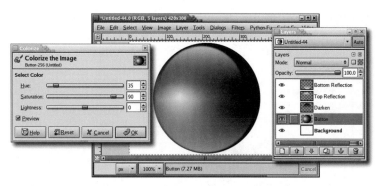

Use the Colorize dialog to put the finishing touch on the metallic button.

Further Exploration

Creating a colored sphere might seem like a simple project, but it's an important one, and it can be the basis for many more sophisticated designs. In fact, it serves as the foundation for another project in this book. Be sure to save this project as an XCF file (the GIMP's native file format) so you can use it again later. In Section 4.1, I'll use this colored sphere to show you how to use the IWarp, Curve Bend, and Whirl and Pinch filters to squeeze a little more out of your project!

3.3 TABS

Gel and metallic buttons can liven up a web page, but practical considerations are often more compelling design criteria. Round buttons can take up valuable screen space, for example. A more compact design might include the use of notebook tabs. Fortunately, using the GIMP to create tabs is even easier than using it to create buttons.

This is one of the most straightforward tutorials in the book. It only takes a few minutes from start to finish, and the effect is easy to reproduce. You'll also learn how to create multiple tabs and colorize them in ways that help visitors navigate your website.

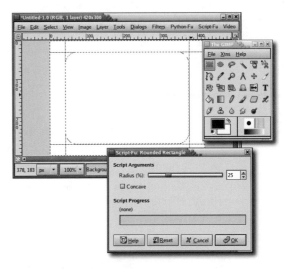

Use guides to make it easier to center the selection.

Tabs are small images, but they can affect your web designs in a big way.

Getting Started

1. Open a new white canvas at the default size (420 × 300 pixels).

2. Add vertical and horizontal guides at **10 percent** and **90 percent** in each direction by selecting **Image ▸ Guides ▸ New Guides (Percent)**.

3. Choose the **Rectangle Select** tool from the toolbox. Create a selection in the center rectangle that is outlined by these guides. Round the selection by **25 percent** (**Select ▸ Rounded Rectangle**).

4. Remove the guides (**Image ▸ Guides ▸ Remove All Guides**).

5. Select **Image ▸ Guides ▸ New Guides (Percent)** to add a new horizontal guide at **70 percent**, just above where the corner begins to be rounded.

6. With the **Rectangle Select** tool still selected, in the Tool Options dialog set the Mode to **Subtract** (highlighted in blue in the image on the next page). Drag to create a rectangular selection that passes through the existing selection below the guide. We now have the basic tab shape.

Adding a Gradient

1. Add a new transparent layer by choosing **Layer ▸ New** and setting the Layer Fill Type to **Transparency**. Name this layer *Tab*.

2. With the toolbox selected, press **D** to reset the foreground and background colors to black and white, respectively.

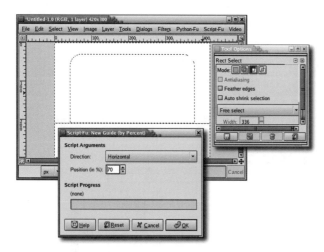

The Rectangle Select tool's Subtract mode lets you drag to create a second selection that is then subtracted from the existing selection.

3. With the canvas selected, press **L** to activate the Blend tool. In the Tool Options dialog, set the Blend tool's Opacity to **70 percent.** Click the canvas near the top of the selection and drag down to the bottom of the selection to apply the gradient.

4. Deselect all (CTRL-SHIFT-A) and remove all guides (**Image ▸ Guide ▸ Remove All Guides**).

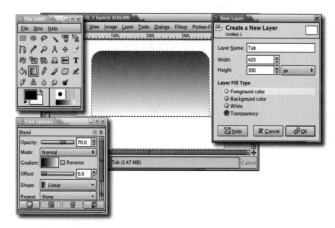

A gradient fills the selection.

Giving the Tab Some Depth

1. Duplicate the Tab layer (**Layer ▸ Duplicate Layer**), and then click the original **Tab** layer in the Layers dialog to make that layer active again.

2. Open the Gaussian Blur filter (**Filters ▸ Blur ▸ Gaussian Blur**). Set the Horizontal and Vertical Blur Radius to **7 pixels,** and then apply this blur to the original Tab layer.

3. Click the **Tab copy** layer in the Layers dialog to make that layer active.

4. Open the Bump Map filter (**Filters ▸ Map ▸ Bump Map**).

5. Set the Azimuth to **180 degrees,** the Elevation to **60,** and the Depth to **30.** Be sure to select the original **Tab** layer from the Bump Map drop-down menu at the top of the dialog.

6. Click **OK** to apply the Bump Map filter, and rename the Tab copy layer *Bump Map.*

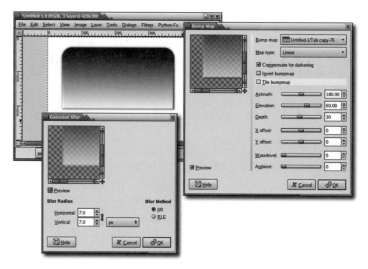

The blurred original tab is used to give depth to the copy layer.

Adding Color and Highlights

1. Duplicate the Bump Map layer (**Layer ▸ Duplicate Layer**). Name this layer *Colorized.*

2. Open the Colorize dialog (**Layer ▸ Colors ▸ Colorize**). Choose a **Hue,** and set its Saturation to **90** and Lightness to **70**.

3. Make a selection of this layer (**Layer ▸ Transparency ▸ Alpha to Selection**). Then shrink the selection by **10 pixels** (**Select ▸ Shrink**).

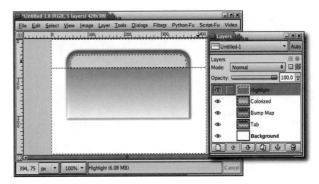

Remove the selection (CTRL-SHIFT-A) before blurring the Highlight layer.

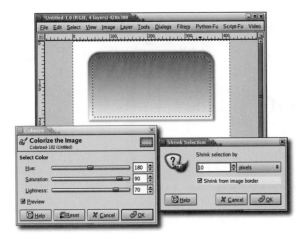

Choose any Hue at this point. You can desaturate this layer and change the color if you decide later that you don't like it.

4. Add a new transparent layer by choosing **Layer ▸ New** and setting the Layer Fill Type to **Transparency**. Call the new layer *Highlight*.

5. Choose **Image ▸ Guides ▸ New Guides** (Percent) to add another horizontal guide at **25 percent** where the rounded edges of the top of the tab straighten out.

6. With the **Rectangle Select** tool selected, in the Tool Options dialog set the Mode to **Subtract** to cut off the existing selection from the guide on down. (Be sure to change the Rectangle Select tool's Mode back to Replace when you're done.) Drag the background color (white) into the selection to fill the selection.

7. Deselect all (CTRL-SHIFT-A).

8. Open the Gaussian Blur filter (**Filters ▸ Blur ▸ Gaussian Blur**), and apply a blur of **5 pixels** to the Highlight layer to soften the reflected highlight.

Adding Text

The basic tab is now complete. All that's left is to add some text.

1. Remove all guides (**Image ▸ Guide ▸ Remove All Guides**).

2. Select the **Text** tool from the toolbox. Choose an appropriate font (this tutorial used Serif Bold set to 80 pixels with a black color). As when choosing a font size for button text, the font size should allow for the longest piece of tab text to fit. Keep in mind that a sans-serif font might be more appropriate if you plan to scale down the tab's size.

3. Click the canvas to open the Text Editor. Type some text, and then click the **Close** button.

4. Use the **Move** tool to position the text in the center of the tab.

5. If you like, add a drop shadow (**Script-Fu ▸ Shadow ▸ Drop Shadow**). Set the Offset X and Offset Y values to **3 pixels,** the Blur Radius to **8 pixels,** and the Opacity to **80 percent.**

Creating More Tabs

In the real world, web pages usually have multiple tabs. A colored tab could indicate the page being viewed while gray tabs represent other pages available to your website visitor.

1. To create a series of tabs, start by turning off the visibility of the Background, drop shadow, and text layers. Then merge the visible layers (**Image ▸ Merge Visible Layers**).

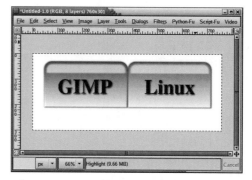

After the addition of a drop shadow, the text appears to rest on a semi-transparent tab.

2. Copy this new layer and paste it onto the canvas, where it will appear as a floating selection. Create a new layer (**Layer ▸ New**) from this floating selection, and name the new layer *New Tab*.

3. Use the **Move** tool to move this tab to the left of the first tab you created.

4. Resize the canvas (**Image ▸ Fit Canvas to Layers**), and then resize the canvas window (CTRL-E).

5. Move the **New Tab** layer so that it aligns with the left edge of the original Tab layer.

6. Desaturate the New Tab layer if it is to have a different color (**Layer ▸ Colors ▸ Desaturate**), and then colorize it using the Colorize dialog (**Layer ▸ Colors ▸ Colorize**).

7. Add additional text as needed, and then turn back on visibility for the text and drop shadow layers for your original button.

NOTE   *If your Background layer doesn't fill the entire canvas, you can delete it (Layer ▸ Delete) and add a new white layer (Layer ▸ New) that you drag to the bottom of the stack in the Layers dialog.*

When you visit a website, a colored tab often indicates the selected page while noncolored tabs indicate other places you can go.

Further Exploration

Tabs can be placed on websites vertically instead of horizontally. Merge all visible layers and then rotate the image 90 degrees counterclockwise (see Image ▸ Transform). Making text that reads vertically (where the letters are vertical but the word reads from top to bottom instead of from left to right) is more difficult because the GIMP's text alignment features are limited, but you could use a carriage return after each character.

3.4 FANCY BORDERS

If you're looking to enhance your websites, you might consider artistic borders. While the assortment of clipart available on the Internet is nearly endless, finding the perfect border for your project may take longer than you'd like. Fortunately, the GIMP solves this problem in just a few short steps.

Creating fancy borders is one of the easiest tasks you can perform with the GIMP. The process used in this tutorial is also fundamental to many image-merge techniques demonstrated throughout the book. Mastering this border-creation process is an important step toward achieving even more complex effects.

Borders can add elegance to websites and greeting cards.

Getting Started

Creating a border starts with finding workable clipart. The design you choose will, of course, depend on your overall design require-ments. But not all clipart works equally well with this technique. Uniform designs slide right in place with just a little work. Busy images without uniform edges require a bit more effort. For this tutorial, I've chosen two designs, one made up of flowers and one made up of vines. Because the flowers and vines are repeating and nonlinear, these images seamlessly merge with copies of themselves.

The clipart elements consist of repeating, nonlinear patterns that make it easy to blend together copies.

Scanning the Clipart

Most of the really interesting clipart can be found in printed material, such as the Dover Publications collections. You'll need to scan these in order to use them with the GIMP. Linux users will probably use XSane to access a scanner, as described in Section 1.7. Windows and Mac users will use the standard scanner support for those systems. If your scanning software doesn't import directly into the GIMP, save the scanned image as a TIFF or JPEG file and then use the GIMP to open that file.

Cleaning Up the Scan

After importing the clipart or scanned image, you should have a single layer. Name this layer *Original Clipart*.

Scanned images often need minor levels adjustments. For clipart, it should be sufficient to apply the Autolevel option (**Layer ▶ Colors ▶ Levels**). In the Levels dialog, just click the **Auto** button to apply the levels change to the canvas. If you open the Levels dialog again, you'll see that the values are distributed more evenly across the black-to-white histogram.

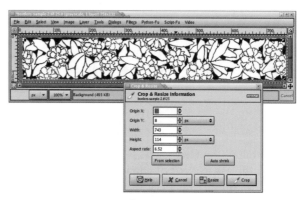

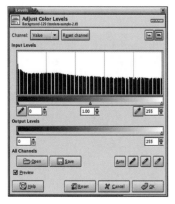

After the Autolevel adjustment is applied, the black-to-white histogram in the Levels dialog reflects the change.

You may also need to rotate and crop the scan if the clipart has distinct edges that need to be uniform. In this tutorial we don't need to do this, but if you do, follow these steps.

1. Pull two horizontal guides from the left ruler and two vertical guides from the top ruler, and then position them appropriately.
2. Choose the **Crop** tool, click the upper-left intersection of the guides, and drag to the bottom-right intersection of the guides. The area to be cropped will be given a dark tint. Click the **Crop** button in the Crop and Resize dialog.
3. Adjust the canvas window to fit the new image size by choosing **Image ▶ Fit Canvas to Layers** and then pressing CTRL-E.
4. Remove all guides (**Image ▶ Guides ▶ Remove All Guides**).

In some cases, cropping and rotating clipart can help align straight edges with canvas edges.

Turning the Clipart Into a Border

1. Duplicate the Original Clipart layer (**Layer ▶ Duplicate**).
2. Rotate the duplicate layer clockwise by 90 degrees (**Layer ▶ Transform ▶ Rotate 90 degrees CW**).
3. To make it easier to move the duplicate layer, adjust the canvas to fit the layers by choosing **Image ▶ Fit Canvas to Layers** and then pressing CTRL-E.

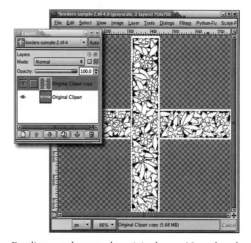

Duplicate and rotate the original scan. Note that the background layer has been removed in order to make the clipart layers easier to see.

4. Open the Align Visible Layers dialog (**Layer ▸ Align Visible Layers**).

5. Choose **Collect** from the Horizontal and Vertical Styles dropdown menus, which will align the edges of the layers with the edges of the canvas. The Horizontal Base option should be set to **Left Edge,** and the Vertical Base option should be set to **Top Edge.** Make sure the two boxes at the bottom of the Align Visible Layers dialog are *not* checked.

6. Click **OK** to align the two layers along the top and left edges of the canvas.

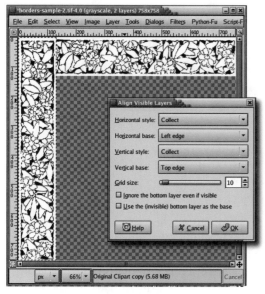

Use the Align Visible Layers dialog to align to layers with the canvas edges.

7. Zoom in (SHIFT-plus) and navigate to the upper-right corner of the window using the Navigation dialog, which is highlighted in red in the lower-right corner of the canvas window.

8. Turn off the Show Layer Boundary option (**View ▸ Show Layer Boundaries**).

9. Add a white layer mask to the top layer (**Layer ▸ Mask ▸ Add Layer Mask**).

10. With the canvas selected, press **D** to reset the foreground and background colors to black and white, respectively.

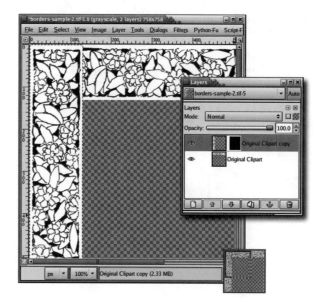

The Navigation dialog is in the lower-right corner of the canvas window.

11. Choose the **Paintbrush** tool from the toolbox. Choose an appropriately sized brush—I start with the Circle Fuzzy (15) brush, but I use several other brushes during the masking process.

12. Click the layer mask to make it active, and then paint until the vertical layer merges with the horizontal layer.

    This is a manual process and should be tailored to the particular clipart element you've chosen. In this example, a large square section is masked first, and then a small section near the bottom of the horizontal layer is masked with the Paintbrush tool. The image on the left shows the masked section with horizontal layer visibility temporarily turned off. The image on the right shows the merged version.

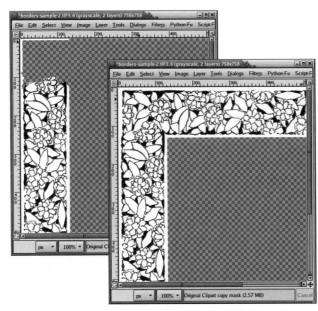

The masked vertical layer (left) merges seamlessly with the horizontal layer (right).

Adding a Colored Layer

1. Add a new white layer by choosing **Layer ▸ New** and setting the Layer Fill Type to **White**.

2. Lower the new layer to the bottom of the layer stack in the Layers dialog. If the bottom layer does not have an alpha channel, you may need to add one manually by clicking the layer and then choosing **Layer ▸ Transparency ▸ Add Alpha Channel**.

3. Add a new transparent layer by choosing **Layer ▸ New** and setting the Layer Fill Type to **Transparency**. Name the new layer *Color*, and move it to the top of the layer stack.

4. Fill the Color layer with red and set its Mode to **Screen**. This will add color to your design without modifying the clipart layers. If you decide to change the color later, you'll only need to modify the Color layer.

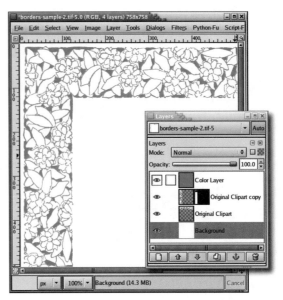

Add a colored layer and set its Mode to Screen to colorize the border. This method works well because the clipart was originally black. Adding color to black in the GIMP will get you that color, while adding color to white gets you white.

Tackling Another Project

A second border is created using the same process, but this time the design poses more difficulties. In this case a block of white is applied directly to the vertical layer and a mask is applied to the horizontal layer. It's necessary to white-out the vertical layer because the horizontal layer mask exposed parts of the vertical clipart element. In this case, we only want the bottom part of the horizontal piece to merge with the vertical piece. If we don't add the white block to the vertical piece, parts of the vertical piece show where we have masked the horizontal piece. If the background were white and matched the background of each clipart layer, then the white-out on the vertical layer could have been replaced with a layer mask instead.

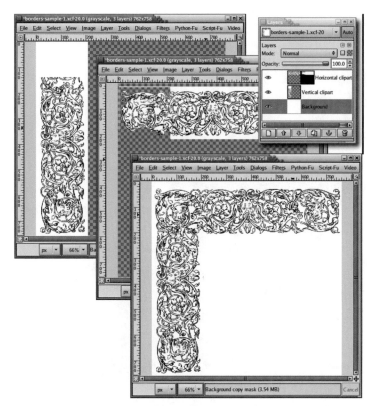

A good mask is the key to merging clipart to create a border. You could even isolate the design in the clipart using the Select by Color tool to create a selection in the same shape as the complex pattern.

Futher Exploration

Border designs like these may not be that common in web designs, but the technique we've used to merge two images will come in handy in both web and print design. When merging any two complex images, you must work to merge intersecting lines. Merging two photos, however, usually requires merging colors or overlaying subject matter, as when you place a person over a backdrop.

Whether you're merging borders or photos, the process is the same: Work with layer masks to remove unnecessary areas in each layer. Using layer masks allows you to make changes without actually modifying the layer content and then edit your changes later by simply editing the layer mask.

3.5 SEAMLESS TILES

The days of obnoxious, page-filling web backgrounds are gone. Now CSS and DHTML let designers spread images across different page components, such as menus and banners, without the background overwhelming the rest of the page. Background images are an important part of web design, and because they can now span multiple CSS divisions on a single page, the need for tiles with no visible edges has become even more important.

NOTE *The Web isn't the only place where these tiles can be used. Much of the work of texturing 3D objects involves the use of seamless tiles.*

The default patterns supplied with the GIMP are nearly all seamless tiles, but few of those patterns are suited for use as background images, so it's likely that web designers will often need to create custom tiles. With the GIMP, it's possible to create seamless tiles from scratch in a few simple steps.

Most raster image editors make creating seamless tiles a point-and-click operation, and the GIMP is no exception. In this tutorial I'll show you how to create tiles the automated way and the manual way.

The Automated Method

The automated method takes advantage of the fact that the Hurl filter generates a tileable pattern by default.

Getting Started

1. Start with a new white canvas (**File ▸ New**). The width and height of the canvas should be equal. For this tutorial I set the canvas size to 300 × 300 pixels, though you could start with a larger canvas.

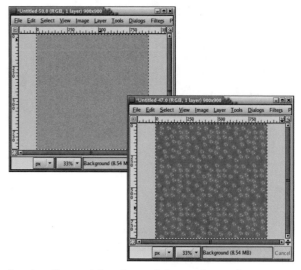

Seamless tiles aren't found on websites as often as they once were, but they can offer your visitors a unique experience if used properly.

2. Open the Change Foreground Color dialog by clicking the foreground color in the toolbox. Set the RGB values to **199/148/103** to match the medium brown shown here, and then click **OK** to close the window. Drag the foreground color onto the canvas.

3. Add a transparent layer by choosing **Layer ▸ New** and setting the Layer Fill Type to **Transparency**. Name the new layer *Noise*.

4. Open the Hurl filter (**Filters ▸ Noise ▸ Hurl**). Set the Random Seed value to **10** and the Randomization to **50 percent**. Set the Repeat level to **2** in order to apply the filter twice. Click **OK** to apply the filter to the new layer.

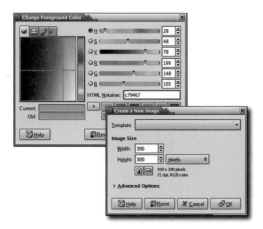

Setting the foreground color before opening a new canvas will fill the canvas with the selected color.

5. Desaturate this layer (**Layer ▸ Colors ▸ Desaturate**).

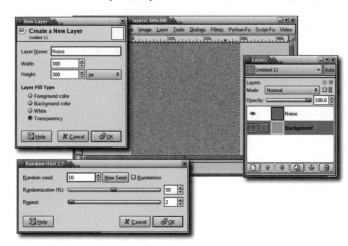

Noise is applied to the new layer and not to the colored layer so the noise can be adjusted before we merge the new layer with the colored layer.

Merging the Layers

1. Make sure the **Noise** layer is active in the Layers dialog.

2. Set the Noise layer's mode to **Grain Merge** and its Opacity to **75 percent**.

3. Merge the Noise layer with the Background layer (**Layer ▸ Merge Down**).

4. Open the Gaussian Blur filter (**Filters ▸ Blur ▸ Gaussian Blur**). Set the Blur Radius to **1 pixel**. Click **OK** to apply this filter to the merged layers.

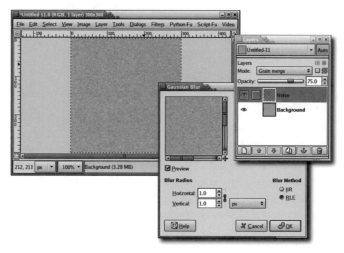

A blur is applied after the two layers have been merged.

Saving and Viewing the Pattern

1. Now let's save this image as a pattern file. Choose **File ▸ Save** to open the Save Image dialog. Browse to the Patterns directory and save the image as *seamless-tile-1.pat*. The *.pat* extension will tell the GIMP to save the file as a pattern file.

2. In the Save As Pattern dialog that pops up, type `Seamless Tile 1` in the Description field. After saving the file, refresh the Patterns dialog by clicking the refresh button (show in red in the image on the next page).

3. To verify that the pattern is seamless, open a new white canvas that is three times the size of the original canvas (in this case, 900 × 900 pixels). In the Patterns dialog (**Dialogs ▸ Patterns** from the canvas window), click the new pattern **Seamless Tile 1**.

4. Choose the **Bucket Fill** tool from the toolbox.

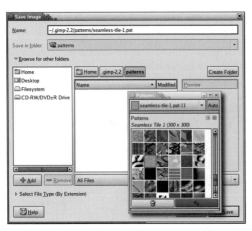

Save the image as a pattern file in the Patterns directory.

5. In the Tool Options dialog, set the Fill Type to **Pattern Fill**. Click the new canvas. The tile should repeat three times across and three times down, and there should be no seams. The original image is shown again for comparison. As you can see from the horizontal ruler and the position of the scrollbars, both images are fully displayed.

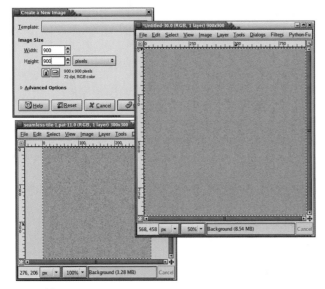

No visible seams!

The Manual Method

The manual method isn't much more difficult than the automated method, but it allows designers far more creative freedom.

Getting Started

1. The manual method starts just as the automated method started, with a white canvas sized to 300×300 pixels. To fill the canvas with the green shown here, click the foreground color box, set the RGB values to **5/138/30**, and then drag the foreground color onto the canvas.

2. Choose the **Paintbrush** tool, and then choose the **Galaxy (AP)** brush from the Brushes dialog.

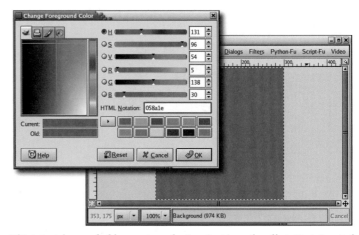

This tutorial uses a bold green to make it easier to see the effect. Keep in mind, however, that seamless patterns used as web page backgrounds should be muted. Most are nearly white.

3. With the canvas selected, press **D** and then **X** to set the foreground color to white. Click the canvas randomly, avoiding the edges of the image.

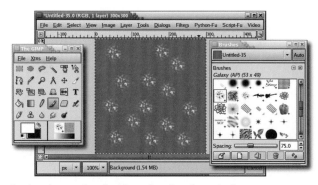

Apply a few random brush strokes directly to the layer.

Offset the Image and Add Brush Strokes

1. Open the Offset dialog (**Layer ▸ Transform ▸ Offset**). Click the **Offset by x/2, y/2** button and leave the **Wrap Around** option selected. Click **OK** to apply the offset.

2. Randomly click the canvas again, targeting blank areas. Again, avoid the edges of the image.

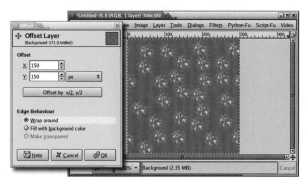

Repeating the process after offsetting the image allows you to apply brush strokes where seams would normally be.

3. Repeat the offsetting and painting processes several times, adding brush strokes until you have what appears to be a seamless tile.

4. As before, save the image as a pattern file and refresh the Patterns dialog.

5. Open a new white canvas that is three times the size of the original (in this case, 900 × 900 pixels), and use the **Bucket Fill** tool to fill the canvas with the new pattern. If there are obvious repetitions in the pattern, edit the original image and repeat the process.

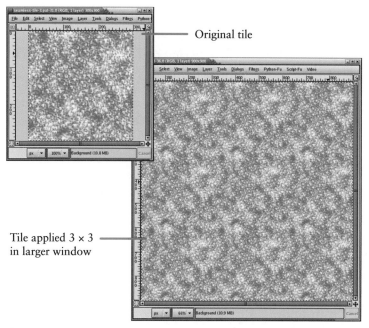

Original tile

Tile applied 3 × 3
in larger window

If the original image is fairly small and applied to a much larger canvas, it can be easy to spot the repeating pattern.

Further Exploration

Two-dimensional patterns like these can add texture to many images. Experiment with different patterns to see how they might be used to add texture to a three-dimensional image. Start by desaturating the patterned image, and then use the Bump Map filter (Filters ▸ Map ▸ Bump Map) to give it depth. Try adding layers above your pattern layer that contain other patterns or solid colors, and then use the layer modes to blend them.

3.6 ROLLOVERS

A web page *rollover* consists of two or more images that are usually the same size and shape but may be different colors or contain different content. They appear in the same location but at different times. One of the images is displayed when the page is loaded. When a visitor moves his or her mouse over the image or clicks the image, JavaScript or CSS code replaces that image with another.

 *Rollovers may be made up of several images, all of which are displayed in the same location on a website, though at different times.*

As CSS is more widely supported by web browsers, fewer web designers are using JavaScript to animate their rollover images. It is far easier to code CSS than it is to write JavaScripts. JavaScript does offers a few more bells and whistles, however, including button up and down states, special images that appear when the mouse is moved over or away from areas on the web page, and even custom-programmed events.

Rollovers are typically used to indicate that an image functions as a link. CSS even allows you to create text links that change characteristics depending on mouse movements. This is a more efficient way of providing feedback because text can move across the Internet faster than images. That said, most CSS- and JavaScript-based rollovers still use images.

This tutorial shows how to create a single button, modify it for different rollover states, and organize your layers for use with rollovers. The rollover states will include Normal, Over, and Click. Normal is the image's default state, Over is the state when the mouse is over the image, and Click is the state when the user clicks the image but does not move the mouse off the image.

This tutorial focuses solely on developing the images for rollovers. There are plenty of other tutorials that explain how to write

CSS or JavaScript code to achieve these simple web effects. I'll leave coding issues to the more advanced and suitably motivated reader.

Getting Started

This rollover consists of a single button on a thin, horizontal button bar. A gradient is used to give the buttons a sense of depth. Start with a white canvas sized to **120 × 50 pixels**. If you have a large display, this may seem like a fairly small workspace. Feel free to zoom in on the canvas (SHIFT-plus) while following along.

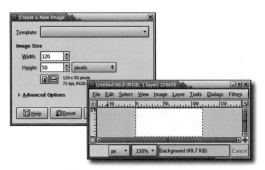

On web pages, rollovers tend to be very small. Start with a small canvas and zoom in as needed.

1. With the canvas selected, press **D** to reset the foreground and background colors.

2. Click the background color box in the toolbox to open the Change Background Color dialog. Set the RGB values to **142/142/142** for a neutral gray, and click **OK** to close the dialog.

3. Choose the **Blend** tool from the toolbox.

4. In the Tool Options dialog, check the box next to the word *Reverse* and choose **Bi-Linear** from the Shape drop-down

menu. The Bi-Linear setting will add a gradient that spreads in two directions along the line you drag in the canvas. In contrast, choosing the Linear shape causes the gradient to spread only in the direction you drag.

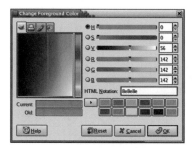

You can choose a recently used color by clicking one of the preview buttons in the Change Foreground color dialog.

5. Set the Opacity to **100 percent**, set the Mode to **Normal**, and choose the default **Foreground to Background** setting for the Gradient.

6. Add a vertical guide at **50 percent** by choosing **Image ▸ Guides ▸ New Guide (By Percent)**. Drag down the canvas along the guide, starting one-third from the top of the canvas and going all the way to the bottom.

7. Turn off the guide (**Image ▸ Guides ▸ Remove All Guides**).

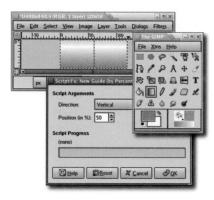

As long as View ▸ Snap to Guides is set, dragging along the vertical guide helps you draw a perfectly vertical gradient stroke.

Creating the Button Text

1. With the canvas selected, press **D** to reset the foreground and background colors once again.

2. Choose the **Text** tool from the toolbox. In the Tool Options dialog, choose a legible font such as Times New Roman Bold sized to 25 pixels.

3. Click the canvas to open the Text Editor. Type `Store Info` and close the window.

4. Use the **Move** tool to position the text layer on the center of the canvas.

Choose a font that's legible when displayed at a small size.

5. Turn off visibility for the Store Info layer. Add another text layer that says *Find one...*, center it on the canvas, and turn off its visibility. Then add another text layer that says *Searching*, center that text layer, and turn off its visibility. Finally, turn on visibility for the Store Info layer.

Multiple text layers are added above the Background layer.

Adding Color to the Layers

1. Add a new transparent layer and name the layer *Color*.

2. Move this layer by dragging it in the Layers dialog so that it is below all of the text layers but above the Background layer.

3. Change the foreground color RGB values to **5/138/30** for the bright green used here for the default state. Drag the foreground color into the new layer. Set that layer's mode to **Grain Merge**.

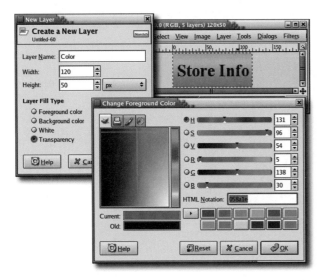

The Color layer is placed above the Background layer but beneath the text layers.

4. Save the image as *Button-Normal.jpg*, using the default settings for the JPEG format.

5. Change the foreground color RGB values to **6/208/44** for a lighter shade of green, and drag the foreground color into the Color layer.

6. Turn off visibility for the Store Info layer and turn it on for the Find one... layer. Save the image as *Button-Over.jpg*.

7. Change the foreground color RGB values to **208/211/10** for the yellow shown here, and drag the foreground color into the Color layer once more.

8. Turn off visibility for the Find One... layer and turn on visibility for the Searching layer. Save the image as *Button-Click.jpg*.

Each of the three buttons is a different color and contains different text, but they are all created as part of the same GIMP project.

Further Exploration

This technique could be modified so that the text color changes when the button is moused over or clicked. If you try this, first create your text with the appropriate color, then duplicate the text layer and change the color of the text in the duplicate layer.

3.7 SIMPLE LOGOS

Logo design is one of the most enjoyable branches of graphic design. For a smaller or newer company, the logo needs to graphically express the company's main product or purpose. For a more established enterprise, the logo might be a unique symbol that has come to be identified with that company and its products. Think of the Nike swoosh or the AT&T globe.

Because they're small, logos are also among the hardest designs to create. Expressing a corporate identity in such a small space is never easy. Fortunately, with a small amount of work, a logo can say a lot.

Custom logos are a snap with the GIMP.

On the Web, small and simple logos work best. At roughly 72 dpi, this medium doesn't leave much room for busy designs. Logos are generally small (but they don't have to be), because they appear on all of the website's pages. When you scale down a large, busy design, detail can be lost, so it's best to keep things simple.

The GIMP provides tools to create logos of all types. For small companies with modest identity needs (web pages and perhaps stationery and business cards), these tools are often sufficient. For larger companies that will use logos in banner advertising, the GIMP is best used only as a prototyping tool. You'll want to transfer the design to vector art later so that it can be scaled to large print sizes easily.

This tutorial will design a simple logo for a small, fictitious biotechnology company named Argonix. The design criteria are that the logo can be no more than two colors, it must emphasize the company name, and it must include a tag line and an icon that represents the company's association with bioengineered plants. The logo will be used on the company's website and must fit in a space that is 400 × 145 pixels.

Getting Started

Start with a new white canvas sized to **400 × 145 pixels**. Choose the **Text** tool from the toolbox. In the Tool Options dialog, choose a serif font. I use Timmons Italic in this example. (A sans-serif font will be easier to trace with a vector tool, should this design need to be converted to vector format later, but I prefer the look of serif fonts.) The choice of font should also reflect the requirements of the client. For example, grungy text might be appropriate for a gaming company, but it probably wouldn't suit a home furnishings chain.

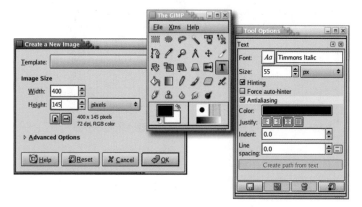

A web page logo doesn't need to be very large, so it's safe to start with the default canvas size.

Creating Text

1. Click the foreground color in the toolbox to open the Change Foreground Color dialog. Set the RGB values to **207/0/0** for the dark red shown here, and then click **OK**.

2. Click the canvas to open the Text Editor. Set the size of the text to **55 pixels**. Type **RGONIX**, and close the Text Editor. The layer will automatically be named to match the text you typed in the Text Editor.

3. In this example, the first character will be larger than the others, so click the **Background** layer in the Layers dialog to make that layer active, and then click the canvas again to create a new text layer for the first letter of the company name. Set the font size to **70 pixels**, and type **A** in the Text Editor. Again, this layer will automatically be named to match the text in the layer.

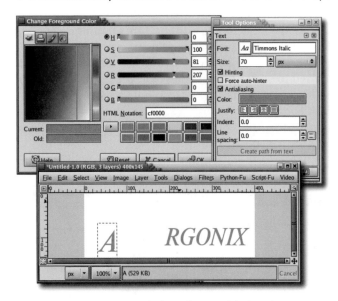

Create the first letter separately from the rest of the brand name so that it can be made larger.

4. Add a horizontal guide at **55 percent** by choosing **Image ▸ Guides ▸ New Guide (by Percent)**.

5. Using the **Move** tool, drag each text layer so the bottom edges of the letters align with the guide. Anchor the two layers together by clicking their anchor icons in the Layers dialog. (The anchor icon is not visible in the Layers dialog by default because by default the layer is not anchored. Just click the blank space between the eye icon and the layer preview to anchor the layer.)

6. Click the **A** layer to make it active, and then drag that layer onto the canvas so the *A* is nearly centered. Make sure to leave a little space on the right side of the text.

Click the space between the eye icon and the layer preview to anchor the layer.

7. Press **D** to reset the foreground and background colors.

8. Select the **Text** tool from the toolbox. In the Tool Options dialog, set the font to Nimbus Sans L (or something similar) and the font size to **15 pixels**.

9. Click the **Background** layer in the Layers dialog, and then click the canvas to open the Text Editor. Type the tag line **Bioengineering for a hungry world**, and click the **Close** button.

10. Use the **Move** tool to drag the tag line below the company name.

11. Add a new transparent layer by choosing **Layer ▸ New** and setting the Layer Fill Type to **Transparency**. Name the new layer *Borders*.

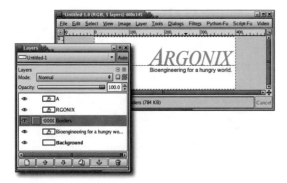

A tag line is added below the brand name.

Adding Borders and Clipart

1. Remove the current guide (**Image ▸ Guides ▸ Remove All Guides**).

2. Add two new horizontal guides, one at **15 percent** and one at **85 percent** by choosing **Image ▸ Guides ▸ New Guide (By Percent)**. Then add two vertical guides, one at **5 percent** and one at **95 percent**.

3. Click the **Paintbrush** tool, and choose **Calligraphic Brush#3** from the Brushes dialog. Click the upper-left intersection of the new guides. Hold down the SHIFT key and click the upper-right intersection to draw a straight line between the two intersections. Repeat this process with the lower-left and lower-right intersections. If necessary, move the text layers so they do not extend past the right edges of the borders.

4. Remove all guides (**Image ▸ Guides ▸ Remove All Guides**).

Use guides and a small brush to draw the horizontal borders in a separate layer.

5. For the leaf icon that appears behind the logo text, we'll use clipart. Open the clipart file you've chosen and copy it into the canvas. Make sure the **Keep Transparency** box in the Layers dialog is checked for this new layer. You may need to scale down the art to fit the available space. In this example, the space between the two borders comfortably fits a clipart image that is 90 pixels high.

6. Depending on the clipart image you've chosen, you may need to cut the shape out of its background to make colorizing easier. Copy the clipart to its own layer, and then desaturate that layer (**Layer ▸ Colors ▸ Desaturate**).

7. Choose the **Bucket Fill** tool and in the Tool Options dialog set the Mode to **Screen**, the Fill Type to **FG Color Fill**, and the Affected Area to **Fill Whole Selection**.

8. Open the Change Foreground Color dialog again, make sure the RGB values are set to **207/0/0** to match the red used for the text, and then close the dialog.

9. Click the layer to colorize the clipart.

A piece of clipart is scaled down to fit between the logo's borders.

Adding a Watermark

1. Click the **Background** layer in the Layers dialog to make that layer active.

2. Add a new transparent layer by choosing **Layer ▸ New** and setting the Layer Fill Type to **Transparency**. Name the new layer *Watermark*.

3. Create a rectangular selection through the middle of this layer. The size of the rectangle makes no difference.

4. In the Change Foreground Color dialog, set the RGB values to **142/142/142** for a neutral gray and close the window.

5. Drag the foreground color into the selection, and then deselect all (CTRL-SHIFT-A).

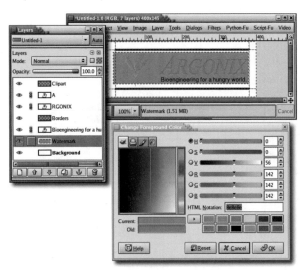

The watermark starts as a gray selection in a layer placed above the Background layer but below all other layers.

6. To convert the new gray background into a watermark, open the Waves filter (**Filters ▸ Distorts ▸ Waves**). Set the Amplitude to **85 pixels** and the Wavelength to **50 pixels**. Click **OK** to apply this filter to the Watermark layer.

7. Open the Curve Bend filter (**Filters ▸ Distorts ▸ Curve Bend**). Make the Upper and Lower curves similar to those shown here and click **OK** to apply them to the layer.

8. Open the Gaussian Blur (**Filters ▸ Blur ▸ Gaussian Blur**) and apply a blur of 1.5 pixels to the layer. Set the layer Opacity to **15 percent**.

9. Use the **Scale** tool to stretch the layer as needed.

Some simple distortions turn the solid gray rectangle into a wavy watermark.

Further Exploration

Creating prototype designs in this way makes it easy to trace the image in a vector program later, should you need to scale the design for larger print media.

This is just one example of how you might create a logo for a small business. And the best part is there's plenty of logo design work out there. Designing simple logos like this for personal use or for small businesses, lawyers, doctors, and other professionals can keep you busy.

3.8 WAVING FLAGS

From time to time I receive requests for images of flags that appear to be waving in the wind. The process for making any item look wrinkled is the same—run it through the Waves and Ripple filters. Both filters will make the image look wrinkled, but you'll need to add shadows to the wrinkles to get a true 3D appearance.

In this tutorial we'll create a simple flag and distort it with the aforementioned filters. Then we'll use a gradient scaled to fit the flag and adjust the layer mode to add depth to the distortion.

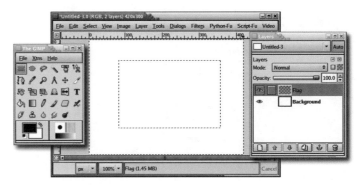

Creating the flag starts with making a rectangular selection.

Use the Waves filter to give simple images a 3D appearance.

Getting Started

1. Start with a white canvas, set to the default size (400 × 320 pixels).

2. Add a new transparent layer by choosing **Layer ▸ New** and setting the Layer Fill Type to **Transparency**. Name the new layer *Flag*.

3. Choose the **Rectangle Select** tool and draw a rectangle about the size of the one shown here on the canvas. Draw the selection slightly to the right of center to leave room for a flagpole.

Adding Color to the Flag

1. Click the foreground color to open the Change Foreground Color dialog. Type **Blue** in the HTML field (you can specify colors by typing a color name in the HTML field or typing part of a color name and then choosing the color you want from the drop-down menu that is presented). Click **OK**. Drag the foreground color into the selection.

2. In the Tool Options dialog for the Rectangle Select tool, change the Mode to **Intersect** by clicking the button on the far right. Starting above the blue selection, drag over the right half of the blue selection.

3. Change the foreground color to red, and then drag the foreground color into the new selection. Deselect all (CTRL-SHIFT-A).

4. Select the entire flag (**Layer ▸ Transparency ▸ Alpha to Selection**).

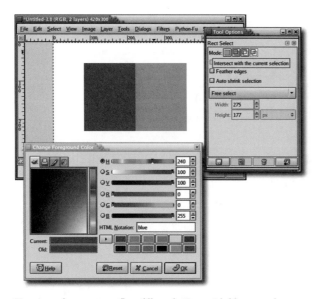

To create the two-tone flag, fill a selection with blue, use the Rectangle Select tool to cut out half of the selection, and fill the new selection with red.

5. Make sure the **Rectangle Select** tool is still active, and click the button on the far right to set the Mode to **Intersect** in the Tool Options dialog. Starting outside the flag, draw a long rectangular box on the canvas through the current selection near the top of the flag.

6. With the canvas selected, press **D** and then **X** to set the foreground color to white. Drag the foreground color into the new selection.

7. Choose the **Move** tool from the toolbox. In the Tool Options dialog set the Affect to **Selection** by clicking the middle of the three buttons next to the Affect label. Click the canvas inside the selection and drag down toward the bottom of the flag.

8. Fill the selection with white. Deselect all (CTRL-SHIFT-A). In the Tool Options dialog set the Affect to **Layer** by clicking the button on the left.

9. Click the **Rectangle Select** tool to make it active again. In the Tool Options dialog set the Mode to **Replace**.

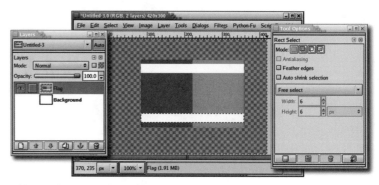

Add two white stripes by creating one rectangular selection, filling it, moving it, and then filling it again.

Adding a Star

You may recall from Section 1.5 that the Gfig filter is the best GIMP tool for drawing complex predefined shapes like stars.

1. Open the Gfig filter (**Filters ▶ Render ▶ Gfig**). This will create a new layer called *Gfig*.

2. Click the star in the icon bar at the top of the window, and then set the Sides slider to **5 sides**.

3. Click the **Browse** button, choose the **Circle (01)** brush, and click the **Close** button.

4. Select **Color Fill** from the Fill drop-down menu, and change the color bar to white (click the bar to change it). The Stroke color box should also be white, and the box next to the word *Stroke* should be checked, as shown in the figure on the next page.

5. Click where the center of the star should be (the middle of the main blue section) and slowly drag down and slightly to the right to draw the star. If you mess up, use CTRL-Z to undo the star and try again. Click the **Close** button when you're ready to apply the star to the flag.

6. In the Layers dialog click the **Gfig** layer and merge it with the Flag layer (**Layer ▶ Merge Down**).

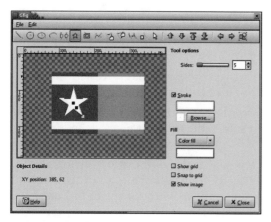

Using the Gfig filter is the easiest way to create common shapes. If you don't make any other changes to the layer, you can even come back later and edit those shapes.

Creating Ripples and Waves

1. Open the Ripple filter (**Filters ▸ Distorts ▸ Ripple**). Set the Orientation to **Vertical,** the Edges to **Smear,** the Period to **195 pixels,** and the Amplitude to **10 pixels.** Click **OK** to apply this filter to the Flag layer.

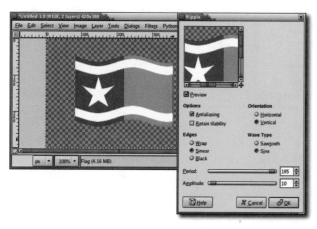

The Ripple filter's Period setting works well for small images, such as those used on web pages. The units of measure are pixels, however, so long periods aren't possible for larger images without using some form of layer or image scaling.

2. Open the Waves filter (**Filters ▸ Distorts ▸ Waves**). Set the Amplitude to **3.5,** the Phase to **180,** and the Wavelength to **50.** The results are good, but the Ripple filter leaves a bit of a stairstep effect on the edges between colors, because it does not handle antialiasing properly. Let's fix that problem.

3. Duplicate the Flag layer (**Layer ▸ Duplicate**) and set the duplicate layer's mode to **Multiply.**

4. Click the original **Flag** layer in the Layers dialog to make that layer active.

5. Open the Gaussian Blur filter (**Filters ▸ Blur ▸ Gaussian Blur**). Set the Blur Radius to **1.5 pixels** and the Blur Method to **RLE.** (The RLE mode is generally used for photographs, while the IIR mode works well for text because text has distinct edges. Despite the distinct edges in this image, the RLE mode is preferred because it handles antialiasing better along curves.) Click **OK** to apply this filter to the Flag layer.

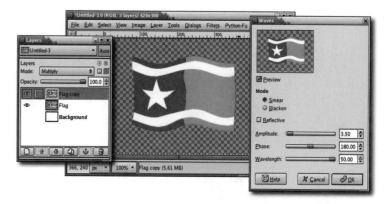

The Waves filter is better suited for larger images than the Ripple filter. The difference is that the Waves filter's effects originate from the center point of the image while the Ripple filter runs the breadth (width or height) of the image.

Adding Depth

We've achieved the basic ripple, but we need to add shadows to complete the 3D effect.

1. Add a new transparent layer to the top of the layer stack by choosing **Layer ▸ New** and setting the Layer Fill Type to **Transparency**. Name the new layer *Shadows*.

2. Select the original **Flag** layer in the Layers dialog and create a selection around it (**Layer ▸ Transparency ▸ Alpha to Selection**).

3. Choose the **Blend** tool and in the Tool Options dialog set the Gradient to **Blinds**. Click the **Shadows** layer to make it active again.

4. With the **Blend** tool selected, drag through the center of the flag. Start outside the selection on the left and drag across to the outside of the selection on the right. This stretches the blinds effect a bit. Reduce the layer opacity to see if the white areas of the gradient corresponds to raised areas of the flag. If necessary, use CTRL-Z to undo the drag and retry until you get this right.

5. When you're ready, open the Gaussian Blur filter (**Filters ▸ Blur ▸ Gaussian Blur**) and, with the selection in place, apply a blur of **50 pixels** to the Shadows layer. Set the Shadows layer mode to **Grain Merge** and adjust the **Opacity** as necessary.

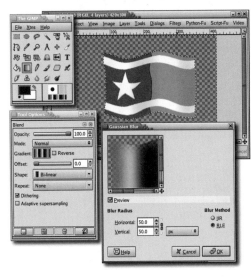

The Blinds gradient is a ready-made lighting effect. By using longer or shorter strokes to apply the gradient, stretch it to fit the wavy structure of the flag. The blur reduces the contrast between light and dark areas.

Adding the Finishing Touches

1. Clear the current selection by choosing **Select ▸ Clear** or pressing CTRL-SHIFT-A.

2. Click the original **Flag** layer to make that layer active. Add a drop shadow (**Script-Fu ▸ Shadow ▸ Drop Shadow**).

3. Add a new transparent layer named *Pole*. Create a rectangular selection on the left side of the flag that just touches the edge of the flag.

4. Choose the **Blend** tool and in the Tool Options dialog set the Gradient to **FG to BG (RGB)**. Check the box next to the word *Reverse* to activate that option. Set the Shape to **Bi-Linear**. With the canvas selected, press **D**. Drag horizontally through the selection, starting at the selection's midpoint and dragging to the right. Deselect all (CTRL-SHIFT-A).

5. Use the Colorize tool (**Layer ▸ Colors ▸ Colorize**) to add color to the pole if desired.

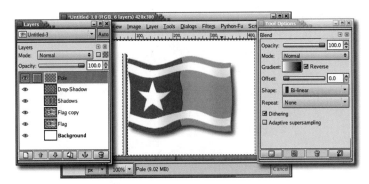

Use the Blend tool to add a flagpole.

Further Exploration

In this section we manually created a simple flag, but the process can be applied to any rectangular image in order to give it the appearance of being imprinted on a flag. You might create a logo that looks like it's flapping in a breeze, for example. Experiment with the Perspective tool to make the flag appear to be blowing away from you.

3.9 TRI-TONE MENUS

Simple menus like this one start with good clipart.

You can achieve just about any kind of page layout using CSS on the Web. One popular CSS technique involves using a background image as part of a block-level element that contains a list and letting the list change from page to page, while the background provides the items that are common to all the lists. For the list text, you should use a font that will be available on all visitors' systems (common fonts like Times New Roman, Verdana, or Georgia). You can use any font family you like for the text in the background image, however, because those items will be embedded in the image itself.

Creating a background image in only three colors helps keep the page's visual clutter to a minimum. You want the page to convey information, not flash with distracting rainbows that annoy visitors at best and scare them away at worst.

In this tutorial we'll create a tri-tone web menu for a travel website. You'll find that the technique is applicable to any type of website—just swap out the clipart as necessary.

Getting Started

Imagine a travel agency has asked you to design a web menu with a South Pacific theme that will showcase its island destination packages. The menu can't be wider than 200 pixels. Start by selecting clipart that matches your site's message and then opening the image in the GIMP. This tutorial uses a piece of retro clipart from a travel collection. It was a print collection, so I had to scan the image at 150 dpi. No matter where the image comes from, it's always a good idea to quickly check its levels. This image has a good distribution of white and black points, so no levels adjustment is needed.

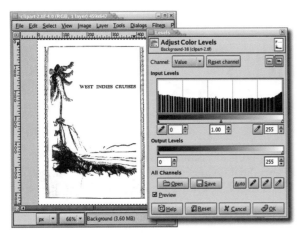

If necessary, make a levels adjustment to increase the contrast between black and white areas of the image.

Prepping the Scanned Image

1. If you've scanned the image, crop the scan so the bottom and left edges are straight. Pull two horizontal guides from the left ruler and two vertical guides from the top ruler and position them appropriately. Select the **Crop** tool, click the upper-left intersection of the guides, and drag to the bottom-right intersection. The area to be cropped will have a dark tint. Click the **Crop** button in the Crop and Resize Information dialog.

2. Adjust the canvas window to fit the new image size by choosing **Image ▸ Fit Canvas to Layers** and then pressing CTRL-E.

3. Remove all guides (**Image ▸ Guides ▸ Remove All Guides**).

4. This clipart element contains some text that we don't want to use in the web menu design. Remove it by using the **Rectangle Select** tool to create a selection around the text you don't want. With the canvas selected, press **D** and then **X** to set the foreground color to white, and then drag the foreground color from the toolbox into the selection to block out the text.

5. This technique works in this example because the white areas of the scan are pure white, not various shades of white. If this isn't true of your scan, use the Curves and Levels tools to adjust the white areas by choosing **Layer ▸ Colors ▸ Levels** and **Layer ▸ Colors ▸ Curves**. Then deselect all (CTRL-SHIFT-A).

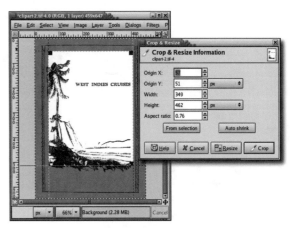

Cropping the clipart removes the unwanted border.

6. Now invert the colors in this layer (**Layer ▸ Colors ▸ Invert**) and add an alpha channel (**Layers ▸ Transparency ▸ Add Alpha Channel**).

7. Set the Mode to **Addition**.

NOTE *If the Add Alpha Channel menu option is not available, the layer you're working in already has an alpha channel. The only layer that ever needs to have an alpha channel added to it is the Background layer, which should be the default (and only) layer when you open a clipart file for the first time.*

Inverting the image gives us an effect similar to a black-and-white film negative, and it allows us to colorize the image's black areas.

Colorizing the Background Image

1. Add a new transparent layer by choosing **Layer ▸ New** and setting the Layer Fill Type to **Transparency**.

2. Click the foreground color to open the Change Foreground Color dialog, and set the RGB values to **109/109/255** to match the purplish blue shown here. Click **OK** to close the dialog.

3. Drag the foreground color into the new layer to fill the layer with that color. In the Layers dialog, drag this layer down below the Background layer.

4. Click the **Background** layer in the Layers dialog to make that layer active. Merge the two layers (**Layer ▸ Merge Down**).

5. Open the Gaussian Blur filter (**Filters ▸ Blur ▸ Gaussian Blur**) and apply a blur of **1 pixel** to the Background layer.

6. Double click the layer name and change it to *Clipart*.

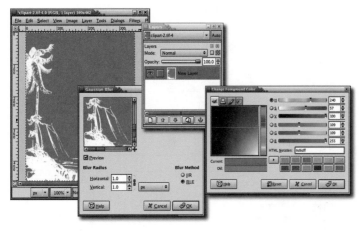

When filling the layer with color, remember that adding color to black gets you that color, while adding color to white leaves you with white.

7. Add a new transparent layer by choosing **Layer ▸ New** and setting the Layer Fill Type to **Transparency**.

8. Again drag the foreground color into the new layer. Set the Opacity to **60 percent**. This new layer colorizes the white area and softens the effect. The background image should be just that—in the background. Click the layer name and change it to *Colorize*.

9. Now drag a vertical guide out to 200 pixels (keep an eye on the status bar below the canvas). Use this to crop the image to 200 pixels, as required by the client. Make sure the box next to the words *Current Layer Only* is not checked in the Tool Options dialog for the Crop and Resize tool.

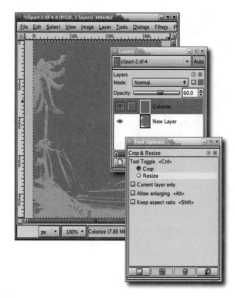

Reducing the layer's opacity allows the colored layer to tint the white clipart.

Adding a Contrasting Color

1. For visual interest, let's add a small geometric figure in a contrasting color. Click the **Rectangle Select** tool. Hold down the SHIFT key, click, and then drag to select a small square.

2. Copy and paste this selection into a new layer (**Layer ▸ New**). Open the Change Foreground Color dialog again. Set the RGB values to **229/133/13** to match the orange shown here and click **OK** to close the dialog. Drag the foreground color into the new layer.

3. Duplicate this layer (**Layer ▸ Duplicate**) and use the Move tool to drag the layer so it is offset to the right and down a little. Duplicate the layer again and drag so it is offset down and to

the left a little. Click the top square layer and merge it down twice (**Layer ▸ Merge Down**). Name this layer *Squares*. Move the layer so to leave space to its right for a menu title.

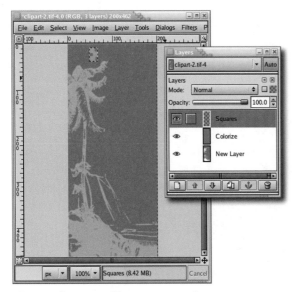

Three small squares add a contrasting color to the design.

Adding a Title and a Border

It's time to add a menu title. You can use any font you like here because the font will be rasterized in the background image, which means the website visitor doesn't need to have that font installed on his or her system in order to see this title correctly. I used TimbrelBroad Ultra-Light Italic sized to 24 pixels in this example. The text is positioned to the right of the squares we just created.

1. Add a new transparent layer.
2. Open the **Change Foreground Color** dialog and select the same orange color used for the Squares layer. Close the dialog.

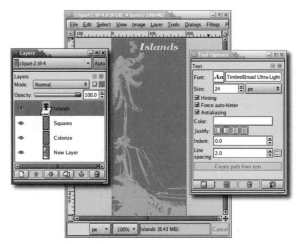

Align the squares with the menu title.

3. Drag the foreground color into the new layer.
4. Scale the layer to **10 pixels** wide (**Layer ▸ Scale Layer**) but leave the height unchanged. Align the new layer with the right edge of the canvas.

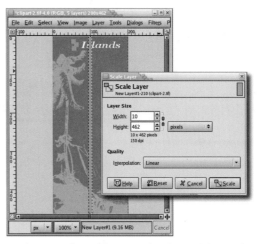

Duplicating a layer, filling it with color, and then scaling it in only one direction is a fast way to create vertical and horizontal bars.

5. Open the Align Visible Layers dialog (**Layer ▸ Align Visible Layers**). Set the Horizontal Style to **Collect** and the Horizontal Base to **Right Edge**. Uncheck the box next to the words *Ignore the bottom layer even if visible* and check the box next to the words *Use the (invisible) bottom layer as the base.*

6. In the Layers dialog turn off visibility for the text and Squares layers. These settings will cause the Background layer and the new layer to align along their right edges. Click **OK** to align the layers.

7. Turn visibility back on for those layers and name the new layer *Sidebar.*

Once you've created it, position the vertical bar using the Align Visible Layers dialog.

8. Next let's merge the Sidebar layer with the Background layer, which includes the island clipart image. Add a layer mask to the Sidebar layer (**Layer ▸ Mask ▸ Add Layer Mask**).

9. Click the **Clipart** layer to make it active.

10. Choose the **Select By Color** tool from the toolbox. Click the white areas of the clipart to create a selection.

11. Click the Sidebar layer mask to make it active again. Press **D** to reset the foreground color to black. Drag this color into the selection.

12. Deselect all (CTRL-SHIFT-A). When these steps have been completed, the lower-right part of the island will have been merged with the orange sidebar.

Merging the Sidebar layer with the Background layer is a subtle effect, but it allows the portion of the clipart image that intersects with the bar to show through.

All that's left is to save the image as a PNG or JPEG image. If you're writing the CSS for this image as well, decide where the menu will be placed and compute the offsets from the image edges. Drag out guides from the rulers to outline the area, and then check the status bar at the bottom of the canvas window for that information.

Use guides to determine the size and location of the area where you'll use HTML and CSS to place the list items on the website.

Further Exploration

Now that we've finished creating the menu background image that will be used on each page of the website, you may be wondering how you can match the font in the title of the background image with the lists of menu items that change from one page to the next. Remember that many visitors to your site will not have the font used in the title of the background image installed on their systems. How can you head off problems? The answer is simple: Use a rollover image for each list item. Instead of creating lists of text and letting the browser choose a font, use rollover images that will look the same in all browser windows. This is a CSS trick that utilizes the skills you developed in Section 3.6.

TIPS FOR WEB DESIGN

The GIMP is a tool capable of producing high-quality images for any design project—no matter what the medium—and its core support for RGB and indexed images makes it ideal for web design. Keep the following tips in mind as you begin using the GIMP to create images for your websites.

Use the GIMP for Images; Use CSS for Design

The GIMP gives you the tools to create a website's images, but you need something more sophisticated to provide layout rules and organize your creations for a coherent user experience. CSS is it. For a more detailed discussion of CSS, see the beginning of this chapter.

Add Contrast Where Necessary

If you're placing text over a background in an image bound for the Web, be certain there is sufficient contrast between the edges of the text and the background. A low-contrast image might look good on a designer's high-end display, but you can't guarantee that all visitors to the website will see the image in the same way. Adding a drop shadow or outline can help separate the text from the background. A text screen is another option. For a more detailed discussion of text screens, see Section 2.9.

Avoid Busy Backgrounds

Backgrounds should be seen but not heard. A loud background is a bad design choice. If your eye is drawn to a background, chances are the background is distracting your visitors from the web content. To make your text pop, first reduce the contrast in the background image. Then desaturate the image and fill it with a light color using the Bucket Fill tool with its Mode set to Color or Grain Merge. You may need to choose a low Opacity setting.

Choose File Formats Wisely

There's a reason so many different image file formats have been developed: Not every format works well in every situation. If you have solid text in an image that has no gradients, use the GIF format. Because it uses only 8 bits per pixel for color information, the GIF format works well for images that have only a few colors (256 or less) and strong contrast (as black text on a white background does). The GIF format also provides lossless compression, which means it compresses the image as much as it can without sacrificing image quality. But skip the GIF format if you have photographs to display.

Photographs are better handled using the JPEG format, which was specifically designed for photographs based upon how the human eye perceives color. Using 24 bits (three 8-bit RGB channels) to represent each pixel, the JPEG format easily handles up to 16 million colors. Unlike the GIF format, the JPEG format's compression is described as *lossy*, which means (theoretically, at least) that by using it you are throwing away data. The actual data loss is usually trivial, however, and you can specify how much to compress an image, depending on the degree of quality loss you're willing to accept. A bigger disadvantage for some GIMP artists may be that the JPEG format doesn't handle transparency information. The GIF format does, but it can only interpret transparency as either on or off for any given pixel, leading to "stairsteps" in nonrectangular regions of your image.

The PNG format, on the other hand, can handle various levels of transparency and millions of colors. It also offers *lossless compression*, so no data is sacrificed. Unfortunately, not all browsers fully support the PNG format. For example, some recent versions of Internet Explorer can't display PNG images if they contain transparency information. If only all of our website visitors used Firefox!

Another option is to force your visitors to use an external program to view your images. Firefox's MIME Type Editor extension allows the visitor to configure external programs to handle various file types. Designers or photographers who provide sample hi-res copies of their work in private web galleries may choose this option. Full-color TIFF images might be appropriate in such a case, though thumbnail previews would still need to be GIF, JPEG, or PNG files because they would be displayed by the browser.

Choose file formats wisely. Using JPEG images for every project just isn't a good enough solution. And if you think choosing among these choices is annoying, just wait until the Web (and all those browsers) finally support vector images. Viva la SVG!

Scan for the Web

If you can't find suitable clipart on the Internet or in a book, you can always scan real-world objects, desaturate the resulting image and then reduce the image's color range using the Levels, Curves, or Posterize tools (Layer ▸ Colors). Scanner support is available from the SANE project at http://www.sane-project.org. The XSane plug-in is required to scan directly from the GIMP and is available at http://www.xsane.org. Both SANE and XSane are included in most recent Linux distributions (such as Fedora and SuSE), though they still require manual configuration. See Section 1.7 for more on working with scanners, and peruse the Web or read the man pages (man sane and man xsane) for more information about configuring your scanner.

Use Web-Safe Colors?

It's debatable whether we still need to limit ourselves to a *web-safe color palette* now that modern desktop monitors and display adapters all support true-color graphics. Many handheld devices, including cell phones with web browsers, may not support the full color range, however. As more handheld devices provide graphical web interfaces and more visitors use those devices to access your website, your GIMP designs must adapt.

You can do an Internet search for web-safe color palettes, or you can use one of those available at http://www.lynda.com/hex.asp. web-safe color palettes are also available here:

O'Reilly Media   http://www.oreilly.com/catalog/wdnut/excerpt/web_palette.html

Victor S. Engel's 6×6×6 Netscape Color Palette Map
http://the-light.com/colclick.html

The GIMP even comes with such a palette (choose Dialogs ▸ Palettes and find the Web entry). To map your image to the palette, convert your RGB image to an Indexed image using Image ▸ Mode ▸ Indexed. The Convert Image to Indexed Colors dialog will open. Choose Use Custom Palette and make sure Web is selected. Then click OK. You can also use this dialog's dithering options to make sure the map to the web-safe palette retains more of the original colors.

Mapping your image to a web-safe palette is still a good idea—if you care about your kid's web phone experience. After all, who else could possibly see the detail in those small displays?

Export Safely

If you'll be using your image in a web design, save it to the appropriate file format: JPEG, GIF, or PNG. When you save a layered image to an image file format suitable for the Web, the GIMP will automatically merge all visible layers. This costs you nothing in effort and won't change your existing layered canvas. But don't forget to save the layered version as an XCF file as well, just in case you need to edit the layers later.

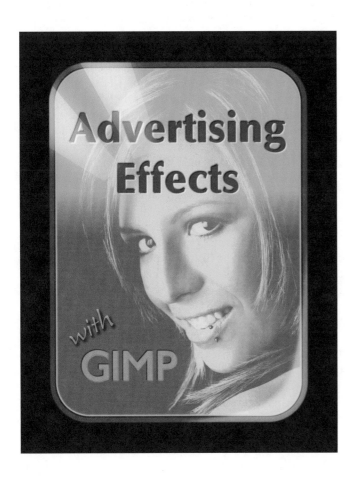

4

ADVERTISING AND SPECIAL EFFECTS

Advertising is about presenting a message to a target audience as effectively as possible and for the least possible cost. The GIMP can't help you rein in your media costs or identify your target audience, but it can help you present a compelling message about a product. The tutorials in this chapter utilize the GIMP tools you've already encountered in this book; they build on skills you've developed and teach you how to apply those skills to common advertising tasks.

Print vs. Web

An advertisement's destination dictates its design. Understanding the requirements and limitations of the destination medium is an important part of the advertising design process. Creating web ads doesn't require as much time, effort, or memory as creating print ads does, but the nature of the Web limits web ads in many ways.

Web ads are designed to be viewed on computer monitors, so the images are usually small and measured at the monitor's resolution (72 dpi). Web ads are also displayed in the same RGB format in which the images were created. For these reasons, web ads are a bit easier to create than print ads, but because both the monitor resolution and screen space are limited, web ads can't show as much detail.

In comparison, print ads are usually larger and measured at higher resolutions (150 dpi to 300 dpi), so they generally require far more computer memory to produce. Additionally, print ads created in RGB usually must be converted to the CMYK format the printer requires. Because the GIMP does not currently support direct manipulation of images in CMYK, your ads will be created in RGB, and the conversion process will have to be handled by the printer or a third-party service bureau.

NOTE *If you're not afraid of the command line, you can also try using the ImageMagick suite of command-line tools to handle image color conversion. If built with the Little CMS (LCMS) library, the convert tool can convert RGB images to CMYK using International Color Consortium (ICC) profiles. GIMP 2.2 can't produce ICC profiles, but GIMP 2.4 will offer tools that can be used to produce ICC profiles for your images.*

Stock Images

Most web and print advertising work starts with stock images. Luckily, the Internet has opened up stock image collections to the masses and reduced the cost of those images in the process. These images are ideal for use in web ads because they are inexpensive, of reasonable quality, and available in many sizes. Most stock image collections provide images in GIMP-supported formats such as TIFF and JPEG, and prices on low-cost stock image websites like BigStockPhoto.com, iStockphoto.com, and CanStockPhoto.com range from $1 to $5 per image.

You can use low-cost stock images for some print ads, though for projects like posters and banners it may be best to use images from professional stock image collections instead. Professional stock image services usually offer much larger images, ones that are big enough to suit large-scale print projects. In addition to per-file downloads, professional stock image services may also sell complete CD collections or provide monthly subscriptions. Prices vary greatly, however. A single image might cost $80 to $200,

while a CD collection might cost around $500. Websites like AbleStock.com, GettyImages.com, and Creatas.com charge approximately $199 per month and $1,200 per year for subscriptions.

Online stock image collections typically offer each image in a few different sizes. These image sizes are generally given in pixels, and you'll want to buy the largest version of the image you can afford. This will allow you to scale down the image to a size appropriate for your project. Remember that the dots per inch (DPI) value is different for print ads (150 dpi to 300 dpi) than it is for web ads (72 dpi). An image that is 1,200 pixels wide is 4 inches wide when printed at 300 dpi for a magazine (300 dpi × 4 inches = 1,200 pixels), but it's over 16½ inches wide when printed at 72 dpi for the Web!

Another issue to consider when using stock images is licensing. Many low-cost stock image collections license all of their images for a wide range of uses, but some allow each photographer to specify his or her own license parameters. Professional stock image services have very specific licensing policies. You'll need to read the licenses carefully to determine whether or not you can use the image as you'd like.

The issue of model releases is also tricky. A *model release* is written permission to use the likeness of a person, place, or identifying mark (such as a logo) that might otherwise have limited rights of use. Model releases are most often used in connection with photos of people and are required if the individual's face is recognizable.

Most stock image websites require that anyone submitting a photo of a person also include a model release giving permission to use the likeness in other projects. A model release allows a designer to use a stock image for a wide range of purposes but protects the model's image from misuse.

NOTE *A very detailed guide to model releases is available at http://www.danheller.com/model-release.html.*

Most advertising projects make use of stock photos.

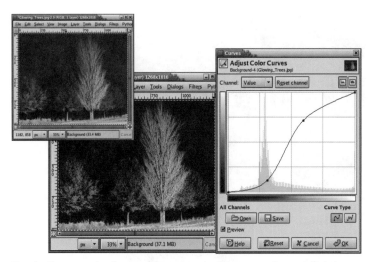

Use the Curves tool to increase contrast and achieve more dramatic lighting effects.

Color, Contrast, and Grayscale

Flip through any glossy trade magazine, and you'll see how color and contrast are used effectively in print advertising. The GIMP offers several tools for enhancing existing colors, among them the Curves, Levels, and Hue-Saturation tools. Each of these can be used to add pizzazz to an image or to alter an image's mood. The Brightness-Contrast tool is often used in conjunction with these other tools to make overall ambient lighting changes.

While color grabs the viewer's attention, you can choose Layer ▶ Colors ▶ Desaturate to desaturate an image and achieve a subtler effect. The level of contrast in a grayscale image sets the mood: A high-contrast grayscale image conveys energy, while a softly blurred grayscale image evokes a feeling of calm and lends the subject a sense of style and class. The GIMP offers many tools for controlling contrast in grayscale images, including numerous layer and tool blend modes.

NOTE   *Note that as it is used in this context,* grayscale *is not the same as the Grayscale mode (Image ▶ Mode ▶ Grayscale). In Grayscale mode an image has no color content, because it only has a gray channel. In the case of desaturated RGB images, the color content has been removed, but because the image is still in RGB mode, color can be added back in.*

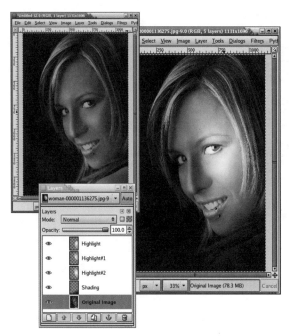

Desaturated images (like the one on the left) are RGB images where the Saturation is set to 0. The Hue and Lightness may be set to any value. The colorized images (center and right) result from changing all three settings.

Lighting plays an important role in advertising, whether the images are color or grayscale.

There's another reason to consider desaturating images with the GIMP: You can add color back in at any time—any color you choose. Colorizing a desaturated image is one more way to set the mood for an advertisement. A range of blues can be cold and harsh, while rich reds and yellows are warm and energetic.

It's Up to You

The GIMP gives the graphic designer many ways to create eye-catching advertisements. The tutorials in this chapter are less about learning new techniques than they are about practicing what you've already learned. Tutorials elsewhere in this book show you how to create 3D images and reflections or enhance color and lighting. Try applying these techniques to stock photographs and you'll soon find that in the hands of a creative designer, the possibilities are endless.

4.1 APPLYING A SQUEEZE

Have an urge to put the squeeze on the government? The GIMP makes this a pretty painless process—at least for you. Several GIMP filters can distort an image, but not all can give you the results you seek.

You can easily pinch and twist images with filters.

Experimenting with Distortion Filters

In this tutorial we'll experiment with the three distortion filters that can pinch an image: the Curve Bend, Whirl and Pinch, and IWarp filters. None of these are difficult to use, but the results can be distinctly different. Each example will show how a filter affects a simple image—the sphere you created in Section 3.2. (Make sure you complete that exercise before trying this one.) Knowing how each of these filters works can help you decide which is appropriate for your project.

Squeezing with the Curve Bend Filter

In general, the Curve Bend filter gives you more control over the pinched shape, but it doesn't provide the wrinkles you'd see with a real pinch.

1. Start by opening the Metal Buttons XCF file you saved in Section 3.2. Make sure the button is in a layer by itself, with the white background layer below it. If there are multiple layers in your Layers dialog, merge them down until you just have a Button layer and a Background layer (**Layer ▸ Merge Down**).

2. Duplicate the Button layer (**Layer ▸ Duplicate**). Turn off the visibility of the original Button layer.

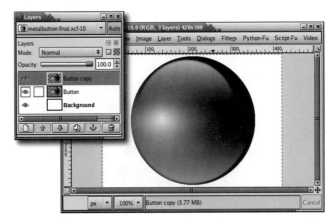

Using a simple object like this button makes it easy to see how you can achieve different effects by using different distortion filters.

3. Open the Curve Bend filter (**Filters ▶ Distorts ▶ Curve Bend**). Click the radio button next to the word *Upper* under the Curve for Border heading. Then drag control points out on the curve, as shown. Check the box next to the words *Automatic Preview* to view the changes as you make them.

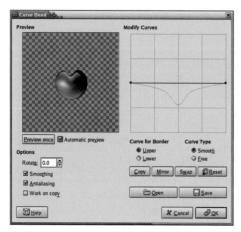

The preview shows how the upper half of the button is bent by the curve in the Curve Bend dialog.

4. Click the **Mirror** button to make the Upper curve mirror the Lower curve and create a symmetrical pinch. Click **OK** in the Curve Bend dialog to apply the changes.

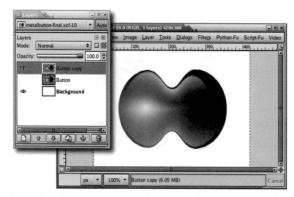

Mirroring the upper curve produces a uniform squeeze on the top and bottom of the button.

If you want to apply the Curve Bend filter's pinch horizontally instead of vertically, you must first rotate your layer by 90 degrees. Then apply your changes in the Curve Bend dialog and rotate the layer to its original orientation.

5. In this example, the edges of the pinched image are jagged. To clean this up, start by making sure the Keep Transparency box for this layer is not checked in the Layers dialog. Then create a selection of the object (**Layer ▶ Transparency ▶ Alpha to Selection**).

6. Shrink the selection by **2 pixels** (**Select ▶ Shrink**), feather the selection by **3 pixels** (**Select ▶ Feather**), and then invert the selection.

7. Open the Gaussian Blur filter (**Filters ▶ Blur ▶ Gaussian Blur**) and apply a blur of **3 pixels**. Deselect all when you're done (CTRL-SHIFT-A).

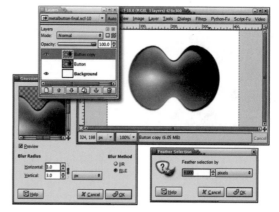

The Keep Transparency button is just to the right of the Mode drop-down menu in the Layers dialog. When there is no check mark in this box, the Keep Transparency option is turned off for the active layer.

Squeezing with the Whirl and Pinch Filter

1. To try out the Whirl and Pinch filter, first turn off the visibility of the Button Copy layer to which the Curve Bend filter was applied. Duplicate the Button layer and name the duplicate layer *Whirl/Pinch*. Turn on the visibility of the new layer.

2. Open the Whirl and Pinch filter (**Filter ▸ Distorts ▸ Whirl and Pinch**). Set the Whirl Angle slider to **0 degrees**, the Pinch Amount slider to **0.82**, and the Radius slider to **1.8**.

3. Click **OK** to apply the filter to the image. The result is that the effect is applied along the horizontal axis and pinches all the way in toward the center of the sphere, converting a highlight into a pinpoint.

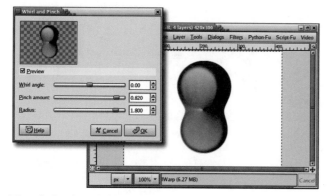

The Whirl and Pinch filter is easier to use than the Curve Bend filter. The effect is just as uniform, if a bit off center.

As with the Curve Bend filter, the Whirl and Pinch filter only works in one direction. This time the direction is horizontal. To apply this pinch vertically, you must rotate the layer, apply the filter, and then rotate the layer back to its original orientation.

Squeezing with the IWarp Filter

The IWarp filter is the only distortion filter that produces a wrinkled pinch effect, much like you'd get if you squeezed a soft ball.

1. To see how it works, first turn off the visibility of the Whirl/Pinch layer. Duplicate the Button layer (**Layer ▸ Duplicate**) and name the duplicate layer *IWarp*. Turn on the visibility of the new layer.

2. Open the IWarp filter (**Filters ▸ Distorts ▸ IWarp**). To apply this filter, configure the various settings and then click and drag inside the preview.

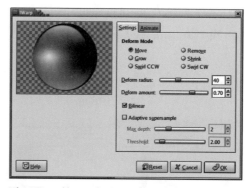

The IWarp filter is the Swiss Army knife of GIMP distortion filters, but its use is far more manual, and there is no simple mechanism for mirroring a distortion on opposite sides of an object.

3. Click above the top edge of the button and drag down a small amount. Multiple drags are usually required to form the desired pinch effect. Do the same on the bottom of the image to squeeze it up.

4. Adjust the **Deform Radius** and **Deform Amount** sliders if you like. With this filter, experimentation is painless—just click Reset to remove all changes made in the preview window. When you are satisfied with the warp, click **OK** to apply the changes.

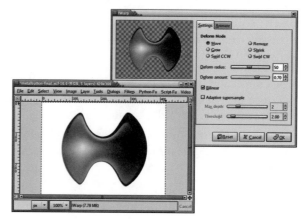

It's easier to set the width of the squeeze using the IWarp filter than it is with the Curve Bend filter. Just increase the Deform Radius setting before dragging through the preview in the IWarp dialog.

Using the IWarp Filter to Squeeze the Capitol Building

Now let's use the IWarp filter to squeeze a photograph of the US Capitol building.

1. Use the **Crop** tool to crop out construction work on the right, leaving the dome and a solid blue background.

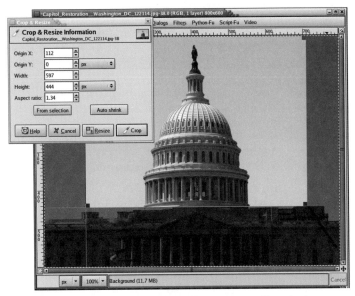

You can leave the lower floors in the picture, but they will just be distracting because we aren't going to squeeze that part of the image.

2. Next let's cut a C-Clamp from a stock photo and add it to this image. Open the clamp image, select the clamp using the **Quick Mask** tool, turn off the Quick Mask, and then copy and paste the selection into the image of the Capitol dome.

3. Use the **Move** tool to position the clamp over the Capitol dome, and then use the **Scale** tool to fit the clamp to the image.

When the clamp is in the right place, make it a new layer (**Layer ▸ New**) and name it *Clamp*.

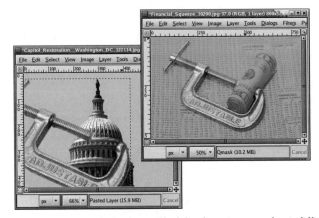

The newspaper in the background of the clamp image makes it difficult to select the clamp with anything other than the Quick Mask tool, but even that takes time and a steady hand. If you're impatient, the next best bet is the Scissors tool.

4. Click the **Background** layer to make it active, and then open the IWarp filter (**Filters ▸ Distorts ▸ IWarp**). Set the **Deform Radius** and **Deform Amount** sliders to low values and begin dragging in the preview window. Experiment with different Deform Radius and Deform Amount values if necessary. Once your preview is satisfactory, click **OK** to apply the warp.

5. Use the **Scale** and **Move** tools to tweak the size of your clamp.

6. Add a layer mask to the Clamp layer to blend the two layers better (**Layer ▸ Mask ▸ Add Layer Mask**). This method is imprecise, and it may take a few trial-and-error attempts to get it right, but the result will be better than you'd get if you used the Curve Bend filter or the Whirl and Pinch filter.

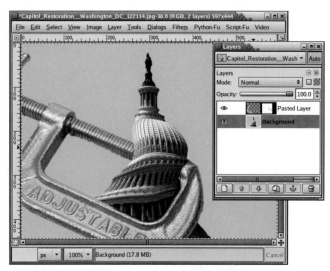

Because of the angle of the clamp in the original image, it's easiest to use the IWarp filter to make the squeeze on the Capitol building fit the clamp.

Further Exploration

The final image shows that white text with a simple drop shadow has been added. The drop shadow uses small values for the X and Y Offsets (2 or 3 pixels for a web design) and the Blur Radius. If the background were not so uniform in color, you might consider adding a text screen as we did in Section 2.9.

Distortions like this squeeze effect are fun to work with, but you have to be careful about the size of the original image. If you distort small images too much, you may notice a stairstep effect along the edges (also known as "the jaggies"). For this reason it's best to apply the distortion to larger images and then scale down the result.

4.2 MOVIE POSTER

The ordinary becomes extraordinary with a little help from the GIMP.

Movie posters are fun fare for the graphic artist. The only limits to the design are your imagination and, of course, the movie's theme. But the movie poster style can lend itself to just about any event: a high school play, Thursday's special at Rocko's Bar and Grill, even the Curmudgeon family garage sale. What you get from a movie poster is something flashy to catch the eye of your target audience. A movie poster is an advertisement. And you want as many people as possible to know about your event.

This tutorial puts a sci-fi spin on a local high school's open house. The goal is to place a eerie light upon the face of a student, with information about the event displayed like credits for the movie. Note that this tutorial, unlike most other tutorials in this book, works on a print-size image (1,900 × 2,850 pixels). This means some of the detail work will be scaled up for the larger image size.

Isolating the Model

1. Let's start with a stock image of a girl, sized to **1,900 × 2,850 pixels** at **300 dpi**. The background is white to start, but that's easy enough to change.

2. Start by using the **Fuzzy Select** tool to create a selection of the white area. Because the white background is nearly uniform, the fuzzy selection grabs most of the white area—and even some of the girl—with just a few clicks.

3. Toggle on the **Quick Mask** to clean up the selection.

4. Feather the selection by **10 pixels** (larger values can be used when working with print-size images) by choosing **Select ▸ Feather.**

Most of the selection is made with the Fuzzy Select tool. The selection is converted to a Quick Mask, refined using paint tools, and then converted back into a selection.

Desaturating and Colorizing the Image

1. Save the selection to a channel (**Select ▸ Save to Channel**), name the channel *Backdrop*, and then deselect the channel (CTRL-SHIFT-A).

2. Click the original layer in the Layers dialog to make it active again. Duplicate the layer (**Layer ▸ Duplicate Layer**), and then name the new layer *Desaturated*.

3. Desaturate this new layer (**Layer ▸ Colors ▸ Desaturate**) and set its mode to **Grain Merge**. This has the effect of enhancing the contrast, as you'd expect if a beam of light were shining directly on the subject at night. We'll add the light itself in just a bit.

4. Duplicate the Desaturated layer and name this layer *Colorized*.

5. Click the foreground color box to open the Change Foreground Color dialog. Set the RGB values to **252/255/0** for the yellow shown here. The color choice is up to you. The unseen alien aircraft could certainly shine a cyan or white light on our subject instead, but choosing yellow helps set an eerie mood. Click **OK** to apply this change.

The girl's skin blends into the white background, but we'll fix this later by adding a dark background.

6. Select the **Bucket Fill** tool from the toolbox. In the Tool Options dialog, set the mode to **Color** and make sure the Fill Type is set to **FG Color Fill**. Click the layer to colorize it. Set this layer's mode to **Multiply**.

A new layer adds a yellow tint to the image. You could apply the Bucket Fill operation to the Desaturated layer instead, but it's helpful to keep each step in its own layer so you can easily reverse changes later.

7. Add a transparent layer by choosing **Layer ▶ New** and setting the Layer Fill Type to **Transparency**. Name this layer *Night* and then move it to the top of the layer stack.

8. Open the **Channels** dialog. Retrieve the selection from the **Backdrop** channel by clicking that channel and then clicking the **Channel to Selection** button (the one with the red box) at the bottom of the dialog.

9. Click the **Night** layer in the Layers dialog to make it the active layer. Grow the selection by **3 pixels** (**Select ▶ Grow**) and feather it by **10 pixels** (**Select ▶ Feather**).

10. With the canvas selected, press **D** to set the foreground color to black, and then drag the foreground color into the selection. Deselect all (SHIFT-CTRL-A).

Adding a black background turns the image from day to night in one easy step.

Creating the Backdrop

1. Add a transparent layer by choosing **Layer ▶ New** and setting the Layer Fill Type to **Transparency**. Name the new layer *Clouds*.

2. Open the Plasma filter (**Filters ▶ Render ▶ Clouds ▶ Plasma**). Set the Turbulence slider to **2.6**, and then click **OK** to apply this filter to the Clouds layer.

3. Desaturate the layer (**Layer ▶ Colors ▶ Desaturate**). Adjust the levels to decrease the white areas and increase the black areas (**Layer ▶ Colors ▶ Levels**). This takes the scene from cloudy to smoke filled. If necessary, use the **Flip** tool to place more clouds on the right side of the image.

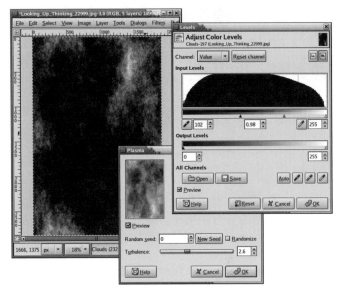

If you don't adjust the levels, the white clouds will overwhelm the black background. We want to break up the solid black background without drawing attention away from the model or the text we'll add later. We want to create the appearance of light smoke, not thick clouds.

4. Retrieve the saved Backdrop selection again by clicking the **Backdrop** channel in the Channels dialog and then clicking the **Channel to Selection** button (the one with the red box). After retrieving the saved selection, click the **Clouds** layer in the Layers dialog to make that layer active.

5. Invert the selection (**Select ▶ Invert**) and feather it by **10 pixels** (**Select ▶ Feather**).

6. With the canvas selected, press CTRL-X to cut the selection from the cloud layer. If the clouds are too bright, reduce the **Opacity** for the Cloud layer.

The clouds add some depth to the scene, making it look as if the model is standing beneath a night sky rather than in front of a black wall.

Adding Light and Highlights

1. The girl is still a little too bright, so we need to add a layer to darken her a bit. With the canvas selected, press **D** to reset the foreground color to black. Add a new layer and name it *Darken*.

2. Fill the layer with black and then add a white layer mask (**Layer ▸ Mask ▸ Add Layer Mask**).

3. Retrieve the saved Backdrop selection and then feather it by **10 pixels**.

4. Click the Darken layer's mask to make it active again. Fill the selection with black, set the layer mode to **Overlay,** and then deselect all (CTRL-SHIFT-A).

Add more contrast to the image by introducing a black masked layer.

5. Add a transparent layer by choosing **Layer ▸ New** and setting the Layer Fill Type to **Transparency**. Name the layer *Beam of light* and move it to the top of the layer stack.

6. Click the foreground color box to open the Change Foreground Color dialog. Set the RBG values to **252/255/0** for the yellow we used earlier.

7. Select the **Blend** tool from the toolbox, and in the Tool Options dialog set the Gradient to **FG to Transparent.** Drag from the upper-right corner of the canvas down past the girl's eyes and toward the back of her neck. It looks like we've added too much light, but we'll mask away most of it in the following steps.

The model is initially bathed in light. In the next step we convert this flood of light into a focused beam.

Creating a Beam of Light

1. Add a black layer mask to the Beam of Light layer by choosing **Layer ▸ Mask ▸ Add Layer Mask**.

2. Use the **Paths** tool to create a triangle, and then click the **Create Selection from Path** button in the Tool Options dialog.

The beam is formed by creating a pyramid-shaped selection.

3. Select the **Rotate** tool and then click the **Transform Selection** button in the Tool Options dialog. The Transform Selection button is the second button from the left, next to the word *Affect*.

4. Click the canvas and then use the Angle slider to rotate the outline of the selection clockwise about **45 degrees**. Click the **Rotate** button to apply the rotation.

Rotations can be applied to images, selections, and paths.

5. Select the **Move** tool from the toolbox. Hold down the ALT key (you may need to hold down the SHIFT key too) and drag up and to the right in the selection so that the bottom of the triangle frames the girl's face.

6. Select the **Scale** tool, and in the Tool Options dialog click the **Transform Selection** button (the first button from the left, next to the word *Affect*). Click the canvas, grab the lower-left drag point, and then drag down and to the left. Click the **Scale** button in the Scaling Information dialog to apply the change.

NOTE   *Whether or not you need to use the SHIFT key depends on your Window Manager settings. If the ALT key is already used by the Window Manager, you may need to hold down the SHIFT key as well so the Window Manager doesn't intercept the ALT keypress. This affects Linux/Unix users more than Windows or Mac users.*

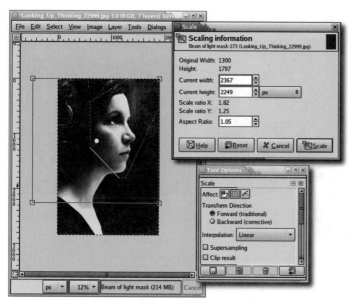

The Scaling Information dialog opens after you've chosen the Scale tool and clicked the canvas. Notice that the selection will be cut off wherever it crosses the boundary of the canvas.

7. With the **Beam of Light** layer mask still active in the Layers dialog and the canvas selected, press **D** and then **X** to set the foreground color to white.

8. Select the **Blend** tool, and in the Tool Options dialog set the Gradient to **FG to Transparent**. Drag on the canvas from the upper-right corner to the lower-left corner. Deselect all (CTRL-SHIFT-A).

9. Open the Gaussian Blur filter (**Filters ▸ Blur ▸ Gaussian Blur**) and apply a blur of **100 pixels** to the mask.

10. If the beam is too large, apply a layer mask (**Layer ▸ Mask ▸ Apply Layer Mask**) and then use the **Scale** tool or the **Perspective** tool to resize and reposition the layer

manually. Reduce the **Opacity** of the layer mask if the light is still too bright. Remember that applying a layer mask in this way actually merges the mask with the layer content.

The flood of yellow light is reduced to a narrow beam.

Adding Text

1. Select the **Text** tool from the toolbox.

2. With the canvas selected, press **D** and then **X** to reset the foreground color to white. Choose an appropriate font in the Tool Options dialog—I used XBAND Rough for the main title and Soutane Ultra-Light for the tag line. Both text elements are right-aligned and positioned in the lower-right corner of the canvas.

A suitably eerie font is used for our poster's tag line. Because the tag line is smaller, it helps to use a font that is legible from a distance.

You can choose View ▸ New View to launch a second canvas window that you can zoom in on. When using multiple views, changes made in one window will show up immediately in all of the other windows.

3. Use the **Text** tool to add credits, along with date and time information for the event. Add a black text screen so that the white words stand out.

Note that if you zoom out to see the full image, the text may appear jagged. Zoom in, and you'll see the text as it will actually appear when the poster is printed.

NOTE *If you need help creating a text screen, see Section 2.9.*

Further Exploration

Much of this project's punch comes from the text at the bottom, which is laid out to simulate the credits you see on real movie posters. Aside from the layout, there isn't anything special about this text. Each name is a text layer that is manually positioned using the Move tool.

If you want to produce the same effect for a postcard, just scale down the process. If you want to create a poster-size image first, choose Image ▸ Scale to resize the final image later. Beware that the resized image won't be as sharp as the original. You might be able to remedy this by using the Unsharp Mask filter (Filters ▸ Enhance ▸ Unsharp Mask), but you'll get much better results if you start with an image that's set to the appropriate size.

4.3 3D PACKAGE DESIGNS

Sometimes an ad needs to include a 3D object that you don't have available to photograph, such as a product package. There are many ways to use the GIMP to simulate three dimensions. The most common method involves using drop shadows to simulate a light source and add a sense of depth. But drop shadows only place one plane above another. They can't add depth to the image itself.

Fortunately, light and shadows aren't the only tricks available to GIMP users. You can also play with perspective. The Perspective tool in the GIMP toolbox provides a simple interface that allows you to change the direction from which an object is viewed; for example, you might choose to view the image from head on or rotate it and view it at an angle. If you need to use 3D packages in your designs, it's best to get familiar with the Perspective tool.

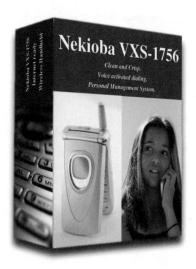

Three-dimensional objects are a snap to create using the Perspective tool.

In this tutorial we create a 3D product package for a fictitious cell phone manufacturer. We take a set of images, arrange them to form the front and sides of the box, align the sides, and then angle the box away from the viewer. As is often the case, you'll save a lot of time if you choose stock images wisely. The actual layout and perspective changes are relatively simple tricks that bring the stock images to life.

This project is scaled for use on the Web, which generally uses 72 dpi for images. To produce the same effect for a print project, leave the original canvas at 300 dpi (150 dpi at the least) and scale up the processes accordingly.

A Quick Look at DPI

DPI stands for *dots per inch*. Most monitors use 72 dpi to display images (CRT displays, that is—LCD monitors tend to be closer to 98 dpi). A monitor that displays at 72 dpi can show 72 dots (one dot is essentially one pixel) in an inch. Printers can squeeze more dots in the same space, so you need to use a higher resolution for printed images. You can get a fairly high-quality print at 300 dpi. If you have an image that is 3 inches across on your 72 dpi display, that would be 216 pixels wide ($3 \times 72 = 216$). To achieve the same result when printing an image that's 3 inches wide at 300 dpi on your printer, the image would need to be 900 pixels wide ($3 \times 300 = 900$).

Preparing the Front of the Box

1. Open a new canvas window by choosing **File ▸ New** in the toolbox. In the Create a New Window dialog that pops up, choose the **US Letter** template. Making this choice will change

the settings in the Advanced Options section. For this project, which is bound for the Web, change the resolution to **72 dpi**.

2. Open your two stock images and scale each one to about **5 inches** wide—a little more than half the width of the new canvas (**Image ▸ Scale Image**). In this example I use a photo of a cell phone and a photo of someone using a cell phone.

3. Copy and paste each stock image into the canvas as a new layer by choosing **Layer ▸ New** after pasting each image. Name one layer *Cell Phone* and the other layer *Girl*.

4. Left-align the Cell Phone layer and right-align the Girl layer, both along the bottom edge of the canvas. You can do this manually, or you can choose **Layers ▸ Align Visible Layers**.

5. Arrange the layer stack so that the **Cell Phone** layer is on top in the Layers dialog. Use the **Move** tool so that the phone and the girl are roughly centered on their halves of the canvas.

You can scale the stock images before you copy and paste them, or you can copy and paste them and then scale the new layers by choosing Layer ▸ Scale. Use the method that is easiest for you, because the result will be the same.

6. Click the **Background** layer in the Layers dialog to make that layer active. Add a vertical guide at **50 percent** by choosing **Image ▸ Guides ▸ New Guide (by Percent)**. Click the **Cell Phone** layer in the Layers dialog.

7. Add a white layer mask (**Layer ▸ Mask ▸ Add Layer Mask**).

8. Use the **Rectangle Select** tool to create a selection to the right of the guide that is as high as the Cell Phone layer.

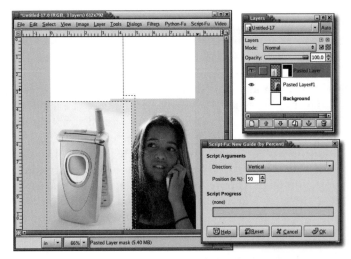

The layer mask on the Cell Phone layer is used to mask out any part of the layer that overlaps the right half of the canvas.

9. With the canvas selected, press **D** to reset the foreground and background colors to black and white, respectively.

10. Make sure the layer mask is still active for the Cell Phone layer by clicking the mask, and then drag the foreground color (black) from the toolbox into the selection. This will cut out a section of the Cell Phone layer, leaving an equal amount of white space on either side of the cell phone and centering it on the left half of the canvas. Then center the image of the girl on the right half of the canvas.

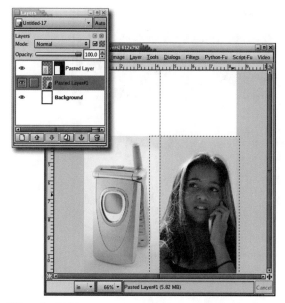

When the Girl layer is active in the Layers dialog, that layer's left edge is hidden by the Cell Phone layer. There is no need to trim off that portion of the image, because the Girl layer is eventually placed below the Cell Phone layer.

Creating a Patch

At this point we need to remove the white strap on the girl's shirt because it distracts from the image. (Even if the image you're using for this project doesn't require a similar fix, you can use this technique whenever you need to remove some distracting element.) While coloring the strap is an option, a much simpler solution is to clone some of the girl's hair and use it to cover the strap.

NOTE *For more cloning practice, see Section 2.10.*

1. Click the **Girl** layer to make that layer active.
2. Zoom in on the image and use the **Free Select** tool to grab a patch of the girl's hair that is large enough to cover the entire length of the strap.
3. Feather the selection by **3 pixels** (**Select ▸ Feather**), and then copy and paste it as a new layer (**Layer ▸ New**).

4. In the Layers dialog move the new layer down to just above the Girl layer, and then use the **Move** tool to position the new layer so that it covers the white strap.
5. Add a white layer mask, and then use the **Airbrush** tool to paint black over the patch and blend the new layer with the original image.
6. Merge down the layer with the original Girl layer (**Layer ▸ Merge Down**).

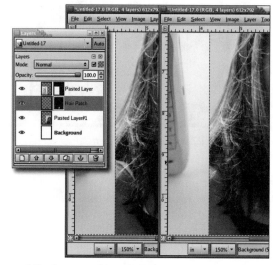

It's difficult to spot the patch because it blends so well with the Girl layer.

Adding Text to the Front of the Box

Now that the images have been cleaned up, we can create the upper half of the package, the portion that contains the product text.

1. Click the **Background** layer to make that layer active.
2. Click the foreground color box to open the Change Foreground Color dialog. Set the RGB values to **6/6/155** for the blue shown here, and then click **OK** to apply the change.
3. Drag the foreground color into the Background layer to add a blue bar that runs across the top of the box.

The product name will be placed inside the blue bar that runs across the top of the box.

Use a larger font for the manufacturer name and model number. Tag lines fill the empty space below.

4. Choose the **Text** tool from the toolbox. With the canvas selected, press **D** and then **X** to reset and then swap the foreground and background colors. Choose an appropriate font and size for the product name and description—I used Nimbus Roman No9 L Bold sized to 72 pixels.

5. Click the canvas to open the Text Editor window. Type a fictitious manufacturer name and model number like `Nekioba VXS-1756`.

6. Use the **Move** tool to center the text layer manually, and then add another text layer that contains some descriptive text set in smaller type.

7. Save this image as *front.xcf*, and then flatten the image (**Image ▸ Flatten Image**).

Creating the Side of the Box

1. Open a new canvas, again using the **US Letter** template set to **72 dpi**. Scale down this canvas to **3 inches** in width, but leave the height at 11 inches.

2. Click the foreground color box and select the blue we used earlier by setting the RGB values to **6/6/155**. Close the Change Foreground Color dialog, and then drag the foreground color onto the new canvas. If you like, add another image to the bottom of the canvas.

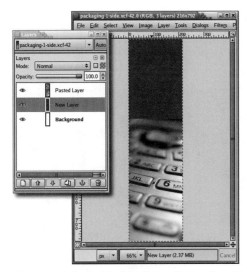

The bottom edges of the blue boxes do not align. If you try to align them now by making the blue boxes the same height, they will become unaligned later when you apply the perspective change. Make your life easy and don't try to align them at all.

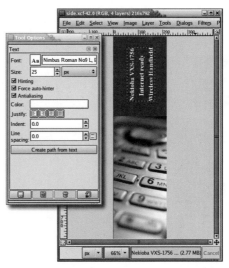

First create the text for the side of the package, then rotate the text. If the text doesn't fit the space well, press CTRL-Z to undo the rotation, choose the Text tool from the Toolbox, click the text layer, adjust the text in the Tool Options dialog, and then rotate the text once more.

3. With the canvas selected, press **D** and then **X** to reset the foreground color to white.

4. Choose the **Text** tool from the toolbox. Choose an appropriate font and size—I used Nimbus Roman No9 L Bold sized to 25 pixels. Retype the text that appears on the front of the box, or modify it if you prefer.

5. Rotate the text layer counterclockwise by 90 degrees (**Layer ▸ Transform ▸ Rotate 90 degrees CCW**) and then use the **Move** tool to manually position the text in the blue area on the side of the package.

6. Save this image as *side.xcf*.

7. Flatten the image (**Image ▸ Flatten Image**) and then scale down the image to **80 percent** of its original size (**Image ▸ Scale Image**).

Merging the Front and Side Panels

1. With the toolbox selected, press **D** to reset the background color to white. Open a new white canvas using the **US Letter** template set to **72 dpi**.

2. Copy and paste the front and side images into this canvas as new layers (**Layer ▸ New**). Name the new layers *Front* and *Side*, respectively.

3. Drag a vertical guide from the left ruler to **3 inches**, and then drag down a horizontal guide from the top ruler to **1 inch**.

4. Click the **Front** layer, and then use the **Move** tool to align the left and top edges of the layer with the intersection of the guides. Click the **Side** layer, and then align the right and top edges of that layer with the intersection of the guides. Make sure that both images fit on the canvas vertically. Don't worry if the sides spill over the edges of the canvas. Just press the minus key to zoom out and make it easier to work on the canvas.

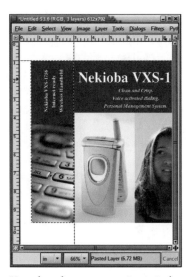

Here the rulers are measuring in inches, though by default they measure in pixels. You can change the units of measure by choosing from the drop-down menu in the lower-left corner of the canvas window.

A perspective transformation makes the front of the box appear to be closer on the left and farther away on the right, as it would be if the box were angled away from the viewer.

5. Drag another vertical guide out to **8 inches**. This marks where the right edge of the box's front will end up.

6. Click the **Front** layer to make that layer active.

7. Choose the **Perspective** tool from the toolbox, and then click the canvas. Drag the top and bottom control points on the right side of the image toward the horizontal center of the canvas until they line up with the vertical guide at 8 inches. Click the **Transform** button in the Perspective Transform Information dialog to apply the changes.

8. Drag a vertical guide from the left ruler out to **1.5 inches** to mark where the left edge of the box's side will end up.

9. Click the **Side** layer in the Layers dialog to make that layer active.

10. Choose the **Perspective** tool from the toolbox, and then click the canvas. Drag the top and bottom control points on the left side of the image toward the horizontal center of the canvas until they line up with the vertical guide at 1 inch.

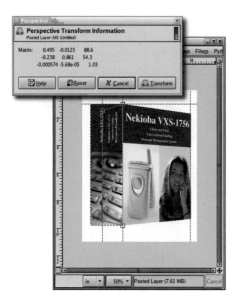

Adding perspective to the side panel transforms the flat images into a realistic box. But we're not quite done with this project.

Cleaning Up the Edges

Zoom in on the bottom edge of the front image—you'll see that it's a bit jagged. Let's fix that now.

NOTE *Even though pixels are alpha blended with transparency when the perspective transformation is performed, it's possible you can still end up with what appear to be jagged edges.*

1. Click the **Front** layer in the Layers dialog. Make sure the **Keep Transparency** box for that layer is not checked.

2. Use the **Rectangle Select** tool to create a selection that spans the guides bounding the left and right edges of the layer.

3. Choose the **Shear** tool from the toolbox, and in the Tool Options dialog set the Affect to **Transform Selection** by clicking the middle button. Click the canvas and drag up the right side of the selection until the top edge of the selection is parallel with the bottom edge of the image. Click the **Shear**

button in the Shearing Information dialog to apply the transformation to the selection.

4. Use the **Move** tool to drag up the selection so that it just barely overlaps the bottom edge of the front image.

5. Open the Gaussian Blur filter (**Filters ▸ Blur ▸ Gaussian Blur**) and apply an RLE blur of 4.5 pixels to the selection. Repeat this process for the top and right edges of the front image and the top, left, and bottom edges of the side image.

Perspective transformations can leave behind jagged edges. Clean them up by applying the Gaussian Blur filter to the areas around each of the transformed edges.

6. Remove all guides (**Image ▸ Guides ▸ Remove All Guides**).

7. Click the Front layer and merge it down with the Side layer—this will merge the front and side panels into a single layer and leave the merged layer separate from the background.

8. Add a drop shadow (**Script-Fu ▸ Shadow ▸ Drop Shadow**), setting the Offset X value to **0 pixels** and the Offset Y value to **12 pixels** to cast a shadow that simulates a light source directly in front and above the box. The Opacity should be

set to **80 percent** so the background can show through it slightly. The Blur Radius is dependent on the size of the image. For this image, which is bound for the Web, a blur of **15 pixels** produces a very soft-edged shadow.

A drop shadow gives the box an even more three-dimensional appearance.

Further Exploration

Consider changing the location of the shadow or adding additional shadows to make it seem as though light is being cast from different directions. A rectangular selection that is modified with the Perspective tool, filled with black, and then placed behind the box with the bottom edges closely aligned can give the appearance that a light source is shining directly on the front of the box and that the box is set atop a surface.

4.4 REFLECTIVE GLASS

Advertising is a name game, and attention spans are running short. If you want to get your message across, you'll need to establish the *who* and the *what* quickly. A logo is the centerpiece of a corporate identity, and it can do a lot to increase name recognition. While logo designs themselves are often quite simple, they can be placed near or inside other objects for added effect. Glass can reflect a company's identity in a big way.

Glass effects are really just tricks with lighting and shadows. In previous tutorials we used lighting to simulate depth in an image. Shadows, too, provide a sense of depth by implying that another surface exists behind or below the main subject. Reflections can also be used to lend texture to a surface. In this tutorial you'll learn how to use reflections to simulate a rounded, glassy surface.

This technique is easy to learn, but you may need to experiment to get the reflections just right. The trick is to create cutouts from an existing selection. And notice the use of paths in this tutorial—the two endpoints of a path will be connected when they are converted to a selection, and in this tutorial we want the line between those two endpoints to be outside an existing selection.

Reflective surfaces can add an unmistakable polish to your logos.

Getting Started

Start with a black canvas set to the default size (420 × 300 pixels). To make sure that the default colors are being used, select the toolbox and then press **D** to reset the foreground and background colors. The techniques used in this tutorial scale up easily enough, so it's okay to work with a canvas that's set to 420 × 300 pixels and 72 dpi until you get it right.

Adding a Border

1. Open the New Guide dialog (**Image ▸ Guides ▸ New Guide**). Select **Vertical** from the Direction drop-down menu, and set the position to **20 pixels**. Click **OK** to add the guide.

2. Repeat this process to add another vertical guide at **400 pixels**. Then choose **Horizontal** from the Direction drop-down menu, and add guides at **10 pixels** and **290 pixels**.

3. Choose the **Ellipse Select** tool from the toolbox. Drag from the upper-left intersection of guides down toward the lower-right intersection of the guides, so that the selection touches each of the guides. (The selection should snap to the guides. If it doesn't, choose **View ▸ Snap to Guides**.)

4. Feather the oval selection by **3 pixels** (**Select ▸ Feather**).

5. Add a new transparent layer by choosing **Layer ▸ New** and setting the Layer Fill Type to **Transparency**. Name the new layer *Border*.

6. Open the Change Foreground Color dialog by clicking the foreground color box in the toolbox. Set the RGB values to **243/217/1** for the bright yellow shown here. Click **OK** to set the foreground color, and then drag the foreground color from the toolbox into the selection.

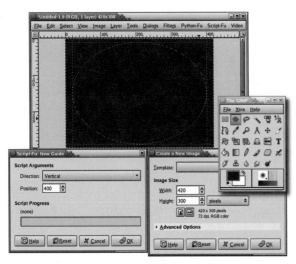

Guides form a bounding box for the elliptical selection. Because the guides are precisely positioned, it's easy to center the oval on the canvas.

7. You don't need the guides anymore, so you can remove them (**Image ▸ Guides ▸ Remove All Guides**).

When you drag the foreground color from the toolbox into the selection, the yellow you've chosen fills the selection in the new transparent layer.

8. Add a new transparent layer by choosing **Layer ▸ New** and setting the Layer Fill Type to **Transparency**. Name this new layer *Edge*.

9. Shrink the selection by **5 pixels** (**Select ▸ Shrink**).

10. With the canvas selected, press **D** to reset the foreground color to black. Drag the foreground color into the selection.

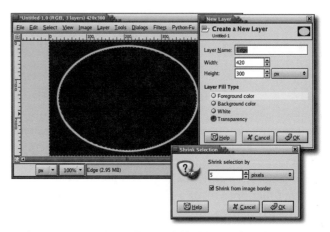

Adding a new layer that is filled with black leaves the yellow oval unchanged. This allows us to make minor changes to the width of the border by modifying the black layer, even long after we've completed the rest of the steps in this tutorial!

Creating a Glassy Surface

Now that we have a border, let's use the Radial gradient to create a glassy surface inside it.

1. Add a new transparent layer by choosing **Layer ▸ New** and setting the Layer Fill Type to **Transparency**. Name this new layer *Green Glass*, and move it to the top of the layer stack in the Layers dialog.

2. Shrink the selection by **2 pixels** (**Select ▸ Shrink**) to leave a thin black edge between the yellow border and green glass.

3. Click the foreground color box in the toolbox to open the **Change Foreground Color** dialog again. This time, set the RGB values to **17/157/43** for the bright-green end of the gradient, and then click **OK** to apply the change.

4. Click the background color box in the toolbox to open the Change Background Color dialog. Set the RGB values to **0/85/16** for the dark-green end of the gradient, and then click **OK** to apply the change.

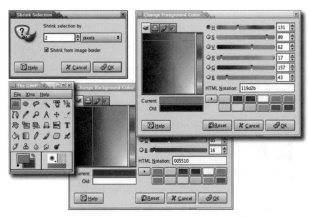

The two shades of green are very similar, but the background color is a bit darker. Higher-contrast colors produce a surface that either looks more reflective or appears to be closer to a stronger, tighter beam of light.

5. Choose the **Blend** tool. In the Tool Options dialog set the Gradient to **FG to BG (RGB)** and set the Shape to **Radial**.

6. Drag inside the selection from the left focus of the oval (just left of center) to the right edge of the oval.

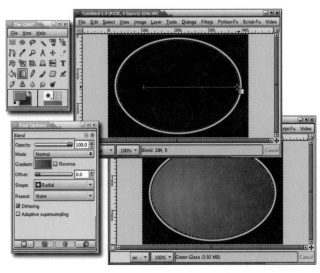

Shrinking the selection slightly and filling it with the Radial gradient simulates a curved surface with an edge that looks like it is in the shadow of a raised yellow border.

Adding Reflective Highlights on the Right

The gradient already simulates lighting changes on the surface of the emblem, but adding highlights will exaggerate this effect even more.

1. Save the selection to a channel (**Select ▸ Save to Channel**).

2. Click the **Green Glass** layer in the Layers dialog to make that layer active.

3. Add a new transparent layer named *Highlight Right*.

4. Reset the foreground and background colors by pressing **D** while the canvas is selected.

5. Choose the **Ellipse Select** tool from the toolbox. In the Tool Options dialog, click the third button from the left to select the **Subtract** mode.

6. Drag over the existing selection to create a new oval that covers all but the lower-right and right edges of the selection. It may take a little experimentation to get this just right. If your first attempt fails, press CTRL-Z to undo the change and try again.

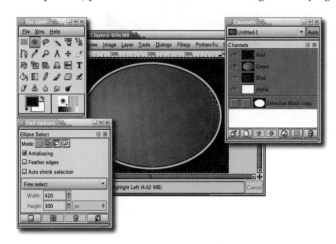

It may take a few attempts to make a cutout from the selection that comes close to the one shown here.

7. Once you have the selection cutout just right, drag the background color box from the toolbox into the selection. Deselect all (CTRL-SHIFT-A).

8. Open the Gaussian Blur filter (**Filters ▸ Blur ▸ Gaussian**). Set the Blur Radius to **10 pixels** for both the Horizontal and Vertical directions, and then click **OK** to apply the blur.

9. Reduce the Opacity of the Highlight Right layer to **15 percent**.

10. Reset the Ellipse tool's mode to **Replace**.

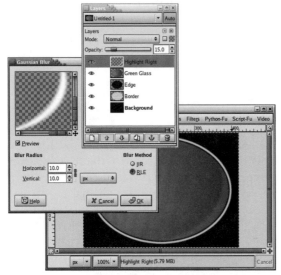

The white area is blurred, and then that layer's Opacity is reduced. This immediately makes the rounded surface look more glass.

Adding Reflective Highlights on the Left

1. Add a new transparent layer and name it *Highlight Left*.

2. Open the Channels dialog (**Dialogs ▸ Channels**). Click the saved channel, which is the last one in the list. Convert this channel to a selection by clicking the **Channel to Selection** button, which is the button that is second from the right at the bottom of the dialog.

3. Return to the Layers dialog and click the **Highlight Left** layer to make it active.

4. Choose the **Path** tool from the toolbox. Click outside the selection, and then trace a path similar to the one shown here. Make sure the first and last grab points in the path

form a straight line outside of the existing selection. While holding down the CTRL and SHIFT keys, click the **Create Selection from Path** button in the Tool Options dialog.

NOTE *If you have trouble working with paths, take a look at Sections 1.8 and 4.2.*

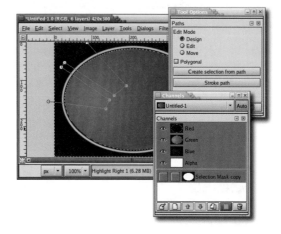

Paths are used to create another selection that intersects the oval. These become additional reflections on the rounded surface.

5. With the canvas selected, press **X** to swap the foreground and background colors and set the foreground color to white.

6. Choose the **Blend** tool from the toolbox. In the Tool Options dialog, set the Gradient to **FG to Transparent** and set the Shape to Linear. Drag from the upper-left edges of the selections to the lower-right edges of the selections. Deselect all (CTRL-SHIFT-A).

7. Open the Gaussian Blur filter (**Filters ▸ Blur ▸ Gaussian Blur**). Apply a blur of **3 pixels** and reduce the Opacity for this layer to **50 percent**.

8. Add a new transparent layer and name it *Highlight Left 2*.

9. As before, retrieve the saved selection by converting it to a channel and then shrink the selection by **20 pixels** (**Select ▸ Shrink**).

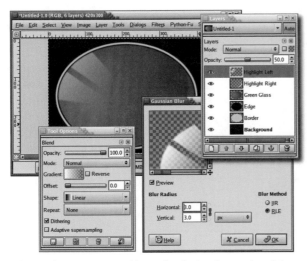

After applying a Gaussian blur and reducing the opacity of the Highlight Left layer, it looks as though a paned window is being reflected on the surface of the object.

10. Click the **Highlight Left 2** layer to make it active again.

11. If the foreground color is not white, press **D** and then **X**, and then drag the foreground color box into the selection to fill the selection with that color. Deselect all (CTRL-SHIFT-A).

12. Open the Gaussian Blur filter (**Filters ▸ Blur ▸ Gaussian Blur**) and apply a blur of **5 pixels**.

13. Add a white layer mask (**Layer ▸ Mask ▸ Add Layer Mask**).

14. Open the Paths dialog (**Dialogs ▸ Paths**). An unnamed path should exist, created when we used the Paths tool earlier in this tutorial. Click the **Path to Selection** button at the bottom of the dialog (it's the fifth button from the left).

15. Invert the selection (**Select ▸ Invert**).

16. Click the layer mask in the **Highlight Left 2** layer to make the mask active, and then fill the selection with black. Deselect all (CTRL-SHIFT-A).

17. Open the Gaussian Blur filter (**Filters ▸ Blur ▸ Gaussian Blur**) and apply a blur of **5 pixels** to the mask.

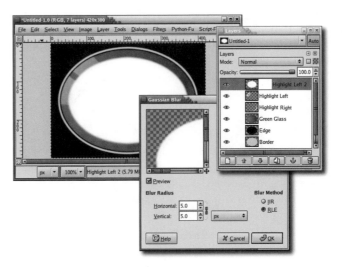

The layer that contains the white oval will be merged with the Highlight Left layer in the next step.

18. In the Layers dialog set the layer mode to **Grain Merge** and the Opacity to **50 percent,** and then drag the **Highlight Left 2** layer down until it is below the Highlight Left 1 layer.

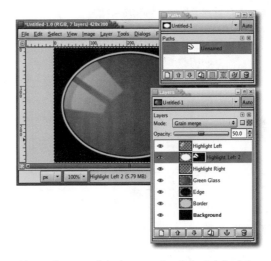

After we've created the layer mask, all that's left of the oval highlight is the area that overlaps the window-shaped highlights.

Adding Text and a Drop Shadow

1. With the canvas selected, press **D** and then **X** to set the foreground color to white.

2. Choose the **Text** tool from the toolbox. In the Tool Options dialog choose an appropriate font and size. Click the canvas to open the Text Editor. Type `Griznak` and close the Text Editor.

3. Use the **Move** tool to center the text on the canvas.

4. Add a drop shadow (**Script-Fu ▸ Shadow ▸ Drop Shadow**). Set the Offset X and Offset Y values to **2 pixels**, and set the Blur Radius to **2 pixels**. Make sure the box next to the words *Allow Resizing* is not checked. Then apply the drop shadow by clicking **OK**.

5. Move the text layer and the Drop-Shadow layer below both of the Highlight Left layers in the Layers dialog.

The text layer is positioned beneath the Left Highlight layers so that the highlights can affect the drop shadow and give the appearance that the text is under the glass.

Further Exploration

This effect works well with oval emblems such as this one, though there isn't any reason why it wouldn't work on a rectangular emblem as well. The key is the soft white layers that simulate reflections of light. These could be reflections of light coming in from a window, or they could be the reflections of nearby surface.

The emblem could also reflect another object, as shown in Sections 2.7 and 2.8. Imagine that this is a car dealership's emblem and a car zooming down the road is reflected in it. With the skills you mastered in Section 2.6, you could even add motion effects to the reflected car.

4.5 POPPING AN IMAGE

Popping is the term used to describe filling a portion of an image's background with white so that the image's subject seems to pop off of the monitor or printed page. Advertisements use this technique extensively. It works much like a type screen does (see Section 2.9) except that in the case of popping the screen is a solid color and its layer is actually placed between the image's subject and background.

This extreme tutorial will take your GIMP skills to the next level. Radical!

Getting Started

Much of the work in this tutorial involves using the Fuzzy Select tool to make a cutout of the subject—in this case, a skateboarder (sans wheels). The process is relatively simple because there is a high contrast between the background and the foreground. Hold down the SHIFT key, click a few times, and you'll be able to select the

background fairly quickly. The same may not be true of the stock image you decide to use for this project, but the basic process will remain the same.

Isolating the Boarder

Let's start with an image of an airborne skateboarder that has a blue sky in the background. The image will be used to advertise a skateboard invitational in the Rocky Mountain region of Colorado. What's missing in the original image is some indication of where the event will take place. Along with popping the boarder from the image, we need to replace the blue sky with a mountain scene.

The blue sky in the background makes for a nice photo, but it will need to be replaced for this project.

1. Open the boarder image in the GIMP and choose the **Fuzzy Select** tool from the toolbox. Click to the left of the boarder and below the board until a solid selection is made. Use the **Quick Mask** to fine-tune the selection.

2. When the entire area left of and below the boarder has been selected, turn the Quick Mask off and invert the selection (**Select ▸ Invert**).

3. Shrink the selection by **1 pixel** (**Select ▸ Shrink**) and feather it by **2 pixels** (**Select ▸ Feather**).

4. Copy and paste the selection as a new layer (**Layer ▸ New**) and name the layer *Boarder*.

5. Open the Unsharp Mask filter (**Filters ▸ Enhance ▸ Unsharp Mask**). Set the Radius to **5 pixels** and the Amount to **0.50**. Click **OK** to apply the changes.

First select the sky. Then invert the selection to isolate the boarder and copy and paste the selection to its own layer (as shown in the Layers dialog).

Enhancing the Board Details

The highlights under the board need to be evened out so that the board doesn't look so washed out.

1. Use the **Fuzzy Select** tool to make a rough selection of the board's bottom.

2. Grow the selection (**Select ▸ Grow**) by **1 pixel**, repeating this process until most of the underside of the board is selected.

3. Feather the selection by **3 pixels** (**Select ▸ Feather**).

4. Use the **Levels** tool to modify the white balance on the board by dragging the right-most slider under the histogram slightly to the left and making sure the middle slider stays centered (**Layer ▸ Colors ▸ Levels**). Modifying the white balance in this way will actually brighten the darker areas of the board and make the hazy underside of the board appear clearer.

5. Deselect all (CTRL-SHIFT-A).

The bottom of the board appears hazy because of a problem with the lighting. Fix this by selecting the board and moving the right slider in the Levels histogram to the left.

Removing the Background

We've isolated the boarder, but there are still patches of sky and clouds between the boarder's legs and along the sides of his torso. These patches need to be removed so we can swap in the Rocky Mountain background.

1. Use the **Fuzzy Select** tool to make selections of the sky on either side of the boarder's torso and in the space between his right arm and each leg.

2. Feather the selection by **3 pixels** (**Select ▸ Feather**).

3. Add a white layer mask (**Layer ▸ Mask ▸ Add Layer Mask**) and fill the selections with black. Deselect all (CTRL-SHIFT-A). Apply the layer mask (**Layer ▸ Mask ▸ Apply Layer Mask**).

When we isolated the boarder, we caught some patches of sky and clouds. Use the Fuzzy Select tool to isolate those areas.

4. Add a new transparent layer and name it *White Backdrop*.

5. Pull a vertical guide from the left ruler until it is just to the right of the boarder's right foot. Choose the **Rectangle Select** tool from the toolbox. Use the guide as the right edge for a selection that covers the left side of the layer. Drag the background color (which should be white) from the toolbox into the selection.

6. Move the **White Backdrop** layer down so it is below the Boarder layer.

7. Deselect all (CTRL-SHIFT-A), and then hide the guide (**View ▸ Show Guides**).

The White Backdrop layer is placed below the Boarder layer. This small detail is what makes the boarder seem to pop out of the Rocky Mountain scene and enter the white poster area.

Adding a Drop Shadow

A drop shadow adds to the pop effect.

1. In the Layers dialog click the **Boarder** layer to make that layer active.

2. Add a drop shadow (**Script-Fu ▸ Shadow ▸ Drop Shadow**). Set the Offset X and Y values to **5 pixels** and the Blur Radius to **15 pixels**. Set the Opacity to **80 percent** and uncheck the box next to the words *Allow Resizing*. Click **OK** to apply these settings and create the drop shadow layer.

3. Click the **Drop Shadow** layer in the Layers dialog to make that layer active. Add a white layer mask (**Layers ▸ Mask ▸ Add Layer Mask**).

4. Click the **White Backdrop** layer in the Layers dialog to make that layer active. Create a selection of the transparent region by first choosing **Layer ▸ Transparency ▸ Alpha to Selection** and then choosing **Select ▸ Invert**.

5. Click the **Drop Shadow** layer again. Drag the foreground color (which should be black) from the toolbox into the selection.

6. Deselect all (CTRL-SHIFT-A).

The drop shadow makes it appear as though there is some distance between boarder and the white background.

Replacing the Background

We want it to be clear from the advertisement that the event is being held in the Rocky Mountain region of Colorado. Let's add in the mountains as a background layer.

1. Click the **Boarder** layer to make that layer active.

2. Open an appropriate background image, such as this one of the Rocky Mountains. Copy and paste the image into a new layer (**Layer ▸ New**) and name the new layer *Mountain*.

3. Use the **Scale** tool to resize the layer so that it is as big as the canvas, and then move the **Mountain** layer below the White Backdrop layer in the Layers dialog. Adjust the placement of the **Mountain** layer as appropriate.

4. Open the Motion Blur filter (**Filters ▸ Blur ▸ Motion Blur**). Set the Blur Type to **Linear**, set the Length to **5 pixels**, and set the Angle to **180 degrees**. Click **OK** to apply these settings to the Mountain layer.

Having removed the sky background, we replace it with an image that is more appropriate for the project. A light motion blur adds depth to the new background and assures that the mountains don't distract from the boarder.

Adding Text

It's time for the finishing touches. Let's add text to the poster. If you want to render the text as I do, you can use the FreeType plug-in, which is available at http://freetype.gimp.org. Duplicate the text twice and color the top version yellow. Offset the two layers by a few pixels to simulate depth. Make sure your text layers are at the top of the layer stack so you can see them over the layer masks and background images.

If the font and color you choose makes it difficult to read the text, you may want to add a drop shadow over the boarder's leg.

Further Exploration

Projects like this one are sometimes the most fun because they aren't particularly difficult. As is true of many of the techniques described in this book, the hard part is creating good selections that isolate your intended subject. The Quick Mask tool is your best bet for objects that have many curves and edges, as this boarder's leg does. If the object you're trying to isolate has straighter edges and the background is a solid color, you can try using the Scissors tool.

4.6 SHINY EMBLEM

Whether you're designing a T-shirt, a website, or letterhead for the company office, chances are good you're going to use some kind of identifying symbol. While printed symbols are often easier (and cheaper) to create in solid colors, designing for the Web allows a bit more flexibility. Color is king on the Web, and because high-resolution, 16M-color monitor screens are the norm, three-dimensional effects are equally widespread.

Even a solitary letter can benefit from reflective techniques.

Symbols play an important role in design, and they can make or break a product or company image—better known in the graphic arts industry as an *identity*. The symbol itself may be flat and solid, flat and textured, or three-dimensional with light effects and shadows. Visual identities are the symbols of the companies we know—just think about McDonald's Golden Arches, a Red Hat for Linux, or IBM's Big Blue.

Logos usually include text that is set in a specific font, and the text is often accompanied by a shape that represents the company, group, or individual. As part of an overall identity campaign, logos are sometimes embedded within other shapes to create emblems.

One of the easiest emblems to create is a round, reflective logo that resembles glass. A glass logo uses soft gradients with little or no grain visible. Many white ovals (or partial ovals) are layered

and placed over the logo to simulate reflections. Sometimes these round reflections are even outlined with distinct edges to simulate a frame in which the logo is set.

A metallic logo is even easier to create. The technique is based on the fact that reflections in metal aren't as wide as reflections in glass, and they have more high-contrast areas between light and shadow. In the case of a metallic logo, the metal might be the focal point—as in a belt buckle or lapel pin—or you might just use metallic edges to accent a nonmetallic design, which is what we do in this tutorial.

Getting Started

When designing these emblems it helps to examine real-world objects like glass buttons or even silver spoons. Notice how the light and colors reflect. One trick is to blur your eyes a little—try to see the reflections without focusing on the shape of the object. Then try to reproduce the effect with the GIMP.

Adding reflectivity and color not only adds style to your design, it's also incredibly easy to do with the GIMP. In this tutorial we work on a small canvas to demonstrate the ease with which the technique can be applied. Remember that raster images—like those we create in the GIMP—don't scale up to larger sizes very well, so start with a larger canvas and scale up the *technique* if you need a bigger emblem.

Creating a Metallic Border

1. With the toolbox selected, press **D** to reset the foreground and background colors to black and white, respectively.

2. Select **File ▸ New**. In the Create a New Image dialog, keep the dimensions set to 420 × 300 pixels. In the Advanced Options

section, choose **Foreground Color** from the drop-down menu next to the words *Fill With* to create a black canvas. Click **OK** to open the new canvas window.

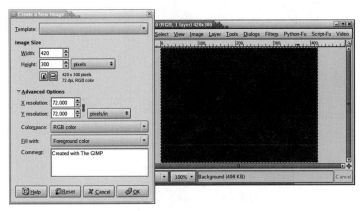

A black canvas provides a high-contrast background for this project.

3. Choose the **Ellipse Select** tool from the toolbox. While holding down the SHIFT key, click and drag on the canvas to create a circular selection in the center of the canvas.

4. If the selection is not exactly centered on the canvas, use the **Move** tool to position the selection. (The cursor should become a selection box with move arrows to indicate that you can reposition the selection.)

5. Choose the **Blend** tool from the toolbox. In the Tool Options dialog, choose the **Crown Molding** gradient. Click and drag from the upper left to the lower right of the selection.

6. Add a new transparent layer by choosing **Layer ▸ New** and setting the Layer Fill Type to **Transparency**. Name the new layer *Ring Color*.

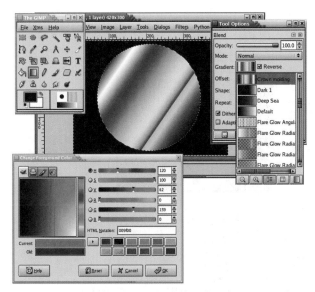

The Crown Molding gradient is applied to the selection. It's okay to apply this effect to the Background layer. Putting the circular selection in its own layer won't make editing it later much easier, because the selection and gradient are pretty easy to reproduce.

7. Click (or double-click) the foreground color box to change the foreground color. In the Change Foreground Color dialog, set the RGB values to **0/159/0** for the green shown here, and then click **OK** to close the dialog. The circular selection should still be active, so just drag the foreground color into the selection.

NOTE *Double-clicking the foreground or background color box is required only when the alternate box is currently active. For example, if the background color box is active (it appears behind the foreground color box in the toolbox) and you want to open the Change Foreground Color dialog, the first click makes the foreground color box active, and the second click opens the Change Foreground Color dialog.*

8. In the Layers dialog set the layer mode to **Soft Light** and the Opacity to **50 percent.**

Use the Soft Light layer mode to blend the colored layer with the circular selection that has been filled with a gradient. Because we use a separate color layer, we can change the color of the image by simply changing the color in that layer.

Creating an Emblem

1. Add another new transparent layer by choosing **Layer ▸ New** and setting the Layer Fill Type to **Transparency.** Name this new layer *Emblem Color.*

2. Shrink the selection by **10 pixels** (**Select ▸ Shrink**), and then feather the selection by **2.5 pixels** (**Select ▸ Feather**).

3. Open the Change Foreground Color dialog again and set the RGB values to **169/7/7** for the red shown here, and then close the dialog. Drag the foreground color into the selection.

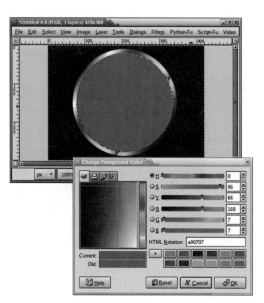

A red selection covers most of the Crown Molding gradient in the Background layer. Where the gradient shows through, the red selection appears to have a metallic border.

Adding an Inner Border

At this point, we have the basic metallic emblem. The rest of the tutorial shows how to get creative with this basic shape. Let's start by adding a slight brushed-metal effect.

1. Add a new transparent layer and name it *Brushed Metal.*

2. Open the Hurl filter (**Filters ▸ Noise ▸ Hurl**). Set the Random Seed to **10,** set the Randomization to **35 percent,** and set the Repeat to **2 times.** Click **OK** to apply this to the new layer.

3. In the Layers dialog set the layer mode to **Multiply** and the Opacity to **50 percent.**

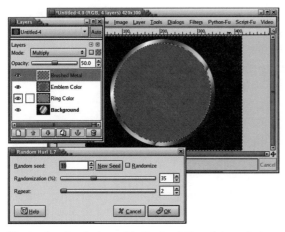

We simulate brushed metal in Section 3.2, and the technique is the same here.

4. Add a new layer and name it *Inner Ring*.

5. Shrink the selection by **25 pixels** (**Select ▸ Shrink**).

6. With the toolbox selected, press **D** to reset the background and foreground colors. Fill the selection with black by dragging the foreground color into the selection.

7. Shrink the selection by **4 pixels**.

8. Press CTRL-X to cut out the selection from the Inner Ring layer and leave behind a thin, black ring.

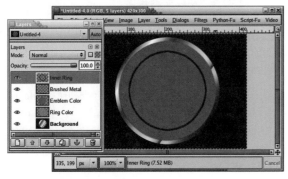

Unlike the outer ring, the inner ring is created by cutting out a selection from a black circle.

9. Open the Gaussian Blur filter (**Filters ▸ Blur ▸ Gaussian Blur**). Set the Blur Radius to **3 pixels**, and then apply the blur to the Inner Ring layer.

10. Create a selection from this layer by choosing **Layer ▸ Transparency ▸ Alpha to Selection**.

11. Add a layer mask to the Emblem Color layer by choosing **Layer ▸ Masks ▸ Add Layer Mask**. In the Add Layer Mask dialog, click the radio button next to the word *Selection* and check the box next to the words *Invert Mask*. This automatically creates a mask in the shape of the black ring.

The black ring is used as a layer mask that is applied to the emblem layer.

Adding Raised Lettering

1. Click the **Inner Ring** layer and invert its colors (**Layer ▸ Colors ▸ Invert**).

2. Set its layer mode to **Grain Extract**.

3. Choose the **Text** tool from the toolbox. In the Tool Options dialog, choose a large, thick font. I used Utopia Bold sized to 150 pixels in this example.

4. Click the canvas to open the Text Editor. Type M and close the dialog. If necessary, use the **Move** tool to align the text layer.

5. Duplicate the text layer (**Layer ▸ Duplicate**), and then invert its color to white by choosing **Layer ▸ Colors ▸ Invert**. Name the duplicate layer *White Outline*.

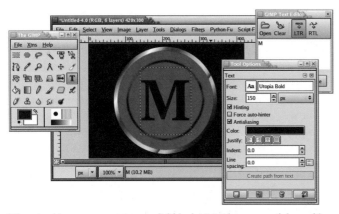

The raised letter starts out as a solid black M in the center of the emblem.

6. Choose **Layer ▸ Transform ▸ Offset** and set the Offset X and Offset Y values to **–1 pixel**.

7. Duplicate the original text layer again, naming the duplicate layer *Black Outline* this time.

8. Choose **Layer ▸ Transform ▸ Offset** once more, but set the Offset X and Offset Y values to **1 pixel** this time.

9. In the Layers dialog move the original text layer so that it is between the White Outline and Black Outline layers.

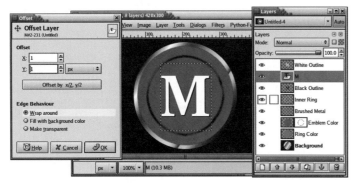

The white letter becomes a highlight for the black letter, making it look as though the letter is raised.

10. Click the **White Outline** layer to make that layer active.

11. Open the Gaussian Blur filter (**Filters ▸ Blur ▸ Gaussian Blur**) and apply a blur of **2.5 pixels** to the White Outline layer.

12. Set the White Outline layer size to match the image size (**Layer ▸ Layer to Image Size**).

13. Click the original text layer and create a selection by choosing **Layer ▸ Transparency ▸ Alpha to Selection**.

14. Click the **White Outline** layer to make that layer active again.

15. Press CTRL-X to cut out the selection from the White Outline layer.

16. Once more click the original text layer and create a selection by choosing **Layer ▸ Transparency ▸ Alpha to Selection**.

17. Click the **Black Outline** layer to make that layer active, and then cut out the selection from that layer.

18. Set the original text layer's mode to **Overlay** and its Opacity to **66.7 percent**.

Create a white border by cutting out the original letter from the blurred and offset White Outline layer.

19. Once more click the original text layer and create a selection by choosing **Layer ▸ Transparency ▸ Alpha to Selection**.

20. Set the RGB values for the foreground color to **172/172/172** for the red shown here.

21. Click the **Emblem Color** layer mask to make it active.

22. Drag the foreground color from the toolbox into the selection and then deselect all (SHIFT-CTRL-A).

The offset black shadow works with the white highlight to complete the raised-letter effect.

Further Exploration

A letter with curves that match the curve of the emblem might look more impressive than this somewhat ordinary *M*. You can also convert paths to selections to create your own curvy letters. If you do so, remember to save the selections so you can recall them when it's time to create the white highlight and black shadow layers.

4.7 A CHANGE OF WEATHER

Companies use advertising to convince consumers to buy their products or use their services. Most advertising is graphics intensive—a picture is worth a thousand words, right? But sometimes a picture by itself is not enough.

This tutorial will show you how to create a print ad for a fictional financial institution. The plan is to set an image of a tropical island against the backdrop of a gloomy, rainy night. To complete the picture, we add a tag line that reads, "Looking for a change in weather?" The ad will be printed in magazines at 150 dpi, and we've been told that it can be no larger than 4.5 inches × 3.25 inches. This means that the image must be no larger than 675 × 487 pixels (rounding down to whole pixel values). With this in mind, let's create an advertisement that is 640 × 480 pixels.

This tutorial will take the gloom out of a rainy day project.

Getting Started

Start with a stock photo of a tropical island, and open the image file in the GIMP. The one I use here is originally larger than 640 × 480 pixels, so it is scaled down to 640 × 480 pixels at a resolution of **150 dpi**.

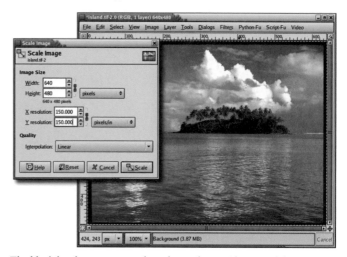

The black borders are cropped out later, along with most of the water.

Creating the Credit Card

1. Drag horizontal and vertical guides from the rulers to outline the portion of the image that looks best—in this case, the island is right of center, leaving room for the raised lettering we'll add later. Use the guides and the **Rectangle Select** tool to

create a selection, and then grow the selection by **6 pixels** (**Select ▸ Grow**). This has the effect of rounding the edges of the selection.

2. Invert this selection (**Select ▸ Invert**) and then add an alpha channel to the image (**Layer ▸ Transparency ▸ Add Alpha Channel**). Press CTRL-X to cut away the rest of the image. This is the basic shape of the credit card.

3. Remove all guides (**Image ▸ Guides ▸ Remove All Guides**).

NOTE *If the Add Alpha Channel option is grayed out, your image already contains transparency information. In this case, you don't need to add an alpha channel.*

We cut away the excess portions of the image, instead of cropping the image, because later we're going to grow this canvas and add additional components, like the stormy weather.

Adding the Company Name

1. In the Layers dialog check the **Keep Transparency** box for this layer.

2. Press **D** to reset the foreground color.

3. Use the **Rectangle Select** tool to create a selection that includes the bottom fourth or so of the island image, and then fill the selection with white by dragging the foreground color from the toolbox into the selection. Deselect all (SHIFT-CTRL-A).

NOTE *If the selection won't cover the entire area you're trying to select, it might be because the Rectangle Select tool isn't set to the correct mode. Look in the Tool Options dialog and set the mode to Replace by clicking the first box from the left next to the word* Mode.

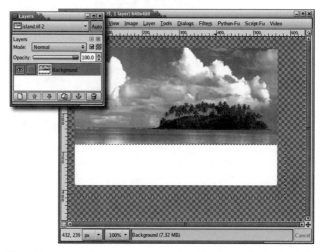

The white box works as a text screen, just like the one in Section 2.9.

4. Choose the **Text** tool from the toolbox and click the image to open the Text Editor. Type the name of the financial institution. In the Tool Options dialog, select an appropriate font, size, and color. I used Times New Roman Bold, sized to 30 pixels and colored light blue (set the RBG values to **129/200/255** to match it).

5. Use the **Move** tool to position the text layer so that it is below the island and vertically centered in the white area at the bottom of the image.

6. Add a drop shadow to the text (**Script-Fu ▸ Shadow ▸ Drop Shadow**). Set the Offset X and Offset Y values to **1 pixel**, set the Blur Radius to **3 pixels**, and set the Opacity to **90 percent**. Click **OK** to apply the drop shadow.

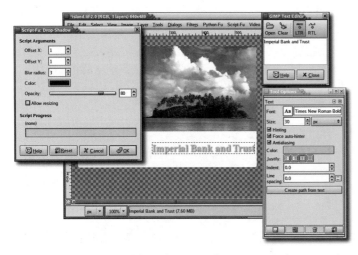

The advertiser's name should stand out. You don't want people to remember "that island ad" but forget the name of the company being advertised!

Adding Raised Lettering

1. Click the **Background** layer to make that layer active.

2. Choose the Text tool from the toolbox. Select an appropriate font. This example uses MagneticCardTwo Bold, which is available from online font archives (search for *MagneticCardTwo font*) and font CD collections. The OCR font family is similar, and it may be easier to find online (search for *OCR font*).

3. Set the font to white and size it to **22 pixels**. Click the canvas and type an imaginary cardholder name. Click **OK** to close the Text Editor.

4. Use the **Move** tool to place the text as shown.

5. Add a drop shadow (**Script-Fu ▸ Shadows ▸ Drop Shadow**). Set the Offset X and Offset Y values to **1 pixel**, set the Radius to **2 pixels**, and set the Opacity to **85 percent**. Click **OK** to apply the drop shadow.

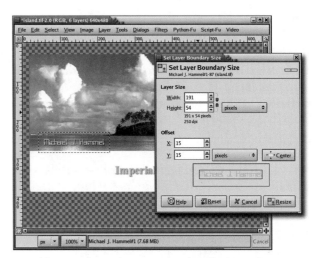

Raised lettering draws the viewer into the advertisement.

6. Duplicate the layer that contains the name. Increase the layer boundary by about **30 pixels** in both width and height by choosing **Layer ▸ Layer Boundary Size**.

7. Open the Gaussian Blur filter (**Filters ▸ Blur ▸ Gaussian Blur**), set the Blur Method to **RLE**, and apply a blur of **10 pixels** to the duplicate layer.

8. Click the original name layer to make that layer active.

9. Open the Bump Map filter (**Filters ▸ Map ▸ Bump Map**) and choose the duplicate layer from the Bump Map drop-down menu. Click **OK** to apply the Bump Map filter. Delete the duplicate layer.

10. Set the name layer's mode to **Grain Merge**.

11. Create a selection of the text by choosing **Layer ▸ Transparency ▸ Alpha to Selection**.

12. Click the **Background** layer to make that layer active. Press CTRL-C to copy from that layer, and then press CTRL-V and choose **Layer ▸ New Layer** to paste the copied selection as a new layer. Set the layer mode for this new layer to **Grain Merge**.

13. Reduce the opacity of the layers as necessary to improve the overall effect.

14. Repeat this process to add an account number.

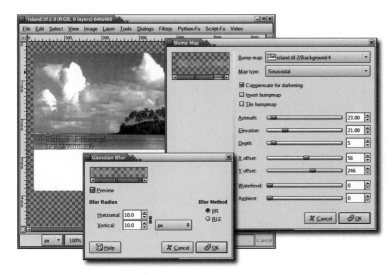

If the combination of the Gaussian Blur and Bump Map filters doesn't produce a suitable raised effect, try using the Emboss filter instead.

Creating the Stormy Background

The last major element we need to create is the stormy background, which will contrast nicely with the image of the tropical island.

1. Merge all of the visible layers (**Image ▸ Merge Visible Layers**) and then turn off the visibility of this layer.

2. Add a new transparent layer by choosing **Layer ▸ New** and setting the Layer Fill Type to **Transparency**. Fill the new layer with dark gray (set the RGB values to **85/84/84** for the gray shown here).

3. Add another new transparent layer.

4. Open the Plasma filter (**Filters ▸ Render ▸ Clouds ▸ Plasma**). Set the Turbulence slider to **1.2** and check the box next to the word *Randomize*. Click **OK** to apply the filter.

5. Desaturate this new layer (**Layer ▸ Colors ▸ Desaturate**).

6. Choose **Layer ▸ Colors ▸ Brightness ▸ Contrast** and adjust the **Brightness** and **Contrast** sliders to reduce the amount of white.

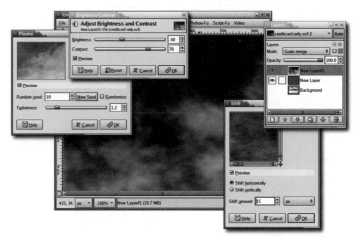

The Plasma filter produces a colored cloud. Desaturating the layer makes the background look like a night scene. You don't have to apply the Shift filter, but doing so spreads the effect across the image.

Adding Rain

1. Add a new transparent layer for the rain.

2. Open the Hurl filter (**Filters ▸ Noise ▸ Hurl**), set the Randomization slider to **75 percent**, but leave the Random Seed and Repeat settings unchanged. Then click **OK** to fill the layer with noise.

3. Use the **Gaussian Blur** filter to apply a blur of **3 pixels**.

4. Open the Motion Blur filter (**Filters ▸ Blur ▸ Motion Blur**). Set the Blur Type to **Linear**, the Length to **20 pixels**, and the Angle to **100 degrees**. Click **OK** to apply the blur.

5. Open the Curves tool (**Layer ▸ Colors ▸ Curves**) and adjust the **Value** curve as shown. You may find that changing the layer mode to Grain Merge helps; but depending on the shape of the clouds in the layer below, that change may not be necessary.

6. Desaturate the layer (**Layer ▸ Colors ▸ Desaturate**).

7. Open the Shift filter (**Filters ▸ Distorts ▸ Shift**). Select **Shift Horizontally** and set the Shift Amount to **15 pixels**. Open the **Gaussian Blur** filter, set the Blur Radius to **10 pixels**, and then click **OK** to apply the blur. Set this layer's mode to **Grain Merge**.

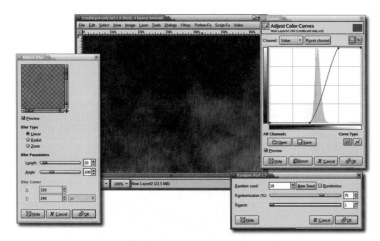

Rain is easy to create, but there has to be enough contrast between the background and the rain for the rain to be visible. In some cases you can make the rain more visible by duplicating the rain layer one or more times, setting the layer mode for each of the duplicate layers to Addition and then merging all of the rain layers.

Adding Lightning

The next step is to create the lightning, a process we covered in Section 2.12. This process is prone to huge variations, so don't be discouraged if your lightning bolts look significantly different. Experiment, experiment, experiment!

1. Add a new transparent layer by choosing **Layer ▸ New** and setting the Layer Fill Type to **Transparency**.

2. Choose the **Blend** tool from the toolbox. In the Tool Options dialog, set the Gradient to **FG to BG (RGB)**. Drag along a short line, a bit left of the middle of the canvas and at a slight downward angle.

3. Add another new transparent layer. Apply the Plasma filter to the layer (**Filters ▸ Render ▸ Clouds ▸ Plasma**), using the same settings used previously for the stormy background, and then desaturate the layer (**Layer ▸ Colors ▸ Desaturate**).

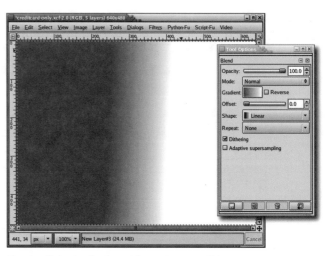

Creating lightning begins with creating a gradient.

4. Set the plasma layer's mode to **Difference** and then use the Curves tool (**Layer ▸ Color ▸ Curves**) to adjust the gradient layer's **Value** curve until you achieve something that looks like a black bolt of lightning.

5. Merge the plasma and gradient layers (**Layer ▸ Merge Down**) and then invert the merged layer (**Layer ▸ Colors ▸ Invert**).

6. Use the Curves tool (**Layer ▸ Colors ▸ Curves**) to adjust the **Value** curve for this layer, as shown on the next page, to pull the lightning bolt from the background noise.

7. Set the merged layer's mode to **Screen**. This will pull out the lightning bolt and remove the layer's black background from the scene.

8. Select and copy portions of the lightning bolt and paste them as new layers. Use layer masks, the Scale tool, or distort filters (**Filters ▸ Distorts**) to modify the pasted layers, and then set the layer mode to Screen to hide the background.

9. Move these layers around to add lightning bolts that fork off from the original.

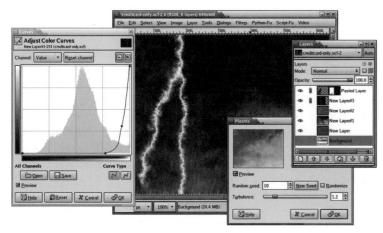

Color will be added to the lighting bolt, though a black-and-white background might make the island image look that much more attractive.

Assembling the Pieces

1. Turn on the visibility of the island layer and move it to the very top of the layer stack.

2. Use the **Scale** tool to resize the island layer so it fits comfortably in the upper two-thirds of the image window and is placed just to the right of the lightning bolts.

3. To give the island even more appeal, use the Curves tool to enhance the color (**Layer ▸ Color ▸ Curves**). You can also add a drop shadow to make that layer stand out in front of the gloomy backdrop.

4. Add color to the lightning bolts by adding a new layer just above the bolts (**Layer ▸ New**) and filling the layer with color. Click the foreground color box, choose a shade of purple, and drag the foreground color into the new layer.

5. Set the layer mode for the purple layer to **Dodge** and reduce its Opacity to about **60 percent**. The Opacity level and layer mode you choose may vary, depending on the shape and intensity of your lightning.

NOTE *If adding the purple layer causes the entire rainy sky to be filled with purple, try adding a layer mask to the purple layer and copying and pasting the lightning layer into that mask.*

Use the Move tool to position the credit card in the upper-right corner of the canvas, leaving room for a tag line below.

6. Click the **Storm** layer to make that layer active.

7. Choose the **Text** tool from the toolbox. Type `Looking for a change in weather?` in white.

8. Add a drop shadow (**Script-Fu ▸ Shadows ▸ Drop Shadow**). Set the Offset X and Offset Y values to **2 pixels,** set the Blur Radius to **3 pixels,** and set the Opacity to **90 percent.** Add multiple drop shadows blurred and offset by slightly different amounts to force the text to stand out against the stormy background.

9. Duplicate the text layer, select and then delete everything except the word *weather*.

10. Check the **Keep Transparency** box for this duplicate layer and fill the layer with a light-blue color.

Placing the layer that contains the tag line text above all the other layers prevents the rain from obscuring the text. If you use a larger font, you may consider placing the text layer below the rain for added effect.

Further Exploration

The color you choose for the lightning is an important variable. Leaving the lightning desaturated might have made that portion of the advertisement feel even drearier. To take this project further, you could make adjustments to the three main components: the lightning, the credit card, and the tag line. The credit card, for example, could be made larger, and the tag line could be centered below the island image instead. These are personal preferences that add to the overall impact of the ad. Once you've learned the tricks to create the initial version, the rest is just where you let your personal touch shine through.

4.8 CLOTH CURTAIN

In Section 4.4 we used light and shadow to simulate reflections. But light and shadow can be used to simulate surfaces that aren't as reflective as glass or metal. They can be used to simulate the texture and folds of a cloth curtain, for example. The technique described in this tutorial can be used to create folded napkins, towels, shirts that wave in the wind, or even giant theater curtains. And it's fairly easy to use the GIMP to produce realistic cloth surfaces. The first trick is to find a suitable texture, and the second is to use gradients to add folds.

Suitable textures can be found just about anywhere. In this tutorial we'll use a stock pattern from the GIMP called Gold Cloth. Textures can also come from photographs, stock image archives, or even scans of interesting patterns.

Gradients are then used to produce highlights—areas of light next to areas of shadow—in the cloth texture. Creating your own gradient is always a possibility, but this tutorial uses the GIMP's Crown Molding gradient, one that has been part of the GIMP package for many versions and provides ready-made waves of light and shadow that map to the folds we seek.

Cloth effects are more common in print advertising because the wrinkles can be difficult to see at the resolution required for web ads. The process for creating cloth is easily scaled, however. Here we work on an image that is slightly smaller than a real-world print ad would be, to illustrate the process in a way that doesn't require a lot of memory.

Get a view of what you can do, with the GIMP!

Getting Started

Eventually we'll make this image twice the size of the default canvas, but let's start with a canvas set to the default size (420 × 300 pixels).

1. Open a new canvas by choosing **File ▸ New** from the toolbox.

2. Choose the **Bucket Fill** tool and in the Tool Options dialog set the Fill Type to **Pattern Fill**. In the text field below this option type **Gold Cloth** and press ENTER. Click the canvas to fill it with the pattern.

3. Desaturate the layer (**Layer ▸ Colors ▸ Desaturate**) and then add an alpha channel to this layer (**Layer ▸ Transparency ▸ Add Alpha Channel**).

NOTE *The Gold Cloth pattern comes in the gimp-data-extras package. Fedora users should try* yum install gimp-data-extras. *If your Linux distribution doesn't have these extras packaged for you, you can download them from one of the GIMP source code mirror sites, such as the one at http://gimp.mirrors.hoobly.com/ gimp/extras.*

6. Scale the image by **200 percent** (**Image ▸ Scale Image**).

7. With the canvas selected, press minus to zoom out once, and then press CTRL-E to resize the window to fit the canvas.

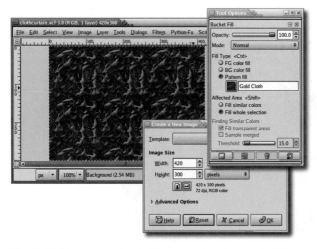

The Gold Cloth pattern is suitable for creating the curtain. We want to change the color, however, and we start by desaturating the layer.

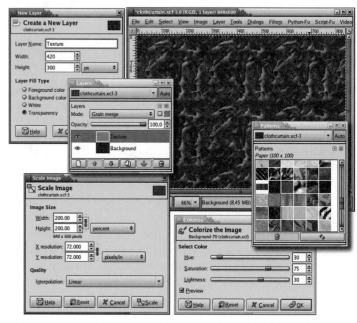

It's usually not a good idea to scale up a raster image like this one, but the details lost when we scale up the Gold Cloth pattern won't be noticeable in the texture of the curtain.

Designing the Cloth

1. Add a new transparent layer by choosing **Layer ▸ New** and setting the Layer Fill Type to Transparency. Name the new layer *Texture*.

2. Open the Patterns dialog (**Dialogs ▸ Patterns**) and select **Paper**.

3. With the **Bucket Fill** tool still active, click the canvas to fill the new layer with this texture.

4. Set the layer mode to **Grain Merge** in the Layers dialog. Merge this layer with the Background layer (**Layer ▸ Merge Down**).

5. Use the Colorize tool to colorize the layer (**Layer ▸ Colors ▸ Colorize**). Set the Hue to **30**, set the Saturation to **75**, and set the Lightness to **30**. You can certainly choose another color, but this one happens to match the freckles of the boy we'll add in later.

Adding Folds

1. Add a new transparent layer by choosing **Layer ▸ New** and setting the Layer Fill Type to **Transparency**. Name the new layer *Curtain*.

2. Choose the **Blend** tool from the toolbox. In the Tool Options dialog set the Gradient to **Crown Molding**, the Shape to **Bi-Linear**, and the Repeat to **Triangular Wave**. Drag from left to right across the middle of the canvas.

3. Open the Gaussian Blur filter (**Filters ▸ Blur ▸ Gaussian Blur**). Set the Blur Radius to **5 pixels** and click **OK** to apply the blur.

4. Duplicate the layer (**Layer ▶ Duplicate**), and then merge the duplicate layer with the original layer (**Layer ▶ Merge Down**). This last step just enhances the appearance of the folds in the curtain. In the Layers dialog set the layer mode for the Curtain layer to **Overlay**.

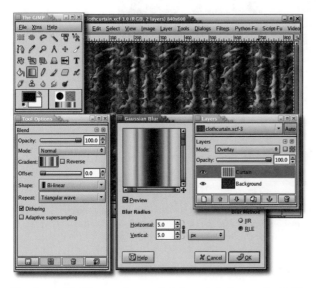

The Crown Molding gradient adds light and shadow to the Gold Cloth texture, giving us a first glimpse at the hanging curtain.

Creating the Left Curtain

1. Duplicate the Curtain layer (**Layer ▶ Duplicate**). Name this layer *Left Curtain*.

2. Temporarily turn off the visibility for the original Curtain layer.

3. Scale the layer to **60 percent** of its original width (**Layer ▶ Scale Layer**), but leave the height unchanged.

4. Align the left edge of the layers (**Layer ▶ Align Visible Layers**) using the settings shown here in the Align Visible Layers dialog.

NOTE *In the Scale Layer dialog there is a small chain link icon to the right of the Width and Height fields. If you click this link, it breaks and allows you to set values in one field without affecting the value in the other field. If the link is intact, changing the value in one field will automatically update the value in the other field because the width-to-height aspect ratio is maintained.*

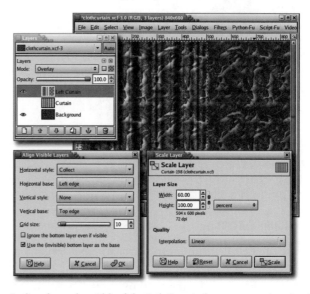

Scaling down the width of the Left Curtain layer squeezes it so its right edge is just right of center on the canvas. This allows the top edge of the Left Curtain layer to overlap the left edge of the Right Curtain layer when we drag the bottom of the Left Curtain layer to the left.

5. Choose the **Perspective** tool from the toolbox. Click the canvas to display the tool's handles, and then drag the duplicate layer's lower-right handle to the left as shown. Click the **Transform** button in the Perspective Transform Information dialog to apply the change.

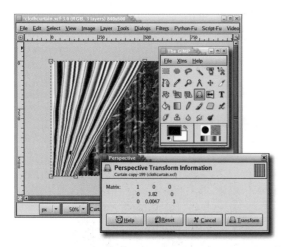

When using the Perspective tool, the canvas displays the layer in raw form so you can see how the changes affect the layer in which you're working. When you click the Transform button, the raw preview is removed and the canvas is displayed as usual.

Creating the Right Curtain

1. Duplicate the Left Curtain layer (**Layer ▸ Duplicate**) and name the new layer *Right Curtain*.

2. Choose the **Flip** tool from the toolbox. In the Tool Options dialog set the Flip Type to **Horizontal**. Set the Affect to **Transform Layer** by clicking the first button from the left. Click the canvas to flip the layer horizontally.

3. Turn off the visibility of the Left Curtain layer. Use the settings shown here to align the visible layers (**Layer ▸ Align Visible Layers**), and then turn on the visibility of the Left Curtain layer.

4. Set the layer mode for both curtain layers to **Normal,** and then merge the Right Curtain layer with the Left Curtain layer (**Layer ▸ Merge Down**). Set the merged layer's mode to **Overlay.**

5. Delete the original Curtain layer from the Layers dialog (**Layer ▸ Delete Layer**). Rename the *Left Curtain* layer *Curtain.*

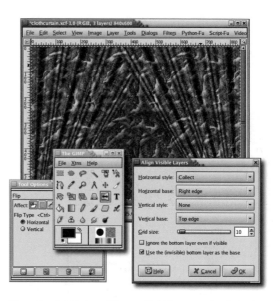

Changing the shape of the gradient layers makes it look as though the curtains have been pulled back. The Gold Cloth layer (which provides the texture for this effect) remains unchanged.

Parting the Curtain

1. Temporarily turn off the visibility of the Background layer.

2. Choose the **Fuzzy Select** tool from the toolbox. Click the **Curtain** layer to make that layer active. Click the transparent region of the canvas to select it.

3. Feather the selection by **3 pixels** (**Select ▸ Feather**).

4. Click the **Background** layer to make that layer active. Add a white layer mask to that layer (**Layer ▸ Mask ▸ Add Layer Mask**).

5. With the canvas selected, press **D** to reset the foreground color to black. Drag the foreground color from the toolbox into the selection to mask out this area.

6. Turn on the visibility of the Background layer.

7. Deselect all (CTRL-SHIFT-A).

8. Apply the layer mask to the Background layer (**Layer ▸ Mask ▸ Apply Layer Mask**).

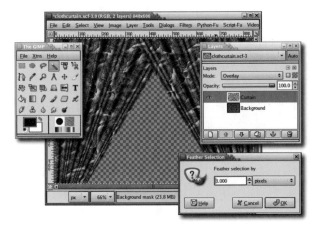

The selection created in the Curtain layer is filled with black in a white layer mask that is added to the Background layer. Where we fill with black in the mask, the Background layer becomes transparent (indicated by the checkered pattern).

9. Click the **Curtain** layer to make that layer active. Merge the Curtain layer with the Background layer (**Layer ▸ Merge Down**).

10. Open the Drop Shadow dialog (**Script-Fu ▸ Shadow ▸ Drop Shadow**). Click **Reset,** and then uncheck the box next to the words *Allow Resizing.* Click **OK** to add the drop shadow.

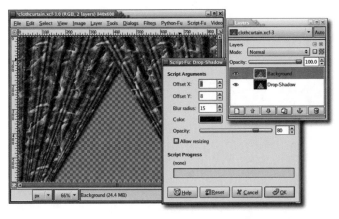

A drop shadow that is only slightly offset from the curtain adds depth to the image.

Adding an Image Behind the Curtain

1. Open the image you've chosen to place behind the curtain—this one is of a freckle-faced boy. Copy the image, click the **Curtain** layer in the Layers dialog to make sure it's the active layer, and then paste the image as a new layer by pressing CTRL-V and then choosing **Layer ▸ New.**

2. Move the new layer below the Drop-Shadow layer in the Layers dialog so the boy looks like he is peeking out from behind the curtain.

3. Resize the layer that contains the boy if necessary and then use the **Move** tool to position the image appropriately.

NOTE   *The pasted layer might need to be moved so its edges overlap the edges of the canvas. Overlapping is fine because any part of the pasted layer outside the bounds of the canvas is unnecessary anyway. When you save the image as a TIFF or JPEG, those areas are simply cropped from the image. If you save the project in the GIMP's native XCF format, however, those overlapping areas are saved in their layer.*

A freckle-faced boy peeks out from behind the parted curtain.

Further Exploration

As you can see, using a wave-filled gradient in combination with a layer that contains texture is the key to simulating cloth. There are many ways to generate a flowing pattern that can then be used to add even more texture to the image. The Crown Molding gradient is only the most obvious choice. The Pattern dialog's Contra Swirl pattern can serve as a blend layer as well. In fact, many of the GIMP's stock patterns can be used with this technique. While the pattern's original form might not be suitable, all that's required is to desaturate it and then use the Gaussian Blur filter to apply a generous blur, mixing in adjustments with the Levels or Curves tools to achieve a smooth gradient.

4.9 CITYSCAPE

As you've seen in previous tutorials, 3D effects are popular in all kinds of advertising, and there are many ways to use the GIMP to create 3D images in a just a few short steps. This tutorial presents one more method, showing you how to use three stock filters to create an imaginary cityscape of high-rise buildings. This tutorial proves that, when used in combination, the noise filters and the Cubism and Wind filters are more than just the sum of their parts.

For larger versions of the cityscape, such as those intended for print, you may need to repeatedly scale, blur, and apply the Unsharp Mask to the image to achieve the desired effect. The exact settings for the Unsharp Mask filter will depend on the results of the Cubism filter, and those results will be different every time because the Cubism filter uses randomization.

You can also incorporate the resulting image into a poster or flier by simply adding text, but make sure to place the text where there is enough contrast so it can be read easily. Placing white text over the solid black background would be best.

This tutorial creates a shimmering, impressionistic cityscape.

Getting Started

Start with a canvas set to **480 × 640** pixels at **250 dpi** (change the resolution in the Advanced Options section of the Create a New Image dialog). You can easily create a canvas of these dimensions by using the 640 × 480 template in the Create a New Image dialog. Just swap the width and height values, or rotate the image 90 degrees (Image ▸ Transform ▸ Rotate 90 degrees CW). This will produce an image that is about 2.5 × 1.9 inches, though you can scale up the techniques used in this tutorial. If you use this tutorial for a print project, the size of the paper can be changed to suit your needs. GIMP 2.*x* users, for example, can use the A4 or US Legal templates for a new image but should be aware that these default to 72 dpi, which is not a suitable resolution for print projects and should be adjusted before going forward. When everything is in order, click **OK** to create the new image and then fill the canvas with black.

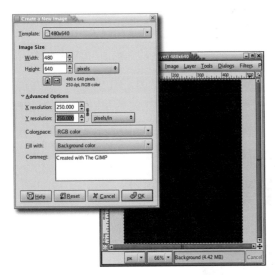

This project starts with a black Background layer.

Adding Noise with the Hurl Filter

1. Choose **Image ▸ Guides ▸ New Guide (by Percent)** to add a horizontal guide at 50 percent.

2. Create a rectangular selection of the bottom half of the canvas. Copy and paste this selection as a new layer. Name the new layer *Cubism*.

3. Use the Hurl filter (**Filters ▸ Noise ▸ Hurl**) to fill the new layer with noise. Set the Random Seed to **10** and the Randomization to **80 percent**. Click **OK** to apply this filter to the new layer.

4. Desaturate the layer (**Layer ▸ Colors ▸ Desaturate**).

5. Remove the guide (**Image ▸ Guides ▸ Remove All Guides**).

Adding a Pattern with the Cubism Filter

1. Center the Cubism layer by choosing **Layer ▸ Align Visible Layers**. Set the Horizontal Style to **None**, set the Horizontal Base to **Left Edge**, set the Vertical Style to **Collect**, and set the Vertical Base to **Center**. Check the box next to the words *Use the (invisible) bottom layer as the base*. Click **OK** to center the layer.

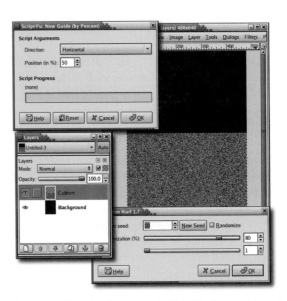

Copying and pasting the bottom half the Background layer is an easy way to create a new layer of the required size. Alternatively, we could add a new layer (Layer ▸ New) scaled to half the size of the canvas.

2. Open the Cubism filter (**Filters ▸ Artistic ▸ Cubism**). Set the Tile Size slider to **35 pixels** and the Tile Saturation slider to **2.7**, and then click **OK** to apply the filter to the Cubism layer.

3. Adjust the layer size so that it equals the size of the full canvas (**Layer ▸ Layer to Image Size**).

4. Add a new transparent layer by choosing **Layer ▸ New** and setting the Layer Fill Type to **Transparency**. Name the new layer *Gradient*.

5. Choose the **Blend** tool from the toolbox. In the Tool Options dialog set the Gradient to **FG to Transparent**, set the Shape to **Linear**, and choose **None** from the Repeat drop-down menu. Fill the new layer with a gradient by clicking the top of the image and dragging downward. The gradient should flow just until it starts to fade the squares generated by the Cubism filter.

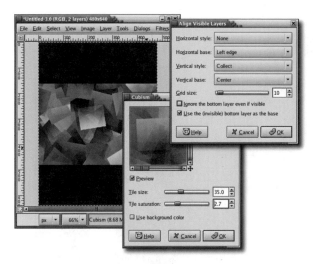

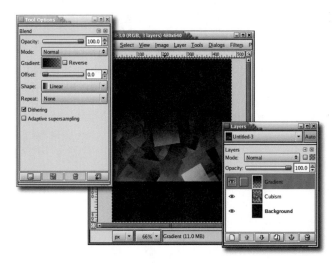

Applying the Cubism filter produces lots of randomly positioned, randomly sized, semi-transparent blocks. Later we extrude these blocks (convert them from two dimensions to three dimensions) to create our skyscraper-filled city.

6. With the Gradient layer active, merge the Gradient layer with the Cubism layer (**Layer ▸ Merge Down**).

The Gradient layer is merged with the Cubism layer so that when we extrude the blocks, the cityscape appears to fade into the distance.

Stretching with the Wind Filter

1. Rotate the Cubism layer 90 degrees clockwise (**Layer ▸ Transform ▸ Rotate 90 degrees CW**).

2. Open the Wind filter (**Filters ▸ Distorts ▸ Wind**). Set the Style to **Wind**, set the Direction to **Right**, and set the Edge Affected to **Leading**. Then set the Threshold slider to **2** and the Strength slider to **50**. Click **OK** to apply the filter.

3. Repeat this process by pressing CTRL-F two or three times, until additional applications of the Wind filter have little or no effect.

4. Rotate the Cubism layer to its original orientation (**Layer ▸ Transform ▸ Rotate 90 degrees CCW**) so that the buildings stand vertically.

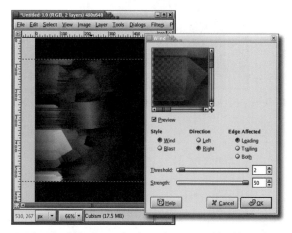

Use the Wind filter to make three-dimensional buildings from the two-dimensional blocks.

Sharpening and Scaling the Image

1. The edges of the buildings can be made more distinct by applying the Unsharp Mask filter (**Filters ▸ Enhance ▸ Unsharp Mask**). Set the Radius slider to **1.2 pixels**, set the Amount slider to **1.50**, and set the Threshold slider to **2**. Click **OK** to apply the filter to the Cubism layer.

   At this point the image is essentially done. Only cleanup and detailing work are left, and neither is required, though they can enhance the final effect. If the buildings are too dim, duplicate the Cubism layer, set the layer mode for the duplicate layer to Dodge, and reduce the layer's Opacity a bit. Then merge the duplicate layer with the original Cubism layer by choosing Layer ▸ Merge Down.

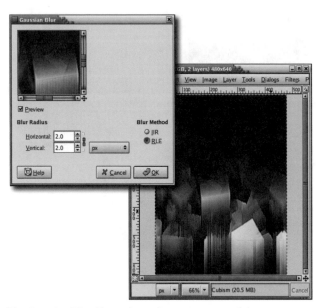

The Gaussian Blur filter reduces the transparency of the buildings' walls.

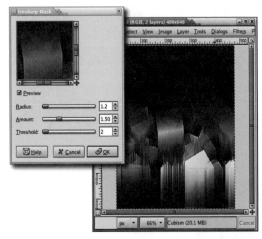

The Unsharp Mask filter enhances the edges of the buildings.

2. Open the Gaussian Blur filter (**Filters ▸ Blur ▸ Gaussian Blur**). Set the Blur Method to **RLE** and the Blur Radius to **2 pixels** for a smaller image. Click **OK** to apply the blur.

3. Now let's make the buildings taller. Choose the **Scale** tool from the toolbox and drag the bottom half of the layer down until the bottom edges of the buildings touch the bottom of the canvas window. If necessary, zoom out on the canvas (**View ▸ Zoom ▸ Zoom Out**).

Adding Color and Intensity

1. If the detail provided by the Unsharp Mask filter is lost after scaling, try duplicating the layer, reducing the duplicate layer's **Opacity**, and setting its layer mode to **Dodge** or **Addition**. Then merge the two layers and reapply the Unsharp Mask filter (**Filters ▸ Enhance ▸ Unsharp Mask**).

2. Add a new transparent layer and name it *Color*. Fill the new layer with a color of your choice (use the RGB value of 201/132/0 to match the color shown here) and set the layer mode to **Color**.

3. Additional depth and detail can be achieved by applying the Bump Map filter to the Color layer using the Cubism layer. Open the Bump Map filter (**Filters ▸ Map ▸ Bump Map**). Choose the **Cubism** layer from the Bump Map drop-down menu as shown. Preview each of the **Map Type** options and choose the most appropriate. Check the box next to the words *Compensate for Darkening*.

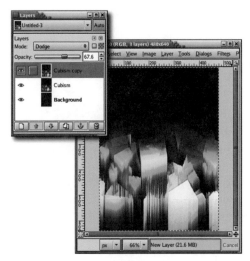

You can use a different color for each building by adding multiple color layers, each with a different layer mask that only affects one building.

4. Adjust the **Azimuth, Elevation,** and **Depth** sliders to produce a preview that looks best. Leave all other settings at their default values and click **OK** to apply the Bump Map filter.

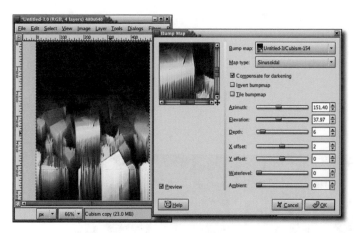

The Bump Map filter adds depth to the image by simulating shadows cast by buildings.

Further Exploration

This tutorial used a few of the GIMP's filters to create a Cubism-inspired skyline full of high-rise buildings. If your project calls for something less experimental, Section 4.10 might prove more helpful. In that section we create a cartoon streetscape. Once again, it's a lot easier than it sounds.

4.10 CUBE CITY

Cartoon buildings are an easy effect to achieve with the GIMP.

What if the last tutorial was a bit too artistic for your project's needs? You could turn to stock imagery for a much more recognizable, if two-dimensional, cityscape. Or you could ditch high art and have a little more fun. Maybe you need something with a little 'toon style to it. Maybe what you need is Cube City.

In this tutorial we create three buildings from simple 3D cubes, and then we bend the buildings a bit to give the design a cartoonish look. The entire image takes only a few minutes to put together—once you're familiar with the tricks of the trade.

The process starts by generating a single 3D cube that is duplicated and stretched to create each of the three buildings. Despite the GIMP's obvious bias toward 2D artwork, creating the cube is far easier than it might seem. This design is created at 250 dpi to produce a print that is 4 × 6 inches. If you're after a larger print, you'll need to create a larger cube. You can scale down the original cube for smaller prints, but the windows in the buildings will become difficult to see if you do, so it's best start with a smaller version of the cube for smaller prints.

Getting Started

Open a new transparent canvas (**File ▶ New**) that is **2 × 2 inches** at **250 dpi**. This layer is used to create the 3D cube. For comparison's sake, note that if you were planning to create a cube city that was 420 × 300 pixels at 72 dpi, you would start with a layer that was 60 × 60 pixels.

Creating the Building's Face

1. Choose the **Blend** tool from the toolbox. In the Tool Options dialog set the Gradient to **FG to BG (RGB)** and the Shape to **Linear**. The rest of the options should be set to their default values.

2. With the canvas selected, press **D** to reset the default foreground and background colors, and then drag on the canvas from left to right.

3. Add a set of four evenly spaced vertical guides and six evenly spaced horizontal guides by choosing **Image ▸ Guides ▸ New Guide** or dragging guides from the top and left rulers. If necessary, press SHIFT-plus to zoom in and get a better look at the gradient layer.

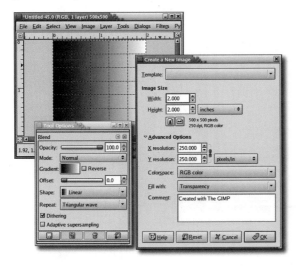

The building starts with a gradient and guides that help outline the windows.

4. Add a new transparent layer by choosing **Layer ▸ New** and setting the Layer Fill Type to **Transparency**.

5. Choose the **Rectangle Select** tool from the toolbox. Using a guide intersection point as the lower-right corner of a selection, drag to create a square selection that is inside the rectangle created by the guides but does not cover the entire rectangle. Leave some space between the selections so the squares will be the windows.

6. Repeat this process for most of the intersection points, leaving a few blank. Selections on the right side of the gradient will be more apparent in the final image, so don't leave those blank. Hold down the SHIFT key as you drag to

create each new selection. This will add the new selection to the existing selections. The selections need not all be the same size. This is, after all, a cartoonish design.

7. After all the selections have been created, click the **Blend** tool again to make it active. Drag from right to left across the width of the gradient layer to fill the selections. Deselect all (CTRL-SHIFT-A).

8. Open the Gaussian Blur filter (**Filters ▸ Blur ▸ Gaussian Blur**), set the Blur Radius to **3 pixels**, and click **OK** apply the blur to the windows.

9. In the Layers dialog set the layer mode to **Hard Light** and merge this layer with the Background layer (**Layer ▸ Merge Down**).

10. Remove all guides (**Image ▸ Guides ▸ Remove All Guides**).

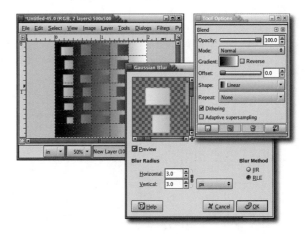

Leaving a few spots blank (without windows) adds some variation to the texture of the cartoonish building.

Making the Face a Cube

1. Open the Map Object filter (**Filters ▸ Map ▸ Map Object**). Choose **Box** from the drop-down menu next to the words *Map to*, and check the box next to the words *Transparent Background*. Make sure the box next to the words *Enable Antialiasing* is also checked.

2. On the Orientation tab set the Y Rotation to **45 degrees**. If the preview does not show that your rectangle has been converted into a nice cube as shown here, check the Box tab and make sure the correct layer is selected for each of the sides' drop-down menus.

3. On the **Box** tab set the Y slider to **0.75**, and then click **OK** to apply the Map Object filter.

4. With the canvas selected, press CTRL-C to copy the cube.

NOTE   *Before continuing, you should save this image (**File ▸ Save**) as an XCF file so that you'll always have a copy of the source cube for future Cube City projects. Saving subcomponents of a project like this is common practice and will, over time, help you build a library of small components suitable for multiple projects.*

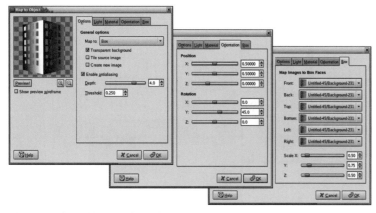

The Map Object filter simplifies this project because it converts the single building face into a cube, giving us a building almost instantly.

Multiplying the Buildings

1. Open a new canvas that is **4 × 6 inches** at **250 dpi**.

2. With the toolbox selected, press **D** to reset the foreground and background colors, and then drag the foreground color onto the canvas to fill the canvas with black.

3. Paste the cube you copied onto the black canvas as a new layer by pressing CTRL-V and then choosing **Layer ▸ New**.

4. Choose the **Scale** tool from the toolbox. Click the cube layer and drag up a bit to make the building taller. Click the **Scale** button in the Scaling Information dialog to apply the change.

5. Duplicate this layer twice by choosing **Layer ▸ Duplicate** twice. Name the three layers *Left*, *Middle*, and *Right*.

6. Click the **Left** layer to make it the active layer, and then use the **Move** tool to drag it left of center on the canvas (hold down the SHIFT key if necessary). Then click the **Right** layer and move it right of center.

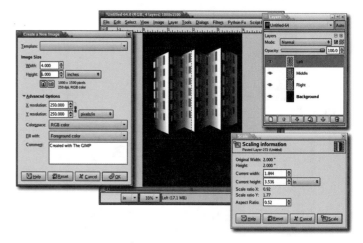

The gradient, which is black on the left and white on the right, works well to simulate shadowed areas on the sides of each building.

7. Choose the **Perspective** tool from the toolbox. In the Layers dialog click the **Left** layer to make that layer active. Then click the canvas to display the drag points around the layer. Drag the top-left and top-right points outward from the center of the layer. In the Perspective Transform Information dialog, click the **Transform** button to apply the change.

8. Repeat this process for the **Right** and **Middle** layers.

9. When all three buildings have been completed, use the **Move** tool to adjust the layers so the bottom edges of the buildings line up.

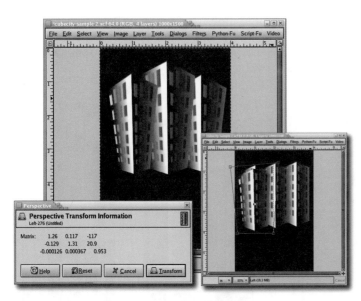

Changing the perspective of the buildings lends the cityscape a cartoonish effect. Because each building's perspective is changed by a different amount, the buildings aren't identical.

Adding Color

We want the buildings to be different colors, but we don't want the colors to clash.

1. For each layer, open the Colorize dialog (**Layer ▸ Colors ▸ Colorize**).

2. For the Left layer, set the Hue to **33**, the Saturation to **66**, and the Lightness to **–15**. For the Middle layer, set the Hue to **180**, the Saturation to **60**, and the Lightness to **–15**. For the Right layer, set the Hue to **100**, the Saturation to **50**, and the Lightness to **–15**.

3. At this point you can use the **Sharpen** filter or the **Unsharp Mask** filter (**Filters ▸ Enhance**) to reduce the fuzziness that was introduced when we modified the perspective.

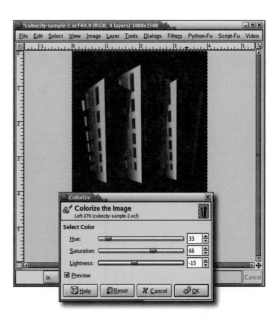

Using the Colorize tool is the easiest way to add color to the buildings, although you could also use the Bucket Fill tool with its mode set to Color.

Adding Highlights

1. Add a drop shadow to the Left and Middle layers by choosing **Script-Fu ▸ Shadow ▸ Drop Shadow**. Set the Offset X value to **15 pixels**, the Offset Y value to **3 pixels**, and the Blur Radius to **15 pixels**. Click **OK** to apply the drop shadow.

2. Click the foreground color box to open the Change Foreground Color dialog. Set the RGB values to **252/255/0** for the yellow shown here and click **OK**.

3. Click the **Left** layer to make that layer active, duplicate the layer (**Layer ▸ Duplicate**), and name the new layer *Left Yellow Oval*. Press CTRL-A and then CTRL-X to clear the layer contents.

4. In the Layers dialog uncheck the **Keep Transparency** box as shown.

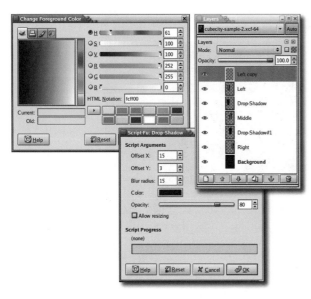

A drop shadow adds even more depth to the image.

5. Choose the **Ellipse Select** tool from the toolbox and use it to create an oval selection on the left side of the building.

6. Feather the selection by **30 pixels** (**Select ▸ Feather**) and then drag the foreground color box into the selection to fill the selection with yellow.

7. Hold down the SHIFT and ALT keys and drag the selection to the right, so it is on the right side of the building. Drag the foreground color box into the new selection. Deselect all (CTRL-SHIFT-A).

8. Open the Gaussian Blur filter (**Filters ▸ Blur ▸ Gaussian Blur**) and apply a blur of **60 pixels**.

9. Set the layer mode to **Grain Merge** and reduce the Opacity to **35 percent**.

10. Duplicate the Left Yellow Oval layer (**Layer ▸ Duplicate**). Name the duplicate layer *Middle Yellow Oval*.

11. Use the **Move** tool to move the Middle Yellow Oval layer over the middle building, and then in the Layers dialog move the **Middle Yellow Oval** layer to just above the Middle layer. Repeat this process for the Right layer, naming the last duplicate layer *Right Yellow Oval*.

12. Adjust the Yellow Oval layers' **Opacity** and **layer mode** and, if necessary, scale them to fit the buildings.

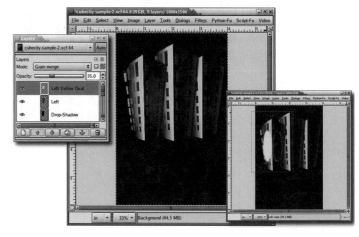

Yellow highlights add a sense of lighting, even though there are no street lamps in the image. This is, after all, a cartoon.

Further Exploration

It's incredibly easy to create 3D objects in the GIMP. As you've seen, it's simply a matter of using gradients and shadows mixed with colored highlights.

And it's easy to take this project to the next level. The first image in this section shows that a man and a zooming car have been added to the cityscape. Both of these elements come from icon collections and were simply cut, pasted into the image, and colorized. The Motion Blur filter is used to make the car look like it's in motion, just as we added motion to the plane in Section 2.6.

4.11 UNDER WATER

We've already discussed how setting the mood in an advertisement is crucial to getting your message across. In Section 4.2 we went outside into the dark night and used yellow light to show that we were about to make contact. Then in Section 4.7 you saw how rain and lightning made a tropical paradise even more appealing in comparison.

This ad's ominous message is enhanced by a murky, watery effect.

Another place we can go to set an eerie mood is under water. Undersea atmosphere is a complex mixture of diminishing light, distorted visuals, and inverted surfaces. In the land of the GIMP, however, the underwater realm is easy to create.

In this section we create an underwater image for use in a print ad. The effect isn't particularly difficult to produce, but it does take some patience and experimentation to get a realistic result. If you don't succeed on the first try, make subtle changes to the Solid Noise filter's settings and try again.

Getting Started

1. Open a new canvas sized to **1,024 × 768 pixels**.

2. Press **D** and then **X** to reset and then swap the default foreground and background colors. In the toolbox, click the foreground color box to open the Change Foreground Color dialog. Set the RGB values to **23/137/125** for the aqua green shown here, and then click **OK**.

3. Choose the **Blend** tool from the toolbox. In the Tool Options dialog set the Gradient to **FG to BG (RGB)**, set the Shape to **Linear,** and choose **None** from the Repeat drop-down menu. Drag vertically from the top of the canvas window to the bottom.

4. In the Layers dialog temporarily turn off the visibility of the **Background** layer. We'll turn it back on when we're done creating the desaturated waves.

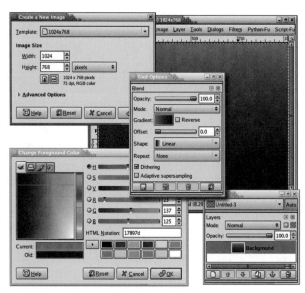

The lightest color is at the top of the canvas so that the waves we add overhead will be visible.

Creating Waves

1. Add a new transparent layer by choosing **Layer ▸ New** and setting the Layer Fill Type to **Transparency**. Name the new layer *Surface*.

2. Open the Solid Noise filter (**Filters ▸ Render ▸ Clouds ▸ Solid Noise**). Check the box next to the word *Randomize*, set the Detail to **5**, set the X Size to **5**, and set the Y Size to **10**. Increasing Detail value increases the contrast in parts of the image, and setting the Y Size value to twice the X Size value stretches the image horizontally. Click **OK** to apply the Solid Noise filter.

3. Repeat this process four more times, creating four new layers and making sure to alternatingly uncheck and check the Randomize box each time so that a new random value changes the shape of each cloud rendering. Set the layer mode to **Difference** for every layer except the original Surface layer.

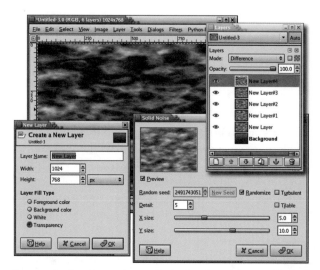

Because the Randomize box is checked in the Solid Noise filter's dialog, your waves won't look exactly like this. You may find that only one noise layer is sufficient, or you may need 10 noise layers. If you aren't achieving the look you want, try selecting a different Random Seed.

4. Merge the visible layers into a single layer (**Image ▸ Merge Visible Layers**). Set the merged layer's mode to **Grain Merge**.

5. If necessary, adjust the Brightness and Contrast to sharpen the edges between the crests and troughs of the waves (**Layer ▸ Colors ▸ Brightness-Contrast**).

6. Turn back on the visibility of the **Background** layer.

7. Choose the **Perspective** tool from the toolbox. Click the canvas to display the drag points at the four corners of the Surface layer. Pull up the lower-left and lower-right points to approximately one-third the height of the canvas. While the mouse is in the canvas window, press SHIFT-minus to zoom out.

8. Drag the upper-left point to the left and drag the upper-right point to the right, as shown here. In the Perspective Transform Information dialog, click the **Transform** button to apply these changes to the layer.

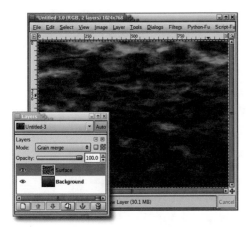

The underwater effect is taking shape, but there are too many waves in the deepest part of our ocean.

9. If the waves appear too small or crowded, use the **Scale** tool to stretch the layer. When this is completed, zoom back in by pressing SHIFT-plus.

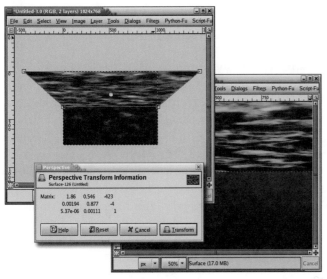

Dragging beyond the edges of the canvas with the Perspective tool doesn't cost you anything unless you save to the XCF format. When you save the file as a TIFF, JPEG, or other image file format, the excess isn't saved.

10. At this point you can use the Gaussian Blur filter (**Filters ▶ Blur ▶ Gaussian Blur**) to apply a blur of **2 to 5 pixels**. You can also use the Ripple filter (**Filters ▶ Distort ▶ Ripple**) to add distortion. Neither of these steps is required—use your own judgment to get the most out of this effect.

11. Add a white layer mask (**Layer ▶ Mask ▶ Add Layer Mask**).

12. Reset and swap the default foreground and background colors by pressing **D** and then **X** while the canvas is selected.

13. Choose the **Blend** tool from the toolbox. In the Tool Options dialog use the same settings you used earlier. Drag vertically from the top of the canvas to the middle. This will fade the Surface layer into the background, making it look as though the surface is disappearing into the distance.

14. Turn off the Layer Boundary (**View ▶ Layer Boundary**) so you can see the underwater effect more clearly. This is also a good time to save a copy of the project for future use (**File ▶ Save**).

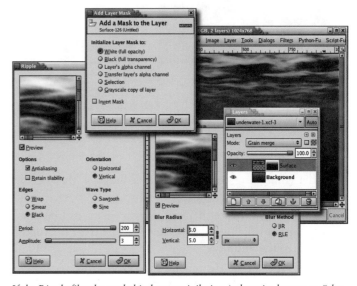

If the Ripple filter leaves behind some pixilation (otherwise known as "the jaggies") you can clean this up by applying a blur to the Surface layer.

Adding Diffused Light

Now it's time to add a light source that appears above the water.

1. Add a new transparent layer by choosing **Layer ▸ New** and setting the Layer Fill Type to **Transparency**.

2. Choose the **Blend** tool from the toolbox again. Set the Gradient to **FG to BG (RGB)**, set the Shape to **Radial**, and choose **None** from the Repeat drop-down menu. Click the top of the canvas near its middle and drag down through the canvas about halfway.

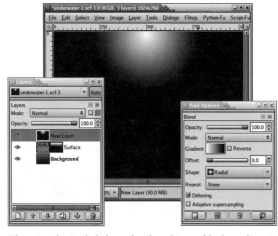

Choosing the Radial shape for the white-to-black gradient is an easy way to create a sphere. In this case, we're creating a radiating light source.

3. Add a white layer mask to this layer (**Layer ▸ Mask ▸ Add Layer Mask**).

4. With the **Blend** tool still active, set the Shape to **Linear** in the Tool Options dialog. Then drag vertically from the top of the canvas to the middle.

5. Set the layer mode for this layer to **Grain Merge**. The black in the layer will darken the waves a bit, but the white will also lighten some of them—giving the overall appearance of a nighttime underwater scene.

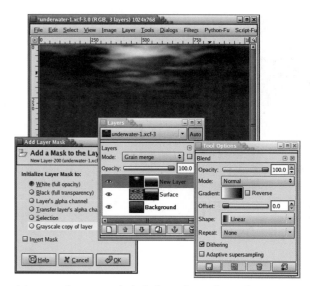

A layer mask prevents the light from shining beyond a certain depth.

Adding Rays of Light

Let's really make this scene shine.

1. Click the **Background** layer to make that layer active.

2. Choose the **Rectangle Select** tool from the toolbox. Drag through the middle of the top of the canvas to create a square selection. The selection should cover the entire light source.

3. Copy and paste the selection, and then choose **Layer ▸ New** to make the pasted selection a new layer. Name this layer *Light Rays*. We won't use the content of the copied layer, but this is a simple way to create a layer of the appropriate size.

4. Choose the **Blend** tool again. This time set the Gradient to **Flare Rays Size 1**, set the Shape to **Bi-Linear**, and choose **Sawtooth Wave** from the Repeat drop-down menu. Drag from left to right in the new layer.

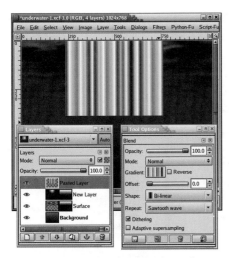

The Flare Rays gradients are similar to the Crown Molding gradient we used in Section 4.8, although the vertical shades of light and dark are closer together in the Flare Rays gradients.

5. Open the Polar Coordinates filter (**Filters ▸ Distorts ▸ Polar Coords**). Set the Circle Depth to **0 percent** and adjust the **Offset Angle** so that the most visible lines are at the bottom of the preview. The box next to the words *To Polar* and the box next to the words *Map from Top* should be checked, but the box next to the words *Map Backwards* should be left unchecked. Click **OK** to apply the filter.

6. Choose the **Scale** tool from the toolbox. Click the canvas to display the drag points on the layer corners. Click near the bottom of the layer and drag down until the center drag point meets the original layer's bottom, as shown here. Drag to extend the sides out toward the edges of the canvas as well. The scaling doesn't have to be exact at this point. Click the center drag point and move it up near the center of the top of the canvas. Click **OK** to apply the scaling changes.

The center point of these radial lines should be moved to the center of the top of the canvas. This will ensure that the lines seem to radiate from the light source we created earlier.

7. Add a white layer mask (**Layer ▸ Mask ▸ Add Layer Mask**), and then press **D** and then **X** to reset and then swap the default foreground and background colors.

8. Choose the **Blend** tool from the toolbox. In the Tool Options dialog set the Gradient to **FG to BG (RGB)**, set the Shape to **Radial,** and choose **None** from the Repeat drop-down menu. Drag from the top of the canvas to the middle to blend the rays of light into the background.

9. Blend this layer with the Background layer by setting the Light Rays layer's mode to **Grain Merge**.

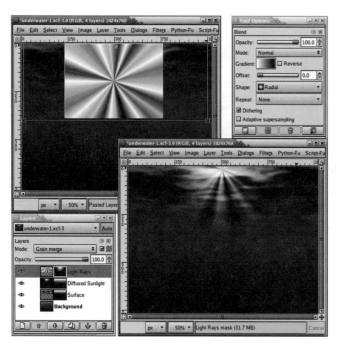

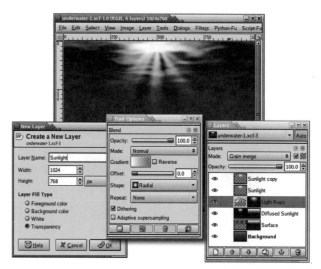

Setting the Light Rays layer's mode to Grain Merge blends the light areas with the Background layer. The layer mask causes the rays to fade as they get farther from the light source.

Because the layer mode is set to Grain Merge, the extra light sources merge with both the rays of light and the Background layer. Don't be afraid to experiment with different layer modes to find the one that produces the most compelling effect for your project.

Intensifying the Light

1. Add a new transparent layer by choosing **Layer ▸ New Layer** and setting the Layer Fill Type to **Transparency**. Name this new layer *Sunlight*.

2. The **Blend** tool should still be active. In the Tool Options dialog change the Gradient to **FG to Transparent**, but leave the other settings unchanged. Click the center of the top of the canvas and drag down through one-fourth to one-third of the canvas.

3. Set the layer mode to **Grain Merge**, and then duplicate this layer (**Layer ▸ Duplicate**). If using the Grain Merge setting for these two layers does not produce the effect you seek, try changing the layer mode to Soft Light or Overlay.

Further Exploration

Some variations on this effect can be achieved by changing the color of the water or the location of the light source above it, but it's what you add below the surface that will really make your ocean come alive. If you like, you can experiment on the final image by applying both the Gaussian Blur filter (Filters ▸ Blur ▸ Gaussian Blur) and the Ripple filter (Filters ▸ Distorts ▸ Ripple) to the Light Rays layer. Both filters will help soften the light rays. You can even add a text layer, as shown in the first image in this section, or cut and paste some ocean life into the scene to complete the project.

4.12 WISPY SMOKE

Smoke can take many forms. There are smoke clouds, like those from car tires spinning on asphalt. There is smog, which is a veil of smoke that is thick like fog. And there is wispy smoke, like that produced by a lit cigarette or the steam that rises from a cup of coffee.

We can use the GIMP to produce clouds of smoke in many ways. Most methods involve either mixing a solid gray Bucket Fill operation with random, desaturated noise or creating clouds with the Solid Noise or Plasma filters. Wispy smoke is produced in a very different way, however.

To create wispy smoke, we repeatedly apply the Ripple and Waves filters. While it is nearly impossible to reproduce the same smoke pattern twice, creating the patterns from scratch is extremely simple, so a bit of trial and error should be fairly painless.

What can you do with this smoke pattern once you've created it? Because the background is black, you can cut out the smoke and paste it into just about any other image. The Grain Merge, Screen, and Overlay layer modes make it easy to blend the smoke with the image you choose.

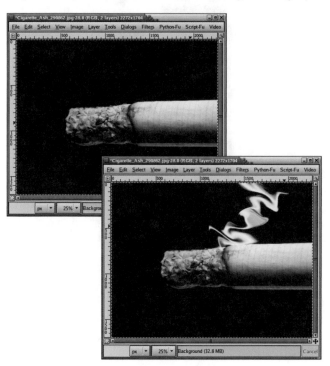

Get a smoky look without a lifetime of addiction.

Getting Ready

Before opening a new canvas window, reset and swap the default foreground and background colors by clicking the toolbox to make it active and pressing **D** and then **X**. Open a new canvas window (**File ▸ New**), and in the Create a New Image dialog click the **Reset** button to retrieve the default canvas settings. Change the orientation of the new window to **Portrait** by clicking the icon below the Height field. Click **OK** to open the new window. We use a portrait orientation for this project so the column of smoke has room to rise. The black background makes the white smoke stand out, but it also allows us to incorporate the final image into other projects easily.

Creating the Column of Smoke

1. Open the Brushes dialog (**Dialogs ▸ Brushes**).
2. Select the **Swirl2** brush and set the Spacing slider to **17**.

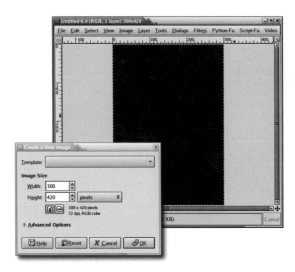

Because smoke rises, a portrait orientation seems appropriate.

3. Choose the **Paintbrush** tool from the toolbox. Click in the upper-right quadrant of the canvas and slowly draw a line that extends down toward the lower-left corner of the canvas. Don't draw a straight line—wiggle the brush lightly as you draw. Retrace the line a few times until it is mostly white, as shown here.

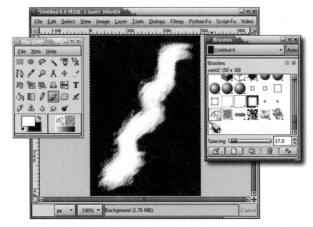

Any oddly shaped brush would work for this tutorial, including one from the collection of Galaxy brushes.

NOTE   *If you're missing the Swirl2 brush, make sure you've installed the gimp-data-extras package for your version of the GIMP.*

Applying a Three-Step Series of Filters

Now let's use two filters to repeatedly distort the image.

1. Open the Waves filter (**Filter ▸ Distorts ▸ Waves**). In this example I set the Amplitude to 8, the Phase to 0, and the Wavelength to 45. Choose values that distort your white line without producing recognizable or repeating forms in the preview window. Click **OK** to apply the filter.

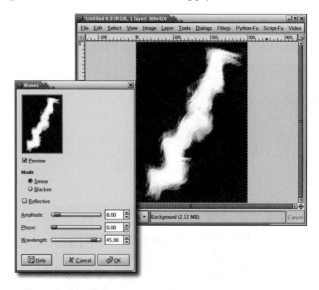

Different Waves filter settings may be appropriate. The goal is to produce sufficiently random shapes.

2. Open the Ripple filter (**Filters ▸ Distorts ▸ Ripple**). Set the Orientation to **Horizontal,** and then choose appropriate **Period** and **Amplitude** values. Pan in the preview window to see how your settings affect the image before clicking **OK** to apply the changes.

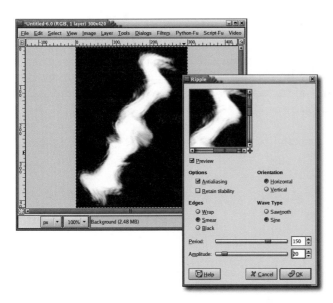

The Ripple filter's preview window won't show the entire image, but you can use the navigate icon to pan around.

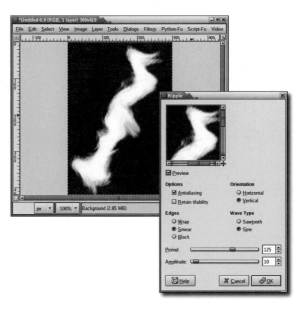

Applying the Ripple filter a second time adds more randomization to the rising column of smoke.

3. Open the Ripple filter again (**Filters ▸ Distorts ▸ Ripple**). This time set the Orientation to **Vertical,** and again choose appropriate Period and Amplitude values. In the example shown here, the same values are used for the Vertical filter as for the Horizontal filter. Click **OK** to apply these settings to the image. Repeat this three-step series as many times as required to achieve the best results.

Blurring the Image

After applying variations on the three-step process five more times, I'm ready to continue.

1. Duplicate the background layer (**Layer ▸ Duplicate**).

2. Open the Gaussian Blur filter (**Filters ▸ Blur ▸ Gaussian Blur**). Set the Blur Radius to **20 pixels** and click **OK** to apply this filter to the duplicate layer.

3. Invert the colors (**Layer ▸ Colors ▸ Invert**) and set the layer mode to **Overlay.**

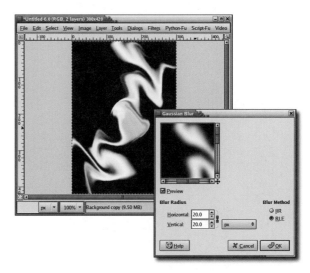

Applying the three-step process several times eventually produces something like cigarette smoke, which is thicker and has smoother edges than the original brush strokes.

4. Feel free to experiment. Choose different layer modes, or see what the result looks like when you don't invert the colors. When you're ready, merge all of the layers into a single layer (**Image ▸ Merge Visible Layers**).

Further Exploration

Cigarette smoke is just one application of this technique. You could use the same method to create steam rising from a cup of coffee, clouds of smoke billowing from a power plant, or the remnants of last night's campfire. You'll be surprised to find how many projects can be enhanced with smoke!

4.13 FLAMES AND EXPLOSIONS

The process for creating fire is much like that for creating smoke, except that when creating fire we stretch vertically to create flames. For fiery explosions, we use a slightly different technique that involves the Plasma filter. In both cases, we use the Curves and Levels tools to add color.

Is it hot in here, or is it just the GIMP?

Creating flames is simple enough, but merging the flames with other images is a bit more complicated. Most advertising projects that require flames need more than just fire, so you'll need to master the art of merging the fire with other objects. In this tutorial we walk through the process for creating ordinary flames and fiery explosions. Then it's up to you to use the blending techniques you've learned elsewhere in the book to merge the resulting image with another image to create a compelling advertisement.

Getting Started

Open a new canvas window (**File ▸ New**) and in the Create a New Image dialog click **Reset** to retrieve the default canvas settings. Change the orientation of the new window to **Portrait** by clicking the icon below the Height field. As when creating smoke, we want a portrait orientation so the flames have room to rise. The size of the canvas doesn't matter for this tutorial, so using the default canvas size makes some trial-and-error experimentation possible.

Creating Flames

1. Open the Solid Noise filter (**Filters ▸ Render ▸ Clouds ▸ Solid Noise**). The X and Y Size sliders should be set to **4**, and the boxes next to the words *Randomize*, *Turbulent*, and *Tilable* should all be unchecked. Set the Detail to **1**. If the preview window doesn't look like the one shown on the next page, adjust the X and Y Size sliders until it does.

2. Add a new transparent layer by choosing **Layer ▸ New** and setting the Layer Fill Type to **Transparency**.

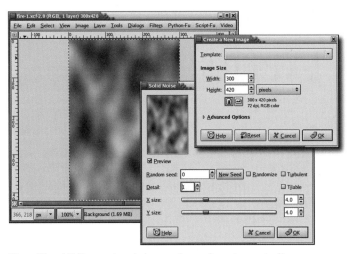

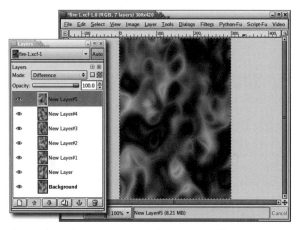

These X and Y Size settings help stretch out the noise vertically.

The number of times you repeat this process will vary. You may want to experiment with different Random Seed values if the Solid Noise filter is not producing an image that looks like flames.

3. Open the Solid Noise filter again (**Filters ▶ Render ▶ Clouds ▶ Solid Noise**), but this time check the box next to the word *Randomization*. For the rest of the settings, use the same values as before. Click **OK** to apply the filter.

4. Change the layer mode to **Difference**.

5. Repeat this process at least four more times, creating new layers and turning the Randomization button on and off each time to reset the randomizer and adjust the way the clouds are rendered. Stop when the shape on the canvas looks like flames, and flatten all of the layers into a single layer (**Image ▶ Flatten Image**).

Adding Color to the Flames

Now let's add some fiery color.

1. Open the Levels dialog (**Layer ▶ Colors ▶ Levels**). The Channel drop-down menu has four options: Value, Red, Green, and Blue. Choose **Red** and move the right drag point (the white one) to the left. Move the middle drag point (the gray one) to the left as well. The degree of adjustment you make will vary, depending on the contents of your canvas.

2. Repeat this process for the **Blue** channel. The **Green** channel might also require minor adjustment, but most of the changes will affect the Red and Blue channels. Adjust these levels until your flames are a reddish orange, as shown here.

3. Click **OK** to apply the levels changes.

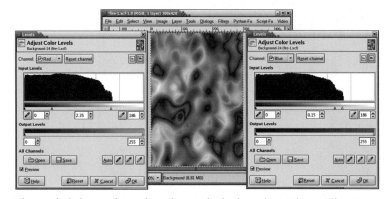

The Levels dialog can be used to adjust multiple channels. Applying different settings to each channel is what colors the flames. The Colorize filter (Layer ▶ Colors ▶ Colorize) can also be used, but the Levels dialog offers more control when creating this flame effect.

Stretching the Flames

1. If the flames are not stretched vertically as much as you'd like, first zoom out a bit (**View ▸ Zoom ▸ Zoom Out**).

2. Choose the **Scale** tool from the toolbox. Click the canvas to display the drag points, and then click the canvas again and stretch the outline vertically. In the Scaling Information dialog click **Scale** to apply the changes.

3. The layer is now larger than the canvas, so adjust the layer size to fit the canvas (**Layer ▸ Layer to Image Size**).

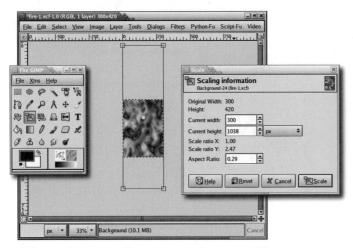

Stretching the layer vertically stretches the flames vertically.

4. Adjusting the size this way may leave transparent edges. To fix this, choose the **Crop** tool from the toolbox and click the canvas to open the Crop and Resize Information dialog. Click the **From Selection** button, and then choose **Auto Shrink**. Click the **Crop** button to apply these changes and cut the canvas down to fit the layer.

Only part of the resized layer is displayed in the canvas window. Move the layer up or down to locate the part of the layer that contains the most realistic flames.

You now have a stock image of a flame that you can incorporate into any project that needs fire. Just use the selection and layer-blending skills you've developed in this book's tutorials to merge the flame with another image.

Creating Explosions

It's a little easier to use the GIMP to create an explosion than it is to use it to create flames. Start by opening a new white canvas, using all of the default settings.

1. Open the Plasma filter (**Filters ▸ Render ▸ Clouds ▸ Plasma**). Use the default settings for this filter, as shown here. Click **OK** to create a cloud on the canvas.

2. Desaturate the cloud layer (**Layer ▸ Colors ▸ Desaturate**).

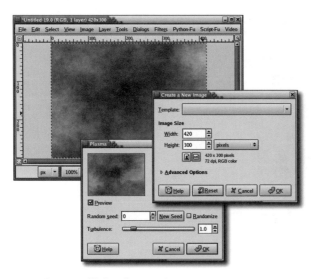

An explosion is filled with particulate matter, so we start by using the Plasma filter instead of the Solid Noise filter.

3. Open the Curves dialog (**Layer ▸ Colors ▸ Curves**). Choose **Value** from the Channel drop-down menu and adjust the curve as shown here to increase the contrast and add more black areas to the canvas.

4. Adjust the Red and Blue channels next. The **Red** channel's curve should be adjusted up and to the left, while the **Blue** channel's curve should be adjusted down and to the right. Once the explosion is a reddish orange, click **OK** to apply the curves changes.

5. Open the Levels dialog (**Layer ▸ Colors ▸ Levels**) and move the left drag point (the black one) to the right. This will make the explosion appear more fiery. Click **OK** to apply the levels change.

As before, you can save this image and use it anywhere a fiery explosion is needed. Practice blending and you'll soon be able to combine the explosion with text and other images effectively.

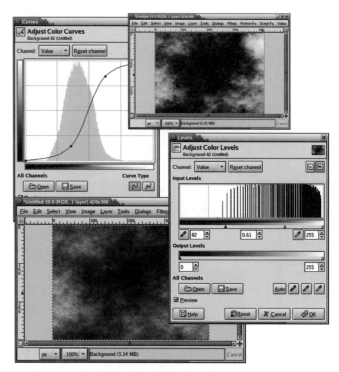

Use the Curves dialog to add color to the explosion, and use the Levels dialog to increase contrast.

Further Exploration

Flames and explosions are some of the simplest effects you can create with the GIMP because they're free-form shapes and leave plenty of room for error. What makes a flame is smooth color transition, and what makes an explosion is appropriately colored particulate matter.

It can be a bit trickier to use the method described in this tutorial to place a single flame on the end of a matchstick, but give it a try. You'll need to add a layer mask to isolate a single flame, and you might want to incorporate additional colors, such as blue and white.

4.14 STUDIO LIGHTING

The studio portrait is a versatile shot, and designers find lots of ways to incorporate it into their advertising projects. Because most studio shots use solid backdrops that are easily selected and removed, it's easy to swap in just about any background image and then use these studio shots for virtually any kind of concept. Most studio portraits need some level of lighting adjustment, however, and you'll often find that the subject's facial features can be enhanced by adding soft shadows.

Lighting effects can quickly change the tone of a photo.

This tutorial takes a studio portrait that's too brightly lit and improves upon it, softening its focus in the style of publicity photos from the era of black-and-white films. Desaturating the image will also make softening the woman's skin tone easier. If you won't be working in grayscale, the same effect can be achieved with the Clone tool, but that process is far more complicated and time consuming. By working in black and white, we streamline our process considerably.

The goal of this tutorial is to make you familiar with a particular process so you can put it to use when you work with any image that has similar characteristics. That said, you may need to adjust some settings if the portrait you're working with is much different from mine.

Getting Started

1. Open the original studio portrait and reset the foreground and background colors by pressing **D** while the toolbox is active.

2. Let's start by selecting the background. Choose the **Fuzzy Select** tool from the toolbox. In the Tool Options dialog set the Threshold to **45**. (You can experiment with different values to find the setting that allows you to grab the background with a single selection.) Click the upper-left corner of the image to create the selection.

3. Grow this selection by **1 pixel** (**Select ▶ Grow**) and then feather it by **3 pixels** (**Select ▶ Feather**).

4. Save the selection to a channel (**Select ▶ Save to Channel**) and name the channel *Old Backdrop*.

5. Deselect all (CTRL-SHIFT-A).

It helps to start with a good studio portrait, but the backdrop is irrelevant because it will be replaced. A solid background that contrasts sharply with the foreground is easily isolated with the Fuzzy Select tool, although you may want to use the Quick Mask tool to clean up.

Making Color and Lighting Adjustments

1. In the Layers dialog click the **Background** layer to make that layer active (it won't be highlighted after you've saved the selection to a channel).

2. This is a full-color image, so the next step is to desaturate it (**Layer ▸ Colors ▸ Desaturate**).

3. This particular image was lit from the front with a bright and direct light. Reducing the contrast (**Layer ▸ Colors ▸ Brightness-Contrast**) reveals detail in the sweater that was hidden in the shadows. Although we don't really need that detail, the fact that the detail emerges tells us that the original lighting was quite harsh. Reducing the contrast is an improvement.

4. Because we'll be adding light back into the scene, let's darken the ambient light by using the Curves dialog (**Layer ▸ Colors ▸ Curves**) as shown here.

It's necessary to darken the subject before adding light back into the scene because the original image was already quite bright, making it difficult to add highlights.

Creating a Replacement Backdrop

1. Add a transparent layer (**Layer ▸ New**) and name it *Portrait Backdrop*.

2. Open the Plasma filter (**Filters ▸ Render ▸ Clouds ▸ Plasma**). The Plasma filter's default settings are fine for this project—just keep the Turbulence value low. Click **OK** to apply the settings to this layer.

3. Desaturate the layer (**Layer ▸ Colors ▸ Desaturate**).

4. Open the Gaussian Blur filter (**Filters ▸ Blur ▸ Gaussian Blur**). Set the Blur Radius to at least **20 pixels**, and then click **OK** to apply this filter to the layer.

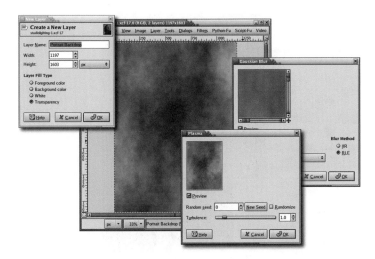

Plasma is placed in its own layer.

5. Add a white layer mask to the Portrait Backdrop layer (**Layer ▸ Mask ▸ Add Layer Mask**).

6. Retrieve the saved selection by opening the Channels dialog (**Dialogs ▸ Channels**). Click the **Old Backdrop** channel to make that channel active, and then click the **Channel to Selection** button at the bottom of the dialog.

7. Feather the selection by **2 pixels** (**Select ▸ Feather**), and then invert the selection (**Select ▸ Invert**).

8. In the Layers dialog click the **Portrait Backdrop** layer mask to make that mask active. Fill the selection with black by dragging the background color from the toolbox into the selection.

9. Deselect all (CTRL-SHIFT-A), and then turn off the visibility of the **Portrait Backdrop** layer by clicking the eye icon for that layer in the Layers dialog.

The plasma layer needs a mask that allows the model to show through. Alternatively, the plasma layer could have been placed below the model and a mask applied to the layer that contains the model. The first approach is the best one for this situation because we'll use the plasma layer to block out other effects later.

Highlighting the Face

1. Add a new transparent layer by choosing **Layer ▸ New** and setting the Layer Fill Type to **Transparency**. Name the new layer *Facial Highlights*. In the Layers dialog move this layer so it is below the Portrait Backdrop layer.

2. Choose the **Ellipse Select** tool from the toolbox. Drag to create a selection around the woman's face.

3. Choose the **Rotate** tool from the toolbox. In the Tool Options dialog click the **Transform Select** button next to the word *Affect* (it's the middle of the three buttons and its icon is a red square with a dotted outline). Click the canvas to open the Rotation Information dialog, and then drag through the

canvas until the bounding box appears to align with the slope of the face, as shown here. Click the **Rotate** button to apply the rotation.

4. If necessary, use the **Move** tool to position the selection over the face.

The selection can be rotated by setting the Affect option to Transform Selection in the Tool Options dialog.

5. Feather the selection by **10 pixels** (**Select ▸ Feather**).

6. Choose the **Blend** tool from the toolbox. In the Tool Options dialog set the Gradient to **FG to Transparent** and set the Shape to **Radial**. If the foreground color box in the toolbox is not white, press **D** and then **X** while the toolbox is active to reset and swap the foreground and background colors. In the canvas window click near the bridge of the subject's nose and drag out toward the edge of the canvas to apply a radial white gradient.

7. Set the layer mode for the Facial Highlights layer to **Soft Light**, and then deselect all (**Select ▸ None**). Don't worry about the highlight that appears on the backdrop itself—that will go away when we turn on the visibility of the Portrait Backdrop layer at the end of the tutorial.

A highlight is applied using a radial gradient within the oval selection.

Highlighting the Hair

Let's apply the same kind of highlight to the woman's hair.

1. Add a new transparent layer by choosing **Layer ▸ New** and setting the Layer Fill Type to **Transparency**. Name the new layer *Hair Highlights* and place it just above the Facial Highlights layer in the Layers dialog.

2. Use the **Ellipse Select** tool to make another selection. Then rotate it as needed and feather it by **10 pixels**.

3. Apply the same white radial gradient to this selection by clicking the outside edge of the woman's hair and dragging in toward her face, and then set the layer mode to **Soft Light**. Again, don't worry about the overlapping highlights on the backdrop. We'll mask those away shortly.

4. If necessary, use the Gaussian Blur filter (**Filters ▸ Blur ▸ Gaussian Blur**) to soften the edges of the hair highlight. The blur should be fairly large in comparison to the canvas size. For this image, I use a blur of 100 pixels.

5. Deselect all (**Select ▸ None**).

The two highlights appear on the backdrop and overlap each other a bit.

Fading the Sweater

The sweater is now too light, so let's add a layer to darken it. The process is the same as for the highlight layers, except that we'll use a black-to-transparent gradient instead of a white-to-transparent gradient.

1. Add another transparent layer below the Portrait Backdrop layer and name it *Sweater Fade*.

2. Use the **Ellipse Select** tool to create a selection of the woman's right shoulder. Rotate the selection as necessary and feather it a bit.

3. With the canvas selected, press **D** to set the foreground color to black.

4. Use the **Blend** tool to fill the selection with a black radial gradient, clicking near the bottom of the layer and dragging toward the woman's left shoulder.

5. Deselect all (**Select ▸ None**).

6. Use the Gaussian Blur filter to soften the edges as necessary (**Filters ▸ Blur ▸ Gaussian Blur**).

7. Set the layer mode to **Soft Light** once again.

The black-to-transparent gradient adds to the impression that the light source is coming from the right.

Softening the Face

1. Click the **Background** layer in the Layers dialog to make it the active layer.

2. Choose the **Ellipse Select** tool from the toolbox. Make a selection of the woman's face.

3. Copy the selection, and then paste it as a new layer by pressing CTRL-V and then choosing **Layer ▸ New**. Name the new layer *Softened Face*.

4. In the Layers dialog uncheck the **Keep Transparency** box for this new layer, and then move the layer so it's just above the Background layer.

5. Open the Gaussian Blur filter again (**Filters ▸ Blur ▸ Gaussian Blur**). Apply a blur of **10 to 20 pixels** to this layer.

6. In the Layers dialog reduce the layer's Opacity to between **60 and 80 percent**.

We could use the Smudge tool to smooth away facial imperfections, but the Gaussian Blur filter handles the situation just as easily.

7. Add a white layer mask to this layer (**Layer ▸ Mask ▸ Add Layer Mask**). In the **Brushes** dialog choose a soft-edged brush, such as **Circle Fuzzy (76)**.

8. Choose the **Airbrush** tool from the toolbox. Make sure that the foreground color is set to black. Spray over the woman's lips, eyes, nostrils, and hair until all of these areas come into focus.

9. Turn on the visibility of the **Portrait Backdrop** layer to view the final effect.

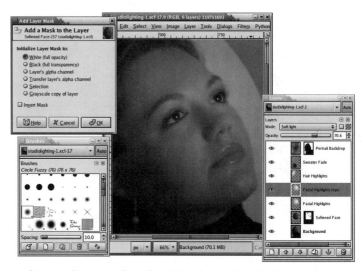

Masking out the eyes in the Softened Face layer allows the details below to show through while keeping the soft glow we added to the skin.

Further Exploration

Black-and-white photographs like this one get most of their impact from contrast. In this case, the black sweater adds plenty of contrast and makes the model's face the focal point of the image. You might even think that the sweater provides too much contrast, and it may be true that a sweater with more texture is more appropriate for your project.

4.15 COLORED LIGHTING

Whether in a portrait studio or while working in the GIMP, colored lighting effects can set the mood. Different colors can evoke different feelings—blues are cool, reds are warm, yellow sets the stage for a sunny day, and green makes you think spring.

Colored lighting can be applied in the same manner that studio lighting is applied, so that the light is directed at the subject and not at the background. But for the most dramatic effect, colored lighting should be ambient lighting. It should be applied to the room, the background, even the open air around the subject.

Digital colored lighting effects are created using radial gradients and a variety of layer modes. The most suitable stock images have two distinct sides to the subject. This allows you to simulate light sources on either side without risk of overlapping.

In this tutorial we add colored lighting to a studio portrait without desaturating the original image. The colored lighting we add will blend with the model's original skin tone.

Yellow and blue tones enhance the model's skin, hair, and eye color.

Getting Started

Open the original image file in the GIMP. The image in this example is very bright, and adding colored lighting will only make it brighter. Let's first use the Levels dialog to reduce the brightness (**Layer ▸ Colors ▸ Levels**). Move the black point about one-third of the way to the right, move the gray point even farther to the right, and click **OK** to apply the levels changes. Not all images will require this kind of adjustment, and with some images you'll get better results using the Curves or Brightness-Contrast tools instead.

Lowering the midpoint of the Levels histogram will darken the image while keeping the contrast high.

Adding Cool Lighting

We want to enhance this image by adding both cool and warm lighting, and we'll start with the cool lighting.

1. Add a new transparent layer by choosing **Layer ▶ New** and setting the Layer Fill Type to **Transparency**. Name the new layer *Left Side - Cool*.

2. Click the foreground color in the toolbox to open the Change Foreground Color dialog. Set the RGB values to **25/59/225** for the blue used in this example, and then click **OK**.

3. Choose the **Blend** tool from the toolbox. In the Tool Options dialog set the Gradient to **FG to Transparent** and the Shape to **Linear**.

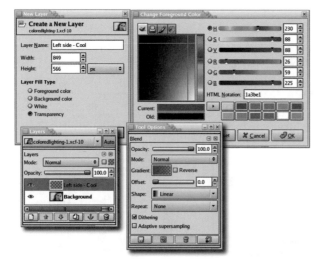

A soft blue blend will give the image a cool feeling.

4. We want to add a blue-to-transparent gradient in the new layer, but in what direction should the gradient flow? Imagine a straight line that goes along the edge of the model's jaw. Starting in the lower-left corner of the canvas, drag a line that passes through and is perpendicular to the imaginary line. Both the imaginary line and the line you should drag are shown. This will apply the gradient to the Left Side - Cool layer.

5. Set the layer mode to **Color** to blend the color in the gradient layer with the colors in the original layer.

The gradient runs from the lower-left corner of the canvas to the upper-right corner, and it is perpendicular to the model's jaw line.

6. This lighting only lights the left side of the image. We need to add a similar lighting effect on the right side. Add another new transparent layer by choosing **Layer ▶ New** and setting the Layer Fill Type to **Transparency**. Name the new layer *Right Side - Cool*.

7. This time imagine a line that goes along the model's left cheek (on the right side of the image). Starting in the lower-right corner of the canvas drag a line that passes through and is perpendicular to the imaginary line.

8. Set this layer's mode to **Color**.

9. The coloring on this side should be a bit darker than on the other side, so duplicate this layer once (**Layer ▶ Duplicate**).

Adding Warm Lighting

Now let's add the warm lighting.

1. Add another new transparent layer and name it *Warm Lighting*. Open the Change Foreground Color dialog again and set the RGB values to **255/222/3** for the warm yellow shown here.

Another gradient runs from the lower-right corner of the canvas up toward the model's left eye.

2. The Blend tool should already be active, but you should change the Shape to **Radial** in the Tool Options dialog before proceeding.

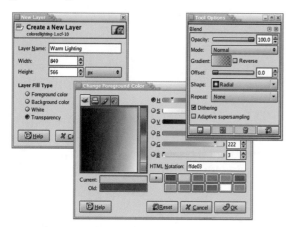

Remember to use the FG to Transparent gradient when creating the colored lighting layers.

3. To apply the warm lighting, click the model's right temple and drag down to the middle of her neck. The result of applying the Radial gradient is shown here in the smaller window.

4. Change this layer's mode to **Soft Light**.

5. To enhance this light further, duplicate the layer once (**Layer ▸ Duplicate**).

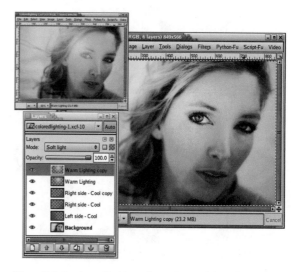

Warm lighting is applied just above the model's right temple so that the brightest points don't overwhelm the color of the model's eyes.

Adding a Highlight

One more highlight is needed. Let's use the Blend tool to add it.

1. Add another new transparent layer and name it *Warm Highlight*.

2. Reset the foreground color to white by pressing **D** and then **X** while the canvas is selected.

3. The Blend tool should still be active, but if it isn't, choose it from the toolbox. Make sure that in the Tool Options dialog the Gradient is set to **FG to Transparent** and the shape is set to **Radial**. Click the outside tip of the model's right eyebrow and

drag toward the inside corner of that eye. The result is shown here in the smaller window).

4. Set this layer's mode to **Soft Light** to produce a brighter yellow over the temple and eyebrow area, making it look as though this is where the light is directed and most intense.

Add intensity to the warm lighting by using the Blend tool to apply a white Radial gradient.

Softening the Image

To add the finishing touch, let's soften the model's face.

1. Duplicate the original layer (**Layer ▸ Duplicate**).

2. Open the Gaussian Blur filter (**Filters ▸ Blur ▸ Gaussian Blur**). Apply a blur of about **8 pixels**. If you aren't satisfied with the result, press CTRL-Z to undo it, and then try again using a different value for the Blur Radius.

    The blur softens the model's face, but we want her eyes and mouth and some of her hair to be in focus.

3. Add a white layer mask (**Layer ▸ Mask ▸ Add Layer Mask**).

4. Reset the foreground color to black by pressing **D** while the canvas is selected.

5. Choose the **Airbrush** tool from the toolbox. Select a soft-edged brush and use it to paint in the mask with black. Paint over the eyes, mouth, and hair until all three are more in focus, but leave the surrounding facial features blurred.

As with the tutorial in Section 4.14, the Gaussian Blur filter is used on a duplicate layer to soften the model's face. A layer mask is also used so that details from the original layer show through the blurred layer.

Further Exploration

Lighting sets the mood in images like this. Experiment with different colored lighting layers to see if you can create images that convey moods of confusion or anger, despite the model's facial expression.

TIPS FOR ADVERTISING DESIGN

Keep the following suggestions in mind as you apply GIMP tools and techniques to designing web and print ads.

Create 3D Effects

Light and shadows are the key components of 3D effects. If you want to add an extra dimension to your work, first determine the direction of the lighting. Then use GIMP tools to increase the light on the surfaces that face the light and decrease the light on the surfaces that would be in shadow.

Add Texture

No surface is completely devoid of texture, not even glass. Wood grains, brushed metal, and scratches can all be created by using the Noise filters in combination with the Motion Blur filter.

Use Layer Modes

Layer modes can be used to merge white reflections with textures. Try the Overlay mode to darken images or the Soft Light and Grain Merge modes to lighten and blend.

Reflect with Gradients

A gradient in a box doesn't look like much. But a gradient applied inside a shape like a circle or a rectangle can look like a reflection. Play with the Blend tool's gradients—many of them can produce reflective effects.

Emboss the Easy Way

The Emboss filter (Filters ▸ Distorts ▸ Emboss) and the Bump Map filter (Filters ▸ Map ▸ Bump Map) both work quite well, but text-embossing effects are so easy to achieve you might as well do things manually. Just duplicate, offset, blur, and cut. To make matters even easier, the blur and cut steps are optional.

Eliminate the Jaggies

Perspective changes can leave behind "the jaggies," but you can apply a light blur to layer edges to clear those up. Zoom out to view the edges of a layer that extends beyond the canvas area. A few jaggies along the edge of a package where the front and side images meet may not be such a bad thing—they can provide contrast to show there is an actual edge where common colors blend. Blurring the jagged edges may give you even better contrast.

Don't Worry About Horizontal Alignment

Don't try to align horizontal elements before applying perspective transformations when creating the front and side images for packaging projects. Applying a perspective change to any side will likely distort those horizontal elements such that they become unaligned. Instead, avoid horizontal lines that need to align on the front and side of an image.

Watch Your Canvas Size

Bigger canvases take up more memory. A plain white canvas that's set to the size of a sheet of legal paper takes up 20 to 30MB just sitting there. Images destined for the Web are usually created at 72 dpi, however, and this greatly reduces the project's file sizes.

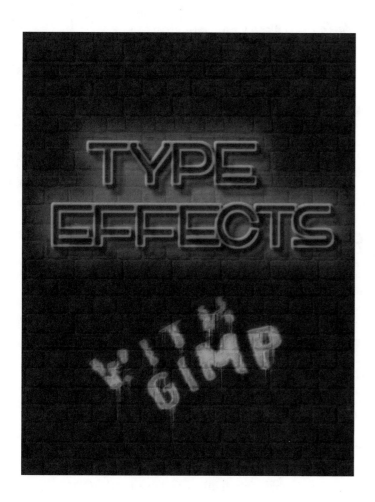

5

TYPE EFFECTS

Chapter 1 covered some of the basics of using text in the GIMP. In Chapter 5, you'll see how you can use lighting, shadows, color, texture, shape, and perspective to make the most of fonts.

The GIMP isn't designed to be used as a font editor; it's a graphic design tool. But what you can do with text in the GIMP is far more interesting than what you can do with a font editor. The GIMP offers you the ability to alter the environment in which the font is displayed. No matter which of the available fonts you use, you can alter the depth, color, and texture for a text string. And that broadens your graphic design possibilities in much more meaningful ways.

The GIMP's Text Tools

The toolbox has a single tool for working with text, and it's the Text tool. When you select this tool, the GIMP launches the Tool Options dialog, which you can use to choose a font and size and adjust other formatting settings, such as color and alignment. In addition, whenever you click a layer while the Text tool is active, the GIMP Text Editor opens. Text you type into this window appears immediately in the current layer and reflects the Text tool's current settings.

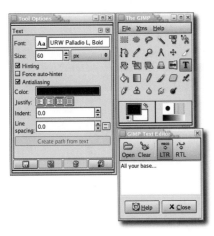

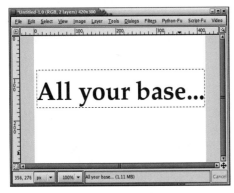

The Tool Options dialog for the Text tool (left) and the Text Editor (lower right)

You'll use the Text tool, its Tool Options dialog, and the Text Editor in all of the tutorials in Chapter 5, but the text itself is only the starting point. Any time you work with text, your goal is to convey a particular message, and the words you choose are only the first step. Where an image editor like the GIMP really allows you to get creative with text is in raster effects.

Text is rendered directly in the layer as you type.

Predefined Text Effects

The GIMP provides a wide set of predefined text effects, from Chalk to Chrome to Frosty to Newsprint. If you need to achieve a certain effect but don't have time to tinker, these predefined effects are the ticket. All of the predefined effects can be accessed by choosing Xtns ▶ Script Fu ▶ Logos from the toolbox. Clicking any option in this menu will open a window in which you can select fonts and colors and set a variety of other options. The truth, however, is that these ready-made tools have their limitations, and we won't rely on them in the following tutorials. If you need to do something really unique, you need to do it yourself.

Create ready-made logos by accessing the Xtns menu in the toolbox.

All of the Script-Fu logos, like the Chrome logo shown here, allow you to adjust a few settings, but the results are usually pretty predictable.

The FreeType Plug-In

If you want to take the Text tool further, you should know that there are additional text plug-ins available for the GIMP. One of these is FreeType, which is available from http://freetype.gimp.org. Once you've installed FreeType, you can access it by choosing Filters ▶ Text ▶ FreeType. It provides options for adjusting rotation, skew, sizing, and letter spacing—options that are not part of the default Text tool. The techniques we'll explore in this book's tutorials don't require the typographic fine-tuning that this plug-in provides, but you're certain to find it useful when working on your own GIMP projects.

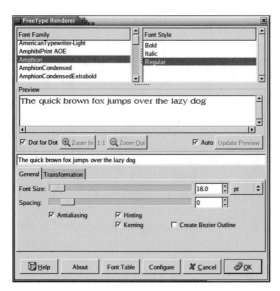

The FreeType plug-in allows you to really fine-tune your text, but the text effects shown in this book's tutorials don't require its features.

Creating Your Own Type Effects

Now it's time for you to explore the GIMP's Text tool while creating your own effects, such as shadows and erosion. The following tutorials will teach you how the GIMP can transform run-of-the-mill characters into a stunning graphic message.

5.1 PERSPECTIVE SHADOW AND REFLECTION

Shadows and reflections give depth to images; they can easily change a two-dimensional image into a three-dimensional design. The Drop Shadow filter (Script-Fu ▶ Shadows ▶ Drop Shadow) places a shadow behind a layer or selection for you. But you'll soon see that if you create a shadow manually, you can position the light source anywhere.

In this tutorial we'll create a white text layer with a perspective shadow over a colored background. The shadow simulates a light source far behind and slightly above the text.

In the final image, the shadow is simply switched from black to white to produce a reflection instead.

Creating the Text

Start with a canvas set to the default size (420 × 300 pixels). Then follow these steps.

1. Turn off the visibility of the Background layer for now by clicking the eye icon in the Layers dialog.

2. Choose the **Text** tool from the toolbox. Set the Color to white, and then choose a font. I've used a font called Alberta Ultra-Light, and I've used a smaller font size for the words *The* and *Of* in order to highlight the more important text in the phrase *The Chronicles Of Mestophanes*. Set the Size to **30 pixels**, click the canvas to open the Text Editor, and type **The**. Close the Text Editor.

3. Use the **Move** tool to drag the new text layer up and to the left.

The text is made up of multiple layers.

4. Click the **Background** layer to make that layer active, and then repeat steps 2 and 3 for the words *Chronicles* and *Mestophanes*, setting the Size to **60 pixels**.

Creating the Shadow

There are now four text layers. Creating the text in multiple layers gives you better control over how each word is positioned.

1. Once all the layers are positioned, merge all visible layers by choosing **Layers ▸ Merge Visible Layers**. Click the radio button next to the words *Expand as necessary* in the pop-up dialog and click **OK** to merge the layers.

After positioning each text layer, merge them into a single layer.

2. It can be helpful to increase the size of the canvas window before you take the next step. A quick way to do this is to zoom in by pressing the plus key three times, press CTRL-E to resize the window frame, and then zoom back out by pressing the minus key three times. Or you can simply resize with the mouse by dragging on the edge of the image window. This image shows the resized canvas window with the original image's text layer. The transparent region is the checkered background behind the text.

Enlarge the canvas window and give yourself more room to work.

3. Now that you have some space in which to work, duplicate the text layer (**Layer ▸ Duplicate**). Click the duplicate layer in the Layers dialog to make that layer active.

4. Use the **Flip** tool to flip the duplicate layer vertically, as shown. In the Tool Options dialog click the **Vertical** radio button, and then click the layer to flip it.

5. Invert the color in the duplicate layer (**Layer ▸ Colors ▸ Invert**). This process will only work if you're using white text—for other colors, try choosing Alpha to Selection (Layer ▸ Transparency ▸ Alpha to Selection) and then using the Bucket Fill tool to fill the shadow with black. If you want to create a reflection instead, you should skip this step.

6. To add perspective to your shadow, choose the **Perspective** tool from the toolbox and then click the canvas. The Perspective Transform Information dialog opens, and a box with handles at its corners appears around the layer. Click the lower-left handle and drag down and to the left. Then click the lower-right handle and drag down and to the right. The line connecting these two drag points should be horizontal, making a trapezoid and making it look as though light is shining somewhere far behind the text. To complete the perspective change, click the **Transform** button.

The duplicate layer will extend beyond the borders of the image itself, but that doesn't matter. You'll snip off the excess later.

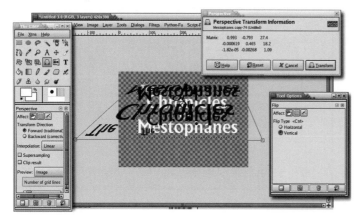

The Perspective tool has its own dialog (upper right), which provides details about the perspective change you are making. The Tool Options dialog for the Flip tool (lower right) allows you to specify the flip direction.

7. Let's blur the shadow twice. The first blur is slight and applies to the upper part of the shadow where it meets the original text. The second blur applies to the lower part of the shadow. In combination, the two blurs make it look as though the shadow is receding from the text and add more depth to the effect.

    Click the duplicate layer to make that layer active. Open the Gaussian Blur filter (**Filters ▸ Blur ▸ Gaussian Blur**). Set the Blur Radius to **4 pixels**, as shown, and click **OK** to apply the blur.

    Choose the **Rectangle Select** tool from the toolbox and draw a square selection around the bottom half of the text in the duplicate layer. Feather this selection by **10 pixels** (**Select ▸ Feather**). Apply the Gaussian Blur filter again, this time setting the Blur Radius to **10 pixels**.

8. Press CTRL-E to resize the window to fit the canvas.

NOTE *The Gaussian Blur filter is better than the simple Blur filter (Filters ▸ Blur ▸ Blur) because it provides precise control over the radius of the blur. You'll probably use the Gaussian Blur filter far more often than the simple Blur filter.*

Feathering the selection (upper-right dialog) will blend the second blur into the first.

9. Turn on visibility for the Background layer in the Layers dialog, and then click the **Background** layer to make that layer active.

10. Select the **Blend** tool from the toolbox. In the Tool Options dialog, click the **Gradient** button and choose a gradient (the Cold Steel gradient is shown here). Click the canvas and drag from the top of the canvas to the bottom.

Use the Cold Steel gradient to create this effect. Simply choose the Blend tool, click the canvas, and drag from the top to the bottom.

Positioning and Reflecting the Shadow

Now let's add the finishing touches.

1. Click the shadow layer in the Layers dialog to make that layer active.

2. The Move tool moves the layer directly beneath the mouse pointer, not necessarily the active (or current) layer. This won't be the correct layer if your mouse isn't exactly over one of the letters in your text. To make it easier for yourself, hold down the SHIFT key to toggle the Move tool's behavior. Now the Move tool only affects the active layer: your text. Check out the Move Tool Options dialog for more options.

3. You may find that the text and shadow are too small compared to the Background layer. If this happens, use the Crop tool to cut away the excess canvas. Choose the **Crop** tool from the toolbox and then click the canvas to open the Crop and Resize Information dialog. Set the Origin X and Origin Y values to **0 pixels**, set the Width to **420 pixels**, and set the Height to **300 pixels**. Click **OK**.

Further Exploration

As an alternative, if you've used white text, you can invert the color of the shadow layer to produce a reflection instead of a shadow. When reflecting your text, the less you blur, the more reflective the surface appears to be.

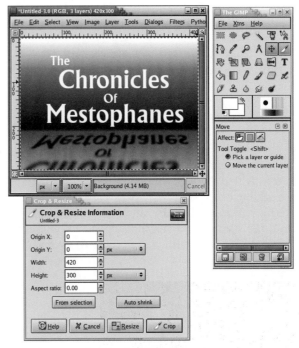

Crop the canvas if you need to fit the text into a smaller background.

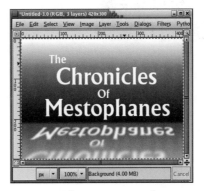

Creating a reflection requires only one additional step: You must invert the color of the shadow. If you knew that you wanted a reflection at the outset, you simply wouldn't change the color of the perspective shadow.

5.2 CHROME AND METAL TEXT

Metallic finishes are most often applied to text, but you can also put these general-purpose textures to use in user interface design. Metallic finishes are created with the Curves dialog. Adjusting the curves of either a gradient or a smooth texture causes gradual changes in tone to become more dramatic and produces the appearance of shiny metal. This set of tutorials shows you how to create three different metal effects, all of which are produced by making adjustments in the Curves dialog.

Metal text samples

Brushed Metal

The brushed-metal effect is the product of two basic processes. First we apply the Motion Blur filter, which makes it look as though the surface is covered with tiny scratches. Applying noise to a layer adds texture to otherwise flat images. Then we adjust the image's gray tones in the Curves dialog. Adjusting the Value curve for an image with variations that are not linear—that is, an image in which gray is somewhat randomly distributed in the layer—accelerates the change from black to white and mimics reflective

metal. This image shows the final effect, which is enhanced by extruding the letter into three dimensions.

The letter S is made to look like brushed metal.

Creating the Text

Begin by opening a new canvas using the default 420 × 300 template.

1. Fill the Background layer with black.
2. Choose the **Text** tool from the toolbox. In the Tool Options dialog, choose an appropriate font. I've used a font called Gilde Ultra-Light sized to 300 pixels in this example. At this size, Gilde Ultra-Light is a thick enough to show the brushed metal texture clearly, which is important because the subtle effect can be lost if you use a font with thinner characters. Change the text color to white.
3. Click the **Background** layer to open the Text Editor, and type **s**. Click the **Close** button to close the Text Editor.
4. Use the **Move** tool to align the text layer manually. Match the text layer to the canvas size (**Layer ▸ Layer to Image Size**).

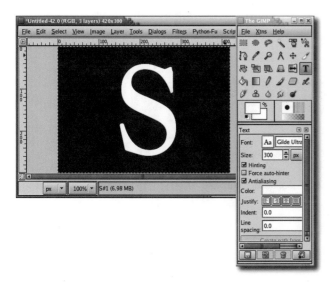

Use the Move tool to position the text on the center of the canvas.

Extruding the Text with the Bump Map Filter

1. Duplicate the text layer (**Layer ▸ Duplicate Layer**).

2. Open the Gaussian Blur filter (**Filters ▸ Blur ▸ Gaussian Blur**) and apply a blur of **10 pixels** to the duplicate layer.

3. Click the original text layer to make that layer active.

4. Open the Bump Map filter (**Filters ▸ Map ▸ Bump Map**). Choose **Sinusoidal** from the Map Type drop-down menu, and then choose the blurred layer from the Bump Map drop-down menu. Set the Azimuth to **132 degrees**, set the Elevation to **30 degrees**, and set the Depth to **7**. Click **OK** to apply the filter, and then delete the blurred layer.

    Sinusoidal mapping produces a more realistic three-dimensional effect with edges that are less rounded than those produced by the Linear and Spherical options. The Azimuth slider sets the direction of lighting within 360 degrees. The Elevation slider changes the roundness of the edges, and the Depth slider sets the softness of the shadowed sides. To get the most out of this tutorial, I've chosen values to accentuate depth.

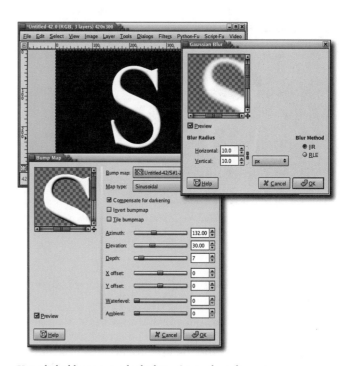

Use a light blur to extrude the letter S into three dimensions.

5. Turn on the **Keep Transparency** option for the layer in which you used the Bump Map filter.

6. Open the Gaussian Blur filter again (**Filters ▸ Blur ▸ Gaussian Blur**) and apply a blur of **10 pixels**. This softens the shadow edges a bit, making the sides appear more rounded.

7. Duplicate this blurred layer (**Layer ▸ Duplicate Layer**).

8. With the duplicate layer active, select the text by choosing **Layer ▸ Transparency ▸ Alpha to Selection**.

9. Press **D** to reset the default foreground and background colors.

10. Choose the **Blend** tool from the toolbox. In the Tool Options dialog set the mode to **Grain Merge** and set the Gradient to **FG to Transparent**. Drag from the upper-left corner of the canvas to the lower-right corner. Then drag from the bottom of the canvas to the top.

11. In the Layers dialog set this layer's mode to **Soft Light**.

12. Press SHIFT-CTRL-A to deselect all.

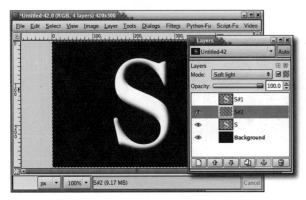

Blending enhances the three-dimensional effect. This isn't required to achieve the brushed-metal appearance, but it gives you an interesting logo.

Adding a Metallic Finish

1. Merge the gradient layer and the layer in which you applied the Bump Map filter (**Layer ▸ Merge Down**).

2. Open the **Curves** dialog and adjust the curve for all channels to closely resemble that shown here. The actual setting will vary, depending on the variation in gray tones in your layer.

3. Duplicate the layer (**Layer ▸ Duplicate Layer**).

4. Select the letter in this duplicate layer by choosing **Layer ▸ Transparency ▸ Alpha to Selection**.

5. Use the Scatter RGB filter to fill the selection with noise (**Filters ▸ Noise ▸ Scatter RGB**). Uncheck the boxes next to the words *Correlated noise* and *Independent RGB*. Set all three color channel sliders to **0.44**, and set the Alpha slider to **0**. Click **OK** to apply this filter.

    The Scatter RGB filter fills the selection with random dots—in this case, all the dots are the same grayish color. Setting the color channel sliders to 0.44 increases the noise. (Higher values mean more noise and lower values mean less noise.) The alpha channel is not used here.

6. Open the Gaussian Blur filter (**Filters ▸ Blur ▸ Gaussian Blur**) and apply a blur of **2 pixels**.

7. The last step is to add the blue tint that gives metal its shiny appearance. With the text still selected, use the Motion Blur

filter to further blur the layer (**Filters ▸ Blur ▸ Motion Blur**). Set the Angle to **45 degrees** and set the Length to **20 pixels**.

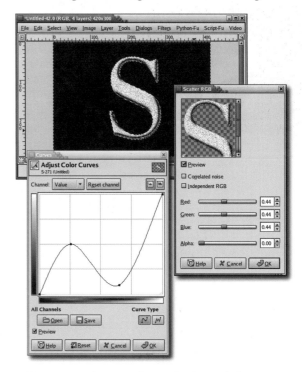

Adding noise to the text and using the Curves dialog to increase the separation of dark and light noise

8. Add a new layer (**Layer ▸ New Layer**).

9. Click the foreground color box to launch the Change Foreground Color dialog, and set the RGB values to **16/59/130**. Click **OK** to close the dialog and then drag the foreground color into the selection in the new layer to fill it with that color. (The letter you selected in step 4 should still be selected.)

10. Deselect all (SHIFT-CTRL-A) and then set the layer mode to **Soft Light** and reduce the Opacity to **52 percent**.

11. Set the layer mode of the next layer down in the Layers dialog to **Grain Merge**. Use the **Gaussian Blur** filter to apply a blur of **2 pixels** to the original text layer. That's it! Just these few steps produce the results you see here.

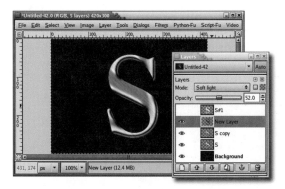

Adding a blue tint completes the effect.

Heavy Metal

The heavy-metal effect is similar to the brushed-metal effect, but it uses the Solid Noise filter to produce a cloudy texture, and it relies on a more dramatic curves adjustment to achieve a very polished, reflective appearance.

Heavy metal looks more polished than brushed metal.

Creating the Text

As in the previous tutorial, start by opening a new canvas using the default 420 × 300 template.

1. Press **D** to reset the default foreground and background colors. Drag the foreground color onto the canvas to fill the canvas with that color.

2. Choose the **Text** tool from the toolbox, and choose an appropriate font. Change the text color to white. For this tutorial, I've chosen Penyae Ultra-Light, a font that uses uppercase characters for lowercase characters (known as *small caps*). This font's wide surfaces make the heavy-metal effect easier to see. I've set the font size to 150 pixels for this example.

NOTE *When trying to achieve this effect, always choose a font that is solid (rather than outlined), and choose a font that has thick characters. If you'd like to use a particular font but the characters seem too thin, the bold version of that font might work.*

3. Click the **Background** layer to launch the Text Editor, and then type `Metal`.

4. Use the **Move** tool to position the text layer manually.

5. Resize the text layer to match the image size (**Layer ▸ Layer to Image Size**).

Using a thick font will make it easier to see the final effect.

Adding Depth

1. Select the text in this layer by choosing **Layer ▸ Transparency ▸ Alpha to Selection**.

2. Grow the selection by **6 pixels** (**Select ▸ Grow**).

3. Save the selection to a channel (**Select ▸ Save to Channel**). Click the channel name and change it to *Outline*. We'll return to the saved channel in just a moment, but for now be sure to click the text layer in the Layers dialog to make that layer active again.

4. Deselect all (SHIFT-CTRL-A).

5. As we did with the brushed metal effect, let's extrude the text. Note that in this tutorial the extruding isn't optional. The depth created along the edges of the text creates variations in the reflections that contribute to the heavy metal effect. Start by duplicating the text layer (**Layer ▸ Duplicate Layer**).

The saved channel appears in the bottom pan of the Channels dialog.

6. Use the **Gaussian Blur** filter to apply a blur of **10 pixels** to the duplicate layer.

7. Click the original text layer to make that layer active.

8. Open the Bump Map filter (**Filters ▸ Map ▸ Bump Map**). Set the Map Type to **Linear** and check the box next to the words *Compensate for darkening*. Set the Azimuth to **130 degrees**, the Elevation to **30 degrees**, and the Depth to 7. Click **OK** to apply this filter to the layer. At this point, you can delete the duplicate layer.

9. Duplicate the layer in which you applied the Bump Map filter (**Layer ▸ Duplicate Layer**).

10. Select the text by choosing **Layer ▸ Transparency ▸ Alpha to Selection**.

11. Fill the selection with a cloud rendered from the Solid Noise filter (**Filters ▸ Render ▸ Clouds ▸ Solid Noise**), as discussed in Section 1.8. Set the Random Seed to **0**. Set the X Size to **10** and the Y Size to **2**.

12. The Random Seed value is used to change the shape of the cloud, so feel free to try different values as you experiment. When set to 0, which is the random seed value used in creating this tutorial, you should end up with the same cloud structure

as I did. However, because the cloud is rendered only within the selection, you won't actually see a cloud. You'll just see various shades of gray inside the selection.

The Bump Map filter makes the original text appear three-dimensional.

13. With the selection still active, open the Motion Blur filter (**Filters ▸ Blur ▸ Motion Blur**). Set the Angle slider to **95 degrees**, set the Length slider to **20**, and then deselect all (SHIFT-CTRL-A). The Motion Blur filter turns the clouds into what look more like reflections of light.

14. Set this layer's mode to **Grain Merge** to brighten the cloud layer and give us the look of a highly reflective metal.

15. Merge this layer with the layer in which you originally applied the Bump Map filter (**Layer ▸ Merge Down**).

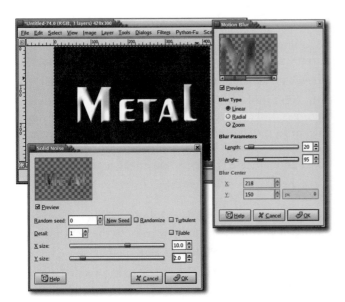

Use the Solid Noise filter to render a cloud on the text. Then apply the Motion Blur filter.

Adding a Metallic Finish

This effect can be improved further by increasing the contrast between light and dark areas.

1. Open the Curves dialog (**Layer ▸ Colors ▸ Curves**) and apply a curve like the one shown here. This gives you the basic metallic effect, but we can still enhance it a bit.

2. Add a white drop shadow (**Script-Fu ▸ Shadow ▸ Drop Shadow**). Set the Offset X and Offset Y values to **–2 pixels** to move the shadow up and to the left, and set the Blur Radius to **10 pixels**. The shadow adds depth to the lit edges of the metallic finish, simulating light that is streaming from above and to the left of the image.

3. Perhaps the soft edges of the text are too soft. It would be nice if the text had a more punched-out look. We can sharpen the edges of the text and get that punched-out appearance by stroking with a gray outline. Start by adding a new transparent layer by choosing **Layer ▸ New** and setting the Layer Fill Type to **Transparency**.

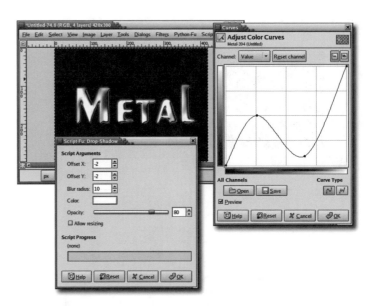

Combining a curves adjustment in the text layer with a blurred white shadow that is slightly offset

4. Open the Channels dialog (**Dialogs ▸ Channels**) and click the **Outline** channel you saved earlier. Select **Channel to Selection** to retrieve the selection of the original text.

5. Click the new transparent layer in the Layers dialog to make that layer active again.

6. Set the foreground color to gray (**#a4a4a4**).

7. Open the Stroke Selection dialog (**Edit ▸ Stroke Selection**) and set the Line Width to **1 pixel**. Click the **Stroke** button to stroke the selection.

8. Deselect all (CTRL-SHIFT-A).

9. Offset this layer (**Layer ▸ Transform ▸ Offset**), setting the Offset X and Offset Y values to **2 pixels**.

10. Shiny metals, like chrome, have a bluish tint, so we'll need to add that for realism. Add a new layer (**Layer ▸ New Layer**) and fill it with blue, setting the RGB values to **16/59/130**.

11. Set the layer mode for this blue layer to **Soft Light** and reduce the Opacity to **53 percent**. The result of our labor is shown on the next page.

Stroke the outline of the original text in gray and blend the layer with
the Soft Light mode to give the text a more punched-out look.

Liquid Metal

As you saw, using the Curves dialog made all the difference in
the last tutorial. You might wonder where you can go from there,
though—what else can you do with metallic text? In this tutorial
I'll show you how to take the process one step further and add
nontext components to your image.

Here we simulate liquid metal. The GIMP provides
the heat, of course.

Creating the Text

1. With the toolbox selected, press **D** and then **X** to reset and
   then swap the default foreground and backgrounds colors.

2. Open a new canvas window (the background will be black).

3. Choose the **Text** tool from the toolbox. Choose a large, thick
   font—I use Arial Black sized to 120 pixels. As in the last tutorial, a thicker font makes the effect easier to see. In this case,
   you also want a font with lowercase letters and "dots" over
   letters like *i* and *j*. These elements will enhance the melting
   effect. Once you've chosen an appropriate font, set the font
   color to white.

4. Click the canvas to launch the Text Editor and then type your
   text. When you've finished, click **OK** to close the Text Editor.

5. Use the **Move** tool to center the text layer manually.

6. Expand the layer boundary to the image size (**Layer ▸ Layer
   to Image Size**).

A thick font is essential for this effect. With thin fonts, the reflective nature
of the metal is more difficult to distinguish.

Liquefying the Letters

1. Use the **Free Select** tool to draw a round selection beneath the
   first letter. Hold down the SHIFT key to draw more selections
   beneath the text. Holding down the SHIFT key allows you to
   add to the new selection to the existing selection, even if the
   new selection does not physically touch the existing selection.
   Make sure the selections overlap portions of each letter.

2. After you have drawn a few selections, grow them by **1 pixel** (**Select ▸ Grow**) to soften the edges of the hand-drawn selections.

3. Fill the selections with white by dragging the foreground color box from the toolbox into the image.

4. Deselect all (CTRL-SHIFT-A).

Hand-drawn selections are added to the text layer and filled with white.

5. Open the Waves filter (**Filters ▸ Distorts ▸ Waves**). Set the Amplitude to **6**, the Phase to **107**, and the Wavelength to **29**. Click **OK** to apply this filter.

    The text and blobs below them will be distorted in a wavy fashion—the effect will depend on which font you chose for this tutorial. If you chose a different font, you may have to experiment with different settings for the Waves filter.

6. Name this layer *Blobs* and then duplicate it (**Layer ▸ Duplicate Layer**).

7. Open the Gaussian Blur filter (**Filters ▸ Blur ▸ Gaussian**) and apply a blur of **10 pixels**. Name this blurred layer *Blur*.

The Waves filter does the real work in this tutorial. The blurred layer sets the stage for us to add depth with the Bump Map filter.

Adding Depth and Polish

1. Open the Bump Map filter (**Filters ▸ Map ▸ Bump Map**) and use the Blur layer to apply the filter to the Blobs layer. Set the Map Type to **Linear** and check the box next to the words *Compensate for darkening*. Set the Azimuth to **130 degrees**, set the Elevation to **30 degrees**, and set the Depth to **7**. Click **OK** to apply this filter. Name this layer *Bump Map*.

2. Turn off the visibility of the Blur layer.

3. Click the **Bump Map** layer to make that layer active, and then duplicate it (**Layer ▸ Duplicate Layer**).

4. Create a selection of the bump map in this duplicate layer by choosing **Layer ▸ Transparency ▸ Alpha to Selection**.

5. Fill the duplicate layer with solid noise (**Filters ▸ Render ▸ Clouds ▸ Solid Noise**).

6. Open the Motion Blur filter (**Filters ▸ Blur ▸ Motion Blur**). Set the Length to **20** and the Angle to **95 degrees**. Click **OK** to apply this filter.

7. Set the layer mode for the duplicate layer to **Grain Merge**, and then merge it with the original text layer (**Layer ▸ Merge Down**).

As in the heavy-metal tutorial, use noise and blurring to simulate reflections.

8. Deselect all (CTRL-SHIFT-A).

9. Open the **Curves** dialog and adjust the **Value** curve as shown here.

10. Open the Gaussian Blur filter (**Filters ▸ Blur ▸ Gaussian Blur**) and apply a blur of **0.7 pixels** to smooth out any rough edges.

11. Add a new layer (**Layer ▸ New Layer**), fill it with blue as before, and set the layer mode for the new layer to **Soft Light**.

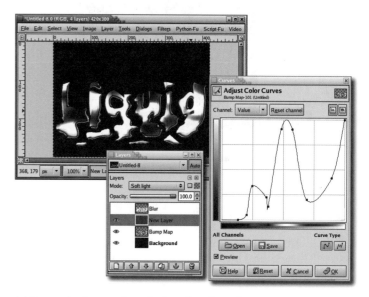

Adding a color layer makes it look as though an object is reflected in the metallic surface.

Further Exploration

This final version could be improved upon by more carefully controlling the distortion of the text. You could do this by using the IWarp filter instead of the Waves filter, for example. Additional color could be added as well. Try adding red and yellow layers with solid noise layer masks to make it look as though the letters are hot—there must be some reason why the metal is liquid, right?

5.3 GEL TYPE

The gel effect shown here is nothing more than soft shadows, smooth surfaces, and white reflections. Imagine how water in a glass tube looks, and you get the idea. Gel effects are especially popular in web design, but you'll see them used in many different contexts. The Mac OS X user interface incorporates what Apple calls the *Aqua* style, which utilizes gel effects in shades of blue.

The process described in this tutorial can be applied to text, borders, and buttons—just about any surface. Depending on the settings you use for the Curves dialog, the Lighting Effects filter, and the Bump Map filter, your results may be different from mine. What you should take away from this process is how to use bump maps, lighting effects, and layer modes.

Looks like gel, doesn't it?

Creating the Text

Start with a canvas set to the default size (420 × 300 pixels).

1. Click the foreground color box to open the Change Foreground Color dialog, and choose a nice blue. I've set the RGB levels to 0/51/222 for this shade.

2. Choose the **Text** tool from the toolbox. In the Tool Options dialog, choose a serifed font and set the font size to **180 pixels**. (Serifed fonts work best for this tutorial because their characters are easily rounded by the process that follows.) Click the canvas, type **GEL** in the Text Editor, and then click **OK** to close that window.

3. Use the **Move** tool to drag the new layer to the center of the canvas.

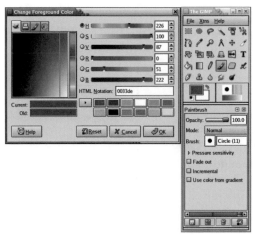

Click the foreground color box in the toolbox to open the Change Foreground Color dialog.

4. Choose **Layer ▸ Layer to Image Size** to expand the text layer to the boundary of the image.

When using the Text tool, you can also change the text color by clicking the color swatch in the Tool Options dialog.

Rounding the Surface of the Text

1. Create a selection around the text by choosing **Layer ▸ Transparency ▸ Alpha to Selection**.

2. Shrink the selection by **2 pixels** (**Select ▸ Shrink**) and feather it by **2 pixels** (**Select ▸ Feather**).

Create a selection of the text, and then shrink and feather that selection.

3. Click the foreground color box to open the Change Foreground Color dialog and set the RGB values to **31/82/255** for a slightly brighter shade of blue.

4. Create a new layer by choosing **Layer ▸ New Layer** or clicking the **New Layer** button in the Layers dialog. Name the new layer *Bump Map*.

5. Click the **Bump Map** layer in the Layers dialog to make that layer active, and then fill the selection with the foreground color by dragging it from the toolbox into the selection.

6. Deselect all (**Select ▸ None**).

7. Duplicate the layer (**Layer ▸ Duplicate**). Name the duplicate layer *Blur*.

8. Open the Gaussian Blur filter (**Filters ▸ Blur ▸ Gaussian Blur**) and apply a blur of **10 pixels** to the duplicate layer.

9. Click the **Bump Map** layer to make that layer active.

10. Open the Bump Map filter (**Filters ▸ Map ▸ Bump Map**). Set the Azimuth to **105 degrees**, set the Elevation to **5.75 degrees**, and set the Depth to **10**. Set the Map Type to **Linear**, check the box next to the words *Compensate for darkening* to turn

on that option, and choose the **Blur** layer from the Bump Map drop-down menu. Click **OK** to apply the filter to the Bump Map layer.

The blurred edges of the duplicate layer are used as input to the Bump Map filter to simulate depth.

11. Set the Bump Map layer's mode to **Addition**.

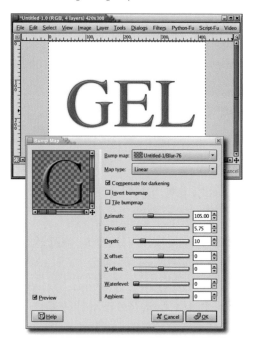

Use the Bump Map filter to add depth.

12. We'll need to make a color adjustment to the Bump Map layer in order to make the text look more gel-like. Open the Curves dialog (**Layer ▸ Colors ▸ Curves**) and set the curve as shown here. Here the visibility of the Blur layer is turned off, and you can see that the Bump Map layer appears brighter.

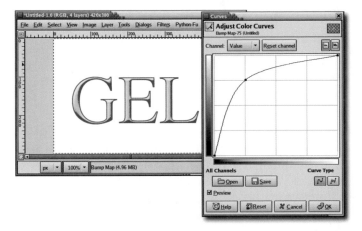

Adjusting the Curves dialog for the Bump Map layer the text a gel-like appearance, but be sure to turn off the visibility of the Blur layer in the Layers dialog.

NOTE *We won't be using the Blur layer again until much later in this project, so we'll make it invisible now to make it easier to see the rest of our work.*

Adding Lighting Effects

Let's apply one more filter to the Bump Map layer.

1. Open the Lighting Effects filter (**Filters ▸ Light Effects ▸ Lighting Effects**). On the **Options** tab, click the upper-left corner of the preview. The blue dot, which represents your light source, will follow the mouse. Position the blue dot so the gel text is lit to personal taste. It's tricky! If you lose the dot, disable this light (by changing the Type in the Light tab to None and then selecting a different light from the Light Settings menu) and create a new one.

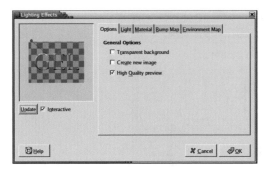

Positioning the light source in the preview can be difficult. Don't be afraid to click Cancel and try again.

2. On the **Light** tab, choose **Directional** from the Type drop-down menu. You can see that your blue dot now has a line associated with it. This line represents the direction of your light source. The Intensity setting you select has a great impact on the overall effect, as do the changes you made in the Curves dialog. I set the Intensity to **1.45**. If you aren't pleased with the gel effect, experiment by adjusting this value. Click **OK** to apply the Lighting Effects filter.

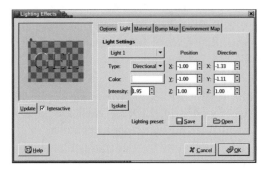

Of all the Lighting Effects filter's settings, the Intensity setting has the greatest impact.

3. Once the Lighting Effects filter has been applied, offset the Bump Map layer by **−2/−2 pixels** (**Layer ▸ Transform ▸ Offset**).

4. Open the Gaussian Blur filter (**Filters ▸ Blur ▸ Gaussian Blur**) and apply a blur of **5 pixels** to that layer.

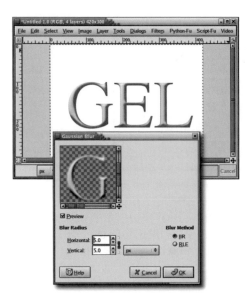

A soft blur smooths the edges, giving the text a more realistic gel-like appearance.

Lightening the Text and Adding a Drop Shadow

To bring out the curved surface of the gel, we can increase the contrast in the text and add a background shadow. If you turned off the visibility of the Blur layer, you'll need to turn it back on to continue with this project.

1. Make sure the **Blur** layer is the active layer in the Layers dialog. Duplicate this layer by choosing **Layer ▸ Duplicate Layer** (the duplicate layer will be named *Blur copy* by default).

2. Offset the Blur copy layer by **2/2 pixels** (**Layer ▸ Transform ▸ Offset**).

3. Click the original **Blur** layer to make that layer active, and then offset it by **–2/–2 pixels** (**Layer ▸ Transform ▸ Offset**).

4. Set the Blur layer's mode to **Addition**, and set the Blur copy layer's mode to **Screen**.

Revisiting the Blur layer and using it to lighten the gel coloring even more

5. Click the **GEL** text layer to make that layer active. Add a drop shadow (**Script-Fu ▸ Shadows ▸ Drop Shadow**) that is offset by **2 pixels** and blurred by **3 pixels**.

Now that the text is so light, it fades into the white background. Adding a drop shadow helps the effect stand out.

Further Exploration

The basic process for creating gel effects is the same no matter what kind of surface you are modifying. To add variety, try using different colors for the gel or using the Waves or IWarp filters to add distortions.

5.4 DISTRESSED TEXT

In interior design, distressing is used to give furniture an aged and weathered appearance. In graphic design, it serves a similar purpose—it takes clean and crisp objects, such as text, and gives them more visual interest. While it would be possible to design a complete font set around this effect, premade effects always limit an artist's design options. You want to add your own personal touches, right? That's tough to do if every *F* in your text looks exactly the same.

BRoKEN
SPARRoWS

An example of distressed text

Creating the Text

1. With the toolbox selected, press **D** to set the foreground color to black.

2. Open white canvas that is set to the default size (420 × 300 pixels).

3. Click the **Text** tool to make that tool active, and then select an appropriate font in the Tool Options dialog. This example uses SoutaneBlack Ultra-Light, which has thick characters that make it easier to see the distressed effect.

4. Click the canvas to launch the Text Editor and type **BRoKEN SPARRoWS**, using lowercase for the letter *o*, just to add a little pizazz. Press ENTER to add a line break between the words and then insert a few spaces before the word *SPARRoWS*. Click the **Close** button to close the Text Editor.

5. Use the **Move** tool to center the text on the canvas.

6. Add a new transparent layer by choosing **Layer ▸ New** and setting the Layer Fill Type to **Transparency**.

The distressed text effect is easier to see if you start with a thick font.

Creating a Distressed Layer

The next part is the hardest. We're going to add a series of vertical lines of varying widths that will be used as the basis for the distressed effect. The difficulty here will be in positioning the lines randomly over the letters.

1. Turn on the image grid (**View ▸ Show Grid**) and set the GIMP to snap to the grid (**View ▸ Snap to Grid**). We'll use the grid to make drawing perfectly vertical (and thus parallel) lines easier.

2. Choose the **Pencil** tool from the toolbox and select the **Circle (01)** brush. Draw a single line that extends from the top of the canvas to the bottom. To do this, click a grid point at the top of the canvas, hold down the SHIFT key, and then click a grid point in the same vertical line as the original point. This will draw a straight line that is 1 pixel in width.

3. Hide the image grid (**View ▸ Show Grid**) and turn off the Snap to Grid option (**View ▸ Snap to Grid**). At this point you may also want to turn off the visibility of the text layer, though that isn't required.

With the help of the image grid and the Snap to Grid option, you can draw straight lines with ease.

4. Choose the **Fuzzy Select** tool from the toolbox and use it to click the line you just drew with the Pencil tool. You may need to zoom in on the line to making clicking it easier.

5. Once you have selected the line, press CTRL-C to copy it, press SHIFT-CTRL-A to deselect all, and press CTRL-V to paste the duplicate line as a floating selection.

6. Use the **Move** tool to move the duplicate line to the right or to the left, and then click outside the floating selection to anchor it to the original layer. Do this a few times, positioning the lines in a random pattern across the width of the canvas. When you've finished, you should have one layer that contains many lines. Duplicate this layer (**Layer ▸ Duplicate**).

7. Offset the duplicate layer by entering **1 pixel** in the Offset X field (**Layer ▸ Transform ▸ Offset**).

8. Merge the active layer with the layer below it by choosing **Layer ▸ Merge Down**. This effectively doubles the width of your lines in a single layer. Of course, you could have simply used a brush that was 2 pixels in width from the start, but knowing how to enhance effects through duplicating and offsetting layers is a useful skill to have at your command.

These randomly positioned lines are used to mask out portions of the original text.

9. With the line layer active, switch to the **Circular (03)** brush and repeat the process described above, this time drawing thicker lines that overlap the lines you've already positioned. Avoid uniformly spacing these thicker lines, and make sure that they intersect the text here and there.

Making a few lines thicker than others adds more randomness to the pattern, but make sure that the lines intersect the text, or you won't be able to see a difference in the final effect.

10. Open the Hurl filter (**Filters ▸ Noise ▸ Hurl**). Set the Random Seed to **150**, set the Randomization to **10 percent**, and set the Repeat to **1 time**. The Hurl filter scatters dots in the current layer, overwriting pixels if necessary. The Randomization value specifies how much of the layer should be filled with dots.

Higher Repeat values indicate that the filter should be applied repeatedly, thus increasing the overall number of dots applied. Click **OK** to apply the Hurl filter to the line layer.

11. Open the Pick filter (**Filters ▸ Noise ▸ Pick**). Set the Random Seed to **10**, set the Randomization to **20 percent**, and set the Repeat to **3 times**. Click **OK** to apply this filter to the line layer.

    The Pick filter is similar to the Hurl filter, but it chooses the pixels and which color to use for them in a slightly different manner. In this case, using the Pick filter makes the dot distribution more random and introduces some larger dots to the pattern. After applying the Hurl and Pick filters, you will be left with a set of distressed lines.

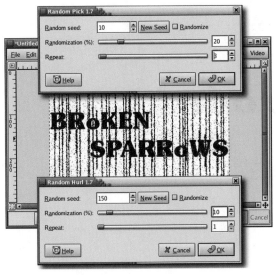

Using the Hurl and Pick filters creates random noise and makes the lines look distressed.

Applying the Distressed Effect to the Text

Now it's time to blend the distressed lines with the text.

1. Invert the colors in the line layer (**Layer ▸ Colors ▸ Invert**).

2. The Hurl and Pick filters scattered colored dots in the line layer, but we're shooting for a black-and-white effect, so go ahead and desaturate the layer (**Layer ▸ Colors ▸ Desaturate**). Make sure to turn back on the visibility of the text layer. Change the line layer's mode to **Addition**.

3. Use the **Move** tool to position the Text layer as necessary to get the best effect.

Because the background is white, the white lines disappear where they don't intersect the text. If your background is a different color, copy the line layer, paste it into a layer mask that you create on the text layer (Layer ▸ Mask ▸ Add Layer Mask), and then turn off the visibility of the line layer.

Further Exploration

There are many other ways to use the distressed line layer to enhance the original text. Try using the distressed line layer as a layer mask on the text layer or as a layer mask on a colored or textured layer above the text. The next tutorial will show you how to let background images show through the "holes" in this effect.

5.5 EROSION

Did you think I was kidding when I suggested trying the last tutorial as a mask? This time I'll take that idea a little further by adding some depth, texture, and color. Despite all this extra flash, the process is still pretty much the same.

Text that has been eroded looks similar to text that has been distressed, but we use a different process to achieve each effect.

Creating the Text

Start with new canvas set to the default size (420 × 300).

1. With the toolbox selected, press **D** to reset the default foreground and background colors. Add an alpha channel to this layer (**Layer ▸ Transparency ▸ Add Alpha Channel**).

2. Choose the **Text** tool from the toolbox and then select an appropriate font. As in the last tutorial, I use SoutaneBlack Ultra-Light here. The font size is set to 110 pixels, and the font color is set to black.

3. Click the canvas to open the Text Editor and type your text. Click the **Close** button to close the Text Editor.

4. Use the **Move** tool to position the text layer in the middle of the canvas, and then expand the boundaries of the canvas to match the image size (**Layer ▸ Layer to Image Size**).

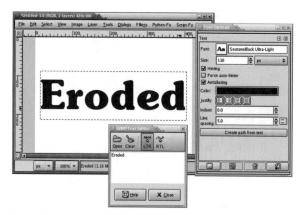

As in the previous tutorials, you'll get the best result if you use a thick font.

Distressing the Text

1. Add a white layer mask (**Layer ▸ Mask ▸ Add Layer Mask**) to the text layer and then click the layer mask in the Layers dialog to make it active.

2. Open the Solid Noise filter (**Filters ▸ Render ▸ Clouds ▸ Solid Noise**). Set the Random Seed to 0, check the box next to the word *Turbulent*, and set the X Size and Y Size sliders to **16**. This will create a smooth, blob-filled cloud in the mask. Click **OK** to apply these settings to the mask.

3. Open the Curves dialog (**Layer ▸ Colors ▸ Curves**) and adjust the curve as shown here to sharpen the edges of the blobs. Click **OK** to apply these changes to the layer mask.

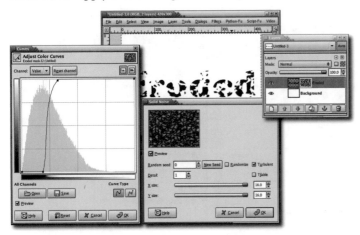

The Solid Noise filter provides a good mask, but making adjustments in the Curves dialog sharpens the edges of the erosion effect.

4. Open the Pick filter (**Filters ▸ Noise ▸ Pick**). Set the Random Seed to **10**, set the Randomization slider to **70 percent**, and set the Repeat slider to **1 time**. This effect should be automatically applied to the layer mask.

5. Apply the layer mask to the layer by choosing **Layer ▸ Mask ▸ Apply Layer Mask**, which merges the mask with the layer content.

Using the Pick filter to add noise gives the text a more crumbled look.

6. Create a selection of the merged layer (**Layer ▸ Transparency ▸ Alpha to Selection**) and save this selection to a channel (**Select ▸ Save to Channel**). Double-click the channel name and change the name to *Outline*. Doing this will make the new channel active, so return to the Layers dialog and click the text layer to make it the active layer once again.

7. Merge the text layer with the Background layer (**Layer ▸ Merge Down**).

8. Deselect all (**Select ▸ None**).

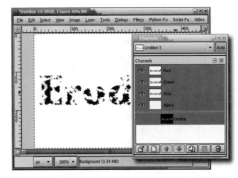

Save the outline of the text to a channel before merging it with the Background layer.

Embossing the Text

1. Use the Emboss filter to add depth to the text (**Filters ▸ Distorts ▸ Emboss**). Choose the **Emboss** option, and then set the Azimuth to **0 degrees**, set the Elevation to **40 degrees**, and set the Depth to **47**.

2. Retrieve the selection you saved earlier by returning to the Channels dialog (**Dialogs ▸ Channels**), clicking the saved channel to make it active, and then clicking the **Channel to Selection** button. This gives us a selection of everything but the text.

3. Grow the selection by **1 pixel** (**Select ▸ Grow**) and invert the selection's colors (**Select ▸ Invert**).

4. Return to the Layers dialog and click the text layer again to make that layer active.

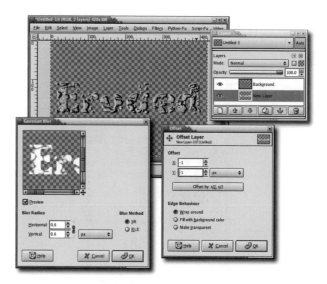

Use the Emboss filter rather than the Bump Map filter to avoid soft edges. The Emboss filter extrudes this text without requiring that we apply a blur as in previous tutorials.

An offset white edge simulates lighting.

5. Press CTRL-X to cut the selection from this layer, leaving just the text over a transparent background. Create a new selection (**Layer ▸ Transparency ▸ Alpha to Selection**).

6. Next we're going to add an edge to the text by creating a white layer, offsetting it, and then positioning it below the text layer. Let's start by creating a new layer (**Layer ▸ New**) and filling it with white. Then deselect all (SHIFT-CTRL-A).

7. Open the Gaussian Blur filter (**Filters ▸ Blur ▸ Gaussian Blur**). Set the Blur Radius to **0.6 pixels** and then click **OK** to apply this blur to the new layer.

8. Use the **Lower Layer** button in the Layers dialog to move this layer below the original text layer.

9. Offset the white layer by **–1 pixel** both horizontally and vertically (**Layer ▸ Transform ▸ Offset**).

Adding Texture

1. Retrieve the saved channel again, and then click the original text layer in the Layers dialog to make that layer active.

2. Select the **Dried Mud** pattern from the Patterns dialog. Drag that pattern into the selection.

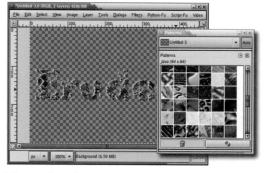

The Dried Mud pattern is a perfect fill texture for this effect.

3. Create a new layer (**Layer ▸ New Layer**). Name this new layer *Mud Color*.

4. Double-click the foreground color to open the Change Foreground Color dialog. Set the RGB values to **171/100/9** and then click **OK**. Drag the foreground color into the selection to fill it with that color.

5. Set the layer mode for the Mud Color layer to **Overlay**.

6. Deselect all (SHIFT-CTRL-A).

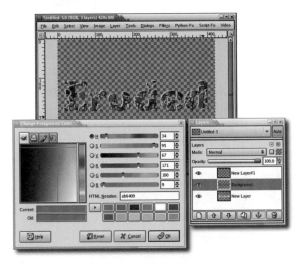

Filling a layer with light brown and setting its layer mode to Overlay enhances the color in the Dried Mud pattern.

7. Click the original text layer to make that layer active.

8. Open the Levels dialog (**Layer ▸ Colors ▸ Levels**). Drag the middle slider a short distance to the left (as shown here) to brighten the text a bit.

9. Create a new layer (**Layer ▸ New Layer**).

10. With the toolbox selected, press **D** to reset the default foreground and background colors.

11. To add the finishing touch, drag the foreground color (black) into the new layer to fill it with that color and then move this black layer to the bottom of the layer stack.

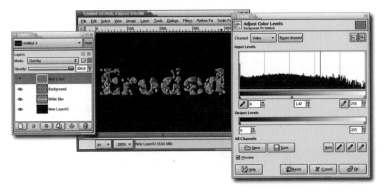

A black background provides some contrast and completes the effect.

Further Exploration

Many variations on this technique are possible. You might try using one of the other noise filters, or you might try choosing the Emboss filter's Bumpmap option (instead of the Emboss option). And while it may not seem to have played a big part in the overall effect, choosing the Dried Mud pattern to provide texture to the text was extremely important. What other patterns can you find in the Patterns dialog that change the feel of this effect just as dramatically?

5.6 FROST

A standard GIMP installation provides several specialty filters, including the Sparkle filter (Filters ▸ Light Effects ▸ Sparkle), which takes specks of white in an image and stretches them out into spokes of light. You can use the Sparkle filter to produce frost, snow, and icicle effects, but the results are not always ideal, because the spokes of light are fairly uniform. This tutorial explores other ways to achieve a frost effect.

Chill out with this cool tutorial.

In this tutorial you'll use the Pick and Slur filters to randomize the edges of selections, and then you'll apply the Wind filter to those selections to generate icicles. You used the Pick filter in Section 5.5, so you should be familiar with it how it works. The Slur filter is a pretty standard noise filter; it works by replacing the color of randomly chosen pixels with the color of nearby pixels.

The lesson here is that you will seldom find a single filter that gives you exactly the effect you need. To get where you really want to go, you'll have to learn to use filters in combination—and in the correct order.

Creating the Background and Text

Open a new white canvas set to the default size (420 × 300 pixels).

1. Choose the **Blend** tool from the toolbox. In the Tool Options dialog, select the **Horizon 2** gradient from the Gradient menu. This gradient will fill the background with what looks like a horizon. Drag down from the top of the canvas window past the bottom.

   When you drag beyond the canvas window, you're effectively stretching the gradient. The result is that the simulated horizon is near the bottom edge of the canvas. The placement of the horizon doesn't matter all that much, as we're just using this blue backdrop to add to the frosty feeling of the design.

2. Duplicate the Background layer (**Layer ▸ Duplicate Layer**). We'll merge the duplicate Background layer with an embossed text layer in a moment.

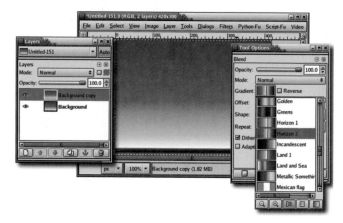

Use the Gradient menu in the Tool Options dialog to choose the Horizon 2 gradient.

3. Choose the **Text** tool. Set the font color to black and choose a thick font. I've chosen SoutaneBlack Ultra-Light set to 65 pixels. Click the canvas to open the Text Editor, type **North Pole**, and click the **Close** button to close the Text Editor.

4. Create a selection of the text by choosing **Layer ▸ Transparency ▸ Alpha to Selection**. Save the selection to a channel (**Select ▸ Save to Channel**). Click the channel name and change it to *Outline*.

5. Deselect all (SHIFT-CTRL-A).

Save the text outline to a channel.

Bringing the Text Forward

1. Click the text layer in the Layers dialog and merge it with the duplicate Background layer by choosing **Layer ▸ Merge Down**. Click the layer name and change it to *Text Layer*.

2. Set the layer mode for the Text Layer to **Grain Merge**. Once the text is embossed, the Grain Merge mode will allow the text's edges to blend with the original Background layer.

3. Now we're ready to emboss the Text Layer (**Filters ▸ Distorts ▸ Emboss**). Use the **Emboss** function, and then set the Azimuth to **313 degrees**, the Elevation to **39 degrees**, and the Depth to **19**. You may wish to change these settings, depending on the font you use, but if you use a thick font, similar settings should work well for you.

4. Right-click the saved **Outline** channel in the Channels dialog, and choose **Channel to Selection**. Remember this process; we'll need to re-create this selection shortly.

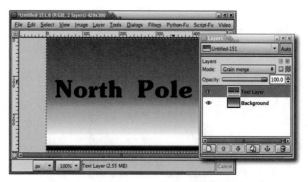

Merge the text layer with a copy of the Background layer in preparation for embossing.

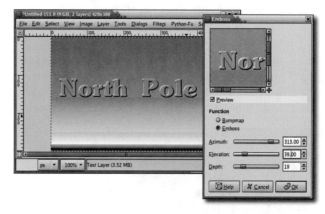

The Emboss filter has two function options: Bumpmap and Emboss. For this tutorial, use the Emboss option. Notice how the innermost areas of the text take on the appearance of the Background layer.

5. Grow the selection by **2 pixels** (**Select ▸ Grow**).

6. Feather the selection by **1.6 pixels** (**Select ▸ Feather**), and then invert its colors (**Select ▸ Invert**). This will select everything but the letters.

7. Click the **Text Layer** in the Layers dialog to make that layer active. Cut this selection from the Text Layer (CTRL-X). This will leave behind the embossed text with the colored background.

8. Retrieve the **Outline** channel selection once again. Grow this selection by **2 pixels** (**Select ▸ Grow**) and save it to another channel. Name this channel *Stroked*.

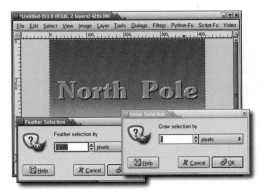

By removing the surrounding portion of the text layer, we get a darker background and lighter text, thanks to the Grain Merge mode on the text layer.

9. Set the foreground color to white.

10. Working in the new Stroked channel, stroke the selection using a Line Width of **3 pixels** (**Edit ▶ Stroke**), and then deselect all (SHIFT-CTRL-A). Temporarily turn on visibility for this channel so you can see what you're doing in the next few steps.

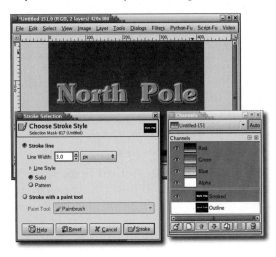

This deviates from the technique we've used in previous tutorials. Here the stroke operation takes place in a channel, not a layer.

11. Open the Pick filter (**Filters ▶ Noise ▶ Pick**). Set the Random Seed to **10**, set the Randomization slider to **30 percent,** and set the Repeat slider to **2 times.** Click **OK** to apply these settings to the Stroked channel.

Working in a channel instead of a layer allows us to easily create a shape that we can turn into a selection later and fill with white in a layer. Not all filters work in channels. Fortunately, the noise filters are an exception, and the results are excellent.

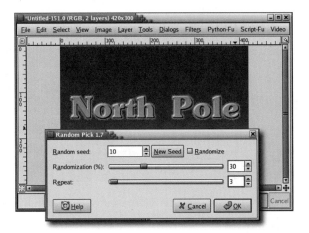

Use the Pick filter to add noise is added to the channel.

12. Open the Slur filter (**Filters ▶ Noise ▶ Slur**). Set the Random Seed to **100**, set the Randomization slider to **30 percent,** and set the Repeat slider to **3 times.** Click **OK** to apply these settings to the Stroked channel.

13. The Pick and Slur filters add some random perturbations to a layer or selection. The noise filters may produce artifacts at the top of the channel. If this happens, make a selection at the top of the channel and fill it with black.

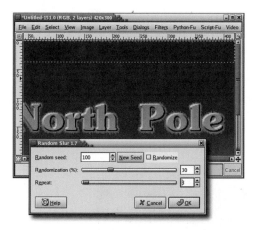

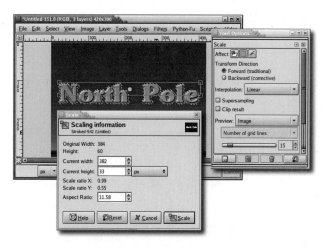

Use a selection to cut artifacts left behind by the Slur filter out of the channel.

Using the Scale tool to resize a selection

Adding Snow

1. In the Layers dialog add a new layer and call it *Snow*.

2. Retrieve the **Stroked** channel as a selection (from the Channels dialog).

3. Use the **Scale** tool to reduce the height of the selection. The transform tools in the Toolbox can be applied to any of three elements—a layer, a selection, or a path—and you need to specify which element you want to transform. Set the Affect to **Transform Selection** by clicking the middle button in the Tool Options dialog for the Scale tool. When you've finished, click the **Scale** button in the Scaling Information dialog to apply the changes.

4. Subtract the Outline channel from the current selection. To do this, select the **Outline** channel in the Channels dialog, and then hold down the CTRL key while you click the **Channel to Selection** button at the bottom of the Channels dialog.

5. Feather the resulting selection by **3 pixels** (**Select ▸ Feather**).

6. Click the **Snow** layer in the Layers dialog, and then fill the selection with white.

7. Deselect all (SHIFT-CTRL-A).

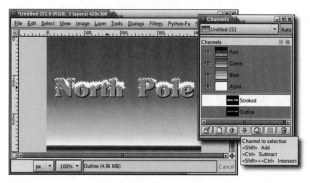

Subtracting the Outline channel from the resized Stroked selection leaves behind a selection that sits on top of the text. When this selection is filled with white, it becomes snow that has fallen on the tops of the letters.

Creating Falling Snow

We've created a cute snow pile on our text, but we can do more to enhance this design's frosty feeling.

1. Rotate the image by 90 degrees clockwise (**Image ▸ Transform ▸ Rotate 90 degrees CW**).

2. Press CTRL-E to fit the window to the image.

3. Open the Wind filter (**Filters ▸ Distorts ▸ Wind**). Set the Style to **Blast** (to achieve thicker streaks), set the Direction to **Right** to indicate the direction from which the wind should blow), and set the Edge Affected to **Leading** (to indicate that the streaks should flow with the wind from the point of impact). Set the Threshold slider to **20** and the Strength slider to **5**. Click **OK** to apply this filter to the Snow layer.

4. Reapply the **Wind** filter, this time setting the Style to **Wind**, the Direction to **Right**, and the Edge Affected to **Leading**. Set the Threshold slider to **20** and the Strength slider to **20**. The second application adds more streaks but softens the overall effect.

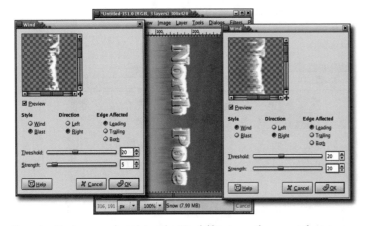

Rotating the image and applying the Wind filter turns the snow piles into falling snow and icicles.

5. To add the finishing touches, start by rotating the image counterclockwise by 90 degrees (**Image ▸ Transform ▸ Rotate 90 degrees CCW**).

6. Press CTRL-E to resize the window to the image size.

7. Open the Slur filter (**Filters ▸ Noise ▸ Slur**) again. Set the Random Seed to **100**, set the Randomization slider to **20 percent**, and set the Repeat slider to **2 times**. Click **OK** to apply this filter to the Snow layer to add icy particles to the snowy streaks.

8. Set the layer mode for the Snow layer to **Grain Merge**.

9. Duplicate the Snow layer (**Layer ▸ Duplicate Layer**), and then set the layer mode of the duplicate layer to **Addition**.

When the duplicate Snow layer is combined with the original Snow layer, there's more snow overall. Set the layer mode to Addition.

Further Exploration

In this tutorial we applied a frosty effect to text, but this effect can be applied to just about any surface, whether straight or curved. You could even apply it to a photo. Using the same techniques on a photo of a house's roof line, you could take the scene from summer to winter in one day!

5.7 NEON SIGNS

One of the most interesting effects in a digital artist's bag of tricks is the glowing neon sign. This was one of the first tricks available to GIMP users, and it's still one of the easiest to master. Neon is a gas that glows reddish-orange when electrically charged. Real neon signs are made to glow in different colors by being filled with gases (often argon) that emit ultraviolet light. The inside of the tube is then lined with phosphors that glow when exposed to the ultraviolet light generated by those gases.

It's time to shed a little light on the subject at hand—neon light, that is.

While science can explain how real neon signs work, using GIMP-generated colored light to simulate a glowing neon sign requires a little magic. There are many ways to perform this magic, but most of them involve using the Emboss filter to transform ordinary lines into 3D tubes, and all of them use some degree of blurring.

Experimenting with the Built-in Neon Effect

Before digging in, let's look at the GIMP's built-in logo generators. The Xtns ▸ Script-Fu ▸ Logos menu offers up a wide array of ready-made logo designs. The Script-Fu logo filter that automatically generates a simple neon effect is shown here, though as you can

see, its default settings produce an effect that is far less interesting than the one you're going to try your hand at. While these ready-made logos are fine for small projects, you're reading this book because you want to create designs that go further than canned effects. Let's see how we can do it better.

The Neon logo provides fast, if somewhat bland, results.

Creating the Background

Let's start by creating a background against which the neon light will shine. Start with a white canvas set to the default size (420 × 300 pixels).

1. Open the Patterns dialog (**Dialogs ▸ Patterns**), find the **Bricks** pattern, and then drag that pattern onto the canvas. This will fill the canvas with the selected pattern.

2. Desaturate this layer (**Layer ▸ Colors ▸ Desaturate**).

3. Double-click the foreground color box to launch the Change Foreground Color dialog and set the RGB values to **244/0/0** for the deep red shown here. Click **OK** to close the dialog.

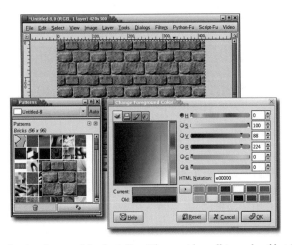

Setting the mood for Joe's Bar: The outside wall is made of brick.

4. Choose the **Bucket Fill** tool from the toolbox. In the Tool Options dialog, set the mode to **Multiply** and set the Affected Area to **Fill Whole Selection**.

5. With the canvas selected, press CTRL-A to select the entire layer. Click inside the selection to color the bricks red.

6. Open the Curves dialog (**Layer ▸ Colors ▸ Curves**), choose **Value** from the Channel drop-down menu, and then drag the curve down and to the right to darken the color, as shown.

7. Deselect all (SHIFT-CTRL-A).

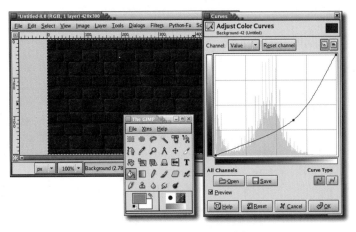

The deep-red background will look striking behind the neon sign.

Preparing the Neon Tubes

Now we're ready to work on the sign itself.

1. Choose the **Text** tool from the toolbox and then choose a font that suits your project. This example uses SoutaneBlack Ultralight sized to 50 pixels. Thick fonts like this one work well, especially when you're still learning how to master this technique, but neon signs can have all sorts of shapes, so feel free to experiment.

2. The text color should be set to the current foreground color, but if it isn't, set the RGB values to **244/0/0** to match the red in the background.

3. Click the canvas to open the Text Editor and type `Joe's Bar`. Click the **Close** button to close the Text Editor.

4. Use the **Move** tool to position the text on the center of the canvas.

5. Expand the text layer boundary to match the image size (**Layer ▸ Layer to Image Size**). Doing this allows us to add elements to the layer that would otherwise be cut off by the original layer boundary.

After positioning the text, don't forget to resize the layer by choosing Layer ▸ Layer to Image Size.

6. Create a selection of the text's outline by choosing **Layer ▸ Transparency ▸ Alpha to Selection**. Save this selection to a channel (**Select ▸ Save to Channel**), and then click the channel name and change it to *Outline*. We'll use this channel again later.

7. Grow the selection by **2 pixels** (**Select ▸ Grow**).

8. Create a new layer (**Layer ▸ New**) and name this layer *Stroke*.

9. Stroke the selection by choosing **Edit ▸ Stroke** and setting the Line Width to **2 pixels**.

10. Delete the original text layer and then deselect all (CTRL-SHIFT-A). We now have the outline we'll use to create the sign's neon tubes.

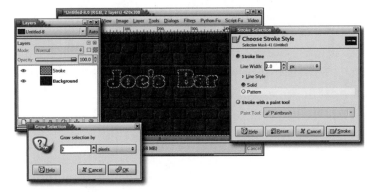

If your image were larger, you would use a thicker stroke.

11. Duplicate the Stroke layer and name the duplicate layer *Emboss*.

12. Open the Gaussian Blur filter (**Filters ▸ Blur ▸ Gaussian Blur**) and apply a blur of **3 pixels** to this layer.

13. Open the Emboss filter (**Filters ▸ Distorts ▸ Emboss**). Set the Function to **Emboss,** the Azimuth slider to **43,** the Elevation slider to **30,** and the Depth slider to **43.** These settings give the duplicate layer a soft glow. Click **OK** to apply this filter to the duplicate layer.

14. Lower the duplicate layer in the Layers dialog by choosing **Layer ▸ Stack ▸ Lower Layer** once.

15. Set the layer mode for the duplicate layer to **Addition.**

16. Open the Gaussian Blur filter (**Filters ▸ Blur ▸ Gaussian Blur**) and apply a blur of **3 pixels** to the original Stroke layer. Set this layer's mode to **Grain Merge.**

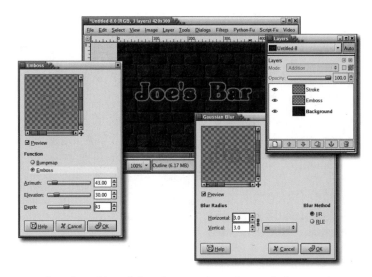

Move the embossed layer below the original text. Setting the layer mode to Addition adds this layer to the Background layer and brightens the embossed areas.

17. Add a drop shadow to this layer (**Script-Fu ▸ Shadows ▸ Drop Shadow**). Offset the drop shadow by setting the Offset X and Offset Y values to **5 pixels.** Set the Blur Radius to **4 pixels,** set the Opacity slider to **100 percent,** and uncheck the box next to the words *Allow resizing.* If you were to instead check the box next to the words *Allow resizing,* the effect would be to resize the canvas and place transparent areas around the edges. That's not what we want for this tutorial.

18. The Stroke layer should still be the active layer, but if it isn't, click the **Stroke** layer in the Layers dialog to make that layer active again.

19. Add a second drop shadow (**Script-Fu ▸ Shadows ▸ Drop Shadow**). This time, set the Offset X and Offset Y values to **6 pixels,** set the Blur Radius to **10 pixels,** and set the Opacity slider to **100 percent.** Again, uncheck the box next to the words *Allow resizing.* Applying these drop shadows raises the neon tubing above the background wall.

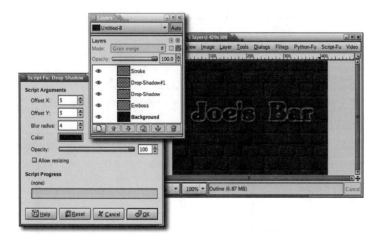

In the Drop Shadow filter, positive Offset X values mean move right and positive Offset Y values mean move down. Note that both drop shadows are applied above the Emboss layer.

Adding the Glow

1. Add a new transparent layer by choosing **Layer ▸ New Layer** and setting the Layer Fill Type to **Transparency.** Name the new layer *Glow.*

2. Retrieve the **Outline** channel selection from the Channels dialog by clicking that channel and then clicking the **Channel to Selection** button.

3. Grow the selection by **25 pixels** (**Select ▸ Grow**). Notice that growing a selection rounds its edges.

4. Feather the selection by **15 pixels** (**Select ▸ Feather**).

5. Click the **Glow** layer in the Layers dialog to make that layer active. Drag the foreground color from the toolbox into the selection to fill the selection with that color, and then deselect all (SHIFT-CTRL-A).

6. Open the Gaussian Blur filter (**Filters ▸ Blur ▸ Gaussian Blur**) and apply a blur of **20 pixels** to the Blur layer. Apply this same blur two more times by pressing CTRL-F twice. The amount to blur is up to you. Apply the blur a few more times if you'd like to soften the edges of the glow even more.

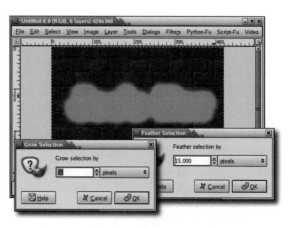

The neon glow starts as a soft-edged, color-filled selection.

7. In the Layers dialog lower the **Glow** layer to just above the Background layer.

8. Set the layer mode for the Glow layer to **Screen**.

If you like, you can apply multiple blurs to the Glow layer.

Adding a Glass-Edged Reflection

1. Add a new layer (**Layer ▸ New Layer**). Move this layer to the top of the layer stack in the Layers dialog and name it *Highlight*.

2. Retrieve the **Outline** channel selection again. Grow this selection by **2 pixels** (**Select ▸ Grow**).

3. Set the foreground color to white, and then click the **Highlight** layer in the Layers dialog to make that layer active again.

4. Stroke the selection by choosing **Edit ▸ Stroke** and setting the Line Width to **2 pixels,** and then deselect all (SHIFT-CTRL-A).

5. Offset this layer by choosing **Layer ▸ Transform ▸ Offset** and setting the Offset X and Offset Y values to **–1 pixel**.

6. Open the Gaussian Blur filter (**Filters ▸ Blur ▸ Gaussian Blur**) and apply a blur of **2 pixels**.

7. In the Layers dialog move the **Highlight** layer to just below the second drop shadow layer.

8. Set the layer mode for the Highlight layer to **Hard Light**.

This last part is what really makes the neon tubes look realistic. By adding light, we make the tubes appear rounded.

The white Stroke layer picks up color when its layer mode is set to Hard Light.

Further Exploration

There are thousands of variations on this technique, and they're applicable to both text and graphic designs. Try using a piece of clipart instead of text. Use the Fuzzy Select tool to make selections of disconnected parts of the clipart. The result will be a neon outline of your clipart!

5.8 SPRAY PAINT

In Section 1.2 you learned the basics of working with layer modes, which provide a unique way of merging one layer with another. While modes are available for use with all of the GIMP paint tools, tool-based modes blend directly within the layer and actually change the layer's pixels. This becomes a problem if you make a long series of brush strokes, for example, and want to backtrack later. If you haven't specified enough undo levels in the Preferences dialog, you might not be able to undo some of those strokes.

Layer modes, on the other hand, don't change any of the underlying pixels. The blending is done only during compositing, which means that it happens when the GIMP combines all of the layers to generate the display on the canvas. This sort of blending is nondestructive and offers greater flexibility for experimentation.

This isn't your average graffiti, but the effect is easy to achieve.

The spray-paint effect makes use of layer modes to blend a painted layer with a textured layer. In the last tutorial we used layer modes to merge the light cast from a neon sign with the brick wall behind it. The same process applies to spray painting a textured surface. First you create the surface, then you add a spray-paint layer above the first layer, and finally you use a layer mode to blend the two together.

Creating the Background

We'll begin just as we did in the last tutorial, by creating and coloring a brick wall. Open a new canvas window, using the default size. Click and drag the **Bricks** pattern from the Patterns dialog onto the canvas, and then Colorize it a deep red, if you're so inclined (Layer ▸ Colors ▸ Colorize).

Adding a Text Outline

1. Choose the **Text** tool from the toolbox, and in the Tool Options dialog, choose a font and font size. This example uses XBAND Rough sized to 160 pixels.

2. Click the canvas to launch the Text Editor, and then type `Kilroy`. Click the **Close** button to close the Text Editor.

3. Use the **Move** tool to center the text on the canvas.

4. Create a selection of the text (**Layer ▸ Transparency ▸ Alpha to Selection**) and save that selection to a channel (**Select ▸ Save to Channel**).

5. Double-click the channel name in the Channels dialog, and change the name to *Outline*.

6. Deselect all (**Select ▸ None**).

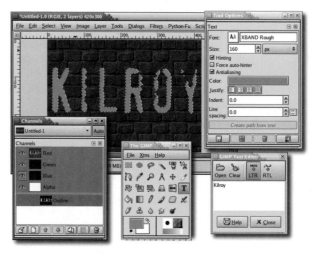

The color of the text doesn't matter yet. We just need an outline at this point.

Converting the Text to Spray Paint

1. Return to the Layers dialog and delete the text layer.

2. Add a new transparent layer by choosing **Layer ▸ New** and setting the layer fill type to **Transparency**. Name the new layer *Paint*.

3. Retrieve the **Outline** channel selection from the Channels dialog, and then grow the selection by **2 pixels** (**Select ▸ Grow**) and feather it by **10 pixels** (**Select ▸ Feather**). These steps will soften the edges of your selection, enhancing the spray-paint effect.

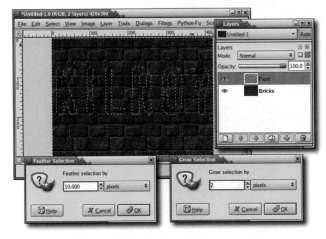

Growing and feathering the text selection

4. Click the **Paint** layer in the Layers dialog to make that layer active again.

5. Choose **Dialog ▸ Brushes** from the canvas menu to open the Brushes dialog, and then choose the **Circle (11)** brush.

6. Choose the **Airbrush** tool from the toolbox.

7. Click the foreground color box in the toolbox to open the Change Foreground Color dialog, type `Yellow` in the HTML field, press ENTER, and then close the dialog.

8. Paint inside the selection with quick, uneven strokes, but don't fill the selection completely. Don't worry if the text doesn't look exactly like spray paint yet. Deselect all (**Select ▸ None**).

The selection acts as a bounding area for your paint strokes.

9. Choose the **Rotate** tool from the toolbox and use it to rotate the Paint layer by **−20 degrees**.

10. Open the IWarp filter (**Filters ▸ Distorts ▸ IWarp**). Set the Deform Radius to **40 pixels,** and then drag the mouse through the lettering to distort it lightly. This step makes the spray painting appear more random.

11. Duplicate the Paint layer (**Layer ▸ Duplicate**). Set the layer mode for the original Paint layer to **Color,** and then set the layer mode for the duplicate layer to **Grain Merge**. These layer modes allow the bricks' shadows and cracks to show through your spray painting.

12. Duplicate the original Paint layer again (**Layer ▸ Duplicate**) and name this layer *Drip*.

13. We'll reuse a technique we used to create frosty icicles in Section 5.6, this time to create paint drips. Start by rotating the Drip layer 90 degrees clockwise (**Layers ▸ Transform ▸ Rotate 90 degrees CW**).

14. Open the Wind filter (**Filters ▸ Distorts ▸ Wind**). Set the Style to **Blast,** the Direction to **Right,** and the Edge Affected to **Leading**. Then set the Threshold to 9 and the Strength to **20**. Click **OK** to apply this filter to the Drip layer.

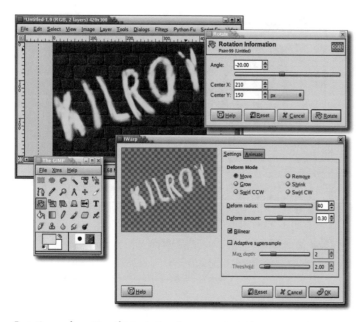

Rotating and warping the text gives it a more sprayed-on appearance.

Changing the layer modes blends the text with the wall beneath it.

15. Rotate the Drip layer 90 degrees counterclockwise (**Layer ▸ Transform ▸ Rotate 90 degrees CCW**).

16. Create a selection of the original Paint layer, using your saved channel. If you leave the original lettering in the Drip layer and then blend that layer with other layers, the lettering will be too bright. Let's remove the lettering from this layer, leaving just the drips behind. Click the **Drip** layer and press CTRL-X to cut the lettering selection from that layer.

17. Set the layer mode for the Drip layer to **Screen**.

The rotated Drip layer is blasted by the Wind filter.

Removing the lettering from the Drip layer keeps it from being too bright and completes the spray-paint effect.

Further Exploration

What can you take away from this tutorial? You've learned that simple tools like the Wind filter can actually serve a wide range of purposes and help you achieve surprisingly numerous effects. We've already used the Wind filter to create both frosty icicles and dripping paint. What will you create next?

5.9 LIGHT BURST

This tutorial simulates lighting that comes from behind text. It also illustrates one of the more interesting uses of the Polar Coordinates filter. Most GIMP users ignore this filter because its purpose isn't obvious. It converts linear effects into circular ones—and it does that extremely well.

The light-burst effect

In this tutorial we'll take black text on a white background and transform it into a dazzling, colorful effect. We'll even take a detour along the way to see how the GIMP can turn wind into light.

Creating the Text

Start with a black canvas set to the default size (420 × 300 pixels).

1. Choose the **Text** tool from the toolbox. Choose a thick sans-serif font—I've used FacetBlack Ultra-Light sized to 80 pixels—and set the font color to white. Whenever you work with textures inside text, you want to use thick fonts so that it's easier to see the texture.

2. Click the canvas to launch the Text Editor. Type **OpenSource** and then click **Close** to close the window.

3. Use the **Move** tool to center the text layer manually.

4. Expand the layer size to fit the canvas (**Layer ▸ Layer to Image Size**).

The Text tool doesn't center the text layer automatically. You'll need to position it manually.

5. Click the text layer to make that layer active, and then create a selection of the text by choosing **Layer ▸ Transparency ▸ Alpha to Selection**. Save the selection to a channel (**Select ▸ Save to Channel**). Double-click the channel name and change it to *Outline*. We'll come back to the saved channel in a moment.

6. Click the text layer in the Layers dialog to make that layer active again and then clear the selection (**Select ▸ None**).

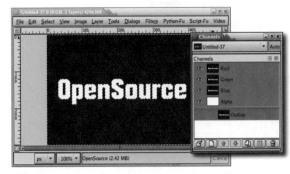

The selection is saved to a channel so we can easily recover it, even if we make changes to the text layer.

7. Open the **Gaussian Blur** filter and apply a blur of **10 pixels** to the text layer. In the Gaussian Blur dialog, specify the **IIR** blur method. (The IIR setting works better with text, whereas the RLE setting works better with photographs.)

8. Merge the text layer with the Background layer (**Layer ▸ Merge Down**).

9. If you'd like, you can enhance the whiteness in the image by applying the Autolevel option. Just choose **Layer ▸ Colors ▸ Levels** and then click the **Auto** button.

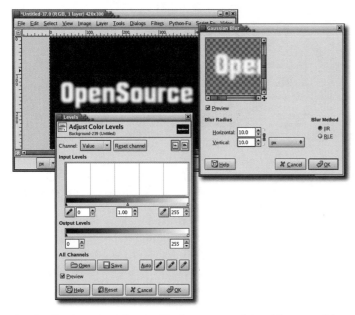

Autoleveling is optional, but it will enhance some of the white areas of the image. How dramatic a change this will make depends on the thickness of the font you choose.

Adding the Light Burst

1. Open the Polar Coordinates filter (**Filters ▸ Distorts ▸ Polar Coordinates**). Set the Depth slider to **0 percent** and set the Offset Angle slider to **0 degrees**. Check the box next to the words *Map from top* and uncheck the boxes next to the words *To polar* and *Map backwards*. Click **OK** to apply these settings to the image.

The Depth setting changes the nature of the effect from rectangular (at the low end) to circular (at the high end). The Angle setting rotates the effect around the layer's central point. Mapping the effect from the top causes each row of the layer, top to bottom, to be mapped from the center of a circle to the outside, with the bottom row mapped to the outermost edge of the effect. This setup allows us to produce a sunburst effect that seems to radiate from the center of the text.

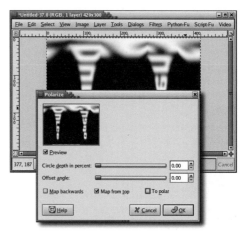

Applying the Polar Coordinates filter to the image produces an interesting effect, but this is just the start.

2. Rotate the image clockwise by 90 degrees (**Image ▸ Transform ▸ Rotate 90 degrees CW**). Then press CTRL-E to resize the canvas to fit the rotated image.

3. Open the Wind filter (**Filters ▸ Distorts ▸ Wind**). Set the Style to **Wind,** the Direction (from which the wind blows) to **Right,** and the Edge Affected to **Leading.** The Wind setting produces softer streaks than the Blast setting, and the streaks originate on the side of the image that is facing the wind.

4. Set the Threshold to 5 so that more of the white pixels are streaked, and then set the Strength to **40** to create longer streaks. Click **OK** to apply these settings to the image.

5. Repeat this process by pressing CTRL-F two more times to strengthen the effect.

NOTE *Pressing CTRL-F reapplies the last filter used. This comes in handy when you need to apply a filter several times in a row.*

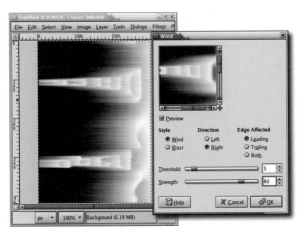

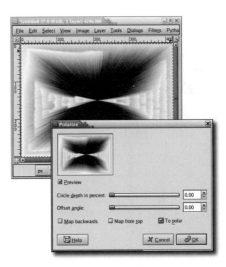

The long streaks created by the Wind filter eventually become bursts of light.

6. Rotate the image counterclockwise by 90 degrees (**Image ▸ Transform ▸ Rotate 90 degrees CCW**). Again resize the canvas by pressing CTRL-E.

7. Open the Polar Coordinates filter again (**Filters ▸ Distorts ▸ Polar Coords**). Set the Depth to **0 percent** and set the Angle to **0 degrees**. Uncheck the boxes next to the words *Map backwards* and *Map from top*, and then check the box next to the words *To polar*. Click **OK** to apply these settings. Now you have something that is beginning to look like a real light burst.

8. Add a new transparent layer by choosing **Layer ▸ New** and setting the Layer Fill Type to **Transparency**.

9. Open the Channels dialog (**Dialogs ▸ Channels**) and click the **Outline** channel at the bottom of the window to make that channel active. Click the **Channel to Selection** button in the Channels dialog.

10. Return to the Layers dialog (**Dialog ▸ Layers**) and click the uppermost layer to make that layer active. Fill the selection you just created with white and then deselect all (**Select ▸ None**).

11. Open the Motion Blur filter (**Filters ▸ Blur ▸ Motion Blur**). Set the Blur Type to **Zoom** and set the Length to **66 pixels**. This long blur will stretch the effect toward the edges of the image. Click **OK** to apply these settings.

Reversing the polar coordinates gives us a light-burst effect.

Enhancing the Text Over the Background

We'd like to make the text stand out a bit against the sunburst background. We'll do that by outlining the text and simulating some depth.

1. Add another new layer (**Layer ▸ New**).

2. Make sure black is the current foreground color by pressing **D** in the canvas to reset the foreground and background colors to black and white, respectively.

3. Click the channel you saved earlier, the one you named *Outline*. Stroke it by **1.5 pixels** to outline the text (**Edit ▸ Stroke**).

4. Deselect all (**Select ▸ None**).

5. Duplicate the layer in which you stroked the outline (**Layer ▸ Duplicate**) and then invert the colors in that layer (**Layer ▸ Colors ▸ Invert**).

6. Open the **Gaussian Blur** filter and apply a blur of **3 pixels** to the original stroke layer.

7. To give the appearance of depth, offset this layer by choosing **Layer ▸ Transform ▸ Offset** and setting the Offset X and Offset Y values to **−1 pixels**.

Outlining the selection with black makes the text easier to read.

Inverting the colors and offsetting the layer gives the lettering an embossed appearance.

Adding a Color Gradient

1. Add a new transparent layer by choosing **Layer ▸ New Layer** and setting the Layer Fill Type to **Transparency**. Move this layer to the top of the layer stack in the Layers dialog.

2. Choose the **Blend** tool from the toolbox. In the Tool Options dialog, select the **Yellow to Orange** gradient and choose **Square** from the Shape drop-down menu. Click the middle of the layer and drag toward any corner of the canvas to apply the gradient. Set the layer mode for this layer to **Color** so you'll be able to see through to the text.

3. Add another layer (**Layer ▸ New Layer**).

4. Choose the saved **Outline** channel and convert it to a selection again. Fill the selection with black.

5. Set the layer mode to **Overlay** and then deselect all (**Select ▸ None**).

Choosing Square from the Shape drop-down menu maps the darker colors over the light streaks while adding lighter colors toward the center, where the light source is supposed to be.

6. Click the **Background** layer in the Layers dialog to make that layer active.

7. Open the Curves dialog (**Layer ▸ Color ▸ Curves**) and adjust the curve as shown here.

8. Open the Brightness-Contrast dialog (**Layer ▸ Colors ▸ Brightness-Contrast**). Set the Brightness to **−56** and the Contrast to **59**. Adjusting contrast increases the streaking effect, as more contrast makes the streaks stand out against the black background. Be careful, though! You'll find that there is a fine line between enhancing the streaks (increasing the contrast) and decreasing the size of the streaks (too much contrast).

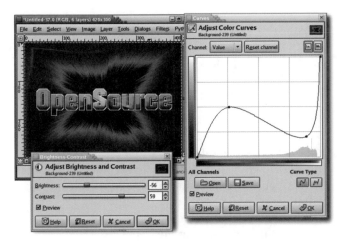

Use the Curves dialog to produce all kinds of bizarre bursts.

Further Exploration

Congratulations! You've created the basic light burst. To test your skills, try adjusting the curves in the Background layer. Doing so will have a dramatic effect on the appearance of the light burst.

TIPS FOR TYPE EFFECTS

Advertising, web design, and many other kinds of projects involve combining text with images. As you begin working with type and the GIMP on your own, consider this food for thought.

Make Alignment Easier

Did you find yourself repeatedly creating a text layer and then centering it on another layer during these tutorials? Use Align Visible Layers (Layer ▸ Align Visible Layers) to make this process a breeze.

Find Good Fonts

A good font will take your message a long way. But there are good fonts and there are not-so-good fonts. While free fonts will often suffice for home, church, club, and school projects, they aren't likely to offer the same quality or features as fonts created by reputable type foundries. High-quality fonts include proper kerning, ligatures, complete character sets, multiple font weights, and even small caps and old-style numerals, all of which can add even more impact to your type designs. If you're trying to make it into print, you're going to need to pay for some high-quality fonts. Some commercial type foundries include:

Linotype   http://www.linotype.com

International Typeface Corporation   http://www.itcfonts.com

Bitstream   http://www.bitstream.com/fonts/index.html

Use Only the Fonts You Need

If you're not publishing your work professionally, free font archives may provide everything you need. Even in that case, you need to decide which fonts to install. Having 1,000 fonts gives you lots of choices, but the GIMP uses simple lists for font selection, so you could be scrolling through them for days. Cut out the useless fonts, such as those that consist of special symbols and nonalphabetic features you don't need.

Use Large Type and High Resolution for Print Projects

If you use a 12-point font at 72 dpi in a project that will ultimately be printed at 300 dpi, you'll need a microscope to read it. Or worse, the printer's rasterizer might blow up the text, making it pixelated and illegible. If your project is destined for print, set the resolution to 300 dpi from the start. Remember that it's easy to scale down gracefully, but it's difficult to scale up without causing problems for yourself.

The tutorials in this chapter all use at least 30-point type. When preparing a design for print, you'll want to use even larger type.

Remember That All GIMP Text Is Rasterized

You can create text in the GIMP and then scale it to a larger size later, but you'll always sacrifice quality because the GIMP doesn't support vector format. It's much better to start with the correct font size and then apply the desired effect.

In a similar vein, when you save your image to JPEG, PNG, or any other raster image format, all layer and text information is lost. As a result, it will be much harder (or even impossible) to edit your file. To retain layer and text information, you must save the file to XCF format, which is the GIMP's native file format.

Practice Copyfitting Manually

Unlike Photoshop, the GIMP does not have bounding boxes for text. To map a paragraph to a specific space, you must create line breaks manually as you type the text in the Text Editor. If you have more than a few words to work with, you'll find it more efficient to lay them out using a vector-based image editor like the open source application Inkscape (http://www.inkscape.org). Once you've finished arranging the text in Inkscape, save the file in SVG format, then import the path (right-click a new path in the Paths dialog). Alternatively, you can save your work in Inkscape to PNG format and open the PNG file in GIMP.

Edit Text Layers Wisely

You can edit a text layer at any point after creating it, but keep in mind that you'll lose any raster effects you've applied to it. When you do need to edit a text layer, click the layer in the Layers dialog to make it active, choose the Text tool from the toolbox, and then click the canvas.

Plan Ahead

As with any project, a graphic design project needs an efficient workflow. Your project has two goals: It's destined for print or for the Web, and it's meant to advertise or inform. In order to reach that goal, you have to be organized. Knowing what your text should say and how it should look before you actually start working in the GIMP will reduce the chance that you'll have to make changes later, when they'll cause excessive reworking. Planning out your text is just the start, however. Think ahead about images, colors, themes, and messages. It's all part of a designer's workflow.

6

USER INTERFACE DESIGN

User interfaces define how we interact with software and hardware tools as varied as a web-based application, a handheld multimedia device, a game console, the word processor running on your computer, and the instruments on your car's dashboard. User interfaces provide the user with visual feedback in meaningful and sometimes even interesting ways.

Practical Applications for User Interfaces

The GIMP can be used to build prototypes for hardware and real interfaces for software. Hardware prototypes help designers and engineers visualize how a product should look when it's complete. The GIMP can easily produce 3D frontal views of a device upon which more complex designs can be based. You'll need to use more sophisticated design tools if you need to create rotating views, and prototype design with the GIMP is often limited to the project's proof-of-concept phase for this reason.

The GIMP is an excellent tool for designing real software interfaces for web applications and native applications, however. Native applications are simply programs written for a specific computer or device and its operating system, such as those that run on MP3 players. By contrast, web applications are intended to work on any system that has a web browser. Web application interfaces are often broken down into rectangular pieces for display on a computer monitor. Some of these rectangular pieces may then be defined as *hot spots*, where mouse clicks and keyboard input are handled by the program displaying the user interface.

The techniques discussed in Chapter 6 are used to design a simple audio player interface.

User interface design is also important in game development, where textures and shapes play an important role in the user experience. This type of design goes beyond prototyping and has much in common with the design of native or web-based applications.

NOTE *It's interesting for graphic designers to note that all computer programs display only rectangular interfaces—those with hard edges—because monitors render images in pixels as opposed to vectors. Various tricks can be used to display nonlinear shapes on computer monitors. One such trick involves mapping a single color to transparency in a GIF file by telling the computer not to display any pixels of that color. Modern operating systems take this trick further by allowing the mapping to define levels of transparency instead of simply turning transparency on or off.*

Support for transparency in modern operating systems allows designers to create unique interface designs for computer applications.

User Interface Design Tutorials

While it's easy to use the GIMP to design hardware prototypes, user interface design will be of the most interest to application, web, and game developers. Because these types of designs will be viewed on computer monitors, many of the web design techniques you've already mastered will be applicable when designing user interfaces. The tutorials in this chapter cover some of the same ground as Chapter 3, but the end result will be very different.

The tutorials in Chapter 6 also take a slightly different approach than the tutorials in the rest of the book. In previous chapters, each section covered a separate project, but in Chapter 6, each section shows you how to create a piece of a larger project—a user interface for a native application that runs on a media player. Each section shows one part of the overall process, with the last section bringing together all the parts in a final design.

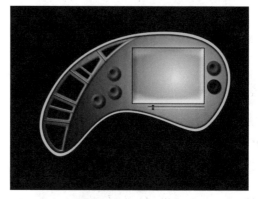

When designing skins for media applications like XMMS, xine, or MPlayer, you don't have to stick to linear layouts. This design uses a square window to display the video, but the rest of the layout is anything but square.

6.1 FACEPLATE

A *faceplate* is a piece of metal or plastic that covers a device like an MP3 player or a handheld game device. The faceplate holds the buttons and display screen in place and serves as a protective cover for the device's innards. Many software media applications incorporate a simulated faceplate that helps users make sense of the application's components.

Creating a faceplate using the GIMP requires laying out the shape of the faceplate, blurring it, and then applying the Emboss or Bump Map filters to make the shape appear three-dimensional. This tutorial walks you through the steps for creating a textured metallic faceplate for a media player.

The display mimics the look of a green LCD.

Getting Started

First reset the foreground and background colors by pressing **D** while the toolbox is selected. The device will be wider than it is tall to accommodate a video display screen, so create a new black canvas sized to **1,024 × 768 pixels** (**File ▸ New**).

Creating the Faceplate

1. Add a new transparent layer above the black layer by choosing **Layer ▸ New** and setting the Layer Fill Type to **Transparency**. Name the new transparent layer *White Frame*.

2. Choose the **Rectangle Select** tool from the toolbox and drag on the canvas to create a selection that takes up approximately two-thirds of the canvas window. (Make sure you leave about 100 pixels of space above and to each side of this selection and about 250 pixels below it to accommodate other features.)

3. To round the corners of the faceplate, grow the selection by **10 pixels** (**Select ▸ Grow**).

4. Fill the selection with white by dragging the background color from the toolbox into the selection.

5. Save this selection (**Select ▸ Save to Channel**) and name it *Frame*. Saving the selection deactivates the active layer, so click the **White Frame** layer in the Layers dialog to make that layer active once again, and then deselect all (SHIFT-CTRL-A).

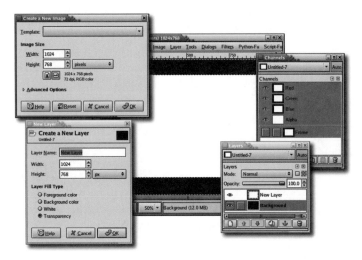

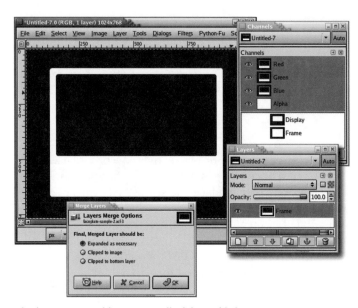

Growing the selection results in rounded corners.

The frame is created by merging all of the visible layers.

6. The next step is to cut out an area for the video display screen. Using the **Rectangle Select** tool again, drag to create a selection in the upper two-thirds of the white frame. Make sure to leave at least 20 pixels above and to the left and right of the selection.

7. Grow the selection by **10 pixels** (**Select ▸ Grow**) to round the corners of this selection as well.

8. Add a white layer mask to the White Frame layer (**Layer ▸ Mask ▸ Add Layer Mask**). Then fill the selection with black to cut a hole in the white frame as shown.

9. Save the selection to a channel (**Select ▸ Save to Channel**) and name the channel *Display*.

10. In the Layers dialog click the **Background** layer to make that layer active.

11. The frame shape is complete, so merge the visible layers by choosing **Image ▸ Merge Visible Layers**. In the Layer Merge Options dialog click the radio button next to the words *Expanded as necessary*, and then click **OK** to merge the layers.

12. Rename this merged layer *Frame* by clicking the layer name and changing it. Deselect all (**Select ▸ None**).

Adding Depth to the Faceplate

Now the design needs some depth.

1. Duplicate the Frame layer (**Layer ▸ Duplicate**).

2. Open the Gaussian Blur filter (**Filters ▸ Blur ▸ Gaussian Blur**). Set the Blur Radius to **20 pixels**, and click **OK** to apply the blur to the duplicate layer. In this case, large blurs round the edges of the user interface more dramatically.

3. Turn off the duplicate layer's visibility, and then click the original **Frame** layer in the Layers dialog.

4. Open the Bump Map filter (**Filters ▸ Map ▸ Bump Map**). Choose the **Frame copy** layer as the Bump Map, the Map Type to **Linear**, the Azimuth to **67 degrees**, the Elevation to **80 degrees**, and the Depth to **52**. Click **OK** to apply the Bump Map filter.

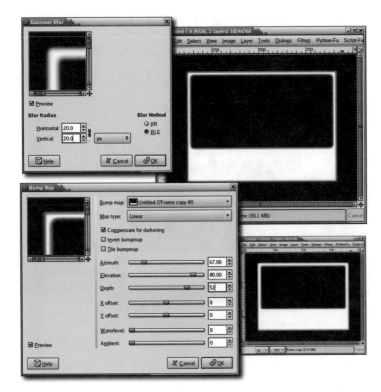

3. Feather the selection by **3 pixels** (**Select ▸ Feather**).

4. In the Layers dialog click the **Frame** layer to make that layer active.

5. Open the Gaussian Blur filter again (**Filters ▸ Blur ▸ Gaussian Blur**). Set the Blur Radius to **15 pixels,** and then click **OK** to apply the blur to the selection.

6. Deselect all (CTRL-SHIFT-A).

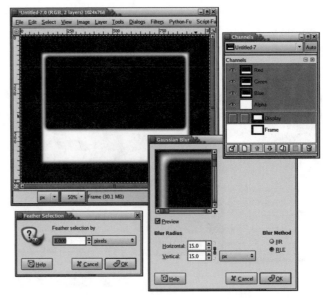

If the edges above and to either side of the video display screen are too thin, you may want to redo the cutout and make the screen smaller.

Applying a Blur to the Frame

The Bump Map filter adds depth to the design, but it can leave behind some jagged edges or even some unexpected lines. To soften the effect, let's apply a blur to the frame.

1. Retrieve the Frame selection from the Channel dialog (**Dialogs ▸ Channels**) by first clicking the **Frame** channel in the Channels dialog to choose that channel and then clicking the **Channel to Selection** button at the bottom of the dialog.

2. Click the **Display** channel to select that channel. Hold down the CTRL key while you click the **Channel to Selection** button again.

Once you've applied the Bump Map filter, you no longer need the Frame copy layer. You may choose to keep it around (with its visibility turned off) as a reminder of the steps you've completed.

Adding a Video Display Screen

The video display screen comes next.

1. Add a new layer by choosing **Layer ▸ New,** and then fill the layer with the foreground color (which should be black) by setting the Layer Fill Type to **Foreground Color.** Name this new layer *Display Screen.*

2. Open the Scatter RGB filter (**Filters ▸ Noise ▸ Scatter RGB**). Uncheck the box next to the words *Independent RGB* and move the Red slider to about **0.20**. With the Independent RGB box unchecked, all of the sliders will move to match the position of the Red slider. Click **OK** to apply this filter to the Display Screen layer.

3. Open the Colorize dialog (**Layers ▸ Color ▸ Colorize**). Set the Hue to **85**, the Saturation to **30**, and the Lightness to **50**. Click **OK** to colorize the image.

4. Open the Gaussian Blur filter (**Filters ▸ Blur ▸ Gaussian Blur**). Set the Blur Radius to **2.5 pixels** and click **OK** to apply the blur.

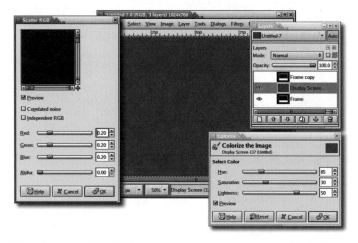

The color of the video display screen color is chosen to match older LCD displays, making the purpose of our player's screen a bit more obvious to the casual observer.

5. Click the **Frame** layer in the Layers dialog. If this layer does not have an alpha channel, add one to the layer (**Layer ▸ Transparency ▸ Add Alpha Channel**), and then drag the **Frame** layer so that it is above the Display Screen layer in the Layers dialog.

6. Add a white layer mask to the Frame layer (**Layer ▸ Mask ▸ Add Layer Mask**).

7. Retrieve the **Display** selection from the Channels dialog by clicking the selection and then clicking the **Channel to Selection** button.

8. Feather the selection by **3 pixels** (**Select ▸ Feather**), and then click the Frame layer's mask to make it active once again.

9. Fill the selection with black by dragging the foreground color from the toolbox into the selection. This will cause the green from the Display Screen layer to show through.

10. Deselect all (SHIFT-CTRL-A).

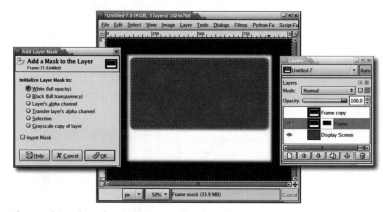

The saved Display selection is retrieved and used to create a layer mask through which the LCD display shows.

Adding Texture to the Faceplate

1. Duplicate the Frame layer (**Layer ▸ Duplicate**) and name the duplicate layer *Texture*.

2. Apply a white layer mask to the duplicate layer (**Layer ▸ Mask ▸ Apply Layer Mask**).

3. Use the **Channel to Selection** button to retrieve the Frame selection from the Channels dialog, and then subtract the Display selection from it just as you did before, by holding down the CTRL key while you click the **Channel to Selection** button for the Display channel. After retrieving the selections, be sure to click the **Texture** layer again to make that layer active.

4. Open the Scatter RGB filter again (**Filters ▸ Noise ▸ Scatter RGB**). This time set the Red slider to **0.25**. Then click **OK** to apply this filter to the selection.

5. Open the Motion Blur filter (**Filters ▸ Blur ▸ Motion Blur**). Set the Length to **10** and the Angle to **45**. Then click **OK** to apply this filter to the selection.

6. Open the Colorize dialog (**Layers ▸ Colors ▸ Colorize**). Set the Hue to **45**, set the Saturation to **75**, and set the Lightness to **−35**. Click **OK** to apply these changes to the layer.

7. Deselect all (CTRL-SHIFT-A).

8. Change the layer mode for the Texture layer to **Hard Light**. If the frame is too dark, duplicate the Frame layer (**Layer ▸ Duplicate**) and set the duplicate layer's mode to **Screen**.

Further Exploration

Now that the faceplate is complete, you're ready to add more components to the media player. It's important to save the work you've done in this section to an XCF file before moving on. The XCF format (which is the GIMP's native file format) saves all layer and channel information. You'll need that information as you move forward with this project.

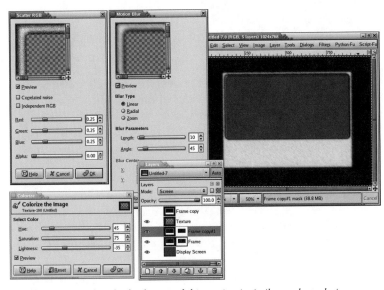

The technique used in the final steps of this section is similar to the technique used in Section 3.2.

6.2 SCREWS, NUTS, AND BOLTS

The faceplate needs some screws to attach it to the rest of the device. In the final design these screws will be small, but let's start by creating them at a larger size. Then we'll scale down the screws and merge them with the faceplate image.

Screws, nuts, and bolts are easy to create as long as you're viewing them head on or directly from the side. Rotated 3D views are more complex and are usually easier to create in an application like Blender. In this tutorial we'll create head-on views of screws and hex nuts, and then we'll create a side view of a threaded bolt.

Small details add to the realism of the design.

Making Hex Nut Heads

Let's start with the object that's easiest to create—the hex nut viewed from above. A hex nut has six sides of equal length. To create them, we need to do a little math (or at least a little approximation).

Creating the Outline

Open a new white canvas set to the default size (420 × 300 pixels). The top, bottom, left, and right sides of the hex nut are easy to define. And the angled sides aren't much more difficult—just remember that they need to be created at a 45 degree angle to the vertical sides. If the length of each side is 80 pixels, the length of each angled side should be 60 pixels.

1. Open the New Guide dialog (**Image ▸ Guides ▸ New Guide**). Choose **Vertical** from the Direction drop-down menu, set the Position to **100 pixels**, and click **OK** to add the new guide. Repeat these steps to create vertical guides at **160 pixels**, **240 pixels**, and **300 pixels**.

2. To add horizontal guides, choose Horizontal from the Direction drop-down menu. Add horizontal guides at **40 pixels**, **100 pixels**, **180 pixels**, and **240 pixels**.

3. Choose the **Path** tool from the toolbox. Click the intersection of the guides as shown. In the Tool Options dialog click the **Create Selection from Path** button to create the paths.

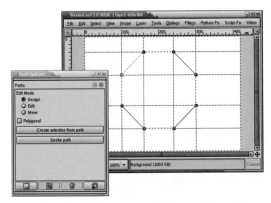

The hex nut head is easy to model if you utilize guides.

Adding a Rounded Head

1. Add a new transparent layer by choosing **Layer ▶ New** and setting the Layer Fill Type to **Transparency.** Name the new layer *Gradient*.

2. With the canvas selected, press **D** to reset the default foreground and background colors.

3. Choose the **Blend** tool from the toolbox. In the Tool Options dialog set the Gradient to **FG to BG (RGB)**, set the Shape to **Radial**, and check the box next to the word *Reverse*. Drag from the upper-left corner of the selection down toward the lower-right corner of the canvas.

4. Because the foreground color is white, the hex nut will initially appear too bright. Use the Brightness-Contrast dialog (**Layer ▶ Colors ▶ Brightness-Contrast**) to darken the image.

5. Deselect all (CTRL-SHIFT-A).

Creating Flat Vertices

1. Choose the **Ellipse Select** tool from the toolbox. Drag on the canvas from the upper-left intersection of the top and leftmost guides down to the intersection of the bottom and rightmost guides.

2. Invert this selection (**Select ▶ Invert**). This will only select small portions of each of the hex nut's vertices.

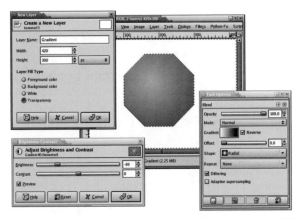

The rounded head of a hex nut is simulated by applying a radial gradient. The gradient is in its own layer and is bounded by the selection that borders the head of the nut.

3. Open the Levels dialog (**Layer ▶ Colors ▶ Levels**). Move the middle slider to the right to darken the corners of the hex nut, and then click **OK** to apply the change.

4. Deselect all (CTRL-SHIFT-A).

5. We don't need the guides anymore, so hide them (**View ▶ Show Guides**).

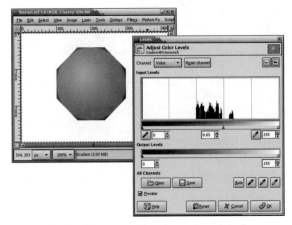

A minor levels adjustment makes the vertices of the hex nut slightly darker than the rounded head, making it look as though those surfaces are flat.

Applying a Metallic Texture

1. Add another new transparent layer and name it *Brushed Metal*.

2. With the canvas selected, press **D** to reset the foreground and background colors. Drag the background color (black) from the toolbox into the new layer.

3. Open the Scatter RGB filter (**Filters ▸ Noise ▸ Scatter RGB**). Make sure the box next to the words *Independent RGB* is unchecked so that all channels are equal and we can create a gray tint. Set the Red slider to **0.35**, and then click **OK** to apply this filter to the Brushed Metal layer.

4. Open the Motion Blur filter (**Filters ▸ Blur ▸ Motion Blur**). Set the Blur Type to **Linear**, set the Length to **50 pixels**, and set the Angle to **45 degrees**. Click **OK** to apply this filter to the noise you just created.

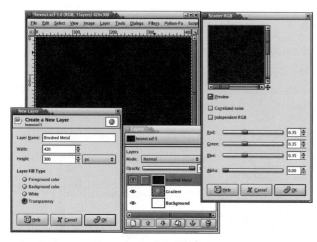

A brushed-metal effect is applied to a black layer. When the layer mode for this layer is set to Overlay, only the light streaks will blend with the medium gray of the rounded nut head.

5. Add a black layer mask (**Layer ▸ Mask ▸ Add Layer Mask**).

6. Click the **Gradient** layer in the Layers dialog to make that layer active.

7. Retrieve the original hex-shaped selection (**Layer ▸ Transparency ▸ Alpha to Selection**).

8. Click the **Brushed Metal** layer in the Layers dialog to make that layer active once again. The layer mask should also be active, but if it isn't, click it in the Layers dialog.

9. Drag the foreground color (white) from the toolbox into the selection. Then set the Brushed Metal layer's mode to **Overlay**, or choose another layer mode that better suits your tastes.

10. Deselect all (SHIFT-CTRL-A).

11. Save the file as *hexhead.xcf*.

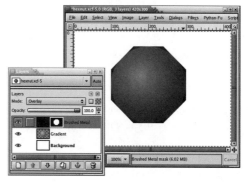

This technique is useful when creating metallic environments for video games. You could also modify the head to include tick marks and use the hex nut as a knob for a media player interface instead.

Making Screw Heads

As I'm sure you know, there are two basic types of screw heads: flat head and Phillips head. The flat head has a single slot that runs across it, whereas the Phillips head has a cross-shaped slot. Because we want to make rounded heads for the screws and the slots are flat, we'll need to apply slightly different types of shading to the different surfaces.

Creating the Outline

1. Start with a new white canvas set to the default size (420 × 300 pixels).

2. Add a new transparent layer by choosing **Layer ▸ New** and setting the Layer Fill Type to **Transparency**. Name the new layer *Rounded Head*.

3. Add two vertical guides at **80 pixels** and **340 pixels** and two horizontal guides at **20 pixels** and **280 pixels** (**Image ▸ Guides ▸ New Guide**).

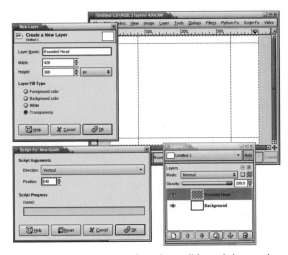

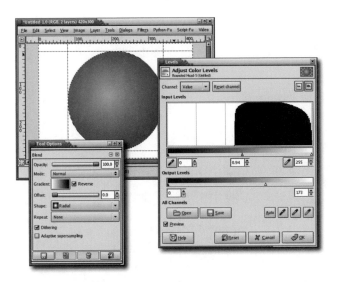

The Levels histogram starts roughly in the center because the darkest pixels in the selection are medium gray, not black.

Guides are used to create a box that will bound the circular selection that will become the screw head.

4. Choose the **Ellipse Select** tool from the toolbox. With the canvas selected, click the intersection of the top and left guides, and drag down to the intersection of the bottom and right guides. The selection should snap to the guides. If it doesn't, choose **View ▸ Snap to Guides**.

Rounding the Screw Head

1. With the canvas selected, press **D** and then **X** to set the colors to background color to black and the foreground color to white.

2. Choose the **Blend** tool from the toolbox. In the Tool Options dialog set the Gradient to **FG to BG (RGB)**, set the Shape to **Radial**, and check the box next to the word *Reverse*. Drag down from the upper-left edge of the selection to the lower-right corner of the canvas. This places a radial gradient inside the selection.

3. Use the Levels dialog (**Layer ▸ Colors ▸ Levels**) to darken the selection slightly by dragging the middle slider to the right.

Designing the Flat Head Screw

It's time to add the slots. We'll need to create two layers, one for the flat head screw's slot and another for the Phillips head screw's slot. This way, we'll have both versions in a single file and we'll be able to easily choose the layer we need.

Adding the Slot

1. Add a new transparent layer called *Flat Head Slot*.

2. Choose **Image ▸ Guides ▸ New Guide** and add two new vertical guides, one at **195 pixels** and the other at **225 pixels**. This marks off space for a slot that is 30 pixels wide and centered in the current selection, which should still be active. The slot selection is created by merging the current selection with a rectangular selection that has the new vertical guides and the old top and bottom guides as edges.

3. Choose the **Rectangle Select** tool from the toolbox. Hold down the ALT and SHIFT keys while you drag to create a new selection. Starting at the intersection of the top guide and the guide you positioned at 195 pixels, drag down to the point where the

bottom guide and the guide you positioned at 225 pixels intersect. What is left is a selection that has a rounded top and bottom. You may need to zoom in to see this clearly.

NOTE   *Linux users take note! If holding down the* ALT *and* SHIFT *keys while you drag to create the new selection doesn't work, try holding down the* CTRL *and* SHIFT *keys. Whether the* ALT *or the* CTRL *key is appropriate depends on the keyboard configuration of your Linux desktop.*

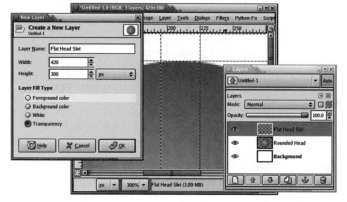

A rectangular selection intersects an oval selection, providing a precise selection for the flat head screw's slot.

4. Click the **Rounded Head** layer in the Layers dialog to make that layer active.

5. Make a copy of the current selection (**Edit ▸ Copy**).

6. Click the **Flat Head Slot** layer in the Layers dialog to make that layer active again.

7. Paste the copied selection (**Edit ▸ Paste**) and anchor it to the Flat Head Slot layer (**Layer ▸ Anchor Layer**).

8. Open the Brightness-Contrast dialog (**Layer ▸ Colors ▸ Brightness-Contrast**). Move the **Contrast** slider to the left so that the gray tones are nearly even throughout the slot. Move the **Brightness** slider to the right to make the slot darker than the rest of the screw head.

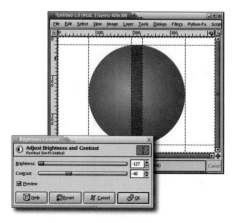

The slot is darker than the rest of the screw head because the slot is in shadow.

Adding Highlights to the Slot

One last thing we need to do is add highlights to the edges of the slot.

1. In the Layers dialog make sure the **Keep Transparency** box checked for the Flat Head Slot layer.

2. Choose the **Paintbrush** tool from the toolbox and choose the **Circle Fuzzy (05)** brush from the Brushes dialog. In the Tool Options dialog set the mode to **Grain Merge**.

3. With the canvas selected, press **D** and then **X** to set the foreground color to white.

4. Click the upper-right corner of the slot. Hold down the SHIFT key and click the lower-right corner to draw a highlight that runs along the guide that marks the right edge of the slot.

5. With the canvas selected, press **D** to reset the foreground color to black.

6. Click the upper-left corner of the slot. Hold down the SHIFT key and click the lower-left corner to draw a shadow that runs along the left edge of the slot.

7. Choose **View ▸ Show Guides** to turn off the guides and make it easier to the results.

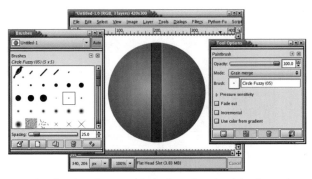

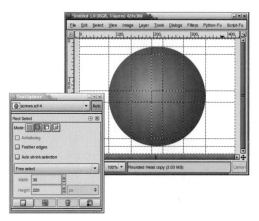

A single white line that runs along the right side of the slot makes it look as though light is shining from the left side of the image.

Designing the Phillips Head Screw

A Phillips head screw can be created using a very similar process. The only differences are that the cross-shaped slot doesn't span the diameter of the screw head, and one side of the cross is longer than the other.

Adding the Cross-Shaped Slot

1. Turn off visibility for the **Flat Head Slot** layer.

2. Create two new vertical guides at **140 pixels** and **280 pixels**, and then create four new horizontal guides at **40 pixels**, **135 pixels**, **165 pixels**, and **260 pixels** (**Image ▸ Guides ▸ New Guide**).

3. Choose the **Rectangle Select** tool from the toolbox. First create a selection for the horizontal slot by dragging through the center rectangle bordered by the guides. In the Tool Options dialog change the mode to **Add** (just click the second button from the left). Then create a selection for the vertical slot by dragging through the upright center rectangle bordered by the guides. You should now have a cross-shaped selection in the center of the rounded head, which is also still selected.

4. Click the **Rounded Head** layer in the Layers dialog to make that layer active.

5. Copy the selection, and paste it as a new layer by choosing **Edit ▸ Paste** and then choosing (**Layer ▸ New**). Name the new layer *Phillips Head Slot*.

Once you've finished creating the cross-shaped selection, don't forget to reset the Rectangle Select tool's mode to Replace by clicking the first button from the left.

6. Click the **Phillips Head Slot** layer in the Layers dialog to make that layer active.

7. Open the Brightness-Contrast dialog (**Layer ▸ Colors ▸ Brightness-Contrast**). Move the **Contrast** slider to the right and move the **Brightness** slider to the left to make the slot darker than the rest of the screw head.

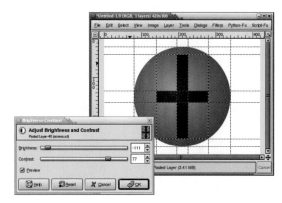

Just as the flat head slot was in shadow, the cross-shaped slot is in shadow.

Adding Highlights to the Cross-Shaped Slot

One more thing we need to do is add highlights to the edge of the slot.

1. Trace the right and bottom edges of the slot with white lines, using the Pencil tool to add highlights.

2. Choose **View ▸ Show Guides** to turn off the guides and better see the results.

3. Save this file as *screwheads.xcf*.

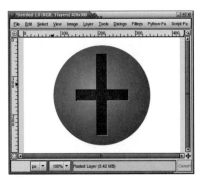

Add highlights to the right and bottom edges of the cross-shaped slot so it looks as though light is shining from the left side of the image. If you'd like the light source to be on the right side of the image, add highlights to the left and top edges.

Making Side-View Bolts

Now that you've mastered the art of creating screws that are viewed from head on, let's create a bolt that is viewed from the side. The pieces include the bolt head—a rectangle with edges that are angled away from the viewer—and the bolt's threaded shaft.

Creating the Bolt Head

1. Start by creating a new white canvas set to the default size (420 × 300 pixels).

2. Choose **Image ▸ Guides ▸ New Guide** to add vertical guides at **110 pixels** and **310 pixels** to create the left and right edges of the bolt head. Then add vertical guides at **150 pixels** and **270 pixels** to create the edges of angled sides and at **170 pixels** and **250 pixels** to mark the width of the shaft.

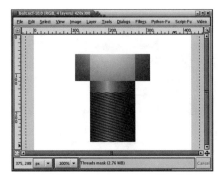

The shading techniques we use to create this side view of a bolt are applicable to any 3D object.

3. Add horizontal guides at **50 pixels** and **120 pixels** to create the top and bottom of the bolt head and at **150 pixels** to create the bottom of the bolt's neck.

4. Add a new transparent layer and name it *Bolt Head*.

5. Choose the **Rectangle Select** tool from the toolbox. Drag from the inside, upper-left intersection of the guides to the inside, lower-right intersection of the guides to create a selection, as shown here.

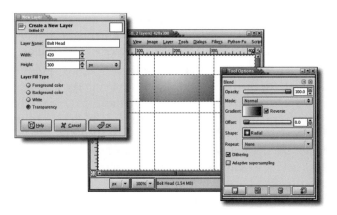

*Make sure to choose **View ▸ Snap to Guides** before making the selection for the bolt head.*

6. Choose the **Blend** tool from the toolbox. With the canvas selected, press **D** to reset the default foreground and background colors. In the Tool Options dialog set the Gradient to **FG to BG (RGB)**, set the Shape to **Radial,** and check the box next to the word *Reverse*. Drag from just left of center at the top of the canvas to just right of center at the bottom of the canvas. Linear gradients that are not perfectly vertical help give the illusion of imperfections on the metal surface.

7. Deselect all (CTRL-SHIFT-A).

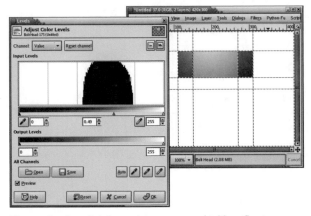

The gradient's radial shape gives us a more highly reflective area on the front of the bolt head, which will be useful as we add the angled sides.

Creating the Bolt Sides

1. Use the **Rectangle Select** tool to select the blocks outlined by guides on either side of the bolt head, as shown here.

2. After making the first selection, hold down the SHIFT key, and then start making the second selection. Let go of the SHIFT key before completing the second selection, so that the second selection is added to the first. Because we've done this, both selections will be active, even though they don't touch each other.

3. Open the Levels dialog (**Layer ▶ Colors ▶ Levels**). Move the middle slider to the right to darken the selections. This makes it look as though the two edges of the hexagon-shaped head are angled away from the viewer.

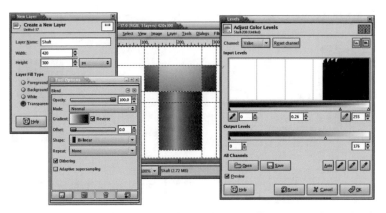

Adjust the Levels dialog to darken each angled side equally. You can select each side separately and adjust them separately if you want to make it look as though light is shining primarily from one side of the bolt.

Creating the Bolt Shaft

1. Add a new transparent layer by choosing **Layer ▶ New** and setting the Layer Fill Type to **Transparency**. Name the new layer *Shaft*.

2. Use the **Rectangle Select** tool to make a selection below the bolt head that extends down to the horizontal guide at 150 pixels and is bounded on the left and right by the innermost vertical guides.

3. Choose the **Blend** tool from the toolbox. In the Tool Options dialog set the Shape to **Bi-Linear**. Drag from just left of center in the selection to the right edge of the canvas.

4. Use the Levels dialog to darken the shaft (**Layer ▶ Colors ▶ Levels**).

5. Deselect all (SHIFT-CTRL-A), and then remove all guides (**Image ▶ Guides ▶ Remove All Guides**).

Creating the Bolt Threads

1. Add a new transparent layer and name it *Threads*.

2. Open the Patterns dialog (**Dialogs ▶ Patterns**) and drag the **Stripes (48 × 48)** preview onto the canvas. This will add a striped pattern to the image.

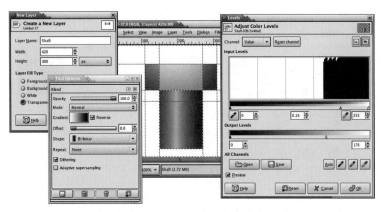

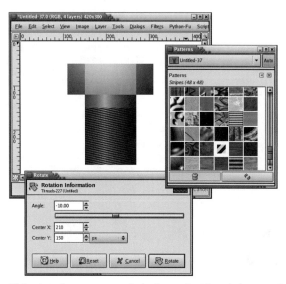

The bolt head is slightly lighter on top, as though the light is shining just above the bolt. That means the shaft should be in the shadow of the bolt head and should therefore be a bit darker than the bolt head.

3. Choose the **Rotate** tool from the toolbox, and click the first button from the left to set the Affect to **Transform Layer.** Click the canvas, and then in the Rotation Information dialog set the Angle to −**10 degrees.**

4. Add a white layer mask (**Layer ▸ Mask ▸ Add Layer Mask**).

5. Click the **Shaft** layer in the Layers dialog to make that layer active.

6. Create a selection of the shaft (**Layer ▸ Transparency ▸ Alpha to Selection**).

7. Click the **Threads** layer mask to make it active again.

8. Invert the selection (**Select ▸ Invert**).

9. Drag the foreground color (black) from the toolbox into the selection.

10. Deselect all (SHIFT-CTRL-A).

11. Use the **Rectangle Select** tool to create a small selection just below the bolt head. Drag the foreground color into this selection.

12. Clear the selection and remove the guides (**Image ▸ Guides ▸ Remove All Guides**).

13. Save this file as *bolt.xcf*.

If the threads appear jagged, duplicate the Threads layer, and then use the Gaussian Blur filter to apply a blur of 2 pixels to the original layer. In the Layers dialog reduce the Opacity of the original layer to between 50 and 75 percent.

Adding Screws to the User Interface

In our user interface project, the rounded head screws are added to corners of the faceplate. Because you created the screws in separate layers, all you need to do is open screwheads.xcf, delete the Background layer (**Layer ▸ Delete**), merge the visible layers (**Image ▸ Merge Visible Layers**), copy the contents of the canvas (CTRL-C), and paste it into the faceplate image as a new layer (press CTRL-V and then choose **Layer ▸ New**). Then just scale down the new layer (**Layer ▸ Scale**) and colorize it so it fits in with the faceplate (**Layer ▸ Colors ▸ Colorize**).

The side-view screws and bolt are not used in the media player project we've been working on, but they could be added to the top edge of the faceplate as decoration. Side-view screws and bolts are more commonly used in game design or when prototyping machine parts like computer cases.

6.3 WIRES AND EAR BUDS

Creating wires for a user interface design is another chance to simulate lighting to add depth to an image. A wire starts as a path that's drawn with a soft-edged brush, then blurred, passed through the Bump Map filter for added depth, and colorized.

In this tutorial, we'll create a wire that connects ear buds to a textured headphone jack for the media player. Then we'll add wires to link the ear buds with the connecting wire, followed by the ear buds themselves. This project consists of four pieces: a connecting wire, a headphone jack, ear bud wires, and ear buds.

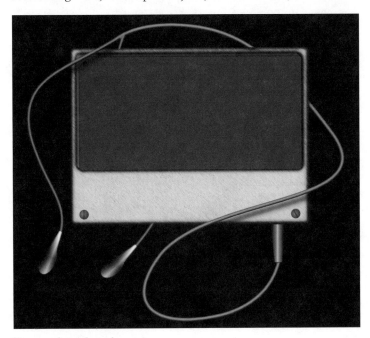

You can almost hear the music.

The Connecting Wire

The wire that connects the jack to the ear buds is created in two parts: First we create the wire that connects the jack and the ear bud wires, and then we create the Y-shaped ear bud wires themselves. The connecting wire starts near the lower-right corner of the media player where the jack will be placed, wraps around and behind the faceplate, and then hangs over the upper-left corner of the faceplate, where it is merged with the ear bud wires.

Creating the Connecting Wire

1. With the canvas selected, press **D** and then **X** to reset and then swap the default foreground and background colors so that the foreground color is white.

2. Open the Brushes dialog (**Dialogs ▸ Brushes**) and choose the **Circle Fuzzy (17)** brush. When creating user interfaces for computer programs or web applications, a brush of this size will produce a suitable wire. Larger brushes won't give you the sort of rounded shape that this brush does, and smaller brushes will make it difficult to see any texture or simulated depth effects you apply to the wire. In addition, using a soft-edged brush allows you to produce a smooth surface, whereas a hard-edged brush like Circle (17) might give you a bumpy result. Once you see how easy it is to put the technique described in this tutorial to work, you can experiment with your own wire designs.

3. Add a new transparent layer to the media player image by choosing **Layer ▸ New** and setting the Layer Fill Type to **Transparency**. Name the new layer *Connecting Wire*.

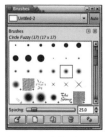

Use one of the GIMP's soft-edged
circular brushes to create wires.
The brushes are named Circle Fuzzy
(XX), where XX is the size.

4. Choose the **Paths** tool from the toolbox. Draw a path in the canvas window that looks like the one shown here. Make sure that the path extends straight down from the lower-right corner of the faceplate for about 100 pixels before it makes its first curve upward. This will allow us to merge the wire with the jack later.

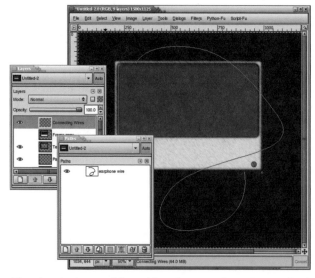

After the wire is created from this path, we mask out the part that inter-sects with the faceplate to make it look as though the wire is wrapped behind the media player.

NOTE *If your canvas is not large enough to accommodate the wires, enlarge the canvas by choosing Image ▸ Canvas Size before adding the Connecting Wire layer. Because the original black layer will not fill the canvas anymore, you'll also want to add a new black layer and move it to the bottom of the stack in the Layers dialog. If you do, you can delete the old black background layer.*

Stroking a Path for the Connecting Wire

1. Open the Channels dialog (**Dialogs ▸ Channels**). At the bottom of the dialog, click the second button from the left to open the New Channel dialog.

2. Name the channel *Connecting Wire*. Set the Fill Opacity to **100 percent,** and then click **OK** to create the new channel. The black channel will be visible initially, making the canvas black.

3. To make the paths we're about to stroke easier to see, add a new white layer by choosing **Layer ▸ New** and then selecting the White option. Move the new white layer below the Connecting Wire layer in the Layers dialog. This is a temporary layer that we'll remove shortly, so it's not necessary to give it a name.

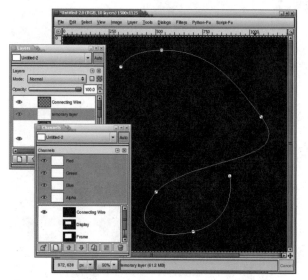

The temporary white layer makes it easier to see the stroked path.

4. Click the **Connecting Wire** channel in the Channels dialog to make that channel active again.

5. With the Path tool and the path still active, click the **Stroke Path** button in the Tool Options dialog to open the Choose Stroke Style dialog.

6. Click the radio button next to the words *Stroke with a paint tool*, and choose **Paintbrush** from the Paint tool drop-down menu. Click the **Stroke** button to stroke the path using the white foreground and the Circle Fuzzy brush you selected earlier.

7. In the Channels dialog duplicate the Connecting Wire channel by clicking the **Duplicate** button (it's the third button from the right at the bottom of the dialog). The new channel will be called *Connecting Wire Copy*.

NOTE *If the path is not active, you will not see any control points along the path. With the Path tool active in the toolbox, clicking the path makes the path active. If you can't even see the path, click the eye icon in the Paths dialog to make the path visible. To avoid confusion, click the eye icon again to turn off the visibility of the path when you've finished stroking it.*

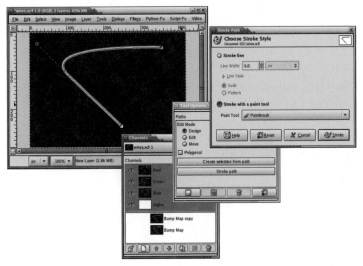

While the path is visible, it may be difficult to see the white stroke. Use the preview in the Channels dialog for the Connecting Wire channel to verify that the stroke was made in that channel.

Extruding the Connecting Wire

1. Click the **Connecting Wire Copy** channel in the Channels dialog to make that channel active.

2. Open the Gaussian Blur filter (**Filters ▸ Blur ▸ Gaussian Blur**). Set the Blur Radius to **5 pixels**, set the Blur Method to **RLE**, and click **OK** to apply the blur.

3. Choose the original **Connecting Wire** channel by clicking its name in the Channels dialog. Create a selection from this channel by clicking the **Channel to Selection** button, which is the second button from right at the bottom of the dialog.

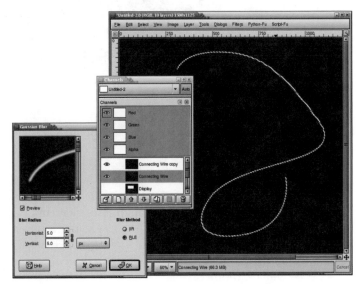

The change the blur makes won't be very noticeable unless you zoom in on the wire.

4. Return to the Layers dialog and click the **Connecting Wire** layer to make that layer active.

5. Click the foreground color in the toolbox to open the Change Foreground Color dialog. Type **C1C1C1** in the HTML field, and then click **OK** to apply the change. Drag the foreground color onto the canvas to fill the selection with gray.

6. Deselect all (CTRL-SHIFT-A) and delete the temporary white layer.

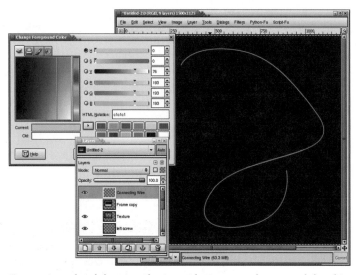

Once we've colored the wire selection with gray we no longer need the white temporary layer.

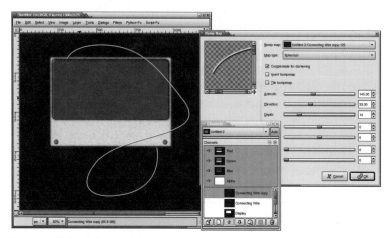

Turning off the visibility of the Connecting Wire and the Connecting Wire Copy channels reveals the wire overlaying the faceplate.

7. Open the Bump Map filter (**Filters ▸ Map ▸ Bump Map**). Adjust the preview window so you can view a portion of the wire clearly. Choosing **Spherical** from the Map Type drop-down menu will likely produce the best, most evenly rounded results. Check the box next to the words *Compensate for darkening* to turn on that option. Adjust the **Azimuth, Elevation,** and **Depth** as necessary. I use an Azimuth value of 145, an Elevation value of 33, and a Depth value of 14, but you may need to use slightly different values to achieve a more three-dimensional appearance.

8. Make sure the **Connecting Wire Copy** channel you blurred earlier is selected from the Bump Map drop-down menu. When the wire looks the way you'd like, click **OK** to apply the filter.

9. In the Channels dialog click the eye icons for the Connecting Wire and Connecting Wire Copy channels to turn off the visibility of those channels. We won't be using them anymore in this tutorial.

Masking and Colorizing the Connecting Wire

1. Add a new white layer mask (**Layer ▸ Mask ▸ Add Layer Mask**) to the Connecting Wire layer.

2. With the canvas selected, press **D** to set the foreground color to black. Using any brush, mask out the section of the wire that actually intersects the faceplate, as shown here.

3. Click the **Connecting Wire** layer preview to make the layer (instead of the mask) active.

4. Now let's colorize the wire. Open the Colorize dialog (**Layer ▸ Colors ▸ Colorize**). Set the Hue to **45**, set the Saturation to **90**, and set the Lightness to **–35**.

5. Add a drop shadow to the wire (**Script-Fu ▸ Shadow ▸ Drop Shadow**). Don't forget to add a layer mask to the drop shadow too!

NOTE *This would be a good time to save the image you've worked so hard to create, just to be safe!*

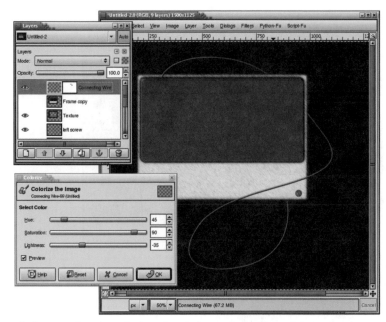

The layer mask makes it look as though the wire wraps behind the media player.

The Headphone Jack

Now we're ready to add a connecting jack between the wire and the faceplate. This process starts with a rectangular selection to which a bit of masking is applied.

Creating the Headphone Jack

1. Create a new layer (**Layer ▸ New**) that is sized to **112 × 172 pixels.** Name the new layer *Jack*.

2. Use the **Move** tool to position the new layer so its top edge is just above the faceplate's bottom edge and so the middle of the Jack layer's bottom edge intersects with the connecting wire.

3. Use the **Rectangle Select** tool to make a selection that spans most of the width of the Jack layer and runs from the top of that layer to just above the bottom of that layer, as shown here.

NOTE   *If you have problems positioning the Jack layer, hold down the* SHIFT *key while you click and drag the layer in the canvas window.*

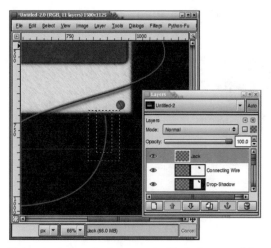

If the wire isn't perfectly centered with the bottom of the selection, don't worry. You'll be able to reposition the Jack layer after you've finished creating the jack itself.

4. Reset the foreground and background colors by pressing **D** with the canvas selected.

5. Choose the **Blend** tool from the toolbox. In the Tool Options dialog set the Gradient to **FG to BG (RGB)** and check the box next to the word *Reverse* to turn on that option. Set the Shape to **Bi-Linear.** The Opacity should be set to **100 percent** and the Repeat option should be set to **None.** Drag inside the selection, starting just left of center and moving to the right edge of the selection.

6. To colorize the gradient, open the Colorize dialog (**Layers ▸ Colors ▸ Colorize**) and use the same settings you used when colorizing the connecting wire.

7. Deselect all (CTRL-SHIFT-A).

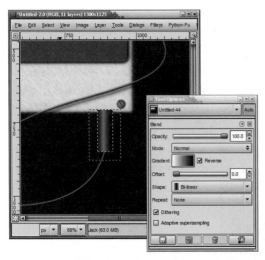

It's not required that the jack match the wire exactly, but it's easy to match the two if you noted the Colorize dialog settings you used when colorizing the connecting wire.

Masking the Headphone Jack

1. Add a new white layer mask to the Jack layer (**Layer ▸ Masks ▸ Add Layer Mask**).

2. Open the Brushes dialog and choose the **Circle Fuzzy (17)** brush.

3. Choose the **Paintbrush** tool from the toolbox. Click the canvas near the upper-left edge of the gradient in the Jack layer. Hold down the SHIFT key and click the bottom of the gradient just left of center, as shown in the image on the left. Repeat this process for the right side, as shown in the second image.

4. Mask out any areas of the jack that are outside the boundaries of the first two lines. Then draw a line in the mask that crosses the top of the Jack layer so the top of the gradient butts up against the bottom of the faceplate. The final mask will look something like the white area in the second image here.

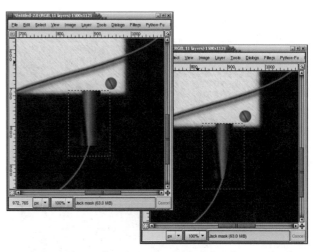

Start creating the mask with two lines that define the outside edges of the jack.

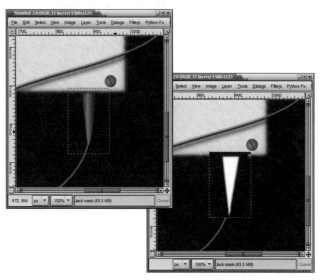

The completed mask makes the rectangular gradient look like a V-shaped connector.

The Ear Bud Wires

The ear bud wires are created just as the connecting wire was created. You obviously need a different path, however. The path used for this portion of the project is shown here.

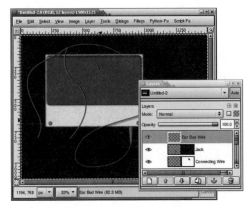

The path for the ear bud wires is an upside down Y, where the lower part of the Y intersects the end of the connecting wire we created earlier.

Creating the Ear Bud Wires

1. Create a new layer and name it *Ear Bud Wire*.
2. Then create a new channel, stroke the path in this channel, and duplicate the channel.
3. Open the **Gaussian Blur** filter and apply a blur of **5 pixels** to the duplicate channel.
4. As before, make a selection from the original channel.
5. In the Ear Bud Wire layer, fill the selection with gray.
6. Use the **Bump Map** filter to extrude the wire, using the blurred duplicate channel as the bump map.

Merging the Ear Bud Wires with the Connecting Wire

In order to merge the ear bud wires with the connecting wire, a layer mask must be added to the Ear Bud Wire layer, and the Connecting Wire layer's existing layer mask must be updated.

1. If the **Ear Bud Wire** layer is not the active layer in the Layers dialog, click that layer to make it active.
2. Add a white layer mask (**Layer ▸ Mask ▸ Add Layer Mask**).
3. Zoom in on the canvas (**View ▸ Zoom**) and center on the intersection of the ear bud wire and the connecting wire, as shown here.

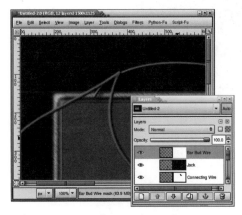

Before you start working on the masks, zoom in to get a good view of the point where the wires intersect.

4. With the canvas selected, press **D** to set the foreground color to black.
5. Choose a brush from the **Brushes** dialog. The Circle Fuzzy (17) brush should work well.
6. Alternate between using the **Paintbrush** tool and the **Airbrush** tool to mask out the tip of the ear bud so it merges with the connecting wire. This will take some patience, and you may need to undo a few strokes before you get it just right, but keep at it. You'll get the hang of it!
7. At this point you've merged the tip of the ear bud wire with the connecting wire, but the excess connecting wire should be removed. Click the **Connecting Wire** layer's mask and repeat the same masking process.
8. Repeat this masking process in the drop shadow mask for the **Connecting Wire** layer.

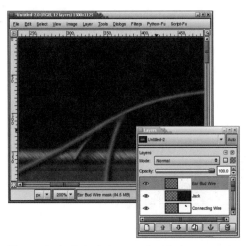

The ear bud wire's tip is merged with the connecting wire, but notice that some excess connecting wire hangs down on the left.

9. Click the **Ear Bud Wire** layer to make that layer active and add a drop shadow (**Script-Fu ▸ Shadow ▸ Drop Shadow**).

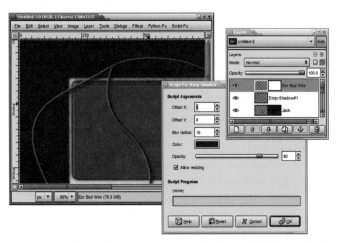

If the drop shadow affects the area you masked out of the Ear Bud Wire layer, delete the drop shadow layer (Layer ▸ Delete), apply the layer mask to the Ear Bud Wire layer by clicking that layer and choosing Layer ▸ Mask ▸ Apply Layer Mask, and then add your drop shadow.

The Ear Buds

The final step is adding the ear buds. These require two pieces: the piece that connects to the ear bud wire and the round ear piece itself. To make it easy on ourselves, let's create both pieces on a separate canvas, merge them into a single layer, and then copy and paste the image into the media player project twice, rotating and positioning each copy to line up with the tips of the ear bud wires.

Creating an Ear Bud

1. Open a new canvas window (**File ▸ New**) that has a black background and is in portrait mode (click the button with the mountain icon below the Height field in the Create a New Image dialog).

2. Add vertical guides at **80 pixels**, **100 pixels**, **150 pixels**, **200 pixels**, and **220 pixels**. Add a horizontal guide at **300 pixels**.

3. Choose the **Ellipse Select** tool from the toolbox. In the Tool Options dialog set the mode to **Replace** by clicking the first box from the left. Choose **Fixed Size** from the drop-down menu in the Tool Options dialog and set the Width and Height to **240 pixels**.

4. Now comes the trickiest selection we've made thus far. Follow along carefully because the sequence of operations is important. Hold down the SHIFT key, press and hold the left mouse button while the cursor is over the intersection of the vertical guide at 150 pixels and the horizontal guide at 300 pixels, and then press down and hold the CTRL key. Move the mouse to draw a circular selection that is 240 pixels in diameter. Let go of the mouse button and release the CTRL and SHIFT keys.

NOTE *This keyboard shortcut is a tricky one. If it doesn't work quite right, just try holding down the SHIFT key, clicking and dragging on the middle of the canvas, and using the Move tool to position the selection as shown here. Make sure to set the Affect to Selection in the Move tool's Tool Options dialog by clicking the middle button.*

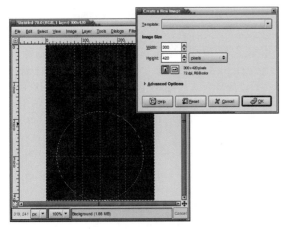

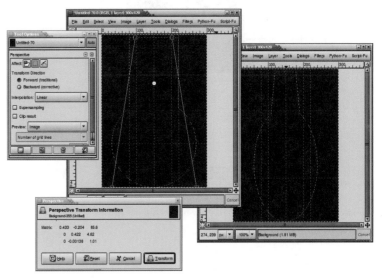

The circular selection serves as the main part of the ear bud. Next we merge that selection with a rectangular selection and use the Perspective tool to transform it.

5. Choose the **Rectangle Select** tool from the toolbox. In the Tool Options dialog click the second button from the left to set the mode to **Add.** Click the leftmost guide near the top of the canvas and drag down to the rightmost guide until the rectangular selection intersects with the oval selection, as shown here.

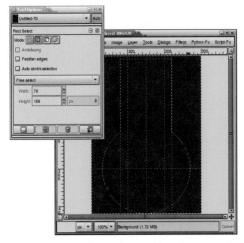

Make sure to set the mode to Add in the Rectangle Select tool's Tool Options dialog before dragging to create the selection.

6. Choose the **Perspective** tool from the toolbox. In the Tool Options dialog set the Affect to **Transform Selection** by clicking the middle button. Click the canvas and drag the upper-left grab point toward the next guide. Repeat this process for the upper-right grab point. Click the Transform button in the Perspective Transform Information dialog to apply the change. The transformed selection is shown here.

The image on the right shows the final shape of the ear bud.

Applying a Colored Gradient to the Ear Bud

1. With the selection still in place, choose the **Blend** tool from the toolbox.

2. In the Tool Options dialog set the Gradient to **FG to BG (RGB)** and set the Shape to **Bi-Linear.**

3. Set the Opacity to **100 percent,** set the mode to **Normal**, and choose **None** from the Repeat drop-down menu.

4. Click the intersection of the horizontal guide and the vertical guide that is second from the left. Drag across to the rightmost vertical guide.

5. Open the **Colorize** dialog and use the same settings you used when colorizing the connecting wire and the ear bud wires.

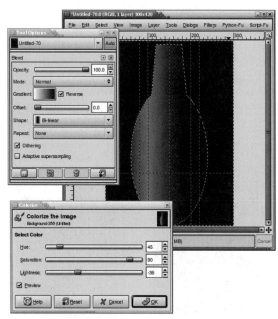

After colorizing the ear bud, keep the selection in place. We'll use the selection to duplicate the ear bud and paste two ear buds into the media player image.

Duplicating and Positioning the Ear Buds

1. With the selection still in place, copy the ear bud.

2. Return to the media player image window and paste the selection. The ear bud might be a bit large. Choose **Layer ▸ Scale Layer** to scale down the ear bud until it is **90 pixels wide** (if the aspect ratio is locked and you positioned all of the guides correctly when you created the ear bud, the height should be 203 pixels).

3. Create a new selection from the pasted layer (**Layer ▸ New**).

4. Duplicate this layer (**Layer ▸ Duplicate**). Name the original layer *Ear Bud Left* and name the duplicate layer *Ear Bud Right*.

5. Use the **Move** tool to drag the **Ear Bud Left** layer so it meets the left tip of the ear bud wire. Then drag the **Ear Bud Right** layer so it meets the right tip of the ear bud wire.

6. Use the **Rotate** tool to align the connectors for each ear bud with their respective wire tips.

6.4 CORRUGATED TUBES

The technique for creating tubes like the ones shown here is similar to the technique we use to create wires—but this is even easier. The trick to achieving the corrugated look shown here is to use a circular or spherical brush, use a small Spacing value, and paint a line so that the circles overlap.

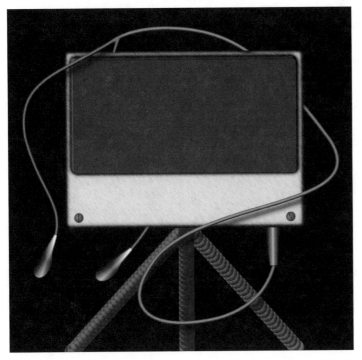

Tubular effects are simple to achieve.

Because soft-edged brushes are used for tubes, and because the lines you paint may contain transparency, it often helps to fill the transparent regions with a background color. This color also adds realistic highlights to the tube.

In this tutorial I'll walk you through the process of creating a simple corrugated tube and then show you how to incorporate tubes into a tripod—the sort of thing that might be used to display the video player at a trade show.

Getting Started

To see how the process for creating a corrugated tube works, let's start with an *S* shape. The video editor project uses uncurved tubes, but it's helpful to practice creating curved tubes first. Open a white canvas at the default settings. Add a transparent layer (**Layer ▸ New**) and name the new layer *Tube*.

Stroking a Path

1. Choose the **Path** tool from the toolbox. Click the canvas three times along a line that runs from upper-right corner of the canvas to the lower-left corner. The second click should be in the center of the canvas.

2. In the Tool Options dialog click the radio button next to the word *Edit*.

3. Click the middle grab point on the canvas and drag away from it to position the handle as shown here. Click inside the same grab point and drag out a second handle, positioning it opposite the first handle. You now have a basic *S* shape.

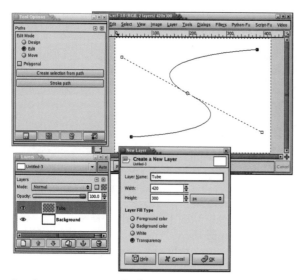

As when creating wires, the first step is to create a path.

4. With the canvas selected, press **D** to reset the default foreground and background colors.

5. Open the Brushes dialog (**Dialogs ▸ Brushes**) and choose the **Sphere (29)** brush. At the bottom of the Brushes dialog set the Spacing slider to **25 pixels**.

6. Choose the **Paintbrush** tool from the toolbox and make sure the mode is set to **Normal** in the Tool Options dialog.

7. If the path is no longer visible in the canvas, open the Paths dialog again (**Dialogs ▸ Paths**) and click the eye icon. Then choose the **Path** tool from the toolbox and click the path on the canvas.

8. In the Tool Options dialog click the **Stroke Path** button. In the Choose Stroke Style dialog click the radio button next to the words *Stroke with a paint tool* and then choose **Paintbrush** from the Paint tool drop-down menu. Click the **Stroke** button to apply the brush stroke to the path.

NOTE   *The Sphere (29) brush is included in the gimp-data-extras package. If you don't have this brush, you may want to install this package.*

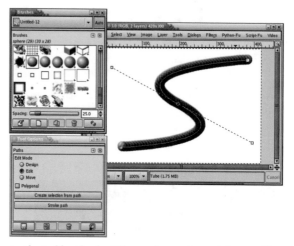

A spherical brush of a different size can be used, but you'll need to adjust the Spacing slider at the bottom of the Brushes dialog if you want to achieve a similar effect.

Removing Transparency

As you can see in the image on the left, the stroked line contains some transparency because of the brush we used to create it. To get rid of this transparency, let's merge the tube with the white background (as shown in the image on the right). Make sure that you only merge the tube—and not the whole Tube layer—with the white background.

1. Choose the **Fuzzy Select** tool from the toolbox and set the Threshold to **45** in the Tool Options dialog. Then click the canvas.

2. Invert the selection (**Select ▸ Invert**) and shrink it by **1 pixel** (**Select ▸ Shrink**).

3. Now that we have a selection of the tube, let's use this selection to grab a copy of the white background layer. First click the **Background** layer in the Layers dialog to make that layer active.

4. Copy the selection, and then paste it as a new layer by pressing CTRL-V and then choosing (**Layer ▸ New**). This places a white tubelike shape in a new layer at the top of the Layer stack.

5. Move the layer that contains the white tubelike shape so that it is below the Tube layer in the Layers dialog.

6. Click the **Tube** layer to make it active, and then merge the Tube layer with the new layer (**Layer ▸ Merge Down**). Rename the merged layer *Tube*. This process effectively fills the transparent regions of the tube image with white so that we can colorize the tube and prevent background colors and images from showing through the tube.

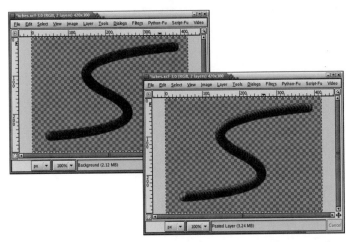

This image shows the tube with the Background layer's visibility turned off so you can see the transparency in the brush stroke.

7. Open the Colorize dialog (**Layer ▸ Colors ▸ Colorize**) and adjust the settings as necessary to add color to the tube.

8. Enhance the contrast of the tube with the Levels dialog (**Layer ▸ Colors ▸ Levels**) or change the ambient lighting with the Curves dialog (**Layer ▸ Colors ▸ Curves**).

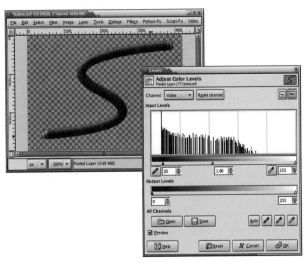

Don't use the Auto option in the Levels dialog. That will adjust the levels so that the brightest areas of the image are white. Instead, just adjust the middle slider as necessary to achieve the corrugated effect.

Adding a Tripod

Now that you've learned how to create a basic corrugated tube, let's use that technique to create a tripod for the video player.

1. Open the video player project you saved in the last section.

2. Add a new transparent layer to the video player project and name it *Tripod*.

3. Add a new vertical guide at 50 percent by choosing **Image ▸ Guides ▸ New Guide (by Percent)**, and then add a new horizontal guide at the bottom edge of the video screen. The three tubes that act as the tripod for the video player will meet at the intersection of these guides.

4. Choose the **Paintbrush** tool from the toolbox, select the **Sphere (29)** brush, and use the same brush settings as before. Draw each of the three legs so they extend to the edge of the canvas.

5. Colorize the layer (**Layer ▸ Colors ▸ Colorize**).

6. Add a layer mask (**Layer ▸ Mask ▸ Add Layer Mask**) and mask out the top of the tripod so it appears to connect to the bottom of the video player.

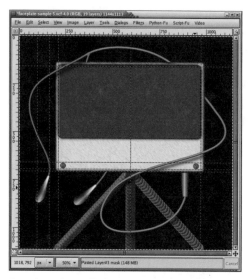

Tripods traditionally have straight legs, but you could just as easily use curved tubes to create a stand for the video player.

6.5 NAVIGATION BAR

So far in the video player project, we've created a display, added audio output, and even attached a small tripod. But there still isn't any way to provide user input. What this player needs is a navigation bar. And that's exactly what we create in this section.

The goal of this navigation bar project is a set of buttons that includes rewind, pause, stop, play, and fast-forward. All of the buttons will fit on a single row that runs across the open area

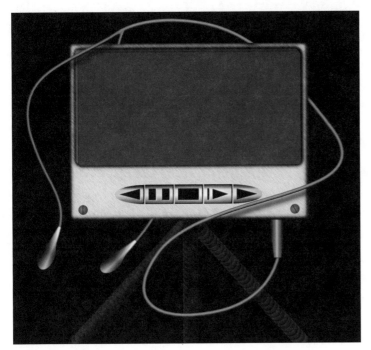

Buttons dictate how users interact with your design. In other words, they're crucial!

beneath the player's video display. The buttons are rounded to give the user some tactile feedback—if this were a real video player, you'd want to be able to find the buttons by simply feeling for them with your fingers.

NOTE *The buttons on this navigation bar are nonstandard. Call it artistic license. You can use the process described here to produce any kind of buttons you like.*

Creating a Gradient-Filled Button Bar

The button bar starts as a rectangular selection. We'll use guides to center the selection and size it in such a way that determining the horizontal positions for rest of the guides will be easy.

1. Open a new image window set to the default size (420 × 300 pixels).

2. The rectangular selection requires two horizontal and two vertical guides. Open the New Guide dialog (**Image ▸ Guides ▸ New Guide**). Choose **Horizontal** from the Direction drop-down menu and set the Position to **60 pixels**. Click **OK** to add the new guide.

3. Repeat these steps to add another horizontal guide at **240 pixels**.

4. Choose **Vertical** from the Direction drop-down menu and add two vertical guides at **25 pixels** and **395 pixels**. In doing this, we've added guides that are 25 pixels from each edge of the canvas.

NOTE *The size of this canvas is chosen to make it easier to work with guides to create the selections that become the video player's buttons. Later, we'll scale down the image to fit the video player project. When creating small elements that require attention to detail, it's usually easier to start at a larger size and scale down. You almost never want to scale up when using a raster image editor like the GIMP.*

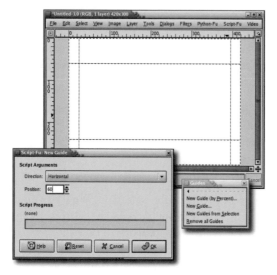

Guides help us center the button bar on the new canvas.

5. With the horizontal and vertical guides in place, use the **Rectangle Select** tool to create a selection that has the intersections of the guides as its corners.

6. Use the Rounded Rectangle dialog to round the sides of the selection (**Selection ▸ Rounded Rectangle**). Set the Radius to **90 percent**, and click **OK** to apply the change.

7. After the sides of the selection have been rounded, add a new transparent layer by choosing **Layer ▸ New Layer** and setting the Layer Fill Type to **Transparency**. Name the new layer *Bar*.

8. With the canvas selected, press **D** to reset the default foreground and background colors. Drag the background color (white) into the selection to fill the selection with that color.

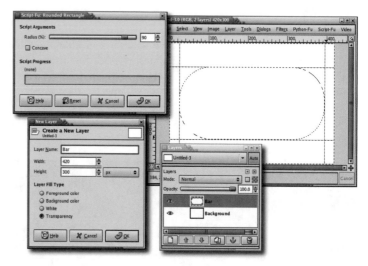

Round the rectangular selection before filling it with gradients.

9. Open the New Guides dialog again (**Image ▸ Guides ▸ New Guide**). This time add horizontal guides at **110 pixels** and **160 pixels**.

10. Choose the **Blend** tool from the toolbox. In the Tool Options dialog set the Gradient to **FG to Transparent** and set the Shape to **Linear**. Drag up from the bottom of the selection to the next horizontal guide. Then drag down from the top of the selection to the next horizontal guide.

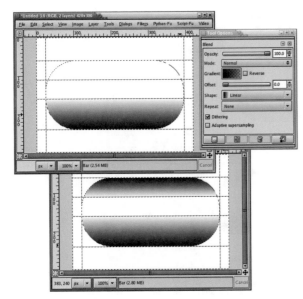

The gradients aren't exactly the same (the lower one is larger than the one at the top), and this makes it look as though we're viewing the button bar from just above its horizontal center.

Adding Shadows to the Button Bar

The next step is to use shadows to add end caps to the bar and give it a more three-dimensional appearance. Because we drag in different directions, the gradients simulate the variations in reflected light—another realistic touch.

1. Add a new transparent layer by choosing **Layer ▸ New Layer** and setting the Layer Fill Type to **Transparency**. Name the new layer *End Caps* and position it above the Bar layer in the Layers dialog.

2. With the Blend tool still active, drag from the right edge of the bar about one-third the length of the selection. Then drag down at a 45-degree angle from the upper-left intersection of the guides that border the selection to the bottom of the selection.

3. Set the End Caps layer's mode to **Grain Merge**.

4. Deselect all (CTRL-SHIFT-A).

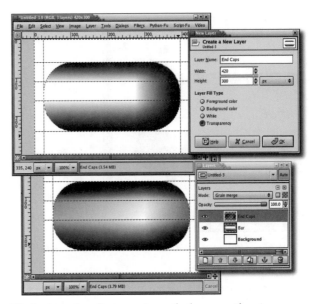

The horizontal gradients aren't exactly the same either. An uneven reflection lends the image a more realistic quality.

Defining the Buttons

The buttons come next. Before we draw their icons, we need to divide up the bar to make spaces for each of them. (For this step you may need to zoom in by choosing View ▸ Zoom ▸ Zoom In and then pressing CTRL-E to resize the canvas to fit).

Each of the five buttons (rewind, pause, stop, play, and fast-forward) should take up the same amount of space on the button bar. The width of the button bar is 370 pixels (420 pixels total, minus 25 pixels on each end). Each button therefore gets 74 pixels. We also need four visual separators—gaps or channels between the buttons. The width of these separators is subtracted from each button's space allowance.

1. Add vertical guides at **97 pixels** and **99 pixels**, **171 pixels** and **173 pixels**, **245 pixels** and **247 pixels**, and **319 pixels** and **321 pixels** (**Image ▸ Guides ▸ New Guide**). Each pair of guides is two pixels apart.

2. Choose the **Paintbrush** tool from the toolbox. In the Brushes dialog choose the Circle **Fuzzy (03)** brush.

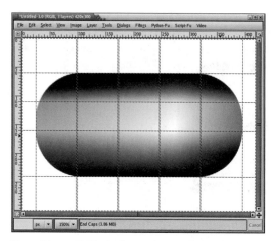

Use guides to divide the button bar evenly.

3. In the Layers dialog click the **Bar** layer to make that layer active, and then make a selection from it by choosing **Layer ▸ Transparency ▸ Alpha to Selection**. This selection will bound the channels we're about to draw, and the small, soft-edged brush will allow the channels to blend with the Bar layer.

4. Add a new transparent layer and name it *Button Channels*. Move the **Button Channels** layer to the top of the stack (**Layer ▸ Stack ▸ Layer to Top**).

5. For each new pair of vertical guides, click the intersection of the pair's upper horizontal guide and left vertical guide, then hold down the SHIFT key while clicking the intersection of the pair's lower horizontal guide and left vertical guide. This draws a shadow edge for a channel that extends from the top of the bar to the bottom.

6. With the canvas selected, press **X** to change the foreground color to white, and then repeat this process for the right vertical guide in each pair. This will brighten the side of the channel that is exposed to the light source. These combinations of black and white lines come together to create the separators between the buttons.

NOTE *Because the Circle Fuzzy (03) brush is so small, it will be difficult to see the lines as you draw them. Toggle the visibility of the guides (View ▸ Show Guides) to see the effect more clearly.*

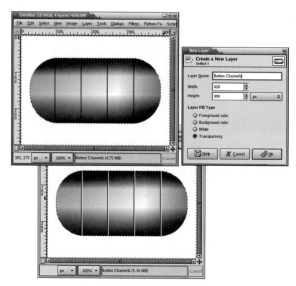

Remember the highlights and shadows we added in the screw head's channels in Section 6.2? Use the same technique to divide up the button bar.

Drawing the Button Icons

Drawing the button icons requires us to work with even more guides. We don't want any of the icons to touch the edges of their buttons, so subtract 10 pixels from each side of each button.

1. Add vertical guides at **35 pixels** and **89 pixels**, **109 pixels** and **163 pixels**, **183 pixels** and **237 pixels**, **257 pixels** and **311 pixels**, and **331 pixels** and **385 pixels**. One additional vertical guide at **267 pixels** is needed for the fast-forward button.

2. Add horizontal guides at **96 pixels** (to mark the top of each icon), **150 pixels** (to mark the middle of each icon), and **204 pixels** (to mark the bottom of each icon).

3. Create a new transparent layer and name it *Button Icons*.

4. With the canvas selected, press **D** to reset the default foreground and background colors.

Having taken these steps, we're ready to draw the icon for each button. Each icon should be drawn in its own layer so you can easily delete the layer and try again if you make a mistake.

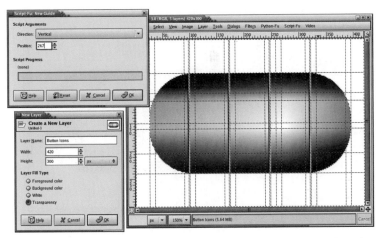

That's a lot of guides! If we'd started with a smaller canvas, just imagine how close all those guides would be.

Rewind   Add a new transparent layer and name it *Rewind*. Choose the **Path** tool from the toolbox. Draw a path for the rewind arrow in the leftmost button, as shown here. Note that only three anchor points are required for this shape. Click the **Create Selection from Path** button in the Tool Options dialog. Fill the selection with black by dragging the foreground color from the toolbox into the selection. Deselect all (CTRL-SHIFT-A).

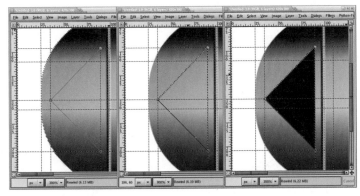

Guides make it easy to position each path. Each path is quickly converted into a selection of the proper shape, and then the selection is filled to create a button icon.

Pause   Add a new transparent layer and name it *Pause*. Choose the **Rectangle Select** tool from the toolbox. Draw a rectangular selection bounded by the guides for this button's icon, as shown here. Fill the selection with black by dragging the foreground color from the toolbox into the selection.

In the Brushes dialog choose the **Circle (13)** brush, and then choose the **Eraser** tool from the toolbox. Click the uppermost horizontal guide in the center of the button. Hold down the SHIFT key, position the mouse over the lower horizontal guide so a straight line is displayed, and then click the mouse. This will erase a straight line that goes through the selection, producing the double bar that is traditionally found on pause buttons. Deselect all (CTRL-SHIFT-A).

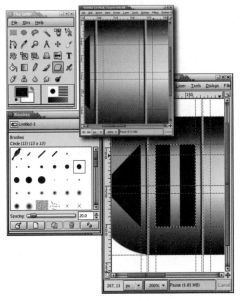

The pause icon is two vertical bars. It's easier to create a rectangular selection and erase a strip from the middle than it is to try to create two identical rectangular selections.

Stop   Creating the stop icon is just like creating the pause icon, except that in this case we don't need to erase part of the selection. Add a new transparent layer and name it *Stop*. Choose the **Rectangle Select** tool from the toolbox. Draw a rectangular selection bounded by the guides for this button's icon, as shown here. Fill the selection with black by dragging the foreground color from the toolbox into the selection. Deselect all (CTRL-SHIFT-A).

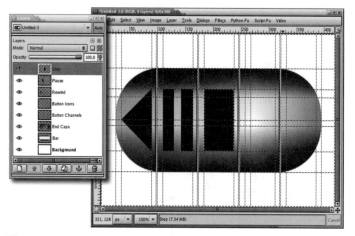

The stop icon is just a pause icon without the center cut out.

Play   Click the Rewind layer in the layers dialog, and then duplicate that layer (**Layer ▶ Duplicate**). Click the duplicate layer name and change it to *Play*. Choose the **Flip** tool from the toolbox. In the Tool Options dialog set the Flip Type to **Horizontal**. Click the canvas to flip the Play layer. It should flip right into place, but if it doesn't, use the **Move** tool to drag the layer into place. Deselect all (CTRL-SHIFT-A).

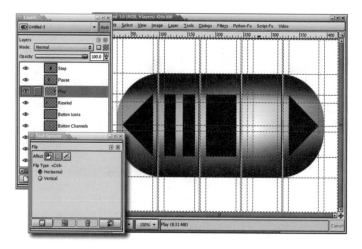

Because the buttons are identical in size, copying and horizontally flipping the rewind icon allows us to create the play icon.

Fast-Forward   Add a new transparent layer and name it *Fast-Forward*. Choose the **Path** tool from the toolbox. Draw a path on the canvas as shown here. In the Tool Options dialog click the **Create Selection from Path** button. Fill the selection with black by dragging the foreground color from the toolbox into the selection. Deselect all (CTRL-SHIFT-A). Choose the **Eraser** tool from the toolbox, and then choose the **Circle (05)** brush in the Brushes dialog. Click where the vertical guide at 267 pixels intersects with the uppermost horizontal guide. Then hold down the SHIFT key and click where the vertical guide at 267 pixels intersects with the lowermost horizontal guide. Deselect all (CTRL-SHIFT-A).

6. Repeat steps 3 through 5 for each of the button icon layers.

7. Save a copy of this image as *navbar.xcf*.

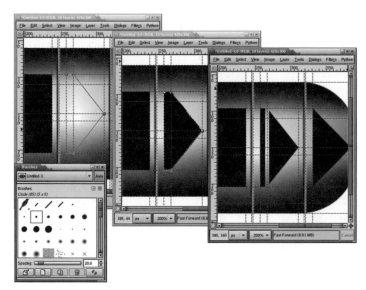

Like the pause icon, the play icon is created by erasing a rectangular selection created from a path.

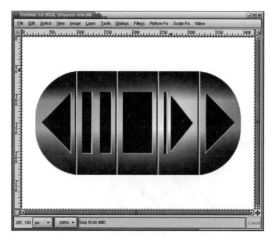

Now that the button bar is complete, we need to copy it into the media player project.

Adding Highlights to the Icons

We've created the basic icon shapes, but highlighting their edges will really make them stand out.

1. With the canvas selected, press **D** and then **X** to set the foreground color to white.

2. Choose the **Paintbrush** tool from the toolbox, and then choose the **Circle Fuzzy (05)** brush in the Brushes dialog.

3. Click the **Rewind** layer in the Layers dialog to make that layer active. Make sure the **Keep Transparency** box is checked for that layer.

4. Create a selection around the icon by choosing **Layer ▸ Transparency ▸ Alpha to Selection**.

5. Use the guides to draw lines along the right and bottom edges of the icon. Toggle the visibility of the guides (**View ▸ Show Guides**) and selection (**View ▸ Show Selection**) as you do this to see the results.

Adding the Button Bar to the Media Player

This button bar is the wrong dimensions for the media player, but because both images were created on canvases sized to 420 × 300 pixels, the button bar can be scaled to fit the player. Turn off the visibility of the Background layer in the button bar's Layers dialog.

1. Merge the remaining visible layers (**Image ▸ Merge Visible Layers**).

2. Copy the button bar by choosing **Select ▸ All** and then choosing **Select ▸ Copy**.

3. Paste the button bar onto the media player canvas as a new layer by pressing CTRL-V and then choosing **Layer ▸ New**. Move the new layer below all of the ear bud layers, and then position the button bar layer on the canvas as shown.

NOTE *If you can't paste the button bar selection as a new layer, a layer mask is probably active on the media player canvas. Just click any layer preview in the Layers dialog, then try pasting the button bar selection as a new layer.*

4. Choose the **Scale** tool from the toolbox. Make sure that in the Tool Options dialog the Affect is set to **Transform Layer** (click the first button from the left). Click the canvas and drag the handles around the button bar layer until it is an appropriate size. Click **Scale** in the Scale Information dialog to apply the change.

5. Use the **Move** tool to center the bar on the player's faceplate.

6. Colorize the layer (**Layer ▶ Colors ▶ Colorize**).

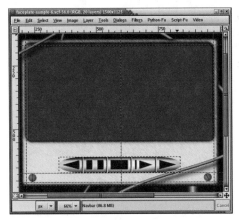

The high-contrast gradients we applied to the button bar may mean that it clashes with the faceplate. If this happens, open the Brightness-Contrast dialog (Layer ▶ Colors ▶ Brightness-Contrast). Reduce the Contrast and adjust the Brightness according to your own taste and then use the Colorize filter to add color to the button bar.

Further Exploration

The button bar adds the last interactive element required to complete the video player project. With the ear buds, video screen, button bar, and faceplate complete, you're ready to hand the project down the production line to the programmers who will turn it into the next great desktop application!

This project has only shown you a small sample of what you can do with user interface design and the GIMP. But it has also shown you how many of the techniques you've encountered throughout the book can come together in a full-scale design project. You've mastered selection and masking techniques, practiced colorizing methods, and learned how to work filter magic. These GIMP tricks have prepared you for your next graphics design project and so much more.

So stand tall and wave your graphic designer banner proudly. You're now a true GIMP expert!

TIPS FOR USER INTERFACE DESIGN

Here are some suggestions and guidelines to keep in mind as you work.

Get Help from Guides

Even if your design has rounded edges and a funky aesthetic, make sure you place your interface components properly. The GIMP workspace provides both vertical and horizontal guides, and it's a good idea to use them whenever you need help positioning components or defining their locations within the larger design.

Add Shadows

You can enhance the experience of using any interface by creating the illusion of three dimensions. Use the Drop Shadow filter to create shadows and highlights and you'll add depth to an otherwise flat design.

Consider Tubes and Wires

The video player project gives you a chance to practice creating both tubes and wires, but the tubes are just for show. They would serve no purpose on an actual device, but they look more industrial than wires and smooth cables, so they suit the overall design. Choose design components carefully to match the device to its audience.

Start Large!

Few components scale up well, so it's best to start large and scale down. When the objects are viewed from head on, images of screws, nuts, and bolts easily scale down to fit most designs. (It's more difficult to create angled views with the GIMP than with other 3D graphics programs.) You'll find that wires and tubes also scale down well.

Use Color Wisely

We use the simplest of techniques to add color to the video player—we do it all with the GIMP's Colorize dialog. When working on more complex designs, you may need to use more than a few colors, and it's important to choose pleasing color combinations. There are a number of color-coordination websites out there—seek one out and learn to use color wisely when designing your user interfaces! Here are two good places to start:

EasyRGB   http://www.easyrgb.com

ColorMixers   http://www.colormixers.com/mixers/cmr

INDEX